THE CARMEN DE PROVIDENTIA DEI
ATTRIBUTED TO PROSPER OF AQUITAINE:
A REVISED TEXT WITH AN INTRODUCTION,
TRANSLATION, AND NOTES

This dissertation was approved by Martin R. P. McGuire, Professor of Greek and Latin, as director, and by Bernard M. Peebles, Professor of Greek and Latin, and Hermigild Dressler, O.F.M., Associate Professor of Greek and Latin, as readers.

THE CATHOLIC UNIVERSITY OF AMERICA
PATRISTIC STUDIES
VOL. XCVIII

The Carmen de Providentia Dei Attributed to Prosper of Aquitaine: A Revised Text With an Introduction, Translation, and Notes

A DISSERTATION

SUBMITTED TO THE FACULTY OF THE GRADUATE SCHOOL OF ARTS AND
SCIENCES OF THE CATHOLIC UNIVERSITY OF AMERICA IN PARTIAL
FULFILLMENT OF THE REQUIREMENTS FOR THE DEGREE OF
DOCTOR OF PHILOSOPHY

BY

MICHAEL P. McHUGH, M.A.

THE CATHOLIC UNIVERSITY OF AMERICA PRESS
WASHINGTON, D. C.
1964

Copyright, 1965
THE CATHOLIC UNIVERSITY OF AMERICA PRESS, INC.

MURRAY AND HEISTER, INC.
WASHINGTON, D. C.

PRINTED BY
TIMES AND NEWS PUBLISHING CO.
GETTYSBURG, PA., U. S. A.

DEO OMNIPOTENTI
ET
SERVAE EIVS
PATRICIAE
VXORI CARISSIMAE

PREFACE

The Carmen de Providentia Dei attributed to St.
Prosper of Aquitaine is an important but relatively neglected literary composition of the early fifth century
A.D. The purpose of the present dissertation is to present a revised Latin text of this work with an introduction, an English translation, and notes.

No new text of the De providentia has appeared
since the Maurist edition of 1711; the Migne text in the
Patrologia latina is simply a reprint of the Maurist text.
The Maurist text itself relies on the editio princeps of
Sebastian Gryphius, published in 1539. The one known
manuscript of portions of the poem is probably copied
from Gryphius' text. Therefore the revised text which appears in this dissertation is essentially Gryphius' text,
with several later emendations.

The introduction deals with the authorship and occasion, date, and place of composition of the poem, and
the biblical allusions and non-biblical parallels in the
work, with a consideration of stylistic and metrical fea-
tures and an outline of content.

The question of authorship has been dealt with in
some detail, but no final decision could be reached. A
full metrical analysis has indicated that the author was
well-trained in classical metrics and a study of the non-
biblical parallels has further indicated that he was well-
acquainted with the earlier Latin poetry. His poetic
style reflects the rhetorical coloring that is so marked
in Latin verse from the days of Lucan.

No complete translation of the work has hitherto
been made into any modern language. Accordingly, I have
tried to render the poem as accurately as possible into
English.

In the notes to the text material treated in the
sections of the introduction dealing with biblical allusions and non-biblical parallels is set out for each relevant verse of the poem, and theological and other material
not treated in the introduction is considered. The dissertation concludes with a complete Index Verborum.

In his monumental work on St. Prosper, Valentin
devoted considerable space to the De providentia, and attempted to show that the poem was composed by Prosper.

But Valentin's work is now some sixty years old, and the great advances in our knowledge of later Latin literature and style during the intervening period have shown that most of Valentin's arguments in favor of Prosperian authorship do not carry sufficient weight. However, he makes many acute and incisive observations on the style of the De providentia, and I have made extensive use of his study throughout this dissertation.

Abbreviations of Latin authors and works are based on the system used in the Thesaurus linguae latinae. Citations of the De providentia are made according to the present text; those of the De ingratis according to Huegelmeyer's text.[1] Quotations from Scripture have been rendered into English from the Confraternity of Christian Doctrine translation, where it has been available, with necessary adjustments to allow for the poetic paraphrasing of scriptural texts in the original Latin.

I wish to express my appreciation to Mlle. J. Veilliard of the Institut de Recherche et d'histoire des Textes and to her associates for providing me with film of the Mazarine manuscript of the De providentia as well as with an invaluable analysis of the manuscript; to Dom E. Dekkers of the Corpus Christianorum and to F. Sciuto for suggestions which led to the finding of the Mazarine manuscript; to Sister Kathryn Clare Krabbe, a fellow student at the Catholic University of America, for providing me with microfilm prints of Antelmy's Dissertationes criticae;[2] to Miss Dorothy Rounds of Cambridge, Massachusetts, and Dr. Max Burckhardt of the Öffentliche Bibliothek der Universität Basel, for their prompt and gracious responses to inquiries, and to Mrs. Carolyn Costa, for typing the manuscript. My appreciation goes also to all my colleagues in the Department of Classics at Howard University for their encouragement, and in particular to Professor Frank M. Snowden, Chairman of the Department of Classics and Dean of the College of Liberal Arts at Howard, for arranging for my partial release from teaching duties

---

[1] C. T. Huegelmeyer, Carmen de Ingratis S. Prosperi Aquitani (CUA Patristic Studies 95; Washington, 1962).

[2] Sister Kathryn Clare's study of the Letter to Demetrias is to appear in the near future in the Patristic Series as Vol. XCVII.

PREFACE

for one semester to further the progress of this study. Above all, I wish to thank my wife, Patricia, for her assistance in ways too numerous to mention here.
I wish further to express my gratitude to Dr. Martin R. P. McGuire, Professor of Greek and Latin in the Catholic University of America, who suggested the topic of the dissertation and guided me throughout its preparation; to Professor Bernard M. Peebles, for reading the dissertation and making many helpful suggestions, particularly in regard to the study of the text of the poem; to Rev. Hermigild Dressler, O.F.M., for reading the dissertation and making a number of suggestions concerning the translation, and to Dr. George J. Siefert, for his assistance on metrical matters.

TABLE OF CONTENTS

ABBREVIATIONS

Benoist	Benoist, E. and H. Goelzer, Nouveau dictionnaire latin-francais
Blaise	Blaise, A. Dictionnaire latin-francais des auteurs chrétiens
BLE	Bulletin de littérature ecclesiastique
CCHS	Orchard, Dom Bernard et al., A Catholic Commentary on Holy Scripture
DTC	Dictionnaire de théologie catholique
Ernout-Meillet	Ernout, A. and A. Meillet, Dictionnaire etymologique de la langue latine
Forcellini	Forcellini-Corradini-Perin, Lexicon totius latinitatis
Georges	Georges, K. E., Ausführliches lateinisch-deutsches Handwörterbuch
K.-Steg.	Kühner, R. and K. Stegmann, Ausführliche Grammatik der lateinischen Sprache
L.-Hof.	Leumann, M. and J. B. Hofmann, Stolz-Schmalz Lateinische Grammatik
Lewis-Short	Lewis, C. T. and C. Short, A Latin Dictionary
PL	Migne, J. P., Patrologia latina
RE	Pauly-Wissowa et al., Realencyclopädie der classischen Altertumswissenschaft
Souter	Souter, A., A Glossary of Later Latin
TLL	Thesaurus linguae latinae
VC	Vigiliae Christianae

SELECT BIBLIOGRAPHY

A. EDITIONS

Gryphius, S., _Divi Prosperi Aquitanici Opera_ (Lyons 1539).

Le Brun des Marettes, J. B. and L. U. Mangeant, _Sancti Prosperi Aquitanici_ . . . _Opera_ (Paris, 1711; reprinted by J. P. Migne, _Patrologiae Cursus Completus: Series Latina_ 51, Paris 1861; earlier 1846).

B. WORKS ON SCRIPTURE

_____ _Biblia Sacra iuxta Latinam Vulgatam Versionem,_ edited by monks of St. Benedict associated with the Pontifical Biblical Institute (Rome 1926-).

_____ _Biblia Sacra iuxta Vulgatam Clementinam,_ edited by A. Colunga and C. Turrado (Madrid 1946).

_____ The _Holy Bible,_ Old Testament, Confraternity Version, Genesis to Ruth, Job to Sirach, and the Prophetical Books; New Testament, Confraternity Version; the remaining books in the Douay Version. (New York 1961).

Dutripon, F. P., _Vulgatae Editionis Bibliorum Sacrorum Concordantiae_ (9th ed. Paris 1880).

Orchard, Dom Bernard, Edmund F. Sutcliffe, S. J. Reginald C. Fuller, and Dom Ralph Russell, _A Catholic Commentary on Holy Scripture_ (New York 1953).

C. WORKS ON LANGUAGE AND STYLE

Arbusow, L., _Colores Rhetorici; Eine Auswahl rhetorischer Figuren und Gemeinplatze_ (Göttingen 1948).

Bennett, C. R., The _Syntax of Early Latin_ (2 vols. Boston 1910, 1914).

Blaise, A., _Manuel du latin chrétien_ (Strasbourg 1955).

BIBLIOGRAPHY

Bogan, Sister Mary Inez, R.S.M., The Vocabulary and Style
of the Soliloquies and Dialogues of St. Augustine
(The Catholic University of America Patristic Studies 42; Washington 1935).

Campbell, J. M., The Influence of the Second Sophistic on
the Style of the Sermons of St. Basil the Great
(The Catholic University of America Patristic
Studies 2; Washington 1922).

Curtius, E. R., European Literature and the Latin Middle
Ages, translated by W. R. Trask (Bollingen Series
36; New York 1953).

Downey, G., "Ekphrasis," Reallexikon für Antike und
Christentum 4 (Stuttgart 1959) 921-944.

Eijkenboom, P., Het Christus Medicusmotief in de Preken
Van Sint Augustinus (Nijmegen 1960).

Holman, Sister Mary John, O.S.U., Nature-Imagery in the
Works of St. Augustine (The Catholic University of
America Patristic Studies 33; Washington 1931).

Kühner, R. and K. Stegmann, Ausfuhrliche Grammatik der
lateinischen Sprache (2nd ed. Hanover 1914-1918).

Lausberg, H., Handbuch der Literarischen Rhetorik
(Munich 1960).

Leumann, M. and J. B. Hofmann, Stolz-Schmalz Lateinische
Grammatik (5th ed. Munich 1928).

Mahoney, Brother Albertus, C.F.X., Vergil in the Works of
Prudentius (The Catholic University of America
Patristic Studies 39; Washington 1934).

Mohrmann, C., Études sur le latin des chrétiens (vol. 1,
2nd ed., Rome 1961; vol. 2, Rome 1961).

_____ "La langue et le style de la poésie latine
chrétienne," Revue des études latines 25 (1947)
280-297; repr. in Etudes 1.151-168.

_____ "Problèmes stylistiques dans la littérature
latine chrétienne," Vigiliae Christianae 9 (1955)
222-246.

BIBLIOGRAPHY

_____ "Quelques traits caractéristiques du latin des chrétiens," Studi e testi 121 (Vatican City 1946) 437-466; repr. in Études 1.21-50.

Neue, F. and C. Wagener, Formenlehre der lateinischen Sprache (4 vols., 3rd ed. Leipzig 1892-1905).

Springer, Sister M. Theresa, S.H.N., Nature-Imagery in the Works of Saint Ambrose (The Catholic University of America Patristic Studies 30; Washington 1931).

Tobin, Sister Mildred Dolores, C.S.C., The Commonitorium of Orientius: An Introduction, Translation, and Commentary (The Catholic University of America Patristic Studies 74; Washington 1945).

Weyman, K., Beiträge zur Geschichte der christlich-lateinischen Poesie (Munich 1926).

Wheeler, A. L., Catullus and the Traditions of Ancient Poetry (Sather Classical Lectures 13; Berkeley 1934).

D. WORKS ON METRICS

Cooper, C. G., An Introduction to the Latin Hexameter (Melbourne 1952).

Cordier, A., Les débuts de l'hexamètre latin: Ennius (Paris 1947).

Harkness, A. G., "Final Monosyllables in Latin Prose and Poetry," American Journal of Philology 31 (1910) 154-174.

_____ "The Word-Group Accent in Latin Hexameters," Classical Philology 3 (1908) 39-58.

Herescu, N. I., La Poésie Latine. Étude des structures phoniques (Paris 1960).

Jackson-Knight, W. F., Accentual Symmetry in Vergil (London 1950).

Kent, R. G., "A problem of Latin prosody," Mélanges de philologie, de littérature et d'histoire anciennes, offerts à J. A. Marouzeau (Paris 1948) 303-308.

BIBLIOGRAPHY

_____ "Likes and Dislikes in Elision," Transactions of the American Philological Association 54 (1923) 86-97.

Marouzeau, J., "Mots longs et mots courts," Revue de philologie 48 (1924) 31-43.

Norberg, D., Introduction à l'étude de la versification latine médiévale (Studia Latina Stockholmiensia 5; Stockholm 1958).

Nougaret, L., Traité de métrique latine classique (Paris 1948).

Platnauer, M., "Elision of atque in Roman poetry," Classical Quarterly 42 (1948) 91-93.

_____ Latin Elegiac Verse: A Study of the Metrical Usages of Tibullus, Propertius and Ovid (Cambridge 1951).

Siefert, G. J., Jr., Meter and Case in the Latin Elegiac Pentameter (Language Dissertation 49 of the Linguistic Society of America; Philadelphia 1948).

_____ "The Reading of Latin Verse," Teaching Latin in the Modern World, edited by M. R. P. McGuire (Washington 1960) 84-101.

Steele, R. B., "Variations in the Latin Dactylic Hexameter," Philological Quarterly 5 (1926) 212-225.

Strecker, K., Introduction to Medieval Latin, translated and revised by R. B. Palmer (Berlin 1957).

Sturtevant, E. H., "Accent and Ictus in Latin Elegiac Distich," Transactions of the American Philological Association 55 (1924) 73-89.

_____ "The Doctrine of Caesura, A Philological Ghost," American Journal of Philology 55 (1924) 329-350.

_____ "Harmony and Clash of Accent and Ictus in the Latin Hexameter," Transactions of the American Philological Association 54 (1923) 51-73.

BIBLIOGRAPHY

Todd, O. J., "Caesura Rediviva," Classical Philology 37
(1942) 22-37.

Vollmer, F., "Römische Metrik," Einleitung in die Altertumswissenschaft, edited by A. Gercke and E. Norden
(Leipzig and Berlin 1927) 1.8.1-22.

E. LEXICA AND CONCORDANCES

Baxter, J. H. and C. Johnson, Medieval Latin Word List
from British and Irish Sources (Oxford 1934).

Benoist, E. and H. Goelzer, Nouveau dictionnaire latin-
francais (n.d. /Paris 1934/).

Blaise, A., Dictionnaire latin-francaise des auteurs
chrétiens (Strasbourg 1954).

Cooper, L., A Concordance to the Works of Horace
(Washington 1916).

Deferrari, R. J., Sister M. Inviolata Barry, and M. R. P.
McGuire, A Concordance of Ovid (Washington 1939).

Deferrari, R. J. and J. M. Campbell, A Concordance of
Prudentius (Cambridge, Mass. 1932).

Deferrari, R. J., Sister Maria Walburg Fanning, and
Sister Anne Stanislaus Sullivan, A Concordance of
Lucan (Washington 1940).

Ernout, A. and A. Meillet, Dictionnaire etymologique de
la langue latine (3rd ed. Paris 1951).

Forcellini, E., F. Corradini, and J. Perin, Lexicon
totius latinitatis (Padua 1864-1867).

Gaffiot, F., Dictionnaire illustré latin-francais (Paris
1934; new ed. n.d. /1957/).

Georges, K. E., Ausführliches lateinisch-deutsches
Handwörterbuch (2 vols. Leipzig 1913-1918).

Lewis, C. T. and C. Short, A Latin Dictionary (New York
1879; reprinted Oxford 1958).

BIBLIOGRAPHY

Merguet, H., Lexikon zu Vergilius (Leipzig 1912).

Paulson, J., Index Lucretianus (Göteborg 1921).

Souter, A., A Glossary of Later Latin to 600 A.D.
(Oxford 1949).

Thesaurus linguae latinae (Leipzig 1900-   ).

Wetmore, M. N., Index Verborum Vergilianus (New Haven
1911).

F. OTHER WORKS

Amann, É., "Semi-Pélagiens," Dictionnaire de théologie
catholique 14.1796-1850.

Antelmy, J., De veris operibus ss. patrum Leonis Magni et
Prosperi Aquitani dissertationes criticae(Paris
1689).

Ballerini, P. and J., "Observationes in Historiam
Pelagianam," H. Noris, Opera Omnia Theologica I
(Venice 1769).

Bardenhewer, O., Geschichte der altkirchlichen Literatur
4 (Freiburg im Breisgau 1924).

Bardy, G., "Prosper d'Aquitaine," Dictionnaire de théologie
catholique 13.1.846-850.

Berger, A., Encyclopedic Dictionary of Roman Law (Transactions of the American Philosophical Society 43.2;
Philadelphia 1953).

Bury, J. B., The Cambridge Medieval History I, edited by
H. M. Gwathin and J. P. Whitney (London 1911).

Cabrol, F. and H. Leclerq, Dictionnaire d'archéologie
chrétienne et de liturgie (15 vols. Paris 1907-1953).

Chéné, J., "Les origines de la controverse semi-pélagienne,"
L'année théologique augustinienne 14 (1953) 56-109.

_____ "Le Semipélagianisme du midi de la Gaule,"
Recherches de science religieuse 43 (1955) 322-
341.

BIBLIOGRAPHY

Courcelle, P., Histoire littéraire des grandes invasions germaniques (Paris 1948).

Couture, L., "S. Prosper d'Aquitaine," Bulletin de littérature ecclésiastique 2 (1900) 269-282; ibid., 3 (1901) 33-49.

Dekkers, E., Clavis Patrum Latinorum (Sacris Erudiri 3; new ed., Steenbrugge and the Hague 1961).

Ebert, A., Allgemeine Geschichte der Literatur des Mittelalters im Abendlande (Leipzig 1889).

Fabricius, J. A., Bibliotheca Latina mediae et infimae aetatis edited by J. D. Mansi (Padua 1754, reprinted Florence 1858).

Fliche, A. and V. Martin, Histoire de l'Église depuis les origines jusqu'à nos jours 4 (2nd ed. Paris 1939; reprinted 1948).

Garrigou-Lagrange, R., O.P., Grace, translated by Dominican Nuns (St. Louis 1952).

_____ Providence, translated by Dom Bede Ross (St. Louis 1937).

Griffe, E., La Gaule chrétienne à l'Époque romaine (Paris 1957).

Hedde, R. and É. Amann, "Pélagianisme," Dictionnaire de théologie catholique 12.675-715.

Helm, R., "Prosper," in Pauly-Wissowa et al. Realencyclopädie der classischen Altertumswissenschaft 45 (1957) 880-897.

Huegelmeyer, C. T., M. M., Carmen de Ingratis S. Prosperi Aquitani (The Catholic University of America Patristic Studies 95; Washington 1962).

Klauser, T., Reallexikon für Antike und Christentum (Leipzig 1941   ).

Labriolle, P. de, Histoire de la littérature latine chrétienne (3rd ed. rev. by G. Bardy, Paris 1947).

xxi

BIBLIOGRAPHY

Lesousky, Sister M. Alphonsine, O.S.U., The De Dono
Perseverantiae of St. Augustine: A Translation
with an Introduction and A Commentary (The Catholic
University of America Patristic Studies 91; Washington 1956).

Letter, P. de, S.J., St. Prosper of Aquitaine, The Call
of All Nations (Ancient Christian Writers 14;
Westminster, Md. and London 1952).

_____ St. Prosper of Aquitaine: Defense of St.
Augustine (Ancient Christian Writers 32; Westminster,
Md. and London 1963).

Manitius, M., "Beiträge zur Geschichte Frühchristlicher
Dichter im Mittelalter," Sitzungberichte der philo-
sophisch-historischen Classe der k. Akademie der
Wissenschaften 117 (Vienna 1889) XII Abh. 8-40.

_____ "Beiträge zur Geschichte Frühchristlicher Dichter
im Mittelalter II," ibid. 121 (Vienna 1890) VII
Abh. 1-30.

_____ Geschichte der christlich-lateinischen Poesie
(Stuttgart 1891).

_____ "Über das Gedicht 'de Providentia divina',"
Zeitschrift für die oesterreichischen Gymnasien 39
(1888) 580-584.

Molinier, M., "Saint Prosper d'Aquitaine," Revue Historique 75 (1901) 114-116.

Moon, Brother A. Anthony, F.S.C., The De Natura Boni of
St. Augustine (The Catholic University of America
Patristic Studies 88; Washington 1955).

Moricca, U., Storia della letteratura latina cristiana
3 (Turin 1932).

Noris, H., Historia Pelagiana (Padua 1673; reprinted in
Opera Omnia Theologica I, Venice 1769).

O'Donnell, J. R., Grace and Free Will by Prosper of
Aquitaine (The Fathers of the Church 7; New York
1949).

BIBLIOGRAPHY

Parsons, Sister Wilfred, S.N.D., Prosper of Aquitaine:
Letter to St. Augustine (The Fathers of the Church
13; New York 1956).

Plinval, G. de, "L'activité doctrinale dans l'église
gallo-romaine," in Fliche-Martin, Histoire de
l'Eglise depuis les origines jusqu'à nos jours
4.379-419.

_____ "Les luttes pélagiennes," ibid. 79-128.

_____ Pélage, ses écrits, sa vie et sa réforme, Étude
d'histoire littéraire et religieuse (Paris and
Lausanne, 1943).

Portalié, E., "Augustinisme," Dictionnaire de théologie
catholique 1.2268-2472.

_____ Guide to the Thought of St. Augustine, translated by R. J. Bastian, S.J. (Chicago 1960).

Redding, J. P., The Influence of St. Augustine on the
Doctrine of the II Council of Orange (Universitas
Catholica Americae Washingtonii, S. Facultas
Theologica 53; Washington 1939).

Schanz, M., C. Hosius and G. Krüger, Geschichte der
römischen Literatur 4.2 (Munich 1920).

Tillemont, L., Mémoires pour servir à l'histoire ecclésiastique des six premiers siècles 16 (Paris 1912).

Tixeront, J., History of Dogmas, translated from the 5th
French edition by H.L.B., I (St. Louis 1910); II
(1914); III (1916).

Vacant, A., E. Mangenot, and É. Amann, Dictionnaire de
théologie catholique (15 vols. Paris 1899-1950).

Valentin, L., Saint Prosper d'Aquitaine, étude sur la
littérature latine ecclésiastique au Ve siècle en
Gaule (Toulouse and Paris 1900).

Wiggers, G. F., Versuch einer pragmatischen Darstellung
des Augustinismus und Pelagianismus II (Hamburg
1833).

BIBLIOGRAPHY

Young, Joseph J., *Studies on the Style of the* 'De vocatione omnium gentium' *Ascribed to Prosper of Aquitaine* (The Catholic University of America Patristic Studies 87; Washington 1952).

INTRODUCTION

INTRODUCTION

A. TEXT

The Bibliothèque Mazarine possesses one manuscript (3896) which contains (fol. 162-167v) a significant portion of the De providentia Dei.[1] The text provided by this manuscript begins at verse 105 of the De providentia, and concludes with verse 520. There are a few lacunae,[2] so that the manuscript contains 340 verses in all. Each page contains 28 or 29 verses, except the title page, which has but 25. There are numerous blank pages in the manuscript, including those immediately following the

---

[1]F. Sciuto, in his article "Nonnulla de codicibus Prosperi Aquitani," Miscellanea di studi di letteratura cristiana antica 9 (1959) 19-24, referred in general terms to manuscripts of Prosper's poems. Dr. Sciuto had sent a provisory list of manuscripts to Dom Dekkers of the Corpus Christianorum in Steenbrugge. After further investigation, Dom Dekkers transmitted the information which led to the discovery of this manuscript to Dr. Bernard Peebles of the Department of Greek and Latin of the Catholic University, at whose request Mlle. J. Vielliard, of the Institut de Recherche et d'Histoire des Textes in Paris, succeeded in bringing the Mazarine manuscript to light. Mlle. Vielliard has since communicated to Dr. Peebles an excellent typewritten study of this MS. The material in this section relating to the content, date and origin of the Mazarine MS. is based on the study furnished by Mlle. Vielliard. The MS. is mentioned in E. Pellegrin, "Manuscrits de Pétrarque dans les bibliothèques de France," Italia medioevale e umanistica 4 (1961) 366. Valentin, Saint Prosper 219, records the absence of manuscripts of the De providentia Dei in the Bibliothèque Nationale and in the Vatican Library.

[2]Viz., vv. 121-146 to munere Christi, 156-174, 191-211, 267-277.

excerpts from the De providentia.[3] The title reads: Ex
libro sancti Prosperi Aquitanici de providentia dei, but
there is no corresponding formula where the excerpts terminate.

The contents of the manuscript, which is essentially an anthology of devotional texts, are quite diverse,
and range from selections from Augustine, Sedulius, and
Venantius Fortunatus to works of such Renaissance figures
as Aeneas Silvius Piccolomini (Pius II), Erasmus, and
Petrarch. It was quite likely composed in a monastery of
the Augustinian canons in Flanders,[4] and is characteristic
of the"devotio moderna" that flourished in the Low Coun-
tries at the time of the Reformation. The manuscript is
a collection for personal use, perhaps belonging at one
time to an Augustinian canon of the priory of Sept-Fontaines
in Flanders.[5] In view of the fact that the scribe often
copies out texts that had long been in print in this era,
and since there is substantial agreement between the
Mazarine manuscript and the first printed edition of the
De providentia in readings, spellings, and punctuation,
it would appear highly probable that the manuscript is a
copy of the printed text (1539). In any event, the manuscript must be dated at some point later than August 27,
1535.[6]

Before the appearance of the first printed text

---

[3]Viz., 168-170^v. Since the MS. breaks off in the
middle of a sentence, it appears that the scribe had intended to use these pages to continue it.

[4]The study furnished by Mlle. Vielliard cites as
evidence of this the nature of the contents of the MS.,
viz., the devotion to St. Augustine and St. Monica as well
as a portion of verse in Flemish in fol. 79.

[5]Cf. the texts of Iacobus Habbekius, added later
to the MS., viz., Carmen in Laudem s. Mariae Magdalenae
fol. 18^v - 19^v, and 266^v - 267. The MS. has 267 leaves
in all. Sept-Fontaines is recorded in L. H. Cottineau,
O.S.B., Repertoire topo-bibliographique des abbayes et
prieurés 2 (Mâcon, 1935) 3011.

[6]Cf. fol. 68^v: "occasione cuiusdam parvi pisci-
culi michi per cellararium oblati anno a sacra Nativitate
tua 1535 kalendarium septembrium die sexto."

of the De providentia, several other printed works were
published under the name of Prosper of Aquitaine.[7] These
included the Epigrams printed at Venice in 1481 and at
Milan in 1495; the Contra collatorem at Mainz in 1524, and
the Epistola ad Rufinum and Responsiones ad excerpta
Genuensium at Paris in 1534. In 1538 a more extensive edition appeared at Venice, including the probably spurious
Poema coniugis ad coniugem.[8] A verse translation of the
Epigrams into Italian was printed at Venice in 1481.[9]

The edition of Prosper's works published at Lyons
by Sebastian Gryphius in 1539 was more comprehensive than
any which had preceded it, for it marked the first appearance of the Carmen de providentia Dei,[10] the Carmen de

---

[7]For additional information on these works see
K. Schoenemann, Bibliotheca historico-litteraria patrum
latinorum 2 (Leipzig, 1794) 1012-1049, and L. Couture,
"Saint Prosper d'Aquitaine," Bulletin de littérature
écclésiastique 2 (1900) 269-282. L. Hain, Repertorium
Bibliographicum 4 (Milan, 1948) 161-163, lists 15th cent.
copies of the Epigrams and also of the De vita contempla-
tiva, a work ascribed by later scholars to Julian Pomerius.

[8]The De vocatione omnium gentium is found in this
early period among the works of St. Ambrose. For further
discussion of the attribution to Ambrose see Young, Studies
on the Style of the De vocatione 6-9.

[9]Hain, op. cit., item 13425.

[10]The title of the poem is listed in the index of
this edition as De providentia Dei, and the page headings
carry the same title, while the entitulature at the opening of the work is De providentia divina D. Prosperi
Opusculum. Vv. 1-96 are printed separately as Prologus,
the remainder of the text following immediately thereafter.
The lines of the poem are numbered. The work ends with
the subscription Finis libri de providentia Dei. Brief
marginal notes are found opposite verses 154, 473, 508, 546,
627, and 721. Gryphius prints three very short elegiac
poems after the De providentia, and following these the
De ingratis and the Expositio psalmorum, which concludes
the volume. No indices or commentaries are provided for
any of the works or for the volume as a whole.

ingratis,[11] and the Expositio psalmorum. The edition appeared under the title Divi Prosperi Aquitanici, Episcopi Regiensis,[12] Opera, accurata vetustiorum exemplarium collatione per viros eruditos recognita. Gryphius wrote to scholars in France and Germany in his search for manuscripts of Prosper's works, but he gives us no details at all on the manuscripts of the three works which came into his hands.[13]

The monumental Lyons edition was reprinted at Cologne in 1540 and again at Louvain in 1565, the latter by Jean Soteaux with the help of the theologian Jean Hassels.[14] Soteaux removes the De providentia from the genuine works of Prosper because it is supposedly tainted with Pelagianism, yet he prints it in the volume itself

---

[11] For the history of the text and translations of the De ingratis see Huegelmeyer, Carmen de Ingratis 1-5.

[12] The notion that Prosper of Aquitaine was Bishop of Reggio is refuted by G. Morin, "Saint Prosper de Reggio," Revue Bénédictine 12 (1895) 241-257.

[13] Cf. Gryphius" preface to the Senate and people of Reggio: ". . . Proinde huc illuc missis litteris, negotium dedi amicis et Gallis, et Germanis, praesertim humaniorum litterarum studiosioribus, ut quicquid huius autoris apud eos in antiquis bibliothecis lateret, tam lacerum, quam integrum, ad me transmitterent. A quibus inter alia eius vetustissima exemplaria allata sunt simul quae desiderabantur opera; nempe duo versu heroico, De providentia Dei unum, alterum /De ingratis/; praeterea, Expositio in postremos quinquaginta psalmos: omnia hactenus, ut opinor, a nostrae tempestatis hominibus non visa."

[14] Intervening between these reprints was another, Pontii Paulini Poemata. Prosperi Tironis Aquitanici Epigrammaton lib. I. De Providentia Dei lib. I. De Ingratis lib. I . . . , which appeared at Antwerp in 1560. This work also contained selections from Hilary and Venantius Fortunatus.

in the same place in which it appears in the Lyons edition.[15] The Louvain edition marks an advance in that it contains a general index and a scriptural index. Jean Olivier, professor of Greek at Douay, published an edition of Prosper in 1577 which is substantially the Louvain text of Soteaux.[16]

Interest among seventeenth-century scholars centered at first in the Chronicon, and later, as a result of the Jansenist controversy, in the De ingratis and Prosper's other treatises on grace.[17] During this period both verse and prose renderings of the De ingratis were produced in French,[18] but no translation of the related De providentia is known, although one might have been expected. Commentaries on the De providentia are also lacking, although the Louvain theologian Martin Steyaert composed one for the De ingratis.

---

[15] Schoenemann, op. cit., 1033: "In eadem praefatione remotum a se dicit /se. editor/ carmen de Providentia, quia Pelagianae doctrinae sit; attamen in ipso volumine eodem ordine impressum extat, quo a praecedenti editione exhibitum fuerat." Couture, op. cit.,272, also remarks on the same fact. Following the Lyons edition, Soteaux titles the poem De providentia divina Opusculum.

[16] Schoenemann, op. cit., 1033: "Superioris editionis substantia non aucta est." But Couture, op. cit., 272, remarks that this edition contains certain new corrections. This Douay edition of Olivier was reprinted at Cologne in 1609 and at Rome in 1611.

[17] As the controversy proceeded, Olivier's Douay edition was again reprinted at Paris in 1671 by Théophile Raynaud, and at Lyons in 1677 in Margarin de la Bigne, Maxima Bibliotheca Veterum Patrum. These reprints are not of great value for the establishment of the text.

[18] Huegelmeyer, op. cit., 3. Add the paraphrase of the De ingratis by Louis Racine, Poème sur la grace (Paris, 1720).

6

J. B. Le Brun des Marettes and his associate, Luc
Urbain Mangeant, edited the Maurist edition of the Opera
Omnia of Prosper, which was printed in Paris in 1711 by
Desprez and Desessartz.[19] The work opens with a Vita
of Prosper, which is essentially a Latin version of the
account given by Tillemont.[20] The De providentia is furnished with an admonitio and divided into twelve sections,
each with a relatively brief note tracing the argument of
the poem. These notes are further broken down into their
component phrases, which are repeated in their appropriate
positions in the margin of the text.[21] There is also a
very rudimentary commentary, actually less than twenty
notes in all, disposed at the bottom of the relevant pages.[22]
The text of the De providentia shows but few substantive
changes from Gryphius' Lyons edition, probably because
the Maurists had no new manuscript evidence.[23] The volume

---

[19]Schoenemann, op. cit., 1023, describes this
edition as "longe semper anteriores excellens."

[20]Tillemont, Mémoires 16 (Paris, 1712) 1-30.
The Maurist editors had seen Tillemont's treatment before
it went to press. Cf. Valentin, Saint Prosper 206.

[21]In the preface, the Maurists describe their im-
provements to the text: "De Providentia Divina Carmen
. . . a nobis primum in capita divisum, et capitum argu-
menta operi praefixa, resque de quibus in singulis eius
partibus tractatur in margine collaterali breviterque
notatae."

[22]Throughout, the title De Providentia Divina is
used, and De Providentia Dei is not found. The De prov.
is printed toward the end of the volume, completely removed from the De ingrat. and identified as Incerti
Auctoris Carmen. Each fifth verse of the poem is numbered. Note an error in the omission of the number 885 between 880 and 890, so that each subsequent number should
be reduced by five. The De prov. contains therefore 972
verses, not 977 as would appear from the Maurist text.

[23]The Maurists employed the Lyons /1539/, Louvain
/1565/, Douay /1577/, and Cologne /1630/ editions.

is, however, furnished with a copious general index as
well as extensive appendices containing biblical and theological material drawn in large measure from the works of
Augustine. It was reprinted at Paris in 1732, and at
Venice in 1744 and 1782.

A renewed interest in the works of Prosper which
burgeoned in eighteenth-century Italy did not extend to
the De providentia. The Roman theologian Salinas published his edition of Prosper in 1732, but it did not
include the De providentia. The Italian theologian and
text critic P. F. Foggini, using Vatican manuscripts, began to publish sundry treatises on grace by Prosper,
Augustine, and others at Rome in 1734, an edition which
was reprinted by Claude Lequeux, prior of St. Yves in
Paris and editor of Bossuet, at Paris in 1760.[24] Lequeux
issued a French translation of these works two years
thereafter, but neither the edition nor the translation
contains the De providentia. Couture cites four verse
translations of the De ingratis into Italian in the
eighteenth century,[25] and Huegelmeyer a fifth, also in
Italian, which appeared in 1818;[26] the De providentia remains untranslated in this period, as far as is known.

The edition of the Abbé Migne in the Patrologia
Latina, issued at Paris in 1846 and reissued there in
1861, virtually terminates the text history of the works
of Prosper considered as a corpus.[27] The Migne text is
essentially a reprint of the Maurist edition of 1711, and
contains only three deviations from the Maurist text of

---

[24]Huegelmeyer, op. cit., 5.

[25]Couture, op. cit., 280-281.

[26]Huegelmeyer, op. cit., 4.

[27]T. Mommsen published the Chronicon in Chronica
minora saec. iv. v. vi. vii. (MGH, auct. antiq. 9; Berlin
1892), and S. H. Hurter published extracts from the De
gratia et libero arbitrio in Patrum sanctorum opuscula
selecta 35 and 36 (Innsbruck,1876-1877). A new and complete edition of the works of Prosper is promised by the
Benedictines of Steenbrugge, Belgium, in the Corpus
Christianorum.

the De providentia.[28] Migne reprints the admonitio of
the Maurists without change, but removes their section
headings to the bottom of the page to join the notes on
the text. The notes are those of the Maurist edition,
and the Maurist entitulature of the poem as Carmen de
Providentia divina remains unchanged. The Migne edition
therefore signals no improvement over the Maurist text.[29]
    The sole known translation of any substantial por-
tion of the De providentia is the French version of
Félix Clément[30] in his Les Poètes chrétiens dupuis le
ive siècle jusqu'au xve, which appeared in Paris in 1857.
The entire work is a translation of the same author's
Carmina e poetis christianis excerpta ad usum scholarum,
issued at Paris in 1854. The work does not include those
passages in the De providentia thought to be of a semipelagian tenor. Valentin provides his own translations

---

[28]At vv. 431, 633, and 947. The change at 431
restores the reading of Gryphius' Lyons edition of 1539
by removing a misprint found in the Maurist text.

[29]Couture, op. cit., 282, comments that Migne
reproduces the Maurist text with some lapses in detail.
Valentin, op. cit.,210, remarks: ". . . le texte de la
Patrologie latine présente quelque fautes, surtout dans
le de Providentia. La question de l'origine de ce poème
n'étant pas résolue, le texte n'a pas été l'objet d'une
recension aussi sérieuse que celui des ouvrages reconnus
comme authentiques de saint Prosper." Cf. Valentin,
op. cit., 845-846.

[30]Clément's interests were wide-ranging, but
centered on church music, musical history, and related
fields; his other works include Introduction à une
méthode de plain chant (Paris,1854); La Poésie latine au
moyen âge (Paris,1853); Histoire abrégée des Beaux-Arts
(Paris,1879); Les grands musiciens (Paris,1882), which
was a school textbook series and contained volumes on
Beethoven and Mozart; a Dictionnaire lyrique, ou
Histoire des opéras (Paris,1869) in collaboration with
Pierre Larousse; and a missal (1864) and short breviary
for the laity (1854). Cf. G. Groves, Dictionary of
Music and Musicians 2 (5th ed., edited by E. Blom;
London and New York,1954) 343-344.

of the suspect passages in his extensive study.[31]
    This survey would suggest that scholars have de-
voted less attention to the De providentia than to the
undoubtedly genuine works of Prosper, and certainly far
less than to the related De ingratis. Surely one reason
for this is that the authenticity of the De providentia
as a work of Prosper has been questioned and often denied.

B. AUTHORSHIP

    No other problem relating to the De providentia is
as controverted as that of the authorship of the poem.
In the ninth century Hincmar of Rheims, in the course of
the controversy over the teachings of Gottschalk on pre-
destination, quoted extracts from the De providentia,
amounting to some sixty verses in all, under the name of
Prosper.[1] Likewise, though centuries later, the Mazarine
manuscript of portions of the De providentia ascribed
the poem to Prosper,[2] doing so in all likelihood on the
basis of the ascription to Prosper which appeared in
Gryphius' Lyons edition (1539).[3]
    Jean Soteaux, who with the theologian Jean Hassels
edited the Louvain edition (1565), was apparently the
first to deny the poem to Prosper.[4] Jean Olivier in his
Douay edition (1577) followed Soteaux in finding Pelagian
doctrine in the De providentia, but was more specific in
listing his objections to the genuineness of the

---

[31]Valentin, op. cit., 786-787; 888-892.

[1]Hincmar, De praedestinatione dissertatio posterior (PL 125.445). The verses cited are 448-457; 467-
472; 497-501; 550-557; 651-654; 659-663; 777-794; 951-
954. For an account of the controversy cf. H. Netzer,
"I. Hincmar," DTC 6.2. 2482-2486.

[2]Cf. Intro.,Text, at n. 3.

[3]Cf. Intro.,Text, n. 10.

[4]Cf. Intro.,Text, at n. 15.

poem.[5]

Cardinal Noris, in his great history of Pelagianism (1673), advanced the view that the De providentia was
composed by an adherent of the semipelagians, a theory
which he observed had already been held by others.[6] The
provencal canon Joseph Antelmy agreed with the Italian
Noris in finding semipelagian elements in the poem, but
showed greater caution by reserving judgment on the question (1689).[7] Antelmy suggested however that the De providentia might have been joined with the De ingratis in
the text tradition in order that the latter work might
serve as a remedy to the former.[8]

Tillemont found certain elements favorable to
Pelagianism in the poem, and expressed succinctly the nub
of the entire issue when he observed that the treatment
of grace in the work raised the one substantial objection

---

[5] Olivier held that the author of the De prov.
teaches that the more just man does not receive more
grace than the less just; that the patriarchs were good
only with the aid of natural law, and not with the help
of grace; and that the activity of the human will in
seeking faith precedes the help of God. Cf. Valentin,
Saint Prosper 769.

[6] H. Noris, Historia Pelagiana 2.14 in Opera omnia
theologica 1 (Venice,1769) 352, orig. published at Padua
in 1673. Noris suspected that the poem was by Hilary of
Arles, a view refuted by Tillemont and the Ballerini;
cf. nn. 9 and 13, below. Cardinal Bellarmine also termed
the De prov. probably semipelagian; cf. 'de scriptoribus
ecclesiasticis' in Opera omnia 12 (Naples,1862) 408, orig.
published at Lyons in 1675.

[7] J. Antelmy, De veris operibus SS. PP. Leonis
Magni et Prosperi Aquitanici dissertationes criticae 9
(Paris,1689) 405-408. Antelmy cited as suspect vv. 296ff;
427-428; 506-507; 238-246; 949ff., but admitted stylistic
resemblances to Prosper, e.g., in vv. 798-805ff. Antelmy
disagreed with Noris by denying the De prov. to Hilary.

[8] Antelmy, ibid.,407.

against attribution to Prosper (1712).[9] Tillemont pro-
posed the theory that Prosper might have composed the
De providentia in his youth, before he had read the
relevant works of Augustine and before the Pelagian
heresy had gained currency in Gaul. While never established as more than an hypothesis, this view was destined
to have some influence on later scholars.[10] The Maurists
in their edition (1711) essentially followed Tillemont
in leaving the genuineness of the poem in doubt.[11] The
Ballerini brothers (1769) also left the issue in doubt,
but tended to assign the De providentia to Prosper on the
theory that it was composed, not in connection with the
Pelagian controversy, but against those who upheld the
power of fate, i.e., the so-called mathematici,[12] and further

---

[9]Tillemont, Mémoires 16.730-731. Tillemont also
refuted Noris' ascription of the De prov. to Hilary.
Cf. n. 6, above.

[10]Tillemont, ibid., 16.731. The hypothesis is open
to the objection that, if Prosp. had indeed composed the
work in his youth, it should be brought up against him
by his opponents at a later point in his career, and he
should retract the unorthodox views which he had expressed therein. Tillemont himself admits this objection,
but attempts to refute it by citing Aug. as a parallel,
and noting that Aug. only issued a retractation of his
earlier works when they were brought against him by his
opponents. But to press the same parallel further, it
would seem that the adversaries of Prosp. should bring
forward De prov. against him as the opponents of Aug.
had brought up his earlier works.

[11]Note again that the Maurist editors had available
a copy of Tillemont's work before it went to press. Cf.
Valentin, Saint Prosper 206. Fabricius listed the De
prov. as Pelagian, and repeated Olivier's suggestion that
it may have been inserted after the De ingrat. by heretics, in order to win for it the prestige of Prosper's
name (1721). Cf. Fabricius, Bibliotheca Latina 6. 320-
321.

[12]The gloss "contra mathematicos" appears at 627
in the Lyons edition.

because of the similarity in style to the undoubtedly genuine works of Prosper.[13] It might be observed that while a part of the De providentia is indeed directed against the mathematici and their followers,[14] the entire work could not be fairly described in this manner.[15]

In the nineteenth century Ebert repeated the accepted view that the poem could not be attributed to Prosper, and suggested further that the author must have been a cleric (1889),[16] a theory accepted by Manitius[17] but convincingly refuted by Valentin.[18]

Against the predominant trend of seventeenth and eighteenth century scholarship, Manitius in a series of works presented evidence to support the ascription of the

---

[13]P. and J. Ballerini, "Observationes in Historiam Pelagianam 2.8," in Noris, op. cit., 497. The Ballerini rejected Noris' ascription of the De prov. to Hilary. Cf. n. 6, above.

[14]De prov. 624-720.

[15]Cf. Intro., Outline of Content, for confirmation of this point.

[16]Ebert, Allgemeine Geschichte 1.316-320. Ebert pointed out that the vocative form fratres occurs in the De prov. as an address to the reader. /Cf. De prov. 956, 972/. But the argument fails, because it is well-known that many Christians adopted a community life in the early centuries of the Church without any thought of becoming clerics or religious.

[17]Manitius, Geschichte 171-172, where the poet's theological erudition is cited in support of this view.

[18]Valentin, Saint Prosper 791. V. rightly termed this view an anachronism, and cited a number of examples of competent lay theologians from the 5th and subsequent centuries.

De providentia to Prosper (1888-1891).[19] Manitius found significant metrical and linguistic similarities between the De providentia and the undoubtedly genuine De ingratis, and relied as well on the citation of the poem under Prosper's name by Hincmar.[20] The work of Manitius opened a number of avenues of approach to the problem which were later explored in considerable detail by Valentin.

The comprehensive work of the Abbé Valentin (1900)[21] treated the question of authorship in such extensive detail and presented such a wealth of data that it would be impossible, within the scope of this dissertation, to do more than list the principle arguments in summary form. Valentin established a framework for his arguments in favor of Prosperian authorship by observing that all who denied the De providentia to Prosper did so on the basis of the purported Pelagian or semipelagian doctrine of the poem.[22] He proceeded to present two negative proofs in favor of ascription to Prosper:

A. The analysis of certain passages suspect of semipelagianism, especially verses 947-954, serves to cast doubt on the purported semipelagian tenor of the work. Further, there are clearly antipelagian passages in the poem, e.g., 960-968; 242-243.[23]

B. If the poem were semipelagian, this would not

---

[19]Manitius, "Uber das Gedicht 'de Providentia divina'," Zeitschrift 580-584 (1888); articles in the Vienna Sitzungsberichte 117 (1889) XII Abh. and 121 (1890) VII Abh.; Geschichte 170-180 (1891).

[20]Cf. n. 1 above. The linguistic and metrical similarities are treated passim in Intro., Biblical Allusions, Non-Biblical Parallels, and Metrics.

[21]Valentin, Saint Prosper.

[22]Ibid., 770.

[23]Ibid., 770-774. For further discussion of suspect passages cf. ibid., 888-892. The passages discussed by V. are De prov. 238-240; 295-302; 427-440; 453-459; 501-504; 550-559; 580-586.

disprove Prosperian authorship, for

a. Augustine even agreed in the beginning of his career with the semipelagian view that the first movement toward conversion must be ascribed to human liberty.

b. As Tillemont had suggested, Prosper might have written the poem in his youth, before he had read Augustine and before Pelagianism had attained prominence in Gaul.

c. There is greater rapport between the doctrine of the De ingratis and the De providentia, than exists between the De ingratis and the /genuine/ Responsiones ad capitula Vincentianorum. There are differences as great between the De ingratis on the one hand and the /equally genuine/ Responsiones ad capitula Gallorum and Epigrams on the other, as those between the De ingratis and the De providentia.[24]

Valentin next enumerated three areas of similarity between the De providentia and the undoubted works of Prosper:

A. Like Prosper, the author of the De providentia is fond of themes dealing with nature and the physical universe.[25]

B. The author of the De providentia accepts the theological ideas of Augustine and presents them with the same method and in the same spirit as Augustine. Specifically:

a. Prosper lacked originality as an interpreter of Augustine; the same lack of originality is evident in the De providentia.

b. The author of the De providentia makes extensive use of the argument from authority and especially from scripture; Prosper and Augustine do this also.

c. The spirit of the De providentia is the same as that of the De ingratis--intolerance for error, compassion for its victims, and especially for the weak (rudes).[26]

C. The author of the De providentia is faulty in

---

[24] Ibid., 774-777.

[25] Ibid., 791-793.

[26] Ibid., 793-798.

his disposition of material, as Prosper often is. That is, the author develops his ideas by reason of their intrinsic importance or the interest which they hold for him, and not according to the logic of the subject itself--a characteristic weakness of Prosper.[27]

Valentin then presented a number of positive proofs of Prosperian authorship:

A. The vocabulary of the De providentia shows many words belonging to Prosper, which the author was not obliged to use and which do not appear in the current language.[28]

B. Similarities in grammatical construction and word order exist between the De providentia and the De ingratis.[29]

C. Stylistic devices are employed in a similar manner in both poems. The rhetorical tone of both poems is similar, and the imagery of both is the same.[30]

D. The metrics of the De providentia is that of the De ingratis.[31]

Valentin concluded his discussion with an ingenious argument by exclusion, by which he established that the De providentia could not be attributed to any known author of the fifth century except Prosper.[32] He did, however, allow for the possibility of composition by an unknown author,[33] and in general admitted that his conclusion could not be considered certain, although noting that it

---

[27] Ibid., 799-802.

[28] Ibid., 802-806. For an extensive list of parallel passages between De prov. and De ingrat., with a few parallels between De prov. and Epigr., Coll., and Resp. ad capit. Gall., cf. ibid. 814-821.

[29] Ibid., 806-808.

[30] Ibid., 808-813.

[31] Ibid., 822-823.

[32] Ibid., 825-831.   [33] Ibid., 830.

was supported in the tradition.[34]

Valentin's arguments have met with a mixed, but generally negative, reception. Molinier asserted that the arguments against the presence of semipelagianism in the poem were simply not convincing, and that the stylistic argument had little value in view of the fact that Prosper's style could not be termed original.[35] Valentin's positive proof doubtless establishes that the De providentia must have had its origins in the same approximate period as the De ingratis, and demonstrates quite clearly that the authors of both poems shared a common educational tradition, but does not prove unity of authorship. As will become evident in subsequent sections of this dissertation, the De providentia, in its vocabulary, metrical structure, and stylistic devices, draws upon a fund of biblical and classical material available to and employed by all Christian authors. And surely the fact that the De providentia is not attributable to any known poet of the fifth century is not sufficient reason to assign it to Prosper, a point noted already by Couture.[36] The question has continued to be discussed since Valentin and divergent views are found in patrologies, histories of literature and special monographs, with most scholars denying the poem to Prosper.[37]

---

[34] Ibid., 823.

[35] M. Molinier, "Saint Prosper d'Aquitaine," a review of V. in Revue Historique 75 (1901) 114-116. The same point is made concerning the semipelagianism of the De prov. by L. Couture, "S. Prosper d'Aquitaine," Bulletin de littérature écclésiastique 3 (1901) 36.

[36] Couture, op. cit., 2 (1901) 37. For Couture's full discussion, which was highly favorable to V.'s work as a whole, cf. BLE 2 (1900) 269-282; 3 (1901) 33-49.

[37] Cf., e.g., Hauck, Realencyclopädie /not by Prosper/; Teuffel, Geschichte /not by Prosper/; Krüger in Schanz-Hosius, Geschichte /brief summary of the argument/; Bardenhewer, Geschichte /semipelagian/; Moricca, Storia della letteratura /probably spurious; the most extensive consideration of the problem since Valentin/; Helm in RE /Valentin is correct in his arguments; poem

17

The problem of the authorship of the De providentia arose early in the history of the printed text, and has continued to be discussed to the present. All authorities who have studied the problem are in agreement that the dispute centers around the interpretation to be given to certain passages in the poem itself. The weight of opinion remains against ascribing authorship to Prosper.

C. OCCASION, DATE, AND PLACE OF AUTHORSHIP

In 406 A.D., the Vandals launched an invasion of Gaul. "The devastation of the extensive provinces and the conquered cities of Gaul was terrible; contemporary writers of prose and verse alike complain bitterly of the atrocities committed by the barbarians in this unhappy country. The oldest people could not remember so disastrous an invasion."[1] A few years later the Visigoths, under their king Ataulf, entered Gaul and captured Narbonne, Toulouse, and Bordeaux, after having attempted to take Marseille without success.[2] The Visigoths moved on to produce further devastation in Spain in 415.

---

by Prosper/; Altaner, Patrology /pelagianizing views in poem/; Dekkers, Clavis /spurious and semipelagian/. De Labriolle compared the argument of the semipelagian Vincent of Lerins in his Commonitorium 26.8 that non-pelagian (orthodox) believers do not "knock" at the door with the assertion in De prov. 953 that one must "knock" to gain admittance to heaven. Cf. de Labriolle, Histoire 2.651. De Plinval asserted that the De prov. faithfully preserved the ideas of Pelagius without addition or deviation, citing vv. 960-967 and 652-657. Cf. de Plinval, Pélage 241.

[1]M. Manitius in J. B. Bury, The Cambridge Medieval History 1.266. Cf. also P. de Labriolle in Fliche-Martin, Histoire de l'Église 4.354.

[2]CMH 1.277. The occupation of Bordeaux occurred in 412, that of Narbonne and Toulouse in 413. Cf. ibid., 1.401-402.

INTRODUCTION

There is strong internal evidence in the De providentia that these were the invasions which occasioned the composition of the poem. Valentin observed that the poet's
reference to a decade in which Gaul had been unable to
withstand the invaders corresponded exactly to the period
406-415.[3] Further, the extensive use of verbs in the present tense suggests that the narrator was an eyewitness
of the events he recounts.[4] Moreover, a number of allusions in the prologue serve to support the hypothesis that
the period 406-415 is in question. The poet refers to
cities located on rivers leading to the sea, which were
unable to withstand the attacks of the barbarians.[5] These
cities may well have been Toulouse and Bordeaux, both
located on the Garonne.[6] And the invasion itself is attributed to the Vandals and Goths;[7] while later interven-
tions of the Goths in the affairs of Gaul are recorded,[8]
there is no other instance of a successive invasion of the
two peoples. Courcelle suggests that the poet's reference

---

[3] Valentin, Saint Prosper 788. Cf. De prov. 33-38:
"si toleranda mali labes, heu! caede decenni
Vandalicis gladiis sternimur et Geticis.
non castella petris, non oppida montibus altis
imposita, aut urbes amnibus aequoreis,
barbarici superare dolos atque arma furoris
evaluere omnes, ultima pertulimus."

[4] Valentin, ibid.,786, citing De prov. 534, 543,
609, 623, 660, 729.

[5] De prov. 35-36.

[6] Valentin, op. cit.,785, citing Ausonius, Ordo
nobilium urbium 18 (Toulouse) and 20 (Bordeaux) for descriptions of the two cities. Cf. n. 2, above.

[7] De prov. 34. For the identification of the Getae
with the Goths, which occurs in the 4th cent. Historia
Augusta and appears again in Isidore of Seville, cf.
Valentin, op. cit.,784 n. 5.

[8] Cf. CMH 1.279 for the Gothic invasion of 425-426
and subsequent disturbances from that quarter in 435-439.

to a bishop who led his flock into exile[9] may be applied to Exuperius, bishop of Toulouse /d. after 410/, who was perhaps exiled for having taken part in the defense of his city,[10] whereas Griffe sees in it a possible application to Bordeaux;[11] the matter remains uncertain.

Therefore 415 is the earliest possible date of composition of the De providentia, and the great majority of scholars have assigned it to the period 415-417, with most placing it in the year 416.[12] But Wiggers, in 1833, sought to place the poem after the Council of Ephesus (431) or perhaps after that of Chalcedon (451).[13] Wiggers' view finds some support in the fact that at first sight certain passages of the poem appear to be directed against the errors of Nestorius and Eutyches, which were condemned, respectively, at the two aforementioned

---

[9]De prov. 59-60: "cum sacer ille senex plebem, usta pulsus ab urbe, / ceu pastor laceras duceret exsul oves." For senex= bishop, cf. Aug. Epist. 128 and 129 and Prosp., De ingrat. 187.

[10]P. Courcelle, Histoire littéraire des grandes invasions germaniques 75. On the life of Exuperius cf. J. Bollandus, Acta Sanctorum Sept. Tom. 7 (Paris 1867) 583-589, orig. published at Antwerp in 1760, and L. Duchesne, Fastes épiscopaux de l'ancienne Gaule 1 (Paris,1894) 296.

[11]E. Griffe, La Gaule chrétienne 2.12 n. 17.

[12]Cf. e.g., P. and J. Ballerini, "Observationes in Historiam Pelagianam 2.8." 497 /A.D. 416/; Tillemont, Mémoires 16.730 /416/; Fabricius, Bibliotheca Latina 6.320 /c. 416/; Manitius, Zeitschrift 580 /416/; Ebert, Allgemeine Geschichte 1.317 /c. 415/; Valentin, op. cit. 289 /c. 416/; Krüger in Schanz-Hosius, Geschichte 4.2.495 /c. 415 or 416/; Bardenhewer, Geschichte 4.540 /c. 415/; Moricca, Storia 3.1.41 /c. 415-416/; Helm in RE 45.887 /c. 417/; Dekkers, Clavis /416/. Tillemont's dating /416/ is followed by the Maurists.

[13]Wiggers, Versuch einer pragmatischen Darstellung 2.201.

councils.[14] But this argument is refuted by Ebert, who observes that the questions raised by Nestorius, at least, were under discussion in Gaul prior to Ephesus, and who further points out the historical inconcinnity in assigning the poem to so late a period, long after the invasion of Goths and Vandals.[15] Valentin essentially follows and expands the position of Ebert.[16] Wiggers' position has in fact found no support and is improbable, given the weight of the evidence which can be adduced against it.

The previously mentioned circumstances of the invasion indicate that the place of authorship of the De providentia is the south of Gaul. Fabricius, Ebert and Valentin suggest that the mention of olive trees in verse 30 may be more appropriate to Provence than to Aquitaine;[17] otherwise there seems little if any special reference to the one area over the other, and both were affected by the invasions.

Acceptance of the date of composition of the De providentia as 416 would not necessarily result in denying the poem to Prosper, even granted that his birthdate

---

[14] Hincmar, De praedestinatione /PL 125.445/, introduces 497-501 with the phrase "in libro contra Eutychen," and vv. 550-557 with "in libro contra Nestorium." Gryphius' Lyons edition prints "contra Eutychem" against v. 473 of the De prov., and "contra Nestorium" at 546. For accounts of the proceedings of Ephesus and of Chalcedon, respectively, cf. Tixeront, History of Dogmas 3.43-51 and 3.84-91.

[15] Ebert, Allgemeine Geschichte 1.317 nn. 3 and 4. Ebert finds evidence of the discussion of questions raised by Nestorius in the Libellus satisfactionis sive emendationis of the Gallic monk Leporius /PL 31.1221-1230/, which is dated in 426. Cf. Dekkers, Clavis, item 515.

[16] Valentin, Saint Prosper 787-788. Cf. ibid., 780 for the relation of De prov. 542-543 to the Libellus satisfactionis.

[17] De prov. 30: "Quodque locus non est vitibus aut oleis." Cf. Fabricius, Bibliotheca Latina 6.321; Ebert, op. cit., 1.317 n. 3 and Valentin, op. cit., 126.

occurred no earlier than the last decade of the fourth century.[18] This is particularly true if a birthdate closer to 390 is admitted, as is done by Valentin and Krüger.[19] The suggestion has been advanced by Tillemont and Valentin that the poem may be a work of Prosper's youth, composed before he had been enlightened by the doctrine of Augustine.[20] Manitius, however, raises the difficulty that the first of Prosper's undoubtedly genuine writings, the Epistola ad Rufinum, must be dated at least ten years after the De providentia, i.e., in 426.[21]

The dating of the De providentia in 416 would not absolutely preclude Pelagian influence upon the poem, either. Pelagius had composed his Epistola ad Demtriadem around 412, and Augustine in the same year issued his earliest writings against Pelagian teachings, the De peccatorum meritis et remissione and the De spiritu et

---

[18] Cf. G. Bardy, "Prosper d'Aquitaine," DTC 13.1. 846-850. Prosper died some time after 463, since the Chronicon of Marcellinus /PL 51.930; MGH, auct. antiq. tom. 11, chron. min. vol. 2/ mentions him under that year.

[19] Valentin, op. cit. 823; Krüger in Schanz-Hosius, Geschichte 4.2.491. Contrast Fabricius, Bibliotheca Latina 6.320, who maintains that Prosp. was scarcely 18 or 20 in 416. Couture, "Saint Prosper," BLE 3 (1901) 35, considers the De prov. a remarkable work for Prosp. if placed in 416.

[20] Tillemont, Mémoires 16.731; Valentin, op. cit.,775.

[21] Manitius, Zeitschrift 580. For further discussion and a translation of the Epist. ad Ruf. cf. Huegelmeyer, Carmen de Ingratis 6-10; 210-220, and P. de Letter, Defense of St. Augustine 21-37; 198-202. The spurious Poema coniugis ad coniugem is dated c. 415. Cf. Krüger in Schanz-Hosius, Geschichte 4.2.491.

littera.[22] Prior to this, Pelagius had been in Rome ex-
pounding his doctrine and making converts from the first
years of the fifth century. But Krüger maintains that
the Pelagian dispute would hardly have affected Gaul by
415 or 416, a judgment in which Moricca concurs.[23]

Greater difficulty occurs in attempting to reconcile
the dating of 416 with the claim of semipelagian influences in the poem. The semipelagian dispute arose
over the import of the decrees of the Council of Carthage
(418).[24] The conflict appears to have started in the
monastery of Hadrumetum in North Africa around 426 through
a misunderstanding on the part of the monks of Augustine's
letter to the Roman priest Sixtus.[25] The earliest direct
statement of the existence of the controversy in Gaul
occurs in Prosper's Epistola ad Rufinum (426),[26] which
contains allusions to the the semi-pelagian views of the
Marseille abbot John Cassian, part of whose Collationes
were circulated privately earlier in 426.[27] And while
Prosper suggests that complaints against Augustine had
been voiced in secret by the monks at Marseille for some

---

[22]For an account of Pelagianism and Aug.'s struggles
against it cf. Tixeront, op. cit. 2.432-505. Tillemont
notes that two Gallic bishops resident at Bethlehem,
Heros of Arles and Lazarus of Aix, presented a libellus
to the Council of Diospolis (415) against the Pelagians.

[23]Krüger in Schanz-Hosius, 4.2.495; Moricca, op.
cit.,3.1.41.

[24]E. Amann, DTC 14.2.1797. For a comprehensive
summary of the dispute cf. Sister M. Alphonsine Lesousky,
The De Dono Perseverantiae of St. Augustine (CUA Patristic Studies 91; Washington,1956) 1-81. Cf. also Tixeront,
op. cit.,3.264-301.

[25]Amann, op. cit. 14.2.1797. Sister M. Alphonsine,
op. cit.,4. The letter itself was composed in 418, and
is Epist. 194 among Aug.'s letters.

[26]Cf. n. 21, above.

[27]Sister M. Alphonsine, op. cit., 12 n. 6.

time,[28] it is doubtful that such dissension should have existed for ten years or more (416-426) without coming to public notice.[29]

The De providentia, then, was composed in southern Gaul in the aftermath of the barbarian invasions of the early fifth century, probably in 416 or thereabouts. The effect of this dating is to allow the possibility of composition by Prosper, and to allow the further possibility of Pelagian influence on the poem, although either of these hypotheses is not without difficulty. It would appear to be more difficult, however, to maintain the possibility of semipelagian influence on the De providentia, given the dating in 416.

D. BIBLICAL ALLUSIONS

Introduction. The biblical material presented below is arranged under three headings: 1. Specific Events; 2. Similarity of Thought; and 3. Verbal Similarity. Specific events may be such as are historically beyond doubt, as in the case of the Crucifixion, or may be susceptible of metaphorical or figurative interpretation, as in the story of the repentance of Ninive. Passages may display similarity of thought in that the same dogmatic teaching, e.g., the Mystical Body of Christ, is involved in each, or may have little or no connection with formal dogma, as in the generalization that man is born to live but a short time, or else the relationship between the biblical passage and the De providentia may be effected through the use of an image or figure, as in that of Christ as the light, or in the depiction of life as a warfare. The indication of verbal similarities is not confined to the section so entitled, but they are supplied also as they occur throughout the two earlier sections of the analysis.

References to verses of the De providentia are arranged in numerical order under each heading in the

---

[28] Epist. ad Ruf. 4-5.

[29] Bardenhewer and Helm recognize the problem. Cf. Bardenhewer, Geschichte 4.540 and Helm in RE 45.887.

INTRODUCTION

left column of the page, with the corresponding biblical
reference in the right. Cross references are supplied to
other verses of the De providentia or to other biblical
passages. Abbreviations of the books of Sacred Scripture
are those used in the Confraternity version. A brief
description of the gist of each set of parallel passages
is given in English, with further references if appropriate. A summary is given for each of the three subdivisions, and a conclusion for the section as a whole.

1. Specific Events

209-23   Gen. 1.1-27; cf. Gen. 2.7-16.
The creation of the universe; the special creation
of man.

258-9
Treated at 264-6, below.

262-3   Gen. 2.19-20
Man's prerogative of assigning names to lower
creatures.

264-6   Gen. 1.26-8; cf. Gen. 9.2-3;
                          Ps. 8.6-9; Sir. 17.3-4.
Man's dominion over the lower animals. Cf. De
prov. 258-59.

273-7   Gen. 2.7-16
The special creation of man; Adam in the garden
of paradise.

278-88   Gen. 2.17; 3.1-13
The temptation and fall of man.

289-90   Rom. 5.12
The transmission of Adam's sin to his descendants.

305-16   Gen. 4.1-8
  306-7 iustus Abel, qui   Abel quoque obtulit de
  primitiis ovium grege ⎫   primogenitis gregis sui
  lectis, / convertit   ⎬   et de adipibus eorum et
  Domini sincera in munera   respexit Dominus ad Abel
  vultum   et ad munera eius
The story of Cain and Abel.

321   Gen. 5.24
. . . transtulit Enoch   ambulavitque /Henoch/ cum
                            Deo, et non apparuit:
                            quia tulit eum Deus.
Henoch's removal from the earth while still living.

327-8   4. Kgs. 2.11
cum raptum ignitis per   . . . ecce currus igneus
inane iugalibus Helim /   et equi ignei diviserunt
scandentem rutilo vide-   utrumque et ascendit
runt aethera curru   Helias per turbinem in
                             caelum
Elias taken up into heaven in a fiery chariot.

329-31   Gen. 6.4; Bar. 3.26-28; cf.
                             Wisd. 14.6
The race of giants begotten by Adam's descendants
through incestuous unions.

335-40   Gen. 6.9 - 8.19
The story of Noe and the flood. Cf. De prov. 826;
842-3.

346-9   Gen. 22.15-18; cf. Gen.
                             15.5-6
The covenant between God and Abraham.

350-5   Gen. 18.16-19.29; Wisd.
                             10.6-7
350 . . . in Pentapolim   10.7: . . . descendente
descenderet igneus imber   igne in Pentapolim
Destruction of Sodom and Gomorrha; deliverance of
Lot. Cf. De prov. 826-7.

356-7   Gen. 41.47-57
357 dira fames, totos   41.54: coeperunt venire
septem toleranda per   septem anni inopiae quos
annos   praedixerat Ioseph et in
                             universo orbe fames
                             praevaluit . . .
The seven years of famine; for the famine as extending with particular severity to Egypt and
Chanaan, cf. Gen. 47.13.

358-69   Gen. 46.1 - 47.12
Migration of the Hebrews into Egypt.

361-2   Gen. 37.5-36
  362 in servum vendunt   37.28: . . . vendiderunt
  pretio . . .   Ismahelitis viginti ar-
                                  genteis
Joseph's dreams; Joseph sold into Egypt; his brothers
deceive Jacob, their father.

363   Gen. 39.1-20
Joseph's virtue in temptation; Joseph cast into
prison.

364-5   Gen. 41.14-46
  365 . . . dignatur   41.43: fecitque ascen-
  honore secundo   dere super currum
                                  secundum
Joseph interprets Pharaoh's dreams and is exalted
in Egypt.

366-7   Gen. 44.1 - 45.8
The cup found in Benjamin's sack; Joseph makes
himself known to his brothers.

377-82   Ex. 1.8-22
The oppression of the Hebrews in Egypt; Pharaoh's
command to the Hebrew midwives to kill all male
Hebrew offspring.

385-8   Ex. 6.10-13.28-30; 7.1-7
The Lord's command to Moses that he order Pharaoh
to allow the departure of the Hebrews; the threat
of stern judgment on Egypt, i.e., the ten plagues.

389-92   Ex. 8.4 (second plague);
                                8.24 (fourth plague); 9.27-9
                                (seventh plague); 10.8-11.
                                16-27 (eighth plague);
                                10.24-5 (ninth plague)
Pharaoh's pretended compliance with the Lord's
command and subsequent hardening of heart.

393-5   Ex. 12.31-51.
Pharaoh's permission to the Hebrews to depart from
Egypt; the exodus. The presentation of gifts to
the Hebrews to hasten their departure, foretold at
Ex. 3.21-2; 11.1-3.

395-9   Ex. 13.21-2
. . . monstrante colum-   13.21: Dominus autem
na / per deserta viam,   praecedebat eos ad osten-
quae formam in tempus   dendam viam per diem in
utrumque / temperat   columna nubis et per noctem
. . . / luce tegens, et   in columna ignis ut dux
nocte regens, eadem ig-   esset itineris utroque
nis et umbra / discutiens   tempore
. . . nube calores.
The column which guided the Hebrews in their wanderings; for the column as settling over the Meeting
Tent, and a further description of the forms of the
column, cf. Ex. 40.34-8 and Num. 9.15-23.

400-4   Ex. 14.10-31; Wisd. 19.6-8
403 . . . illaesae . . .   19.6: . . . ut pueri tui
plebis   custodirentur illaesi.
Crossing of the Red Sea; destruction of the
Egyptians.

410 mannae imbrem . . .   Ex. 16.4-15; cf. Ps. 77
                                (78).24.
The rain of manna on the Hebrews in the desert.

410 . . . et cunctos in   Wisd. 16.20: . . . et para-
caeli pane sapores   tum panem de caelo praesti-
                                tisti illis sine labore,
                                omne delectamentum in se
                                habentem, et omnis saporis
                                suavitatem.
A further reference to the rain of manna; for the
bread as a type of the Eucharist cf. John 6.22-60,
esp. v. 31: . . . sicut scriptum est: panem de
caelo dedit eis manducare, and v. 41: . . . ego sum
panis vivus qui de caelo descendi.

INTRODUCTION

411 siccae rupis aquam . . . Ex. 17.1-7; Num. 20.2-13;
                              cf. Ps. 77 (78).15; Wisd.
                              11.4
The rock of Horeb, a miracle recounted in full twice
in O.T., in Ex. and Num.; for the rock as a type of
Christ, the spiritual rock, cf. 1 Cor. 10.4.

411 . . . et dulcorem   Ex. 15.22-6
fontis amari
The changing of bitter water into fresh at Mara.

412-3   Deut. 8.4; 29.4; 2 Esd. 9.21
Miraculous preservation of the feet and clothing of
the Hebrews in their forty years of wandering in
the desert.

434-5   Ex. 31.18
The giving of the Decalogue to Moses on Sinai, foretold at Ex. 23.12.

435 . . . praesenti . . .   Ex. 32.18-29?
poena
Perhaps a reference to the slaying of 3,000 worshippers of the Golden Calf by the Levites at Moses'
command, shortly after the giving of the Ten Commandments.

436-8   Ex. 34.10-28
The covenant between the Lord and Moses made upon
the renewal of the Commandments.

443-4   3 Kgs. 10.1-10
Visit of the Queen of Saba to Solomon in Jerusalem.

445-7   Jon. 3.1-10
  445-6 sic Ninive . . ./   3.3: . . . et Ninive erat
  credidit, et tribus in   civitas magna itinere
  luctu ieiuna diebus /   trium dierum
                                 3.5: et crediderunt viri
                                 Ninivitae in Deum, et
                                 praedicaverunt ieiunium.

The conversion of Ninive.

29

465
. . . et Verbum caro
fit . . .
The Incarnation.

John 1.14
et Verbum caro factum
est . . .

516-8
. . . pauperis egit /
in specie . . . / . . .
dives egenis.
Christ's life as a poor man.

2 Cor. 8.9
. . . propter vos egenus
factus est, cum esset
dives, ut illius inopia
vos divites essetis.

520-33

Matt. 26.1 - 27.66; Mark
14.1 - 15.47; Luke 22.1 -
23.56; John 13.1 - 19.42.
The passion and death of Christ.

523-4
. . . felque et acetum /
dulcius ille favis
haurit . . .

Matt. 27.34: . . . vinum . . .
cum felle mixtum; Luke
23.36: . . . acetum offer-
entes . . . John 19.29-30
19.29: . . . spongiam
plenam aceto . . .
19.30: cum ergo accepisset
Iesus acetum . . .
The soldiers offer Jesus vinegar and gall at the
Crucifixion.

527-8
. . . sol fugit ab
orbe / et medio nox
facta die est

Matt. 27.45: . . . tenebrae
factae sunt . . . Mark 15.33:
. . . tenebrae factae sunt
Luke 23.44-5
23.44: . . . tenebrae
factae sunt . . .
23.45: et obscuratus est
sol . . .
Darkness over Jerusalem immediately preceding the
death of Christ.

528-31
530-1 excita sanctorum
sumpserunt corpora vitam/
velum etiam templi
scissum est . . .

Matt. 27.51-2
27.51: et ecce velum
templi scissum est
27.52: . . . et multa
corpora sanctorum, qui
dormierant, surrexerunt

Mark 15.38: et velum templi
scissum est; Luke 23.45:
. . . et velum templi scissum
est . . .

Miraculous occurrences accompanying the death of
Christ.

536

Mark 16.12 (appearance before
two of the disciples); Mark
16.13-4 (appearance before
the eleven apostles); Luke
24.13-31 (appearance before
the disciples traveling to
Emmaus); Luke 24.36-7
(appearance before the eleven apostles); John 20.19-
23 (appearance before the
apostles)

Appearances of Christ before his apostles and other
disciples immediately after the Resurrection.

537-9

Luke 24.39-40 (to the apostles); John 20.24-9 (to
Thomas)

Christ's invitation to the Apostles, and later to
Thomas, to touch his wounds as a proof of his
Resurrection.

539

John 19.34

Christ's body pierced by the lance at the Crucifixion.

540-1

John 20.24 - 21.25; Acts
1.1-8

Events of the forty days between the Resurrection
and Ascension.

619-21

Apoc. 12.1-9

620-1 . . . rueritque   12.4: et cauda eius tra-
illo pars tertia pulso /   hebat tertiam partem
astrorum . . .   stellarum caeli . . .

Satan's banishment from heaven after a great battle.

680-3   3 Kgs. 17.1; cf. Sir. 48.
                              1-3; Jas. 5.17
Elias closes the heavens from raining.

683-5   3 Kgs. 18.1-40; cf. Sir.
685 quem /ignem/   48.1-3
dederat sacris . . .
Elias brings fire upon the altar.

685 . . . ignem immisisse   4 Kgs. 1.1-15
profanis
Fire brought down by Elias against two companies of
troops sent to apprehend him.

826
Treated at 335-40, above.

826-7
Treated at 350-5, above.

827-9   Ex. 12.1-30
Sparing of the firstborn of the Hebrews from the
tenth plague.

830-1   Jos. 2.1-24; 6.15-25
Hebrew spies spared by Rahab the Harlot; Rahab and
her family spared by the Hebrews when Jericho was
taken.

832   Jos. 3.7-17
The Hebrews cross the Jordan on dry ground to take
possession of the promised land.

833-4   Dan. 14.33-9
Habacuc is conveyed to the lions' den to supply
Daniel with food.

836-7   Acts 12.6-11; Acts 16.16-34
836 . . . vinctos la-   16.26: . . . et univer-
bentia vincula solvunt   sorum vincula soluta
                                 sunt.
Miraculous deliverance of Peter from prison by an
angel.

INTRODUCTION

838 deficit . . . ignes   Dan. 3.1-97
calor . . .
Sidrach, Misach and Abdenago in the fiery furnace.

838 deficit . . . ira   Dan. 6.2-29
leones
Daniel in the lions' den.

842-3
Treated at 335-40, above.

Summary: The De providentia relies heavily on
material from Scripture, with more events recounted from
the Old Testament than from the New. While the incidents
related in the poem have been derived from a number of
the sacred books, chief reliance has been placed on
Genesis, Exodus and the Gospels. In general the employment of the biblical material corresponds to the pattern
of the poem as described by the content analysis, i.e.,
the events of the Old Testament are related first, then
those of the New, with special emphasis on the life of
Christ, and finally there is a recapitulation of events
of the Old Testament already narrated together with the
addition of other O.T. incidents. Relatively few verbal
parallels occur; the most notable of these are in the
accounts of the destruction of Sodom (De prov. 350-5),
the Incarnation (De prov. 465) and the tearing of the
veil of the temple upon Christ's death (De prov. 528-31).
Occasionally a single verse in the De providentia shows
verbal similarity to two biblical passages (De prov. 410-
411, 685, 838).

2. Similarity of Thought

93-4   John 14.2-7
94 inque viam . . . re-   14.6: ego sum via . . .
ferre pedem   Heb. 10.19-21
Figure of the way; the biblical texts cited designate
Christ himself as the Way.

94 . . . visa luce . . .   John 1.15; 1.9; 3.19-21;
                           8.12; 12.34-36; 12.46; cf.
                           Heb. 1.2-3

Figure of Christ the Light, a favorite theme of
John's Gospel. For God as Light in O.T. cf. Ps. 26
(27).1. For the Messias as Light cf. Isa. 9.1;
42.6-7; 49.6; Luke 1.78-9 ("The Orient"). Christ
appears to Saul as light in Acts 9.3. For the contrast between light and darkness implied in De prov.
94-5 cf. John 12.31-6; Eph. 5.8-13; Col. 1.11-14;
1 John 1.5-7 (God as the light). Cf. also 160 and
544, below.

159   Job 37.19: . . . nos quippe
o mersi in tenebras . . . involvimur tenebris; cf.
                            1 Tim. 6.9: . . . desideria
                            . . . quae mergunt homines
                            in interitum et perditionem
Depiction of man as sunk in darkness.

160   Matt. 6.22-3; Luke 11.33-6
Bodily and spiritual illumination cast in figurative
terms; for other contrasts between light and darkness,
cf. De prov. 94, above.

183-94   Sir. 42.15-25
190 nec de noscendis   42.22: Et non eget
egeat manifesta doceri   alicuius consilio·
The works and attributes of God.

194 . . . et peccata   Ps. 31 (32). 5: . . . et tu
remittat   remisisti impietatem peccati
                             mei; Ps. 84 (85).3: remisisti
                             iniquitatem plebis tuae,
                             operuisti omnia peccata eorum;
                             Sir. 2.13: . . . et remittet
                             /Deus/ in die tribulationis
                             peccata
The power of God to forgive sin; for Christ's power
and his exercise of it, cf. Matt. 9.2; Luke 5.20;
7.47; 1 John 1.9; 2.12.

197-8   Wisd. 9.5: . . . homo infirmus,
. . . hominis . . . in   et exigui temporis
tempora nati /
exigua . . .
Man is born for a short time. In De prov., a generalization applicable to all men; in Wisd., Solomon's
portrayal of self. The theme is a common one in all
literature.

204-5   <u>1 Tim.</u> 6.12; 6.19
  205 immortale decus,   6.12: . . . apprehende
  superato <u>apprendite</u>   vitam aeternam
  caelo   6.19: . . . ut <u>apprehen-</u>
                                    dant veram vitam
The Christian must lay hold of eternal life.

229-34   <u>Rom.</u> 7.13-23; <u>Gal.</u> 5.16-7;
                               cf. <u>2 Tim.</u> 4.7
The warfare in man between the flesh and the spirit.
Cf. <u>De prov.</u> 660-1; 918-20; 958-64.

255
Treated at 604-5, below.

319
Treated at 604-5, below.

343   <u>1 Cor.</u> 12.12-27; cf. <u>Rom.</u>
                               12.5; <u>1 Cor.</u> 6.15, 10.17;
                               <u>Eph.</u> 4.1-16, 5.29-30; <u>Col.</u>
                               1.18, 1.24
The doctrine of the Mystical Body of Christ, a
favorite theme in the Pauline epistles, Cf. <u>De
prov.</u> 697.

419-21   <u>Rom.</u> 2.14-15
  420-1 . . . scripta vo-   2.15: qui ostendunt opus
  lumina <u>cordis</u> / inspicite,   legis <u>scriptum</u> in <u>cordi-</u>
  et genitam vobiscum   bus suis . . .
  agnoscite <u>legem</u>
Natural law written in the heart of man. For a
statement of the natural law, cf. <u>Sir.</u> 17.12: "He
says to them, 'Avoid all evil'; each of them he
gives precepts about his fellow man."

455-7   <u>Gal.</u> 3.28: non est <u>Iudaeus</u>,
  . . . vir, femina, ser-   neque <u>Graecus</u>: non est <u>ser-</u>
  <u>vus</u> / <u>liber</u>, <u>Iudaeus</u>,   <u>vus</u>, neque <u>liber</u>: non est
  <u>Graecus</u>, <u>Scytha</u>, <u>barbarus</u>,masculus, neque <u>femina</u>.
  <u>omnes</u> / in <u>Christo</u> sumus   Omnes enim vos <u>unum estis</u> in
  <u>unum</u> . . .   Christo.

Col. 3.11: ubi non est gentilis et Iudaeus, circumcisio
et praeputium, barbarus et
Scytha, servus et liber: sed
omnia, et in omnibus Christus.

The unity of all Christians in Christ.

457-9
. . . non persona po-
tentis / nec domini,
regisve prior; distan-
tia nulla / luminis
unius . . .

Lev. 19.15: . . . ne consideres personam pauperis nec
honores vultum potentis
Deut. 1.17: nulla erit distantia personarum . . .
Prov. 24.23; Jas. 2.1-13

Impartiality toward persons.

462 . . . confessi Christi

Matt. 10.32: "omnis ergo
qui confitebitur me coram
hominibus, confitebor et ego
eum coram Patre meo, qui in
caelis est."
Luke 12.8 . . . "omnis quicumque confessus fuerit me coram
hominibus, et filius hominis
confitebitur illum coram
angelis Dei."

The Christian's acknowledgement of Christ.

464-5   Phil. 2.7
Christ's assumption of human nature.

470-1
venturum ad terrena
Deum, qui morte per-
empta, / solveret in-
ferni leges . . .

Rom. 7.6: nunc autem soluti
sumus a lege mortis . . .

Christians freed from slavery to the law.

487-8
. . . et non ego iam
in me / vivam, sed
Christus . . .

Gal. 2.20: vivo autem, iam
non ego, vivit vero in me
Christus
Cf. John 17.23

Christ's life in the Christian.

489-91   Rom. 5.12-14
   489-90 . . . transfu-   5.12: . . . in omnes
   dit in omnes / mortem   homines mors pertransiit.
   homines . . .
The reign of death over all men a result of Adam's
sin.

506-7   1 Cor. 6.19-20
   . . . nec tuus ipse   6.19: . . . et non estis
   es. / emptus enim es,   vestri?
   pretiumque tui resolvere   6.20: empti enim estis
   fas est   pretio magno . . .
                  1 Cor. 7.23: pretio empti
                  estis . . .
Christ has redeemed man at a great price, that of
his own blood. Cf. De prov. 947-8.

511   Matt. 11.30: iugum enim
   sub durum iubet ire   meum suave est . . .
   iugum . . .
In De prov., the harsh yoke of the law; in Matt.,
the gentle yoke of Christ.

524-5   Gal. 3.13: Christus nos
   . . . sanctus maledictum / redemit de maledicto legis,
   fit crucis, et moritur   factus pro nobis maledictum
   Christus . . .   . . .
                  Cf. Deut. 21.23: . . . male-
                  dictus a Deo est qui pendet
                  in ligno . . .
Christ became the curse of the cross for man's
salvation.

534   1 Cor 15.55: . . . ubi est
                  mors stimulus tuus?
                  Cf. Os. 13.14
The stings of death. Cf. De prov. 611.

544   John 1.4-5
   . . . dum vita in vita   1.4: In ipso vita erat. . .
   est, in lumine lumen   Cf. Ps. 35 (36).10: . . .
                  et in lumine tuo videbimus
                  lumen
Christ as life and light. Reference in Ps. is to
God and divine providence. For further references
to the figure of Christ the Light, cf. De prov. 94,
above.

548 . . . curramus . . .   Gal. 2.2: . . . ne forte in
                                  vacuum cucurrerem, aut
                                  cucurissem.
                                  Phil. 2.16: . . . quia non
                                  in vacuum cucurri . .
                                  1 Cor. 9.24; Rom. 9.16
The Christian's life as a race toward salvation.
Cf. De prov. 648.

551   1 Tim. 2.4
God's universal salvific will. Cf. De prov. 781-3.

561   2 Pet. 2.15: derelinquentes
error enim est eius qui   rectam viam, erraverunt . . .
cessit limite recti   Cf. Prov. 2.13
Image of the Christian "path" and man straying from
it. In De prov., the application is general; in
2 Pet., to certain particular heretics.

603   Gen. 1.31: viditque Deus
omnia quae fecit bona   cuncta quae fecit et erant
valde . . .   valde bona . . .
                                  Cf. 1 Tim. 4.4: . . . omnis
                                  creatura Dei bona est
All creation is good, because it was made by God.

604-5   1 Cor. 9.25: omnis autem
. . . ut superas caper-   qui in agone contendit, ab
emus in illis, hic de-   omnibus se abstinuit, et illi
certato virtutis agone,   quidem ut corruptibilem coro-
coronas   nam accipiant; nos autem
                                  incorruptam.
                                  Cf. 2 Tim. 4.8: . . . corona
                                  iustitiae . . .
                                  1 Pet. 5.4; . . . percipietis
                                  immarcescibilem coronam
                                  gloriae
                                  Jas. 1.12; Apoc. 2.10:
                                  coronam vitae
Image of the Christian life as a contest, and the
(athlete's) crown as its reward. Cf. De prov. 663
for the image of reward in general; for the crown,
cf. De prov. 255, 319, 852, 900.

610-1   Eph. 6.10-7
  610 . . . gladio verbi,   6.16: . . . scutum fidei
  fideique umbone potenti   6.17: . . . et gladium
                                    spiritus (quod est verbum
                                    Dei)
The armor of God, based on the image of Christian
life as a warfare, for which cf. De prov. 229-34.

611
The stings of death, treated at 534, above.

612-6   Deut. 4.19, 17.3; 4 Kgs.
                                    23.5; Job 31.26-8; Jer.
                                      19.3; Am. 5.26, quoted at
                                      Acts 7.43
References to worship of heavenly bodies and warnings
against the practice. Cf. De prov. 674-5.

640   2 Pet. 1.3-4
  . . . cunctos eadem ad   1.3: . . . qui vocavit
  promissa vocare   nos
                                      1.4: . . . maxima et pre-
                                      tiosa nobis promissa
                                      donavit
Christ's call to the Christian; in De prov. in a
general sense, in 2 Pet. with stress on the fulfillment of the promise through the Christian's parti-
cipation in the divine nature.

648 . . . currentem . . .
Treated at 548, above.

649-50   Deut. 6.13-4
  'solum,' inquit, 've-   6.13: . . . Dominum Deum
  nerare Deum, solique   tuum timebis et ipsi
  memento / servire . . ."   servies
                                      The passage from Deut. is
                                      cited Matt. 4.10, Luke 4.8,
                                      in the form: Dominum Deum
                                      tuum adorabis, et illi soli
                                      servies
Worship is to be given to God alone.

651
        1 Tim. 6.4-12
'hoc operis <u>sectare</u> boni,   6.11: . . . <u>haec</u> <u>fuge</u>:
hoc <u>fuge</u> cautus iniqui'   sectare vero . . .
       Cf. <u>Sir</u>. 17.12
The command to do good and avoid evil, with discussion of specific virtues and vices in <u>1 Tim</u>.

660-1
Treated at 229-34, above.

663 . . . <u>bravio</u>que poti- 1 Cor. 9.24-5
tos   9.24: . . . unus accipit
        bravium
      Phil. 3.13-4
       3.14: . . . ad <u>bravium</u>
       supernae vocationis Dei
       in Christo Iesu
Figure of the prize, taken from athletic contests.
Cf. <u>De</u> <u>prov</u>. 604-5; 852.

665 . . . <u>callidus</u> hostis Gen. 3.1: sed et serpens
        erat <u>callidior</u> cunctis ani-
        mantibus terrae . . .
Cunning as a quality of Satan.

674   Acts 7.43: . . . et <u>sidus</u>
 <u>sidus</u> adoratum <u>Rempham</u> dei vestri <u>Rempham</u>
 . . .   Am. 5.26: . . . <u>sidus</u> dei
        vestri . . .
Worship of Rempham (probably the planet Saturn).

674-5   Deut. 17.3: ut . . . ador-
 . . . venerataque <u>caeli</u> ent eos, <u>solem</u> et <u>lunam</u> et
 militia et cultus <u>Soli</u> omnem <u>militiam</u> <u>caeli</u> . . .
 <u>Lunae</u>que dicatus.   4 Kgs. 23.5: et eos qui
        adolebant incensum Baal et
        soli et <u>lunae</u> et duodecim
        signis et omni <u>militiae</u>
        caeli
        Job 31.26-8
        Jer. 19.13: . . . sacrifica-
        verunt omni <u>militiae</u> <u>caeli</u>
        Acts 7.42-3
        7.42: . . . /Deus/ tradi-
        dit eos servire <u>militiae</u>
        caeli

The worship of heavenly bodies. Cf. De prov. 612-6.

694

. . . renovavit
.Spiritus . . .

Tit. 3.5-6
3.5: . . . per lavacrum
regenerationis et renova-
tionis Spiritus Sancti
Our salvation through renewal by the Holy Spirit.

695

. . . mortali ex stir-
pe recisos

Rom. 11.24: . . . tu ex
naturali excisus es
oleastro . . .
The figure of grafting; the Christian is cut off
from his old life. In Rom. the image is carried
through to the Christian's engraftment onto the new
tree, Christ.

697

. . . templum in
Domini . . .

John 2.19: . . . solvite
templum hoc . . .
John 2.21: . . . dicebat de
templo corporis sui
1 Cor. 3.9; 3.16
3.16: . . . templum Dei
estis . . .
2 Cor. 6.16: . . . Vos enim
estis templum Dei vivi . . .
Apoc. 3.12: . . . in templo
Dei mei
The Church as the Temple of God. For the image of
the Christians as stones in the building which is
the Church cf. Eph. 2.19-22; 1 Pet. 2.1-10; for God
and Christ as the temple of the New Jerusalem, Apoc.
20.22.

697

. . . in Domini corpusque . . .
The doctrine of the Mystical Body, treated at 343,
above.

721

. . . laqueis . . .

1 Tim. 3.7 and 6.9: . . . in
laqueum diaboli
2 Tim. 2.26: . . . a diaboli
laqueis . . .

The snares of Satan.

41

739   Gen. 2.7
  In De prov., God is depicted as breathing life into
  the universe; in Gen. the passage refers only to
  the creation of man.

745   Gen. 1.26-7, 5.1, 9.6; Wisd.
                              2.23; Sir. 17.1; 1 Cor.
                              11.7; Jas. 3.9
  Man is created in the image of God.

770   1 Cor. 1.17-31
  The wisdom of Christ is the foolishness of the world.

781-3   Ezech. 18.23, 18.32
  781 ' mortem,' inquit   18.32: ' quia nolo mortem
  Dominus, 'peccantis   morientis,' dicit Dominus
  nolo . . .'   Deus . . .
                              Ezech. 33.11: . . . dicit
                              Dominus Deus, 'nolo mortem
                              impii . . .'
                              2 Pet. 3.9: . . . Dominus
                              . . . nolens aliquos perire
                              . . .
                              Cf. 1 Tim. 2.4
  The universal salvific will of God. Cf. De prov. 551.

785-6   Rom. 12.19: . . . date locum
  785 ;. . . vindictam,'   irae. scriptum est enim,
  inquit, 'mihi cedite   mihi vindicta . . .
  . . .'   Heb. 10.30: . . . mihi vin-
  786 '. . . detur lo-   dicta
  cus irae'   Deut. 32.35
  "'Vengeance is mine,' saith the Lord."

794   Matt. 5.26; Luke 12.59
  Man must face a complete reckoning of all his actions;
  the passages from Matt. and Luke are cast in the form
  of a parable.

802-3   Sir. 42.18-9
  The omniscience of God.

805-6   Rom. 2.16; 1 Cor. 4.5
  The general judgment.

811-2   Luke 1.46-55 (the Magnificat);
                                          1 Kgs. 2.1-10; Ps. 74 (75).8,
                                          112 (113). 6-7, 145 (146).7-9.
Manifestations of the justice of God.

816-20   Ezech. 21.3-4
820 . . . iniustorum   21.3: . . . occidam in te
iustos mala ferre   iustum et impium
necesse est   Eccles. 9.2-3
The just and the unjust receive the same rewards and
punishments in this life.

852
Treated at 604-5, above.

859   Phil. 3.19-20
 . . . et caelo ascrip-   3.19: . . . qui terrena
ti terrena fovemus   sapiunt
                                          3.20: nostra autem con-
                                          versatio in caelis est . . .
                                          Heb. 12.22-6
                                          12.23: et ecclesiam pri-
                                          mitivorum, qui conscripti
                                          sunt in caelis . . .
The citizenship of the Christian in the Kingdom of
Heaven.

875   Matt. 20.20-3; Mark 10.35-40
The challenge of drinking from Christ's cup, i.e.,
his cup of suffering.

877-8   Jas. 1.15: . . . peccatum
878 quae morbos mor-   vero cum consummatum fuerit,
temque animae generant-   generat mortem
que foventque
Sin and sinful objects bring about the death of the
soul.

887-8   Jdt. 8.27: . . . flagella
888 diligit, et patrio   Domini, quibus quasi servi
vult emendare flagello   corripimur ad emendationem
                                          . . .
                                          Prov. 3.12; Heb. 12.6;
                                          Apoc. 3.19
God's punishment of sinners a sign of his love for
them.

892-4   Eccles. 7.16
The attribution of a long lifespan to the wicked.

900
  Treated at 604-5, above.

912   Phil. 1.23: . . . desiderium
  . . . cupidus victo cer-   habens dissolvi, et esse cum
  tamine solvi   Christo . . .
  Desire of the Christian to depart this life and be
with Christ; expressed as a personal desire of Paul
in Phil.; cf. 3. Verbal Similarity, below, at this
verse.
918-20
  Treated at 229-34, above.

927-8   Rom. 9.22-3
  . . . nos splendida   9.22: . . . vasa irae . . .
  quondam / vasa Dei . . .   9.23: . . . vasa miseri-
                        cordiae . . .
                     2 Tim. 2.21: . . . vas in
                     honorem sanctificatum
                     Acts 9.15: . . . vas elect-
                     ionis . . .
  Figure of men as vessels; for man as a potsherd cf.
Isa. 45.9. For the figure of the potter cf. Wisd.
15.7; Isa. 29.16; Jer. 18.6.

930   Wisd. 5.16: ideo accipient
  . . . et diadema   regnum decoris, et diadema
  decoris   speciei de manu Domini.
  The beauteous diadem an ornament of the just. For
the diadem as an adornment of Jerusalem, the Lord's
Bride, cf. Isa. 62.3.

932-3   Ps. 35 (36).7: . . . iudicia
  iudicium . . . Dei,   tua abyssus multa
  quod mentis et oris /   Sir. 24.27: . . . consilium
  officium multa transcen-   illius ab abysso magna
  dit maius abysso
  The power of God's judgments.

934-7   Ps. 72 (73).1-12
  The apparent prosperity of the wicked.

938   Col. 3.11: . . . sed omnia
nos, quibus in Christo   et in omnibus Christus
sunt omnia . . .
For the Christian, Christ is everything.

943   Rom. 8.21: . . . in liberta-
in libertatem et patri-   tem gloriae filiorum Dei
ae redeamus honorem   Rom. 15.7: . . . Christus
                         suscepit vos in honorem Dei.
The liberty and honor of the Christian.

947-8   Acts 20.28: . . . ecclesiam
948 sanguine quos pro-   Dei, quam acquisivit san-
prio quaesivit prodigus   guine suo
emptor
Christ purchased his people with his blood. Cf. De
prov. 506-7.

953   Matt. 7.7-8; Luke 11.9-10
The image of man knocking at the gate, i.e., seeking
and gaining his request in prayer. Matt. 7.7 is the
same text as Luke 11.9; Matt. 7.8 corresponds exactly
to Luke 11.10. Each citation is cast in the form of a
quotation of Christ.

958-64
Treated at 229-34, above.

962-3   Eph. 4.22: . . . veterem
. . . si carne vetusta/   hominem
exuti . . .   Col. 3.9: . . . veterem
                       hominem
Man is to put aside his old human nature which is
under the domination of sin.

968   Matt. 12.30: . . . qui non
. . . sparsi . . .   congreget mecum, spargit
                       Luke 11.23: . . . qui non
                       colligit mecum, dispergit
Those who are separated from Christ are "scattered."

970   John 4.14: . . . fons aquae
. . . vivo de fonte   salientis in vitam aeternam
                       Cf. Ps. 35 (36). 9-10; Isa.
                       55.1

The water of Baptism, or divine revelation and the
Holy Spirit under the figure of living water. Cf.
R. E. Brown, S.S., The Gospel of St. John (New
Testament Reading Guides 13; Collegeville, Minnesota
1960) ad loc.

Summary: The author of the De providentia shows
his familiarity with both the Old and New Testaments,
as in the preceding subdivision, but especially evident
is his thorough acquaintance with the Pauline Epistles
and Pauline theology.[1] Verbal parallels occur more frequently than in the earlier subsection, and are sometimes quite close (e.g., 506-7). At times the poet
seems to go out of his way to use a specific word from
the biblical text (e.g., 524, maledictum; 603, valde;
663, bravium); he tends also to use a simple verb where
Scripture uses a compound (e.g., 912, solvere; 947-8,
quaerere).

3. Verbal Similarity

307
convertit Domini sin-
cera in munera vultum

Num. 6.26: convertat Dominus
vultum ad te et det tibi
pacem

In De prov., the Lord's acknowledgement of Abel's
offering; in Num., the priestly blessing which the
Lord gives to Moses for use in the rites of the
Hebrews.

438
et promissorum Domini
succederet heres

Gal. 3.29: . . . secundum
promissionem heredes

In De prov., the covenant with Moses; in Gal., that
with Abraham.

513
in tabulis cordis de-
scribat sanguine Christi

Prov. 3.3: . . . describe in
tabulis cordis tui

In De prov. the activity of the Holy Spirit in en-
lightening men's minds; in Prov., kindness and fidel-
ity as virtues to be treasured in the heart.

---

[1] Valentin, Saint Prosper 809, points to the
imitation of Paul.

566   1 Kgs. 15.10: factum est
fit verbum Domini . . . autem verbum Domini . . .
"'The word of the Lord' is the consecrated phrase
which describes the experience of every man who is
called a prophet." R. L. MacKenzie, The Two-Edged
Sword (Milwaukee 1956) 29.

871-2   2 Mach. 6.30: . . . duras
. . . et dolor aegri / corporis sustineo dolores
corporis . . .
In De prov. in a general sense; in 2 Mach., the
martyrdom of Eleazer. The phrase occurs frequently
in literature.

912   Wisd. 10.12: . . . certamen
. . . victo certamine forte dedit illi ut vinceret
In De prov., desire of the Christian to win the
battle of earthly life so as to depart to Christ;
in Wisd., a gift of Wisdom to the just man.

952   Acts 16.30: . . . ut salvus
fit salvus . . .   fiam
         1 Cor. 7.16: . . . salvum
         facies . . . salvam facies
         1 Cor. 9.22: . . . ut omnes
         facerem salvos
The idiom used to express the act of salvation.

  Summary: The small number of instances makes
any conclusion impossible. Most of the phrases cited
are short and occur frequently in Christian literature;
one (De prov. 871-2) is as likely to be derived from a
classical as from a biblical source.

  Conclusion: The author of the De providentia
was steeped in the biblical tradition, as were all the
Christian authors; he is equally familiar with both
Old and New Testaments, and uses material derived from
many books of the Old Testament and almost every book
of the New, with the possible exception of some of the
shorter Epistles. The total number of verbal similarities noted in all three subsections is rather more
than might have been expected, considering the exigencies of metrics and of poetic diction; very few of
these are word-for-word renderings, however.

The distribution of biblical allusions throughout the middle and end of the poem is fairly even, but fewer by far occur at the beginning; this may be accounted for by the disposition of subject matter within the poem and the fact that the poet is concerned in the beginning chiefly with a description of contemporary events in Gaul.

E. NON-BIBLICAL PARALLELS

Introduction. The material presented below is divided into longer and briefer parallels for each author considered. Longer parallels frequently involve both adaptation of the thought expressed in the imitated passage and verbal relationship, but sometimes adaptation of thought alone, i.e., higher imitation. Briefer parallels most often involve verbal relationship only, i.e., lower imitation. The briefer parallels have been further classified on the basis of correspondence in verse position as initial, internal, and final, or as having no correspondence.[1] A summary is given for each major author or group of authors considered.

In the treatment of parallels of greater length, the relevant text of the De providentia has been set out first, and the corresponding text of the author under discussion follows. Other parallels show the text of the De providentia in the left column, the corresponding text in the right. Variant readings have been enclosed between double lines. Parallels between the De providentia and the works of Vergil and Orientius noted by Valentin have been marked by /V_7, parallels between the De providentia and the works of Vergil, Ovid, and other poets noted by Manitius by /M_7.[2]

---

[1] The treatment of parallels is based on that adopted by Brother Albertus Mahoney, C.F.X., Vergil in the Works of Prudentius (C.U.A. Patristic Studies 39; Washington, 1934).

[2] Valentin, Saint Prosper 893 (Verg.) and 787 (Orient.) and Manitius, Zeitschrift 39 (1888) 580-584.

INTRODUCTION

1. **Lucretius**. De providentia 755-8 is an answer
to those who seek immediate and perfect justice from God
in this life. The poet notes that if each person received his just due now, the world would no longer continue, since the just and the unjust alike would have
been removed from it to receive their respective reward
or punishment and offspring could not be produced to
prolong the race:

sic mundi meta abruptis properata fuisset
temporibus, neque in subolem generanda veniret
posteritas, pariter cum iustos atque nocentes
aut promissus honos aut poena auferret ab orbe.
(De prov. 755-8)

Lucretius 5.1026-7 is the conclusion of that author's
discussion of the evolution of family life. The poet
seems to accept a social contract theory of society; if
the greater part of mankind had not adhered to the contract, the race would have been destroyed, and there
would have been no offspring to prolong it:

aut genus humanum iam tum foret omne peremptum,
nec potuisset adhuc perducere saecla propago.
(Lucr. 5.1026-7)

De providentia 570-4 makes the point that all
things remain in the form in which God created them,
and none change into other forms:

sic etiam quae non spirant sunt semper in illo
in quo sunt formata modo; non plana tumescunt
collibus, aut celsi sternuntur in aequora montes;
non veniunt Alpes in pontum, aut pontus in agros;
saxa iacent, amnes decurrunt, stantque paludes.
(Dc prov. 570-4)

In order to make his atomic theory correspond to the
reality of things, Lucretius accepts, at least implicitly,
a natural law or foedus Naturai by which each element
maintains its own properties:

denique in aethere non arbor, non aequore in alto
nubes esse queunt nec pisces vivere in arvis
nec cruor in lignis neque saxis sucus inesse.
(Lucr. 3.784-6)

It might be noted in passing that another characteristic Lucretian term, the "shores of light," or luminis
orae, used to refer to birth (Lucr. 1.22; 1.170; 1.179;
2.577; 5.224; 5.781) or the passage into knowledge (5.1455),
is matched in the De providentia, where the extremae vitae
orae (De prov. 894) are the shores of death that one approaches in old age.

49

An example of a passage in the De providentia which contains verbal parallels with several passages of Lucretius' poem occurs in the description of the contents of the universe:

115-7 quidquid inest caelo, quidquid terrae- que marique, / quidquid quocumque est in corpore, sive animatum, / sive expers animae . . .	Lucr. 4.43 terrai maris et caeli generisque animantum Lucr. 6.678 . . . omnia cum caelo terraque marique Lucr. 3.837; 5.219 . . . terraque marique

Another is found in the description of various human misfortunes:

871-2 . . . durus labor urgeat, et dolor aegri / corporis, . . . et turpes egestas.	Lucr. 3.999; 5.1272; 5.1359 . . . durum sufferre laborem Lucr. 4.1079-80 . . . dolorem / corporis . . . Lucr. 3.65 turpis . . . con- temptus et acris egestas

Briefer Parallels

Initial

803 ante oculos . . .	Lucr. 2.113; 3.185; 4.979 ante oculos . . .

Internal

39 . . . nullo discrimine . . .	Lucr. 5.1314 . . . nullo discrimine . . .
305 . . . onerans altaria sacris	Lucr. 4.1237 . . . adolentque altaria donis
367 . . . cognoscere fratrem	Lucr. 2.349 . . . cognoscere matrem . . .
479 . . . sine Numine . . .	Lucr. 2.168 . . . sine numine . . .

Final

35 . . . montibus   Lucr. 5.313 . . . a montibus
    altis   altis
                           Lucr. 5.492 . . . montibus
                               altis
                           Lucr. 5.663 . . . e montibus
                               altis
                           Lucr. 4.1020; 6.735 . . .
                               de montibus altis
                           Lucr. 1.897 . . . montibus
                               . . . altis
                           Lucr. 2.331; 6.963 . . .
                               altis montibus . . .
                           Lucr. 1.283 montibus ex
                               altis . . .
114 . . . semina rebus   Lucr. 1.59 . . . semina
                               rerum

213 . . . origine   Lucr. 5.548 . . . ab origine
    mundus   mundi

260 . . . sidera noctis   Lucr. 1.1065 . . . sidera
                               noctis

560 . . . rationis egenum Lucr. 4.502 . . . rationis
                               egentem
                           Lucr. 5.1211 . . . rationis
                               egestas

818 . . . frigora et   Lucr. 6.364 . . . frigus et
    aestus   aestum

901 . . . quidquid mundanis Lucr. 3.53 . . . in rebus
    rebus acerbum   acerbis

No Correspondence

12 . . . tali tempore   Lucr. 1.93 . . . in tali
    . . .   tempore . . .

260 . . . solis lunaeque   Lucr. 5.751 solis item quo-
    vices . . .   que defectus lunaeque . . .

381 . . . <u>durus labor</u> . . .	Lucr. 3.999; 5.1272; 5.1359 . . . <u>durum</u> sufferre <u>laborem</u>
608 . . . <u>motus animi</u> . . .	Lucr. 4.1072 . . . <u>animi</u> traducere <u>motus</u>
641 . . . natis violentum <u>affigere sidus</u>	Lucr. 4.391 <u>sidera</u> . . . aetheriis <u>adfixa</u> cavernis

<u>Summary</u>: The totality of evidence in regard to Lucretian source material is not as impressive as might at first appear. The two longer parallels discussed at the opening of the section contain virtually no verbal resemblances; the two passages of the <u>De providentia</u> which do contain verbal resemblances with several Lucretian passages can be duplicated in Vergil; the first in particular (<u>De prov</u>. 115-7) contains several stock phrases. Almost all the briefer parallels are duplicated in Vergil.[3]

2. Vergil and the <u>Appendix Vergiliana</u>. <u>De providentia</u> 772-6 is a description of those who have departed from true faith and then return to it, cast in the metaphor of a voyage from the harbor--reason--into the sea, where the travelers are tossed about through many wanderings--a play on two senses of the word <u>error</u>--and from which they finally gain a safe return:

quam multos procul a portu rationis in altum
dedecorum <u>turbo</u> abstulerat, quos <u>aequore toto</u>
iactatos, nimiumque vagis <u>erroribus actos</u>,
nunc <u>reduces</u> iuvat <u>excipere</u>, amplexuque paterno
confotos, nusquam statione abscedere vitae!
(<u>De prov</u>. 772-6)

The passage depends heavily on Vergil's famous description of Juno's spiteful vengeance on Aeneas and his men, whom she drove over all the seas for many years (<u>Aen</u>. 1.23-32); the friendly reception which the voyagers receive on their return is modeled on Acestes' reception of the Trojans in Sicily (<u>Aen</u>. 5.35-41):

---

[3] For an extensive list of briefer parallels between Lucr. and Verg., cf. W. A. Merrill, "Parallels and Coincidences in Lucretius and Vergil," <u>University of California Publications in Classical Philology</u> 3 (1918) 135-247.

INTRODUCTION

Aen. 1.29-32
    his accensa super iactatos aequore toto /V 7
    Troas, reliquias Danaum atque immitis Achilli
    arcebat longe Latio, multosque per annos
    errabant acti fatis maria omnia circum
Aen. 1.511-2
    . . . ater quos aequore turbo
    dispulerat . . .
Aen. 10.665; Georg. 3.470
    . . . aequore turbo
Ciris 480
    . . . in aequore turbo
Aen. 5.456
    . . . agit aequore toto
Aen. 11.599
    . . . fremit aequore toto
Aen. 12.501-2
    . . . quos aequore toto
    inque vicem nunc Turnus agit, nunc Troius heros
Aen. 6.532
    . . . . pelagine venis erroribus actus
Aen. 7.199
    sive errore viae seu tempestatibus acti
Aen. 5.40-1
    gratatur reduces et . . .
    excipit
        Contaminatio, or the fashioning of a single pas-
sage from several sources, appears evident in the preced-
ing passage. A similar example of contaminatio occurs in
the account of the appearance of birds in the works of
creation:

217 . . . liquidum volucres   Georg. 1.404 . . . liquido
    innabant aera pennis   sublimis in aere Nisus
                                        /V 7
                                    Georg. 1.406 . . . aethera
                                        pennis
                                    Aen. 5.215-7 . . . /columba7
                                        plausumque exterrita
                                        pennis / dat tecto ingen-
                                        tem, mox aere lapsa quieto
                                        / radit inter liquidum . . .
                                    Aen. 6.202 . . . /columbae7
                                        liquidumque per aera
                                        lapsae
                                    Aen. 11.272 . . . aethera
                                        pennis

53

Ciris 541 illa levem fugiens
raptim secat aethera //
aera // pennis

The following passage, where only two possible
Vergilian sources are involved, is a more typical example
of contaminatio; the first parallel cited (Aen. 1.208) is
merely verbal, the second (Aen. 12.487) involves resemblance in thought:

166-7 . . . insomnibus 　aegram / partiri curis 　in multa negotia mentem	Aen. 1.208 . . . curisque 　ingentibus aeger Aen. 12.487 diversaeque 　vocant animum in contraria 　curae

There is one instance in which two separate verses
in the De providentia appear to depend on the same Vergilian
verse. An aged bishop is weighted down by his heavy pack
on the sorrowful journey away from his city, which has been
destroyed by the barbarians; in a more general observation,
the poet of the De providentia notes that the wayfarer
under his heavy pack dreads the rain; both verses show
verbal similarity with Vergil's description of the stalwart
Roman soldier who takes to the road under his pack:

58　carpebas duram iniusto 　　sub fasce viam	Georg. 3.347 iniusto sub 　　fasce viam cum carpit . . .
138 iniusto pluviam 　　metuit sub fasce viator	Georg. 3.347 iniusto sub 　　fasce viam cum carpit 　　. . . /v_/

There is a more striking instance where two
separate verses of the De providentia may each depend on
the same two verses from Vergil. The first of these verses
(De prov. 17) describes the image produced on the poet's
mind by seeing his fatherland put to the torch by the
Goths; the Vergilian passages describe the image produced
by a father's pietas. Contaminatio is evident:

17　. . . animum patriae 　　subiit fumantis imago	Aen. 9.294 . . . animum pa- 　　triae strinxit pietatis 　　imago

                              Aen. 10.824 . . . mentem
                              <u>patriae</u> <u>subiit</u> pietatis
                              <u>imago</u>
                         Cf. Aen. 2.560 . . . <u>subiit</u>
                              cari genitoris <u>imago</u> /M_7

The second verse (<u>De</u> <u>prov</u>. 244) occurs in a discussion of man's ancestral virtues and the possibilities
for good consequent upon their exercise; God implanted
virtue in man, but man failed to realize his potentialities
under the Old Law. There is no evidence of <u>contaminatio</u>;
the verse may have been borrowed as well from the one
Vergilian verse as from the other:

244 insita sic nobis   Aen. 9.294 . . . animum
     <u>patriae</u> virtutis   <u>patriae</u> <u>strinxit</u> pietatis
     <u>imago</u> est   <u>imago</u> /V_7
                             Aen. 10.824 . . . mentem
                                  <u>patriae</u> <u>subiit</u> pietatis
                                  <u>imago</u>

        The parallels set out immediately below illustrate
another aspect of the technique of the poet of the <u>De</u>
<u>providentia</u>, namely the use of verses from Vergil with
relatively little change in wording, and essential, although not perfect, correspondence in thought:

381 ut <u>durus</u> <u>labor</u> <u>et</u>   Georg. 3.68 et <u>labor</u> et
     saevae <u>inclementia</u>   durae rapit <u>inclementia</u>
     <u>mortis</u>   <u>mortis</u> /V_7 /M_7
                             Georg. 2.412 <u>durus</u> uterque
                                  <u>labor</u> . . . /V_7

537 nec <u>dubiis</u> Dominum   Georg. 4.253 . . . non
     licuit <u>cognoscere</u>   <u>dubiis</u> poteris <u>cognoscere</u>
     <u>signis</u>   <u>signis</u>
                             Georg. 1.394 . . . certis
                                  poteris <u>cognoscere</u> <u>signis</u>
                             Ciris 243 . . . ut nullo
                                  passim <u>cognoscere</u> <u>signo</u>

718 dum nullum <u>curare</u>   Ecl. 8.35 nec <u>curare</u> <u>deum</u>
    <u>Deum</u> <u>mortalia</u> suadet   credis <u>mortalia</u> quemquam

871-2 iustitiam <u>durus</u>   Georg. 1.145-6 . . . <u>labor</u>
     <u>labor</u> urgeat . . . /   omnia vicit / improbus et
     . . . et <u>turpis</u> egestas   <u>duris</u> <u>urgens</u> in rebus

egestas

Aen. 6.276 . . . turpis
egestas /V_7 /M_7

At times the thought contained in a Vergilian passage of less than a verse appears to be expanded in the
De providentia into a full verse or more, as in these
examples:

529-30 . . . sepulchris /
excita sanctorum sump-
serunt corpora vitam

Ecl. 8.98 . . . animas imis
excire sepulchris

944-6 impia non oberunt
cum saevo pacta tyranno /
. . . resolubile Christo
est / hoc foedus . . .

Georg. 4.492-3 . . . immitis
rupta tyranni / foedera
. . .

960 cuncta licet variis
terroribus impleat
hostis

Aen. 11.448 . . . magnisque
urbem terroribus implet

Contraction of one or several Vergilian verses into shorter passages in the De providentia also occurs,
at times with a pronounced shift in thought:

123-4 . . . contraria
discors / omnia motus
alit . . .

Aen. 6.724-6 . . . caelum
ac terram corpusque li-
quentis / lucentemque
globum, lunam Titaniaque
astra / Spiritus intus
alit . . .

263 . . . ingenium varias
augere per artes

Georg. 1.133 ut varias usus
meditando extunderet artes

407-8 . . . cunctas per-
currere formas /
virtutum . . .

Aen. 6.626-7 . . . omnes
scelerum comprendere
formas / omnia poenarum
percurrere nomina . . .

730 . . . a prisco divi-
sum foedere rerum

Georg. 1.60-1 . . . aeternaque foedera certis /
imposuit natura locis . . .

56

941 sed si quis superest   Aen. 5.363 nunc si cui
  animi vigor . . .   virtus animusque in pec-
                              tore praesens

    Frequently the appropriation of pagan elements
into a Christian context becomes especially noticeable.
Thus the complaint in the De providentia that innocent
children must suffer the wrath of the barbarians is cast
in terms reminiscent of Venus' complaint to Jupiter in
the Aeneid:

43 quid pueri insontes,   Aen. 1.231-2 quid meus
  quid commisere puellas?   Aeneas in te committere
                               tantum / quid Troes
                               potuere? . . .

    Likewise, the life of just men under holy customs
in the Old Law may be suggested by the life of the bees
under their mighty laws:

430 . . . sanctis agerent   Georg. 4.154 . . . /apes_7
  in moribus aevum   magnisque agitant sub
                               legibus aevum

    Similarly, the Christian poet depicts the end of
the world in terms derived from the last age--the new
Golden Age--portrayed in the fourth Eclogue:

469 ultima cum mundi   Ecl. 4.4 ultima Cumaei
  finem prope curreret   venit iam carminis aetas
  aetas

    The fact that all knowledge, past, present, and
future, is immediately present to God is expressed in a
manner which may be derived from Vergil's description
of the prophetic powers of Proteus:

802-3 nam quod ubique   Georg. 4.392-3 . . . novit
  agitur, quod gestum est,   namque omnia vates / quae
  quodque gerendum est /   sint, quae fuerint, quae
  ante oculos Domini   mox ventura trahantur
  puncto subsistit in uno.

    As the wrath of a deity might prove a trial to a
pagan, so the darts of God try the faithful:

897 namque eadem cunctos   Georg. 4.453 non te nullius
  exercent tela fideles   exercent numinis irae /V_

Such appropriation may extend even to a passage
based on the biblical narrative, so that Elias' ascent
into heaven could perhaps be suggested by Neptune's
travels over the sea in his chariot:

327-8 . . . raptum igni- tis per inane iugalibus Helim / scandentem rutilo viderunt aethera curru	Aen. 5.819 caeruleo per summa levis volat aequora curru Cf. Culex 212 . . . rapior per inania

All nature is at the service of God who is its
author; similarly, all the world receives Caesar, the
author of crops and mighty tempests:

405 omnis enim auctori servit natura potenti	Georg. 1.26-8 . . . te /Caesarem/ maximus orbis / auctorem frugum tempes- tatumque potentem / accipiat . . .

Even the birth of Christ is portrayed in terms
which recall the fourth Eclogue; Christ is the new man
from the heavens, just as a new offspring is sent down
from high heaven upon the Romans:

492-3 sed novus e caelis per sacrae Virginis alvum / natus homo est . . .	Ecl. 4.7 iam nova progenies caelo demittitur alto

Transference of literal Vergilian expressions into figurative terminology descriptive of the Christian
life may also occur. Brutus the avenger put his sons
to death in the name of liberty when they plotted civil
war against the Republic, but man's very liberty causes
him to be shaken by civil war within himself:

660-1 . . . ipsaque bellum / libertas movet, et quatimur civilibus armis	Aen. 6.820-1 . . . natosque pater nova bella moventes / ad poenam pulchra pro libertate vocabit

Man desires perishable things--one day can give
these gifts, another take them away; the Christian poet
makes his point in language reminiscent of Vergil's

description of the tragic young Pallas--one day brought
him to battle, that same day took him away in death:

866-7 . . . ut dare	Aen. 10.508 haec te prima
quivit / una dies, sic	dies bello dedit, haec
una potest auferre . . .	eadem aufert

A shepherd refuses prompt treatment to his
wounded beast, but God sends a medicinal cure from
heaven and cuts out the foul matter of man's sins:

880-1 cumque Deus medicam	Georg. 3.455-6 dum medicas
caelo demittere curam /	adhibere manus ad vulnera
dignatur, penitusque	pastor / abnegat . . .
putres abscindere fibras	

Man's enemy besieges the gates of his heart, just
as Idomeneus besieged the Sallentini and, on another
occasion, Messapus was ordered to set a guard around the
gates of his own camp:

961 et vigili clausas	Aen. 3.400 . . . obsedit
obsidat milite portas	milite campos
	Aen. 9.159 . . . vigilum
	excubiis obsidere portas

Occasionally parallelism is conveyed by the use
of a synonym, as may be the case with these two short
passages:

399 discutiens flammis	Georg. 3.357 . . . sol . . .
tenebras . . .	discutit umbras

670-1 . . . prisci /	Ecl. 4.31 . . . priscae
. . . commenta doli	vestigia fraudis

In the first, tenebras may stand for umbras; in the
second, doli may represent the fraudis of the classical
poet.

Two briefer parallels deserve special mention,
because in each case a variant manuscript reading is in-
involved:

655 . . . vatum scripta	Aen. 4.464 . . . vatum prae-
piorum	dicta priorum //piorum//

696-7 . . . nec <u>terrea</u>   <u>Georg.</u> 2.341 <u>terrea</u> //ferrea//
nectit / <u>progenies</u>   progenies . . .

The first passage suggests the reading <u>piorum</u>,[4] the
second <u>terrea</u>.[5]

Briefer Parallels

Initial

192 <u>det</u> vitas <u>adimatque</u>   Aen. 4.244 <u>dat</u> somnos <u>adimit</u>-
. . .   que . . .

262 <u>scire potestates</u>   Aen. 12.396 <u>scire potestates</u>
<u>herbarum</u> . . .   <u>herbarum</u> . . . /M/

400 <u>quid loquar</u> . . .   Ecl. 6.74 <u>quid loquar</u> . . .

402 <u>instar montis</u>   Aen. 2.15 <u>instar montis</u>
<u>aquas</u> . . .   . . . /V /
                                   Aen. 1.105 . . . praeruptus
                                   <u>aquae mons</u>

536 <u>tertia</u> . . . <u>lux</u>   Aen. 3.117; 11.210 <u>tertia</u>
                                   <u>lux</u> . . .

680 <u>novimus et</u> . . .   Ecl. 3.8 <u>novimus et</u> . . .

817 <u>indignos dignosque</u> . . . Aen. 12.811 <u>digna indigna</u>
                                   . . .
                                   Aen. 9.595; <u>Ciris</u> 247 . . .
                                   <u>digna atque indigna</u>

845 <u>progenies auctura</u>   Aen. 5.565 <u>progenies</u>
<u>malos</u>   <u>auctura</u> Italos . . .

_____

[4] Modern editors tend to prefer <u>priorum</u>, which has
more MS. support. Cf., e.g., Hirtzel's Oxford text.
Serv. recognized both readings. Cf. J. Conington, <u>P.</u>
<u>Vergili Maronis Opera</u> II (London,1884) <u>ad loc.</u>

[5] The Oxford text accepts <u>terrea</u>, which was read
by Lact., although most MSS. give <u>ferrea</u>. Cf. E. C. Page,
<u>P. Vergili Maronis Bucolica et Georgica</u> (London 1898,
repr. 1954) <u>ad loc.</u>

896 <u>bella</u> <u>excita</u> . . .   Aen. 1.541 <u>bella</u> <u>cient</u> . . .

903-4 . . . <u>talentis</u> /   Aen. 10.531 <u>argenti</u> <u>atque</u>
<u>argenti</u> <u>atque</u> <u>auri</u>   <u>auri</u> . . . <u>talenta</u>
<u>amissis</u> . . .   Aen. 5.112 . . . <u>argenti</u>
                            <u>aurique</u> <u>talentum</u>

969 <u>haec</u> <u>sat</u> <u>erit</u> . . .   Aen. 3.602 <u>hoc</u> <u>sat</u> <u>erit</u>
                            . . . /V̲ ̲/

Internal

11 . . . <u>cui</u> <u>tanta</u> Deo   Aen. 9.97 . . . <u>cui</u> <u>tanta</u>
<u>tribuente</u> <u>facultas</u>   <u>deo</u> permissa potestas /M̲ ̲/

33 . . . <u>mali</u> <u>labes</u> . . .   Aen. 2.97 . . . <u>mali</u> <u>labes</u> . . .

39 . . . <u>nullo</u> <u>discri</u>   Aen. 1.574; 10.108; 12.498;
<u>mine</u> . . .   12.770 . . . <u>nullo</u>
                            <u>discrimine</u> . . .

213 . . . <u>pulchra</u> verna-   Aen. 1.286 . . . <u>pulchra</u>
bat <u>origine</u> <u>mundus</u>   Troianus <u>origine</u> Caesar
                            Georg. 2.336 . . . prima
                            crescentis <u>origine</u> <u>mundi</u>

230 . . . <u>manet</u> <u>exitus</u>   Aen. 10.630 nunc <u>manet</u>
unus utrumque   insontem gravis <u>exitus</u>
                            . . .

249 totaque <u>res</u> <u>effecta</u>   Aen. 11.14 maxima res
Dei . . .   <u>effecta</u> viri . . .

254 . . . quo promissis   Aen. 10.152 . . . humanis
<u>adsit</u> <u>fiducia</u> magnis   quae <u>sit</u> <u>fiducia</u> rebus

260-1 huic <u>solis</u> <u>lunaeque</u>   Georg. 2.477-8 . . . caeli-
vices, et <u>sidera</u> noctis /   que vias et <u>sidera</u>
nosse datum . . .   monstrent / defectus
                            <u>solis</u> varios <u>lunaeque</u>
                            labores

305 . . . <u>onerans</u> <u>altaria</u>   Aen. 5.101 . . . <u>onerant</u>
sacris   aras . . .
                            Aen. 11.50 . . . cumulatque
                            <u>altaria</u> donis

61

367 . . . venia　　　　　　　Ecl. 4.60 . . . risu
cognoscere fratrem　　　　　cognoscere matrem /V 7

479 . . . sine Numine　　　　Aen. 2.777; 6.368 . . .
. . .　　　　　　　　　　　　sine numine . . .

516 . . . rerum dominus　　　Aen. 1.282 . . . rerum
. . .　　　　　　　　　　　　dominos . . .

649 . . . venerare　　　　　　Georg. 1.338 . . . venerare
Deum . . .　　　　　　　　　　deos . . .

664 ardua quaeque piget　　　Aen. 11.437 ut tanta quid-
pro spe temptare　　　　　　 quam pro spe temptare
latenti　　　　　　　　　　　 recusem

668 . . . frustraque　　　　　Ecl. 7.69 . . . victum
homines contendere　　　　　 frustra contendere
dives　　　　　　　　　　　　 Thyrsim /V 7
　　　　　　　　　　　　　　　Ciris 329 . . . neque est
　　　　　　　　　　　　　　　cum dis contendere nos-
　　　　　　　　　　　　　　　trum

736 . . . nec abest ab　　　　Georg. 3.48 . . . abest ab
origine rerum　　　　　　　　 origine Caesar

880 . . . caelo demittere　　 Georg. 1.23 . . . caelo
curam　　　　　　　　　　　　 demittitis imbrem

928 . . . et sacraria　　　　　Aen. 12.199 . . . et duri
Christi　　　　　　　　　　　　sacraria Ditis

Final

1 . . . lapsis . . .　　　　　Georg. 1.64 . . . a mensi-
iam mensibus anni　　　　　　 bus anni
　　　　　　　　　　　　　　　Aen. 2.14 . . . tot iam
　　　　　　　　　　　　　　　labentibus annis

5 . . . carmina curis　　　　 Ecl. 3.61 . . . carmina
　　　　　　　　　　　　　　　curae

19 . . . fletibus ora　　　　 Aen. 6.699 . . . largo fletu
rigamus　　　　　　　　　　　 simul ora rigabat /M 7
　　　　　　　　　　　　　　　Aen. 9.251 . . . vultum la-
　　　　　　　　　　　　　　　crimis atque ora rigabat

23 . . . rerum <u>hominumque</u>
<u>labores</u>

Aen. 2.284 . . . hominumque
urbisque <u>labores</u> /M /

35 . . . <u>montibus</u> <u>altis</u>

Aen. 3.675 . . . <u>montibus</u>
<u>altis</u>
Aen. 7.563 . . . sub <u>monti-</u>
<u>bus altis</u>
Aen. 10.707 . . . de <u>monti-</u>
<u>bus altis</u>
Aen. 12.523 . . . de <u>monti-</u>
<u>bus altis</u>
Georg. 4.112 . . . de <u>mon-</u>
<u>tibus altis</u>
Ecl. 7.66 . . . in <u>montibus</u>
<u>altis</u>

65 . . . <u>veterum</u>
recolamus <u>avorum</u>

Aen. 7.177 . . . <u>veterum</u>
effigies ex ordine <u>avorum</u>

73 . . . sine <u>crimine</u>
<u>vitam</u>

Aen. 4.550 . . . sine
<u>crimine vitam</u> /M /

75 . . . <u>iuvenumque</u>
<u>senumque</u>

Aen. 9.309 . . . <u>iuvenumque</u>
<u>senumque</u>

83 . . . <u>celsa</u> spectaret
ab <u>arce</u>

Aen. 1.56 . . . <u>celsa</u> sedet
Aeolus <u>arce</u>

87 talia cum facilis
<u>vulgi</u> <u>spargantur</u> in
<u>aures</u>

Aen. 2.119 . . . <u>vulgi</u> quae
vox ut venit ad <u>aures</u>
Aen. 2.90-9 . . . hinc
<u>spargere</u> voces / in
<u>vulgum</u> ambiguas . . .

91 <u>prome</u> . . . <u>tela</u>
<u>pharetris</u>

Aen. 5.501 . . . de<u>promunt</u>
<u>tela pharetris</u> /M /
Ciris 160 . . . de<u>promens</u>
<u>tela pharetra</u>

98 . . . in <u>aequore</u>
<u>aperto</u>

Aen. 12.333 . . . <u>aequore</u>
<u>aperto</u>

99 . . . <u>ventis</u> dare
libera <u>vela</u> secundis

Aen. 7.23 . . . <u>ventis</u> implevit <u>vela</u> <u>secundis</u> /M /
Aen. 3.683 . . . <u>ventis</u>
intendere <u>vela</u> secundis

63

115 . . . terraeque marique	Aen. 1.598 . . . terraeque marisque Aen. 10.162 . . . terraque marique Aen. 9.492 . . . terraque marique . . .
144 . . . vellere Serum	Georg. 2.121 velleraque ut foliis depectant tenuia Seres
145 . . . tergis horrere ferarum	Aen. 7.20 . . . terga ferarum
148 . . . quidquid variatur in herbis	Moretum 106 . . . tot variatur ab herbis
239 . . . discrimina rerum	Aen. 1.204 . . . discrimina rerum
292 non uno tantum . . . errore parentum	Ciris 240 . . . uno . . . errore parentum
409 . . . miracula rerum	Georg. 4.441 . . . in miracula rerum $/\overline{V}\_/$
507 . . . fas est	Aen. 1.77 . . . fas est Aen. 6.63 . . . fas erit . . .
535 . . . referentem carne tropaeum	Aen. 10.542 . . . refert . . . tropaeum
560 . . . rationis egenum	Aen. 8.299 . . . rationis egentem
566 . . . lege tenentur	Aen. 12.819 . . . lege tenetur
598 . . . nullum procedat in aequor	Aen. 10.451 . . . medium procedit in aequor
599 . . . effusis . . . habenis	Aen. 5.818; 12.499 . . . omnes effundit habenas

613 . . . sidera caeli   Georg. 2.1 . . . sidera
                          caeli

632-3 . . . qua pontum   Georg. 1.130 . . . iussit
lege moveri / iusserit   pontumque moveri
. . .

684 . . . altaria flamma   Ecl. 8.105 . . . altaria
                            flammis

695 . . . mortali ex   Aen. 12.208 . . . imo de
stirpe recisos   stirpe recisum

710 . . . cardine rerum   Aen. 1.672 . . . cardine
                          rerum

728 . . . quid ab ordine   Aen. 3.447 . . . neque ab
cessit   ordine cedunt

731 . . . solis . . .   Georg. 3.277 . . . solis ad
in ortum   ortus
                          Aen. 6.255 . . . sub lumina
                          solis et ortus

734 . . . nubibus   Aen. 11.548; Georg. 4.312
imber   . . . nubibus imber
                          Ecl. 6.38 . . . nubibus
                          imbres

750 . . . immitis   Georg. 4.492-3 . . . immitis
feritate tyranni   rupta tyranni / foedera
                          . . .

767 . . . errore   Ciris 240 . . . errore
parentum   parentum

808-9 . . . maxima   Aen. 9.608 . . . quatit
bellis / regna quatit   oppida bello
. . .

835 . . . vertitur ordo   Aen. 3.376 . . . is verti-
                          tur ordo

838 . . . ira leones   Aen. 7.15 . . . iraeque
                          leonum

840 . . . more parentum   Aen. 6.223 . . . more parentum

858 . . . culpamque decusque   Aen. 2.89 . . . nomenque decusque

863 . . . totum res fusa per orbem   Aen. 1.457 . . . totum vulgata per orbem

901-2 . . . quidquid mundanis rebus acer- bum / accidit . . .   Aen. 12.678 . . . quidquid acerbi est

909 . . . caeloque prius translata locavit   Aen. 12.145 . . . caelique libens in parte locarim

942 . . . ruptisque catenis   Aen. 8.225 . . . ruptisque immane catenis

No Correspondence

1 Maxima pars . . .   Aen. 7.686 . . . pars maxima . . .
Georg. 2.40 . . . pars maxima . . .

35-6 . . . oppida montibus altis / imposita . . .   Aen. 6.774 . . . imponent montibus arces

57 . . . inter et arma . . .   Aen. 9.557 inter et arma . . .

113 . . . numerosque modosque   Aen. 11.328 . . . numerum- que modumque . . .

140 caeruleos angues . . .   Georg. 4.482 . . . caeruleos- que angues . . . /M /

174 . . . genita et gignentia . . .   Aen. 9.642 . . . genite et geniture . . .

261 . . . numerisque . . . comprendere . . .   Georg. 2.104 . . . numero comprendere . . .

287 . . . acceperat   Aen. 3.242-3 . . . neque
   hanc vim   vim plumis ullam . . . /
                        accipiunt . . .

291 . . . antiqua . . .   Aen. 3.342 . . . in anti-
   virtutis ab arce   quam virtutem . . .

320 . . . aeterni . . .   Ciris 100 . . . aeterno
   honoris   . . . honore . . .

357 dira fames . . .   Aen. 3.256 . . . dira
                        fames . . .

360 . . . populi   Ecl. 4.49; Ciris 398 . . .
   incrementa futuri   magnum Iovis incrementum

372-3 . . . mentes /   Aen. 12.246 turbavit
   non possunt turbare   mentes . . .
   pias   Aen. 12.160 . . . turbatam
                        vulnere mentis
                        Aen. 12.599 . . . mentem
                        turbata dolore

393 donec vi victus . . . Aen. 12.254 . . . donec vi
                        victus . . .

411 siccae rupis . . .   Aen. 5.180 . . . siccaque
                        in rupe . . .

526 impia gens tantum   Aen. 6.624 ausi omnes
   ausa nefas . . .   immane nefas . . .

567 . . . faciunt   Aen. 1.302 . . . iussa
   iussa . . .   facit . . .

574 . . . amnes   Aen. 12.524 . . . amnes et
   decurrunt . . .   in aequora currunt

587-8 . . . variis   Georg. 4.406 . . . variae
   rerum speciebus /   eludent species . . .
   suscipimur . . .

608 . . . motus animi   Georg. 4.86 . . . motus
  . . .   animorum . . .

653 coram adsunt . . .   Aen. 1.595 . . . coram,
                                     quem quaeritis, adsum

674 sidus adoratum . . .   Aen. 2.700 . . . sanctum
                                     sidus adorat

708-9 . . . fas omne   Aen. 5.800 fas omne . . .
   nefasque / confundant   Georg. 1.505 . . . fas
   . . .   versum atque nefas . . .

735-6 laeta . . . /   Georg. 1.1 . . . laetas
   semina . . .   segetes . . .

778 . . . implacabilis   Culex 238 implacabilis
   irae   ira nimis . . .

838 deficit humor . . .   Georg. 1.290 . . . deficit
                                     humor

950 . . . fletu Dominum   Aen. 4.438-9 . . . sed
   motura fideli   nullis ille movetur /
                                     fletibus . . .

966 . . . non humanis   Aen. 10.152 . . . humanis
   fidens homo   quae sit fiducia rebus

        Summary: The evidence of pervasive Vergilian
influence on the poet of the De providentia is impres-
sive; the total number of all parallels found for the
Aeneid is 125, for the Georgics 42, and for the Eclogues
14. Among the works in the Vergilian Appendix, the Ciris
furnishes ten parallels, the Culex two, and the Moretum
one; while the small number of cases where the Appendix
poem supplied the parallel does not definitely establish
that the author of the De providentia knew these minor
poems, the parallels themselves are as close as those
for the major works in virtually every instance. The distribution of all Vergilian parallels from the major works
throughout the De providentia is very even. Granted that
individual parallels may not be too striking--for many
are simply verse tags, epithets, or conventional phrases--
the totality of the evidence suggests heavy reliance,
whether conscious or not, on Vergil, even in passages
with a distinct biblical tone.

INTRODUCTION

Mahoney provides a clear explanation for this remarkable Vergilian influence: "In the educational system
of the late Empire Vergil was one of the most important
authors studied and certainly the favorite. In the schools
of the grammarians Vergil was the final authority in syntax
and prosody. The Roman or provincial schoolboy, Christian
and pagan alike, practically learned his Vergil by heart
and composed after Vergilian models. No less dominant
was Vergil's position in the rhetorical schools, where
the advanced students received an intensive training in
declamation, often on Vergilian themes."[6] Mohrmann sum-
marizes the matter well when she remarks, "Pour le
chrétien comme pour le paien,Virgile était le source
principale de toute connaissance humaine."[7]

3. Ovid. De providentia 212-23 is an account
of the work of creation, concluding with the special
creation of man; Ovid's creation account (Met. 1.69-86)
is so closely parallel in thought as to leave no doubt
that it, along with Genesis, has inspired the ordering
and structuring of the passage in the De providentia.[8]
This is true despite the fact that there are no significant verbal parallels between the two passages. Each
passage is set out in order below and an analysis of the
two passages follows:

---

[6]Brother Albertus Mahoney, C.F.X., op. cit.,3.
B other Mahoney concludes that the reminiscences of Verg.
in Prud. are more abundant than those of any other author.
Sister Mildred Dolores Tobin, C.S.C., Orientii Commonitorium (C.U.A. Patristic Studies 74; Washington,1945) 13-22,
reached a similar conclusion for Orient. in her investigation of the sources for that author.

[7]C. Mohrmann, "La langue et le style de la poésie
latine chrétienne," Revue des études latines 25 (1947)
283; also in Etudes sur le latin des chrétiens I (Rome,
1961) 151-168.

[8]The parallel was noticed by Valentin, Saint
Prosper 894, and by Manitius, Geschichte 174 n. 1 and
Zeitschrift 581-582.

Dispositis rebus, totum iam conditor orbem
fecerat, et pulchra vernabat origine mundus.
iam sol dimensis in tempora cursibus ibat,
lunaque cum stellis praebebat lumina nocti;
iam pecudes tellus, iam pisces pontus alebat,
et liquidum volucres innabant aera pennis.
sed quod divina posset ratione potiri,
nondum erat in terris animal; dedit optimus auctor
hoc homini speciale decus, cumque omnia verbo
conderet, hunc manibus, quo plus genitoris haberet,
dignatur formare suis; substantia duplex
iungitur, inque unam coeunt contraria vitam.
                                        (De prov. 212-23)
Vix ita limitibus dissaepserat omnia certis,
cum, quae pressa diu fuerant caligine caeca,
sidera coeperunt toto effervescere caelo;
neu regio foret ulla suis animalibus orba,
astra tenent caeleste solum formaeque deorum,
cesserunt nitidis habitandae piscibus undae,
terra feras cepit, volucres agitabilis aer.
  Sanctius his animal mentisque capacius altae
deerat adhuc et quod dominari in cetera posset:
natus homo est, sive hunc divino semine fecit
ille opifex rerum, mundi melioris origo,
sive recens tellus seductaque nuper ab alto
aethere cognati retinebat semina caeli.
quam satus Iapeto, mixtam pluvialibus undis,
finxit in effigiem moderantum cuncta deorum,
pronaque cum spectent animalia cetera terram,
os homini sublime dedit caelumque videre
iussit et erectos ad sidera tollere vultus.
                                        (Met. 1.69-86)

212-223

a. The Creator made the
world and disposed its elements.

b. The sun proceeded
in its course, the moon and
stars gave light.

Met. 1.69-86

a. The creator /fabri-
cator, Met. 1.57/ brought
all things out of chaos and
divided them.

b. The stars began to
glow, and took their places
in heaven together with the
gods.

c. The land supported its flocks, the sea its fishes, and birds flew through the air.

c. The sea received its fishes, the land its beasts, the air its birds.

d. There was no creature on earth capable of reason.

d. There was no creature on earth capable of thought or able to rule the others.

e. The Creator gave the glory of reason to man, and fashioned him with His own hands. Two contrary substances--flesh and spirit-- were joined in a single life.

e. Man was born; the creator either fashioned man from his own divine substance, or else Prometheus made man out of earth and water in the likeness of the gods. The creator ordered man to stand erect and look up to the heavens.

De providentia 113-129 is a description of the elements of creation and the strife that exists among them; the same description occurs in Ovid (Met. 1.7-9, 15-20); in this instance there is considerable verbal correspondence, particularly in the listing of the elements involved in strife.[9] The two passages are set out below:

Condidit ut voluit, formas, numerosque, modosque,
et genera, et vitas statuens et semina rebus.
quidquid inest caelo, quidquid terraeque marique,
quidquid quocumque est in corpore, sive animatum,
sive expers animae, calida, humida, frigida, sicca,
uno exstant auctore Deo, qui divite Verbo,
quod Deus est, rerum naturas atque elementa
protulit, et summis opifex intentus et imis.
Quod vero adversis compugnant condita causis,
atque aliis alia obsistunt, contraria discors
omnia motus alit; dumque illi occurritur illo,
vitalem capiunt cuncta exagitata vigorem;
quae vel pigra situ, vel prono lubrica lapsu,
aut cursu instabili, stabili aut torpore perirent.

---

[9]This parallel has been observed by Valentin, Saint Prosper 894 and by Manitius, Geschichte 173 n. 1 and Zeitschrift 581-582.

mollia sic duris, sic raris densa resistunt,
et liquidis solida, et tardis velocia, claro
obscurum objectum, et dulci contendit amarum.
(De prov. 113-29)

. . . chaos: rudis indigestaque moles
nec quicquam nisi pondus iners congestaque eodem
non bene iunctarum discordia semina rerum.
(Met. 1.7-9)

utque erat et tellus illic et pontus et aer,
sic erat instabilis tellus, innabilis unda,
lucis egens aer; nulli sua forma manebat,
obstabatque aliis aliud, quia corpore in uno
frigida pugnabant calidis, umentia siccis,
mollia cum duris, sine pondere, habentia pondus.
(Met. 1.15-20)

Perhaps the simplest type of longer parallel--it
may be termed one-for-one correspondence--is that which
exists between two verses, one in each author under consideration. Such a parallel, with considerable verbal
similarity, is the following:

115 quidquid inest caelo, quidquid terraeque marique	Fast. 1.117 quidquid ubique vides, caelum, mare, nubila, terras

It should be noted that the thought involved in the two
verses is different; the verse from the De providentia
pertains to creation, whereas the Ovidian verse is part
of a statement of Janus to the effect that he opens all
things as god of the doors.

An Ovidian verse with a quite specific and local-
ized reference may be used in the De providentia in a
more general sense. Thus Ovid, in one of his innumerable
letters from exile to influential persons in Rome, flat-
ters Fabius Maximus by reminding him that "a single day
/i.e. the battle of Veii/ did not take away in death all
of the /great/ Fabii"; the poet of the De providentia,
composing with a more universal thought in mind, observes
that "a single day can take it all away," i.e., all the
possessions men cherish so dearly. Contaminatio may be
involved in the passage:

867 una dies . . . potest auferre	Pont. 1.2.4 non omnis Fabias abstulit una dies Cf. Ibis 132 /auferet illa dies . . ./

INTRODUCTION

The poet of the De providentia may expand or contract a passage, just as he did in his use of Vergilian
material. Thus the thought, expressed in a single verse
by Ovid, that Jupiter overwhelms many men by shipwreck,
appears in the De providentia over two verses as the observation that God often overwhelms great cities and
peoples with water:

809-10 . . . saepe urbes,   Pont. 3.6.29 obruerit cum
    populosque potentes /   tot saevis deus aequoris
    . . . obruit undis   undis

Ovid's lament to his wife from exile, in which he
expresses the hope that he may retain some of his old
strength, extends over an entire verse of the Tristia; the
hope that man may have strength of spirit--so as to shake
off the yoke of sin--is expressed in the first four feet
of a verse in the De providentia:

941   sed si quis superest   Trist. 1.6.31 si quid et in
    animi vigor . . .   nobis vivi fuit ante
                                   vigoris
                                Cf. Her. 16.51 . . .
                                   vigorque animi

A considerable number of passages in the De providentia which are based on the biblical narrative are couch-
ed in Ovidian terminology or otherwise derive their inspiration from Ovidian thought; contaminatio, either
certain or possible, appears in some of these passages.
Ovid's complaint to his wife from exile that the number of
his sorrows is as great as the wild creatures in the
forest, or the fishes in the sea, may be a possible source
for one verse in the creation account of the De providentia, to the effect that the land supported its flocks, and
the sea its fishes:

216   iam pecudes tellus,   Trist. 5.2.25 silva feras
    iam pisces pontus alebat   quot alit, quot piscibus
                                   unda natatur

Adam and Eve were forbidden to eat the fruit of the
tree in the garden; the language of the prohibition recalls Ovid's portrayal of Proserpina's action in eating of
a forbidden tree, thus preventing her return from the
underworld:

73

284-5 mandato exclusum quia noverat arbore ab una, / perpulit a vetitis pomum decerpere ramis	Met. 5.536 poeniceum curva decerpserat arbore pomum

The parallel between the monstrous race of giants, the offspring of sinful man, in the De providentia, and the race of giants, offspring of earth, who fought against Jupiter, is so obvious that one would perhaps be surprised not to find it:

331 dira toris vetitis generaret monstra gigantas	Fast. 5.35-6 terra feros partus, immania monstra Gigantes / edidit . . .

Glaucus undergoes a change into a sea divinity in the Metamorphoses; his reception by the gods of the sea, who associate him with themselves, is recalled by Pharaoh's reception of Joseph, who is similarly associated with the Egyptian ruler by receiving the second place of honor in that land; there is considerable possibility of contamin- atio in the De providentia passage:

365 exemptum vatem digna- tur honore secundo	Met. 13.949 di maris exempt- um socio . . . dignantur honore Met. 1.194 . . . dignamur honore Pont. 2.9.23 . . . solito dignemur honore Pont. 4.12.3 . . . hoc dignarer honore Met. 3.521; 8.569 . . . dignatus honore

The earth shook and trembled as Christ died, just as it does in Ovid when Neptune wields his trident:

528-9 . . . concussaque tellus / intremuit . . .	Met. 1.283-4 ipse tridente suo terram percussit at illa / intremuit . . .

When Pentheus ordered the torture of Acoetas in the
Metamorphoses, the chains fell of their own accord from
the prisoner; so by God's power chains fall from captives
through an inversion of the natural order. The Christian
poet is probably thinking of Peter's miraculous release
from prison (Acts 12.6-11):

836 . . . vinctos   Met. 3.699-700 . . .
   labentia vincula   lapsasque lacertis /
   solvunt   sponte sua fama est nullo
         solvente catenas

Another type of parallel is found in the present
discussion with special reference to the Christian life,
although it need not have such reference in itself. This
is the use of a literal statement, with more or less verbal adaptation, in a figurative sense. Helen informs
Paris that Menelaus has set sail for Crete under favorable winds; so, in the open sea of the law, i.e., in
scripture especially, man could readily set sail under
favorable winds, but he is afraid to enter upon that
depth:

99 . . . ventis dare   Her. 16.163 /17.163_7 vela
   libera vela secundis   quidem Creten ventis
         dedit ille secundis

Man stirs up verbal strife with his complaints
against providence; when it is spring in Tomis, the site
of Ovid's exile, verbal battles cease in the marketplace:

552-3 . . . querulis,   Trist. 3.12.18 cedunt
   homo, garrula verbis /   verbosi garrula bella
   bella moves . . .   fori

As a result of his many complaints, man wounds his
vitals with his own darts, as it were. The young
Cyparissus literally wounded a stag with his dart in the
Metamorphoses; as a result, the stag died and Cyparissus
was changed into a tree, but the parallel in the De
providentia does not extend so far:

553 . . . iaculisque tuis   Met. 10.130-1 hunc puer
   tua viscera figis   imprudens iaculo Cypar-
         issus acuto / fixit . . .

As was noted in the discussion of Vergil, man's very freedom is a source of the warfare and civil strife within him; Ovid expresses his pride in the Paeligni, a native people of Italy who were prominent in the Social War against Rome, because of their love of liberty. In this instance the verbal parallel is not particularly close:

660-1 . . . ipsaque   Am. 3.15.8-9 . . . gentis
   bellum / libertas   . . . / quam sua libertas
   movet   ad honesta coegerat arma

Laodamia's expectation of giving a fond embrace to her husband Protesilaus upon his return from battle with the Greeks at Troy is echoed in the De providentia by the fond embrace the Christian community will bestow on those who have returned from their sinful errors:

775-6 nunc reduces iuvat   Her. 13.115 quando ego te
   excipere, amplexuque   reducem cupidis amplexa
   paterno / confotos . . .   lacertis
                         Cf. Her. 17.101 excipis
                         amplexu

The enemy, Satan, besieges the gates of the Christian's heart with his legions; Ovid beseeches the janitor to open the door to his lover's chamber, for "closed doors avail /only/ as defenses of cities under siege." The passage in the De providentia shows some evidence of contaminatio:

961 et vigili clausas ob-   Am. 1.6.29-30 urbibus
   sidat milite portas   obsessis clausae munimina
                         portae / prosunt . . .
                         Met. 3.449 . . . clausis
                         . . . portis
                         Trist. 5.10.21 . . .
                         clausis . . . portis
                         Pont. 1.8.62 . . . clausa-
                         que porta . . .
                         Trist. 3.14.41-2 . . .
                         custodia muri / submovet
                         infestos clausaque porta
                         Getas
                         Met. 3.560 . . . claudere
                         portas

INTRODUCTION

In the following briefer parallel the use of a synonym, viz., scelerum for the Ovidian malorum, is observable,
a practice that has already been noted in the discussion
of Vergilian parallels:

334 . . . scelerum   Met. 4.564 . . . serieque
   seriem . . .   malorum
                    Pont. 1.4.19 . . . series
                    immensa malorum

No discussion of Ovidian parallelism would be complete which failed to take special notice of Medea's un-
forgettable lament, "I see and approve the better, but
follow the worse," re-echoed in the De providentia, "although you can distinguish right from wrong, you choose
the worse," and thus elevated into the lament of every
sinner:

557 . . . sed cum recta   Met. 7.20-1 . . . video
  queas discernere pravis,   meliora proboque /
  / deteriora legis   deteriora sequor . . .

Briefer Parallels

Initial

1 Maxima pars . . .   Met. 1.311; Pont. 1.2.83
                      Maxima pars . . .
                  Met. 2.672; 6.380; Ars 3.229
                    . . . pars maxima . . .

400 quid loquar . . .   Her. 18.39; Trist. 2.399;
                    3.10.25; 5.10.51 quid
                    loquar . . .

493 natus homo est . . .   Met. 1.78 natus homo est
                    . . .

536 tertia . . . lux   Fast. 3.713 tertia post
                    Idus lux . . .
                  Fast. 4.629; 4.679 tertia
                    . . . lux . . .
                  Fast. 4.377 **tertia** lux
                    . . .

680 <u>novimus</u> et . . .   <u>Pont</u>. 4.13.12 <u>novimus</u>
                                         atque . . .

969 haec sat <u>erit</u> . . .   <u>Am</u>. 3.2.84 <u>hic satis</u>
                                         <u>est</u> . . .
                                     <u>Met</u>. 11.211 . . . <u>haec</u>
                                         <u>satis est</u> . . .
                                     <u>Trist</u>. 4.10.91 . . . <u>hoc</u>
                                         <u>satis est</u> . . .
                                     <u>Trist</u>. 3.3.77 <u>hoc satis</u> in
                                         titulo <u>est</u> . . .

Internal

18 et <u>stetit ante</u>   <u>Am</u>. 1.5.17 ut <u>stetit ante</u>
    <u>oculos</u> . . .   <u>oculos</u> . . . /M /

                                     <u>Am</u>. 3.5.10; <u>Her</u>. 15.162
                                         <u>constitit ante</u>
                                         <u>oculos</u> . . . 10

39 . . . <u>nullo</u>   <u>Met</u>. 1.291 . . . <u>nullum</u>
    <u>discrimine</u> . . .   <u>discrimen</u> . . .
                                     <u>Trist</u>. 5.10.29 . . .
                                         <u>discrimine nullo</u>

215 . . . <u>praebebat</u>   <u>Met</u>. 1.10 . . . <u>praebebat</u>
    <u>lumina</u> . . .   <u>lumina</u> . . .

253 . . . <u>nullisque</u>   <u>Met</u>. 15.853 . . . <u>nullisque</u>
    <u>obnoxia</u> damnia   <u>obnoxia</u> iussis

254 . . . <u>quo</u> promissis   <u>Met</u>. 7.309 . . . <u>quo sit</u>
    adsit <u>fiducia</u> magnis   <u>fiducia</u> maior

261 . . . <u>numerisque</u>   <u>Trist</u>. 5.11.19 . . . <u>numerum</u>
    . . . <u>comprendere</u> . . .   <u>comprendere</u> . . .
                                     <u>Ars</u> 2.447; 3.151 . . .
                                         <u>numero comprendere</u>

479 . . . <u>sine Numine</u>   <u>Met</u>. 11.263 . . . <u>sine</u>
    . . .   <u>numine</u> . . .

---

[10]This phrase reoccurs in Paul. Nol., <u>Carm</u>. 6.114;
Ven. Fort., <u>Vit. Mart</u>. 2.285; Drac., <u>Laud. Dei</u> 1. 393.
Cf. C. Weyman, <u>Beiträge</u> 147 and n. 1.

620 . . . <u>pars</u> <u>tertia</u>   Met. 5.372 . . . <u>pars</u>
. . .   <u>tertia</u> . . .

735-6 . . . <u>negant</u> . . .   Trist. 3.10.73 poma <u>negat</u>
flores / <u>semina</u> . . .   regio . . .

750 . . . <u>saeva</u> . . .   Trist. 5.7.46 . . . <u>saevae</u>
<u>feritate</u> . . .   plus <u>feritatis</u> . . .

918 . . . <u>captivae</u>   Am. 1.2.30 . . . <u>captiva</u>
<u>mentis</u> . . .   vincula <u>mente</u> . . .

Final

19 . . . <u>fletibus</u> <u>ora</u>   Met. 11.419 . . . <u>fletibus</u>
<u>rigamus</u>   ora rigavit
                         Pont. 2.11.9 . . . <u>ora</u>
                         rigabas

35 . . . <u>montibus</u>   Met. 1.133 . . . in <u>monti</u>-
<u>altis</u>   bus altis
                         Fast. 3.315-6 . . . in
                         <u>altis</u> / <u>montibus</u> . . .

73 . . . <u>sine</u> <u>crimine</u>   Nux 1 . . . <u>sine</u> <u>crimine</u>
<u>vitam</u>   vitae

75 . . . <u>iuvenumque</u>   Met. 7.612 . . . <u>iuvenumque</u>
<u>senumque</u>   senumque
                         Met. 8.526 . . . <u>iuvenesque</u>
                         senesque
                         Met. 12.464; 15.210 . . .
                         inter <u>iuvenemque</u>
                         senemque

91 <u>prome</u> . . . <u>tela</u>   Met. 1.468 . . . <u>prompsit</u>
<u>pharetris</u>   duo <u>tela</u> <u>pharetra</u>
                         Met. 5.620; Pont. 3.8.19
                         . . . <u>tela</u> <u>pharetra</u>

98 . . . <u>in</u> <u>aequore</u>   Met. 4.527; 11.555 . . . <u>in</u>
<u>aperto</u>   <u>apertum</u> . . . <u>aequor</u>

102 . . . <u>tellus</u> <u>cir</u>-   Met. 2.272 . . . <u>tellus</u> . . .
<u>cumdata</u> <u>ponto</u>   <u>circumdata</u> <u>ponto</u> /M /

115 . . . terraeque
marique

Met. 2.96 . . . terraeque
marisque

145 . . . tergis horrere
ferarum

Met. 14.66 . . . terga
ferarum

213 . . . origine mundus

Met. 1.3; Trist. 2.559
. . . ab origine mundi

217 liquidum volucres
innabant aera pennis

Met. 7.354; 7.379 . . . in
aera pennis
Met. 11.732 . . . aera
pennis
Met. 8.253; Pont. 2.7.27
. . . in aere pennis
Met. 1.466; 10.159 . . .
aere pennis
Met. 4.677 . . . in aere
pennas
Met. 15.99 . . . per aera
pennas
Met. 11.194 . . . liquidumque per aera vectus

316 . . . primordia
mundi

Met. 15.67 . . . primordia
mundi

360 . . . populi incre-
menta futuri

Met. 3.103 . . . populi incrementa futuri

507 . . . fas est

Ars 3.151; Trist. 3.5.27;
4.10.89 . . . fas est

521 . . . convicia
linguae

Met. 11.601 . . . convicia
linguae

560 . . . rationis
egenum

Met. 15.150 . . . rationis
egentes

566 . . . lege tenentur

Met. 10.203 . . . lege
tenemur

602 . . . reddemus
honorem

Met. 13.272 . . . reddat
honorem
Fast. 2.555 . . . redduntur
honores

613 . . . sidera caeli   Met. 7.580 /. . . ad sidera
                          caeli_7

727 . . . moderantis   Met. 6.223 . . . graves
habenis   moderantur habenas

731 . . . solis . . .   Met. 5.455 . . . solis . . .
in ortum   ad ortus
                          Ibis 429 . . . solis ad
                          ortus
                          Met. 6.49; Her. 15.143; Pont.
                          1.4.29; 3.1.127; Trist.
                          5.8.25 . . . solis ab
                          ortu

731 . . . revocatur   Her. 20.87 . . . revocavit
in ortum   ad ortus

734 . . . nubibus imber   Met. 11.516 . . . nubibus
                          imbres

774 . . . vagis errori-   Met. 4.567 . . . longisque
bus actos   erroribus actus
—   Met. 15.771 . . . longis
                          erroribus actum
                          Her. 2.107; Trist. 4.10.109
                          . . . longis erroribus
                          acto

778 . . . implacabilis   Pont. 3.3.63 . . . non
irae   implacabilis ira

838 . . . ira leones   Trist. 4.6.5 . . . ira
                          leonum
                          Met. 15.86 . . . iracundique
                          leones
                          Met. 10.551 . . . leonibus
                          ira

840 . . . more parentum   Met. 15.366 . . . more
                          parentum

847 . . . noxia culpa   Ars 1.395 . . . /noxia
                          culpa_7

81

863 . . . totum res fusa Pont. 2.5.17 . . . totum,
 per orbem   mihi crede, per orbem
          Met. 5.481 . . . latum
          vulgata per orbem
          Met. 1.727; Am. 1.3.25 . . .
          per totum . . . orbem

944 . . . cum saevo   Met. 6.581 . . . saevi . . .
 . . . tyranno   tyranni

Final and Initial

708-9 . . . fas omne   Met. 6.585-6 . . . fasque
 nefasque / confundant nefasque / confusura
 . . .   ruit . . . /M /
          Ars 1.739 . . . fas omne
          nefasque
          Met. 9.551-2 . . . nefasque
          / fasque . . .

No Correspondence

1 . . . mensibus anni   Fast. 3.100 . . . mensibus
          annus . . .

182 . . . meta est . . . Met. 10.597 . . . meta est

185 . . . moderamina   Met. 6.677 . . . rerumque
 rerum   capit moderamen . . .

192 det vitas adimatque Met. 8.615 . . . si dant
 . . .   adimuntque figuras

230 . . . manet exitus   Met. 8.60 . . . manet
 . . .   exitus
          Met. 9.726 . . . quis me
          manet exitus, inquit

244 insita . . . patriae Pont. 2.8.31 . . . virtutis
 virtutis imago est   imagine natum /M /

260 . . . sidera noctis   Am. 1.6.44 . . . sidera
          noctis . . .

291 . . . antiqua . . .   Met. 11.343 virtutem anti-
 virtutis ab arce   quam . . .

357 dira fames . . .   Met. 8.845 . . . dira
                           fames . . .
                           Met. 11.371 . . . diramque
                           famem . . .

516 . . . rerum   Pont. 2.2.12 in rerum
     dominus . . .   dominos . . .

526 impia gens . . .   Met. 10.232 . . . gens
                           impia . . .

540 . . . firmans   Met. 10.430 . . . promissa-
     promissa . . .   que numine firmat

567 . . . faciunt   Met. 2.798; Fast. 1.379
     iussa . . .   iussa facit . . .
                           Met. 3.154 iussa viri
                           faciunt . . .

587 . . . variis rerum   Rem. 526 mille mali
     speciebus   species . . .

634 sidereosque ignes   Met. 15.665 . . . sidereos
     . . .   . . . ignes /M /

644 . . . aetheriis   Fast. 1.473 . . . aethereos
     . . . ignibus . . .   . . . ignes

666 . . . vires capit   Met. 7.417 . . . vires
     . . .   cepisse . . .

720 . . . plebem . . .   Met. 1.595 nec de plebe
     deorum   deo . . .
                           Ibis 81 . . . plebs
                           superum . . .

774 . . . vagis   Met. 4.502 erroresque
     erroribus . . .   vagos . . .

809 regna quatit . . .   Her. 8.118 . . . et sua
                           regna quatit

838 deficit humor . . .   Met. 9.567 . . . linguam
                           defecerat humor

871 . . . durus labor . . .	Trist. 4.10.115 . . . durisque laboribus
880 . . . medicam . . . curam	Pont. 1.6.35 . . . medicorum cura . . .
880 . . . caelo demittere curam	Met. 1.261 . . . demittere caelo

Summary: The two long parallels cited in the beginning of this discussion, one in thought (De prov. 212-23; Met. 1.69-86), the other in both thought and choice of words (De prov. 113-29; Met. 1.7-9; 15-20), are strong evidence for the existence of a distinct Ovidian influence in the De providentia. But many of the briefer parallels, and even a few of the longer ones, could have come with equal or even greater probability from Vergil. Still other longer parallels have a clear Ovidian ring, and a few of the briefer ones sound the same Ovidian note (e.g., deteriora legis, De prov. 557). The total number of all parallels noted for Ovid by individual works is as follows:

Metamorphoses - 84	Amores - 9
Tristia - 22	Ars Amatoria - 6
Epistulae ex Ponto - 18	Ibis - 3
Fasti - 11	Nux - 1
Heroides (Epistulae)-10	Remedia Amoris - 1

Parallels are found with all the longer works of Ovid with the Metamorphoses holding first place by a wide margin; there are far fewer parallels with the shorter works in the Ovidian corpus, and none at all for the Halieuticon, Medicamina Faciei Femineae or for the fragments.

The distribution of Ovidian parallels throughout the De providentia is also even, and extends to passages that have an obviously Christian or biblical inspiration as well; in these respects the Ovidian parallels are similar to the Vergilian.[11]

---

[11]Sister Mildred Dolores Tobin, C.S.C., in Orientii Commonitorium 13, reports that the number of Ovidian imitations in the Commonitorium of Orient. is only slightly less than the Vergilian. For further evidence of Ovidian

4. **Other Classical Poets**. No evidence has been discovered for imitation of passages in the De providentia from Propertius,[12] and virtually none from the Tibullan corpus.[13] A few parallels from Horace are noted below; the close verbal correspondence of some does suggest that the poet of the De providentia knew Horace, although the instances cited are doubtless too few in themselves to establish the point with certainty:[14]

448	verum ne longo sermone moremur . . .	Epist. 2.1.4 si longo sermone morer . . .
467	. . . volumina vatum	Epist. 2.1.26 . . . annosa volumina vatum
591	. . . patulas intrant stipata per aures	Epist. 2.2.105 . . . patulas . . . aures Epist. 1.18.70 . . . patulae . . . aures

---

influence in later Latin poetry, cf. Sister Marie Liguori Ewald, Ovid in the Contra Orationem Symmachi of Prudentius (C.U.A. Patristic Studies 66; Washington,1942) and A. H. Eaton, The Influence of Ovid on Claudian (C.U.A. Patristic Studies 69; Washington,1943).

[12]D. R. Shackleton-Bailey, "Echoes of Propertius," Mnemosyne ser. 4.5 (1952) 307-333, concludes that the evidence for the Propertian influence on Prud. is doubtful; it would seem, a fortiori, that Propertian imitation in the De prov. is unlikely.

[13]One parallel is found: De prov. 217 . . . liquidum volucres innabant aera pennis and /Tib. 7 4.1.209 /Panegyricus Messallae/: . . . per liquidum volucris vehar aera pennis. Cf. the numerous parallels to De prov. 217 cited for Verg. and Ov.; the Tibullan parallel is slightly closer to the wording in De prov., however.

[14]C. Mohrmann, "Le langue et le style de la poésie latine," 283, notes in passing that Hor., along with Verg., held a high place in 4th cent. pedagogy; thus it is highly probable that the poet of De prov. had studied Hor. in school. Horatian influence in the Commonitorium of Orient.

773-4 . . . quos aequore   Carm. 4.4.53-4 gens . . . /
    toto / iactatos . . .   iactata Tuscis aequoribus

951 . . . somnove quietus   Sat. 2.1.8 . . . somno
    in alto   quibus est opus alto

A few instances of possible parallels from authors of the Silver Age follow. The small number of parallels leaves the question of imitation open:

204 degeneri . . . metu   Lucan 3.149 degenerisque
                                      metus . . .

876 vipereum obducto   Lucan 9.635 vipereumque
    melle potamus venenum   fluit depexo crine
                                      venenum

702 . . . transcendet   Sil. 1.226 . . . transcendit
    Nestoris annos   florentes viribus annos
                                  Sil. 4.426 . . . annos
                                      transcendere factis

941 . . . animi vigor   Sil. 15.355 . . . animorum-
                                      que vigoribus . . .

399 discutiens flammis   Sen., Thy. 896-7 . . .
    tenebras . . .   discutiam tibi / tenebras
                                      . . .

19 . . . immodicis et   Stat., Silv. 5.1.247 . . .
    fletibus . . .   immodicos . . . fletus

695 . . . mortali ex   Stat., Theb. 4.747 mortali
    stirpe . . .   de stirpe . . . /M/

773-4 . . . aequore   Stat., Theb. 12.12 . . . ad-
    toto / iactatos   siduo iactatis aequore . . .

---

ranks third after Vergilian and Ovidian, and it is significant that Orient. was active in Gaul about or shortly after the date of composition of the De prov. Cf. Sister Mildred Dolores Tobin, op. cit., 2-3; 13-22.

137 inter <u>hyperboreas</u> Val. Fl. 8.211 <u>hyperboreas</u>
   mavult algere <u>pruinas</u>   movit . . . <u>pruinas</u> /M/

876 . . . <u>mella</u> veneno Val. Fl. 1.63 . . . <u>mella</u>
                <u>veneno</u> /M/

5. <u>Classical Prose Authors</u>. Serious evidence for
imitation in the <u>De providentia</u> of any prose writer before Cicero is tenuous;15 the evidence for imitation of
Cicero consists of only a few citations:

238-9 . . . discernere De orat. 3.50.195 . . .
   <u>rectis</u> / <u>prava</u>   <u>rectis</u> ac <u>prava</u> diiudicare
                <u>Ac</u>. 2.11.33 . . . inter
                   <u>rectum</u> et <u>pravum</u> . . .
                <u>Ac</u>. 1.15.9 . . . <u>rectum</u>
                   . . . <u>pravumve</u> . . .

364 . . . aenigmate De div. 2.64.132 . . .
   somni   <u>aenigmata somniorum</u>

703 <u>falsum</u> . . . aut <u>Ac</u>. 1.15.9 . . . rationem
   <u>verum</u> . . .   veri et <u>falsi</u>

941-2 . . . excutiamus / <u>Phil</u>. 1.2.6 . . . <u>iugum</u>
   peccati <u>servile iugum</u>   <u>servile</u> deiecerant

   There is one substantial parallel to Livy. When
Hannibal captured Saguntum, he sent off to Carthage a
great quantity of furniture and clothing; in the <u>De</u>
<u>providentia</u>, the worldly man who values others by external
possessions esteems rich clothing and fine furniture.
Both passages have a Vergilian ring, but neither

15For the sake of completeness, two possible parallels to Enn. and Varro, respectively, are set out here.
The example from Enn. refers to birth, the corresponding
citation from <u>De prov</u>. to the end of life.

894 extremas turpis vitae Enn., <u>Ann</u>. 114 (Warmington
   <u>produxit</u> <u>in</u> <u>oras</u>   121) tu <u>produxisti</u> nos
                   <u>intra</u> luminis <u>oras</u>

200 in <u>pecudum</u> <u>genus</u> et Varro, <u>Rust</u>. 2.1.5 . . .
   sortem transire <u>ferarum</u>   <u>genera pecudum</u> <u>ferarum</u>
                   . . .

corresponds precisely to anything in Vergil:

864 . . . vestes pre-   Liv. 21.15.2 . . . multam
    tiosae et pulchra   pretiosam supellectilem
    supellex   vestemque missam Cartha-
                               ginam

A few briefer parallels from Livy follow:

516 . . . rerum   Liv. 9.18.16 . . . domini
    dominus . . .   rerum . . .

657 . . . vis externa   Liv. 5.33.3 . . . externa
    . . .   vis . . .

880 . . . caelo demittere   Liv. 5.54.7 . . . ancilia
    curam . . .   caelo demissa . . .

    The following citations have been noted from
Seneca, Tacitus, Pliny the Elder, and Quintilian, respectively:

147 scire datum . . .   Sen., Epist. 124.20 . . .
                               quibus datum est scire
                               . . .

390 . . . obsequium   Tac., Ann. 12.47 . . .
    simulat . . .   simulare obsequium . . .
                               Tac., Hist. 4.56
                               simulatum ipsis obsequium

641 . . . violentum   Plin., Nat. 2.28 . . .
    affigere sidus   sidera adfixa mundo . . .

707 dent sese scelerum   Quint., Inst. 10.7.23 . . .
    potius torrentibus   se inani verborum
    omnes   torrenti dare

    Summary of 4 and 5: It is probable that the author
of the De providentia knew and made use of Horace; imitation of Livy appears possible. The small number of instances cited for other authors, in both prose and poetry,
and the fact that none of these instances involves a
longer parallel, makes any judgment impossible.

6. Juvencus. Manitius has set out a series of
parallels which exist between the De providentia and the
De historia evangelica, the work of the fourth-century
Spanish Christian poet Juvencus.[16] These parallels are
not considered further here.

7. Prudentius. A consideration of the literary
relationship between the De providentia and the works of
Prudentius must rely heavily on the biblical material
which is treated extensively by both poets.[17] Often both
poets treat the same biblical incidents in similar language and with correspondence of thought, as when God the
Father forbids Adam and Eve to eat the forbidden fruit:

285 . . . vetitis pomum   Cath. 3.109 stipite carpere
       decerpere ramis   poma veto

or when Elias is conveyed to heaven in his fiery chariot:

327-8 cum raptum ignitis   Cath. 7.31-2 sed mox in
        per inane iugalibus   auras igneis iugalibus /
        Helim / scandentem   curruque raptus evolavit
        rutilo viderunt aethera   praepete
        curru

---

[16]Manitius, Zeitschrift 583:

De prov.	Iuvenc.
33	4.262
159	4.334
160	1.319
194	2.88
205	praef. 18
419	4.43
420	1.213
502	1.68
528	4.704
613	praef. 3
916f.	4.7

[17]Mohrmann, op. cit., 284, observes that Christian
poetry was intended to supplement pagan poetry, not to
replace it; the most important themes of Christian poetry
are derived from the biblical narrative.

In the immediately preceding example, the De providentia has the classical phrase per inane, Prudentius the equally classical per auras. This use of classical phraseology is characteristic, in varying degrees, of virtually all the Christian Latin poets.[18]

The same similarity of language and thought in treatment of the biblical narrative occurs in phrases of less than a verse, as when Joseph's brothers recognize him by his act of forgiveness:

367 . . . venia cogno-	Ditt. 28 . . . agnoscunt
scere fratrem	fratrem veniaque pudescunt

The same biblical incident may be given the same emphasis by Prudentius and the author of the De providentia. For example, of all the consequences of Adam's sin--physical and mental disturbances in man, the disordering of the physical universe, etc.--the one stressed by both poets is the transmission of original sin to subsequent generations; in this, both poets come to the heart of the matter, and are in full agreement with the traditional teaching:[19]

489-90 . . . Adam trans-	Apoth. 911-2 exim tincta
fudit in omnes / mortem	malo peccamine principis
homines, quoniam cuncti	Adae / infecit genus
nascuntur ab illo	omne hominum, quod
	pullulat inde.

But the same incident may be treated with different emphases to accord with differing contexts. Thus the poet of the De providentia stresses the fact that Christ after

---

[18]Prud. employed traditional poetic language in a religious sense. Cf. his terms for God the Father, the resurrected Christ, and the Holy Spirit, verus tonans, dux redivivus, and tonans spiritus, respectively, cited in Mohrmann, op. cit.,287. One has the impression that the De prov. is less strict in this regard; compare De prov. 492-3-Prud., Cath. 3.136-7, with Verg.,Ecl. 4.7; also De prov. 802-Prud., Cath. 9.12, with Verg., Georg. 4.393. The two comparisons between Prud. and the De prov. are discussed at nn. 20 and 21, below.

[19]Cf. Rom. 5.12-21, where Paul lays great stress

his Resurrection appeared to his disciples; Prudentius in
the Apotheosis approaches the same mystery of the Resurrection as restoring Christ in the majesty of the Father,
of course without denying that Christ enjoyed the Beatific
Vision while on earth. In both accounts the tertia lux,
the day of Resurrection, provides a starting point:

536 tertia discipulis,   Apoth. 531 maiestate patris
     Iesu, dedit attonitis   vivum lux tertia reddit
     lux

Similarly, in the De providentia Christ is portrayed
as coming to raise the human race; Prudentius portrays
faith as raising the descendants of the race in the age
to come. In the one case the Redemption is considered
from the viewpoint of Christ's redemptive acitivity present now among men; in the other, the future effects of
redemption are stressed:

471-2 . . . longamque   Symm. 1.559-60 . . . stipem-
     ruinam / humani generis   que superbam / gentis pa-
     meliore attolleret ortu   triciae venturo attollere
                                   saeclo

The same incident may be recounted with some verbal
similarity but also with considerable difference in
language. In the following accounts of Christ's birth,
the word homo is the same, but the De providentia uses
the apparently more natural terms novus homo and natus,
and alludes to the role of Mary; Prudentius employs the
Vergilian terms nova progenies and aethere proditus, which
appear somewhat artificial in this context, and seemingly
finds nothing in the classical language which would serve
as a suitable model for a reference to the Virgin at this
point:[20]

---

on this consequence of Adam's sin in a comparison between
Adam and Christ.

[20] Cf. n. 17,above, and Verg., Ecl. 4.7.

492-3 sed novus e caelis
    per Sacrae Virginis
    alvum / natus homo
    est . . .

Cath. 3.136-7 ecce venit
    nova progenies / aethere
    proditus alter homo

The same point may be made by both poets in similar language, and yet the context may differ. Man must serve God alone, and worship only him--this thought is conveyed as a direct quotation from the Author of Life in the De providentia, at the conclusion of a passage directed against the astrologers and their claim that the stars deserve worship as influencing human life. Prudentius expresses the same thought in the Contra orationem Symmachi, but there God is speaking of his wonderful works and ordering that man construct a temple in the heart in his honor:

649-50 'solum,' inquit,
    'venerare Deum, solique
    memento / servire . . .'

Symm. 2.244-5 'soli mihi
    construe templum / meque
    unum venerare Deum . . .'
Cf. Apoth. 385 . . .
    venerata Deum

There are lists of contrasting physical elements in both the De providentia and the Hamartigenia. If the Hamartigenia was indeed a source for the list of physical elements in the later poem, some expansion has taken place:

127-9 mollia sic duris,
    sic raris densa resis-
    tunt, / et liquidis
    solida, et tardis
    velocia, claro / obscurum
    obiectum, et dulci con-
    tendit amarum

Ham. 325-6 quid durum, quid
    molle foret, quid lene,
    quid horrens, / quid
    calidum gelidumve . . .

Contraction of Prudentian expressions may also occur in the De providentia. Abel's offering of the choicest of his flock to God is expressed over two verses in the De providentia, but over three in the Peristephanon:

306-7 iustus Abel, qui
    primitiis ovium grege
    lectis / convertit
    Domini sincera in
    munera vultum

Peri. 10.828-30 ut primi-
    tivum crederes fetum
    geri / Deo offerendum
    sancti Abelis ferculo /
    lectum ex ovili, puriorem
    ceteris

Similarly, the giving of the Law to Moses is expressed by a brief phrase in the De providentia, while it is recounted more explicitly over more than a verse in the Dittochaeon:

434-5 . . . tradita	Ditt. 38-9 scripta decem
Mosi / littera . . .	verbis saxorum pagina
	Moysi / traditur

The reference to the elements of creation discussed above (127-9; Ham. 325-6) raises the question of items in series and their treatment by the two poets. One series of terms in the De providentia depicts the unjust man in general as violent, cruel, crafty and greedy; the portrayal may be a contaminatio of two descriptions in Prudentius, one of a certain Eumorphius, a pagan soldier involved in the martyrdom of St. Vincent, portrayed as violent, unrestrained, and barbarous, and the other of the Emperor Galerius, a persecutor of Christians, depicted as heartless, cruel, gross and intransigent:

69 . . . violentus,	Peri. 5.467 violentus,
atrox, versutus, avarus	audax, barbarus
	Peri. 10.33 immitis, atrox,
	asper, implacabilis

Another series found in each poet enumerates the various races of men, who are all united in Christ; in Prudentius the enumeration occurs, most appropriately, as part of a hymn for the Epiphany:

455-7 . . . vir, femina,	Cath. 12.202-4 Iudaea, Roma,
servus, / liber,	et Graecia / Aegypta,
Iudaeus, Graecus,	Thrax, Persa, Scytha, /
Scytha, barbarus,	Rex unus omnes possidet
omnes / in Christo	
sumus unum . . .	

The tripartite division of events into past, present, and future is also found in both the De providentia and the Cathemerinon:[21]

---

[21] Cf. n. 17, above, and Verg., Georg. 4.393.

802   nam quod ubique   Cath. 9.12 . . . quae sunt,
      agitur, quod gestum   fuerunt, quaeque post
      est, quodque gerendum   futura sunt
      est

    There is, finally, an example of the same thought, that of God's omnipresence, expressed by both poets, and in similar language, but in the De providentia through the use of the double negative and in Prudentius by a simple positive assertion:

183   sed nusquam non esse   Apoth. 638 . . . Deus est,
      Dei est, qui totus   qui totus ubique est
      ubique

Briefer Parallels

Initial

399   discutiens flammis   Peri. 13.26 discutit et
      tenebras . . .   tenebras . . .

400   quid loquar . . .   Ham. 230; Symm. 1.271; Peri.
                                   1.112 quid loquar . . .

402   instar montis   Cath. 5.93 instar fellis
      aquas . . .   aqua . . .
                               Psych. 654 mons . . .
                                   pendentis aquae . . .

520   sacrilegis manibus   Apoth. 199 sacrilegisque
      . . .   . . . manibus . . .

558   'erro,' ais . . .   Ham. 509 'errat,' ait . . .

680   novimus et . . .   Ham. 366 novimus et . . .
                               Apoth. 433 novit et . . .

904   argenti atque   Peri. 14.102 argenti et
      auri . . .   auri . . .

Internal

39   . . . nullo discri-   Ham. 72; 99 . . . nullo
      mine . . .   discrimine . . .

94

	Symm. 2.826 . . . discrimine nullo
138 . . . sub fasce viator	Apoth. 720 . . . sub fasce minister
230 . . . manet exitus . . .	Ditt. 159 . . . manet exitus . . . 22
454 . . . cuius generis . . .	Symm. 2.823 . . . cuius generis . . .
516 . . . rerum dominus . . .	Apoth. 227 . . . rerum dominum . . .
928 . . . sacraria Christi	Symm. 1.379 . . . sacraria Ditis

Final

1 . . . mensibus anni	Peri. 11.195 . . . mensibus annus
19 . . . fletibus ora rigamus	Peri. 11.194 . . . fletibus ora rigant
48 . . . religionis amor	Peri. 11.192 . . . religion- is amor Symm. 2.591 religionis amor . . .
65 . . . veterum recolamus avorum	Symm. 1.39 . . . veterum procul absit avorum
73 . . . sine crimine vitam	Symm. 1.95 . . . crimine vitam
83 . . . celsa spectaret ab arce	Ham. 494 . . . celsa stans eminus arce
87 . . . spargantur in aures	Peri. 1.78 . . . per aures posterorum spargerent

---

22 This parallel is noted in Manitius, Geschichte 174 n. 2.

115 . . . terraeque   Symm. 2.579 . . . terraque
     marique   marique
                               Symm. 2, praef. 25 terrae-
                                   que et maris . . .

145 . . . tergis horrere   Symm. 1.128 . . . terga
     ferarum   ferarum

194 . . . et peccata   Apoth. 964 . . . et
     remittat   peccata remitto

217 . . . liquidum   Ham. 816; Psych. 305 . . .
     volucres innabant   aera pennis
     aera pennis   Ham. 535 . . . volucres
                                   dum pennis transvolat
                                   auras

263 . . . ingenium varias   Symm. 2.390 . . . varias
     augere per artes   agitetur ad artes

402 . . . vacuo   Ham. 471 . . . aequoreum
     cessisse profundo   pelago cedente profundum

409 . . . miracula rerum   Apoth. 138 . . . miracula
                                   rerum

507 . . . fas est   Apoth. 18 . . . fas sit

523-4 . . . felque et   Apoth. 99 . . . fel potat
     acetum / . . . haurit   et haurit acetum

535 . . . referentem   Psych. 64 . . . referens
     carne tropaeum   ex hoste tropaeum

541 . . . tractabilis   Symm. 2.588 . . . quidquid
     esset   tractabile moribus esset

560 . . . rationis   Symm. 1.81 . . . diae
     egenum   rationis egenum
                               Cath. 10.82 . . . rationis
                                   egenis

566 . . . lege tenentur   Psych. 343 . . . lege teneri
                               Symm. 2.70-1 . . . teneri /
                                   lege sua . . .

586 . . . luminat omnes   Symm. 2.831 . . . luminat
                            omnes

591 . . . patulas intrant Apoth. 399 . . . stolidas
    stipata per aures   intrare per aures

603 . . . ut non   Apoth. 934 . . . sed non
    vitiorum   vitiorum

721 . . . fraudis   Psych. 268 . . . ad fraudis
    opertae   opertum

731 . . . solis . . .   Peri. 13.102-3 . . . in
    in ortum   ortum / solis . . .

750 . . . feritate   Symm. 1.46 . . . feritate
    tyranni   tyranni

759 . . . generis nostri   Symm. 2.341-2 . . . nostrae
    profunda propago   porrecta propago /
                               stirpis . . .
                           Symm. 2.224 . . . generisque
                               propagine . . .

768 . . . submissus   Apoth. 598 . . . submissus
    adorat   adoro

838 deficit . . . ira   Cath. 4.86 . . . languente
    leones   truci leonis ira

863 . . . totum res fusa   Symm. 2.915 . . . totumque
    per orbem   per orbem

876 vipereum . . .   Peri. 13.57 . . . vipereis
    venenum   . . . venenis

909 . . . caeloque   Symm. 2.868 . . . caeli
    prius translata   super astra locare
    locavit   Symm. 1.271 . . . caelesti
                               in sede locatum

944 . . . cum saevo   Symm. 2.876 . . . saevo
    pacta tyranno   vivens captiva tyranno

No Correspondence

22 . . . saucia corda petunt	Psych. 322 saucia . . . capiebat corda . . .
78 . . . ulcera dira . . .	Ham. 928 . . . post ulcera dira . . .
205 immortale decus . . .	Symm. 2.757 . . . decus immortale . . .
222 . . . substantia duplex	Psych. 909 . . . duplex substantia . . .
244 . . . patriae virtutis . . .	Psych. 2 . . . patria virtute . . .
249 totaque res effecta Dei . . .	Cath. 11.23-4 virtute verbi effecta sunt / haec cuncta . . .
264-5 . . . uni / sub- iectum servire Deo . . .	Peri. 5.172 solique subiectum Deo
372-3 . . . mentes / non possunt turbare pias . . .	Symm. 2.102-3 vimque fatigatae mentis . . . / turbari . . .
394 ditia . . . gazis	Psych. praef. 24 . . . gaza dives . . .
443 . . . regina austri . . .	Ditt. 82 . . . regina austri . . .
465 . . . rerumque creator	Peri. 10.469 rerum creator . . .
467 . . . volumina vatum	Apoth. 219 . . . volumini- bus vatum . . .
546 . . . alter et alter	Peri. 8.18 . . . alter et alter . . .
587 . . . variis rerum speciebus	Apoth. 733 exiguas rerum species . . .

624 sed quo te praeceps   Ham. 1 quo te praecipitat
     rapit orbita . . .   rabies tua . . .

695. . . mortali ex   Symm. 1.268 mortali de
     stirpe . . .   stirpe . . .

708 . . . fas omne   Cath. 3.134 fasque nefasque . . .
     nefasque

731 . . . revocatur in   Cath. 10.10 . . . revocantur
     ortum   in ortus . . .

827 arsuris . . .   Ham. 725 . . . Sodomis
     Sodomis . . .   ardentibus

901-2 . . . quidquid   Ep. 33 quidquid illud
     mundanis rebus acerbum   accidit
     / accidit . . .

916 . . . penetralia   Ham. 542 . . . cordis
     cordis   penetralia . . .

926 . . . congesta   Symm. 2.718 . . . congesta
     iacent . . .   iacent . . .

969 haec sat erit . . .   Peri. 12.65 . . . sat est
                                      . . .
                                  Apoth. 893 . . . sat sit

Summary: Prudentian influence on the De providentia
is clearly evident in some of the parallels, both the
longer and the shorter. In the longer parallels this influence exists above all with reference to the treatment
of material derived from the biblical narrative. It is
interesting to observe that Prudentius and Vergil stand
closer to each other in the language of certain of these
parallels than either does to the De providentia; doubtless a gradual lessening of the restrictions against the
use of distinctly Christian terminology even in Christian
poems accounts for this fact. Many of the briefer parallels are of such a nature that they could have been derived indifferently from Prudentius or Vergil, and some
from Ovid; others are distinctly Prudentian. Briefer
parallels are found to every part of the De providentia.

99

The total number of all parallels from each work of Prudentius is as follows:

Contra orationem Symmachi - 27
Apotheosis - 18
Peristephanon - 16
Hamartigenia - 13
Cathemerinon - 11
Psychomachia - 9
Dittochaeon (Tituli historiarum) - 4
Epilogue - 1

Parallels have been found with every work of Prudentius, but only a few to the shorter works, as might be expected.

8. Paulinus of Nola. In the fourth of his Natalicia, or birthday hymns in honor of the martyr Felix (Carm. 15), Paulinus of Nola portrays the delivery of Peter from prison by an angel; it would appear that the poet of the De providentia had the same incident in mind in listing miraculous jail delivery as one of the wonders God performs for the saints. In the De providentia, chains fall off and release their captives, an idiom that is found elsewhere in the fourth Natalicium of Paulinus.[23] In the present account, Paulinus portrays Peter as going out of the chains and confines of his prison;[24] there is thus a transition from a more specific reference in Paulinus to a more generalized one in the De providentia:

---

[23]Carm. 15.250 ". . . molles manibus fluxere catenae."

[24]The biblical source is Acts 12.6-10. Carm. 15 was probably composed in 398. Cf. R. C. Goldschmidt, Paulinus' Churches at Nola (Amsterdam, 1940) 11. For an English translation and commentary on Carm. 12 through 15, see M. P. McHugh, Paulinus of Nola: Natalicia I-IV (unpublished Master's thesis, The Catholic University of America, Washington, 1956).

836-7 . . . vinctos
   labentia vincula
   solvunt; / carcer
   sponte patet . . .

Carm. 15.263-4 Petrus
   sponte sua vinclis
   labentibus eque / carcere
   processit clauso . . .

The contrast between the aversi, or those who have
turned away from Christ, and the conversi, or those who
have turned toward him, is found both in the De providentia and in the Epistles of Paulinus. Christ receives those
who have turned toward him, and in the Epistles he illumines
them with the light of glory. There is a difference in the
treatment of the aversi, however; in the De providentia
Christ calls them back to himself, in the Epistles he
punishes them with further blindness:

947 aversos revocans et
   suscipiens conversos

Epist. 32.23 . . . ut conversos ad se reficit lumine, ita aversos adficit
   caecitate.

Briefer Parallels

Initial

804;867 una dies . . .

Carm. 14.82 una dies . . .

Internal

18 et stetit ante oculos
   . . .

Carm. 6.114 constitit ante
   oculos . . .

211 . . . Christo
   donante . . .

Carm. 12.35 . . . Christo
   donante . . .

Final

285 . . . decerpere
   ramis

Carm. 15.291 . . . decerpere
   ramo

350 . . . igneus imber

Carm. 28.92 . . . igneus
   imber

734 . . . nubibus imber

Carm. 18.18 . . . a nubibus
   imber

No Correspondence

115 . . . terraeque marique	Carm. 13.10 . . . terraeque marique . . .
306 . . . ovium grege . . .	Carm. 14.131 . . . ovium grege . . .
419 . . . penetralia mentis . . .	Carm. 6.237 . . . sacrae ad penetralia mentis

Summary: The possibility that Paulinus served as a source for the De providentia should not be discounted. After Juvencus, Paulinus stands with Prudentius as one of the Fathers of Christian Latin poetry. At the same time, the number and texture of the examples discovered does not suffice to establish Paulinus' influence on the De providentia with any certainty.

9. Claudius Marius Victor. Claudius Marius Victor's work, the Alethia, was in all likelihood composed after the De providentia.[25] In the Alethia, God is addressed as "without beginning and likewise perduring without end, always the same and subject to no age, beyond the bounds of all space that penetration of mind can reach, not confined by any limit;"[26] in the De providentia God is described as "without author or limit of time, remaining ever the same, and not confined by time or place in his immensity." The passage in the Alethia may be an expansion of the thought of the earlier poem:

---

[25]Dating the De providentia c. 416, the Alethia was composed probably c. 424-455. On the dating of the Alethia cf. G. Bardy, "Claudius Marius Victor," DTC 15.2877-80.

[26]The translation is that of J. C. Schnaubelt, O.S.A., Claudius Marius Victor, Alethia: Prayer and Book I (unpublished Master's thesis, The Catholic University of America, Washington, 1960). For an English translation and commentary on Book II cf. K. A. Gersbach, O.S.A., Claudius Marius Victor, Alethia, Liber II (unpublished Master's thesis, The Catholic University of America, Washington, 1962).

hic auctore carens, et tempore, permanet idem
semper, et immensum nec saecula nec loca claudunt.
(De prov. 109-10)
solus semper idem nullique obnoxius aevo,
tu spatium rerum, mentis quocumque recessus
tenditur, excedis spatio neque cingeris ullo,
(Aleth., prec. 9-11)

In the Alethia narrative, when the Almighty made
hell, the heavens and earth and sea trembled and opened
their vast recesses at the shock; in the De providentia
the earth trembles at the shock of Christ's death:

| 528-9 . . . concussaque | Aleth. 1.473 intremit et |
| tellus / intremuit . . . | vastos concussa recessus |

Hovingh has noted two other parallels of greater
length between the two poems in his recent edition of the
Alethia.[27] In one of these, Adam speaks in the Alethia of
his condemnation as the just penalty for his sin; there
is considerable verbal similarity to the passage in the
De providentia where Moses receives the ten commandments,
which condemn sins to swift punishment:

434-5 . . . cum tradita	Aleth. 2.63 . . . cum
Mosi / littera prae-	damnarer iusta pro
senti damnaret crimina	crimine poena
poena	

The other parallel is one of thought with no verbal correspondence. The author of the De providentia
observes that after the fall of Adam, man confounded all
right and wrong, i.e., lost all moral sense; likewise,
in the Alethia, the race of giants had lost all sense
of right and wrong, and did not consider it either licit
or illicit in conscience to commit any sin:

708-9 . . . fas omne	Aleth.2.368-9 non illis
nefasque / confundant	quicquam illiciti
	temerasse profanum /
	aut licitum cordi . . .

---

[27] P. F. Hovingh, ed., Claudii Marii Victorii Alethia
(CC, Series Latina 128; Turnholt,1960) 271.

In the list of briefer parallels, those noted by Hovingh are indicated by /H_7.[28]

Briefer Parallels

Initial

536 tertia . . . lux	1.85 tertia lux . . .
948 sanguine quos proprio . . .	prec. 88 sanguine mox proprio . . .

Final

115 . . . terraeque marique	1.335 . . . terraeque marisque
183 . . . qui totus ubique	2.54 . . . qui semper totus ubique es
	prec. 16 . . . quia totus semper ubique es
217 . . . aera pennis	2.524 . . . aera pennis /H_7
292 . . . errore parentum	3.497 . . . errore parentum /H_7
316 . . . primordia mundi	prec. 107; 2.1 . . . primordia mundi /H_7
356 . . . regna teneret	3.402 . . . regna tenebis
	3.539 . . . regna tenentis /H_7
477 . . . miracula divinorum	1.428 . . . secretorum miracula divinorum /H_7
507 . . . resolvere fas est	prec. 3. . . . comprendere fas est
512 . . . spiritus almus	prec. 124 . . . spiritus almus
	1.5-6 . . . almus / spiritus /H_7

---

[28]Cf. Hovingh, ibid. All of Hovingh's parallels to the De prov. are included here.

692 . . . tempora vitae   prec. 80 . . . per lubrica
tempora vitae /H 7

734 . . . nubibus imber   2.463 . . . nubibus effluit
imber

767 . . . errore parentum   3.497 . . . errore parentum

779 . . . melioris tempora   prec. 80 . . . per lubrica
vitae   tempora vitae /H 7

787 . . . poena malorum   prec. 77 . . . poena
malorum /H 7

876 vipereum . . .   1.419 . . . vipereo . . .
venenum   veneno

No Correspondence

33 . . . mali labes   2.43 . . . labe mali . . .
. . .

177 . . . tempora   1.21 . . . tempora
condens   conderet . . . /H 7

735-6 laeta . . . /   1.264 . . . laeto . . .
semina . . .   semine . . .

786 iudicio quae digna   prec. 76 . . . iudice digna
meo . . .   severo /H 7

Summary: There is some evidence to indicate that the author of the Alethia was acquainted with the De providentia. Parallels with the De providentia are found in the introductory prayer and in each of the three books of the Alethia; the total number of possible borrowings noted is 29.

10. Other Christian Authors. The purpose of this section is to set out a number of parallels between the De providentia and several other works of Christian authors of the fifth century. Orientius, the poet of the Commonitorium, appears to have known and used the De providentia;[29] in the other instances cited, relationship with the

---

[29] Cf. Teuffel, Geschichte 3.430.

De providentia is doubtful. The relationship between the De providentia and the works of Sedulius, which is not considered here, has been studied to some extent by Manitius.[30]

17 . . . animum patriae subiit fumantis imago	Orient., Comm. 2.184 uno fumarit Gallia tota rogo. /V_/
35-8 non castella petris, non oppida montibus altis / imposita, aut urbes amnibus ae- quoreis, / barbarici superare dolos atque arma furoris / evaluere omnes, ultima pertulimus.	Orient., Comm. 2.167-72 non densi nemoris, celsi non aspera montis, / flu- mina non rapidis fortia gurgitibus, / non castella locis, non tutae montibus urbes, / invia non pelago, tristia non heremo, / non cava, non etiam tetricis sub rupibus antra, / ludere barbaricas prae- valuere manus. /V_/ /M_/
217 et liquidum volucres innabant aera pennis	Cypr. Gall., Gen. 20 et volucres varias sus- pendunt aere pennas
619 . . . excelso deiectus Lucifer axe	Cypr. Gall., Gen.160 . . . celsumque ascendit ad axem

---

[30]Manitius,Zeitschrift 581-584, notes the following parallels between the De prov. and the Carmen Paschale and Hymni duo:

De prov.	Sedul.
47	Carm. 2.67
289-90; 298	Hymn. 1.5; 1.69
321	Carm. 1.103; 1.106
465	Carm. 1.38; 1.43
528	Carm. 5.245; 5.268
531	Carm. 5.270
808	Carm. 3.2
876	Carm. 2.186
941	Carm. 2.54

Most of the parallels involve biblical passages.

901 . . . mundanis   Cypr. Gall., Gen. 26 . . .
   rebus . . .   . . . mundanis defore
                     rebus

695 . . . mortali ex   Claud. Mamert., In Ruf. 56
   stirpe ricisos   . . . vitiisque a stirpe
                     recisis

603-4 . . . non   Salv., Eccl. 1.12 . . . sed
   vitiorum / incentiva   incentiva vitiorum

     Conclusion: The existence of a strong Vergilian in-
fluence on the De providentia is established without
question; the influence of Ovid ranks second only to that
of Vergil. Evidence of Lucretian influence, while present,
could be somewhat misleading, but it is probable that the
author of the De providentia knew and made use of Horace.
Among the Christian poets, Prudentius made the largest
contribution, but other influences, particularly that of
Paulinus of Nola, should not be excluded. The De providentia itself quite possibly had some bearing in the composition of the Commonitorium of Orientius and of the
Alethia of Claudius Marius Victor.

F. STYLE[1]

     1. Vocabulary. Valentin[2] supplies a full treat-
ment of the vocabulary and grammar of the De providentia
with extensive cross-references to the De ingratis. He

---

[1] The arrangement of material in this section is suggested in part by that adopted by A. Blaise, Manuel du
latin chrétien. The subsections on rhetorical figures and
on figurative language owe much to H. Lausberg, Handbuch
der literarischen Rhetorik.

[2] Valentin, Saint Prosper 802-808. The material and
examples included in this subsection are taken from V.
The examples, cited by V. in their standard grammatical
form, are cited here in the form in which they actually
appear in the poem. Other occurrences of all examples
cited may be controlled through reference to the Index
Verborum.

finds that the De providentia contains many classical
words employed with modification in sense (e.g., assertoris 949, and servatos 954). Simple forms of the verb
are preferred to compounds (e.g., tersa est 460, trudentia 735, quatit 809, quivit 866) and archaic forms are
occasionally found (viz., popularier 45, consumier 89,
mage 460).[3] Abstracts occur with some frequency (e.g.,
substantia 324, reverentia 53), and the poet shows a
preference for inchoative verbs (e.g., tumescunt 571,
brutescere 770, senescant 792, tabescere 882) and a lik-
ing for adjectives in -ilis (viz., instabili and stabili
126, cruciabilis 225, mutabilis 713, implacabilis 778,
resolubile 945). Derivatives in -tor and -sor occur often
in the De providentia (e.g., sator 132, auctoris 149,
conditor 212, 466, transgressoris 491, messor 834); syncopated forms and polysyllabic words are not uncommon.
In both the De providentia and the De ingratis words tend
to retain their etymological senses (e.g., compugnant,
De prov. 121, and compugnantia, De ingrat. 740). Words
susceptible of different meanings are often employed in
the same sense in both poems (e.g., in both De prov. and
De ingrat., aversi are those who have turned away from
God, insontes are sinless persons, pius refers to one
who has the faith, and reus is a sinner).

There are few grammatical irregularities in the
De providentia; perfect participles of deponent verbs
occasionally appear in a passive sense (e.g., confessi
462, scrutatis 716, populati 926) and intransitive verbs
are used at times in the passive (e.g., sileantur 61,
properata 755, festinata 800). Adjectives are treated
as substantives and modified by other adjectival forms
(e.g., vacuo profundo 402, mortale meun 486), and adjectives terminating in -ilis are followed by the dative
of agent (e.g., Domino cruciabilis 225, resolubile
Christo 945).

2. Structure of the Period. The ordering of the
period in the De providentia is simple while the periods
themselves tend to be somewhat lengthy. A salient feature
of the structure is the author's practice of appending a
subordinate clause to conclude the period.

---

[3] Another is peremptor, 295, if V.'s reading is accepted.

Clauses appended in this manner may be descriptive (2,
quo scripta est versu pagina nulla tuo), or may express
result (12, ut tali tempore liber agat) or condition
(548-9, si calle tamen curramus eodem, / edocti non posse
capi nisi de cruce caelum; cf. 949-50; 962-4) or may be
temporal (855-6 dum non nostrarum curanda negotia rerum /
suscipimus, propriisque iuvant aliena relictis; cf. 898-900).
Valentin has noted that phrases in the period often terminate with a participle in apposition to the subject of the
principal proposition.[4] An example of the two preceding
phenomena occurs at verses 548-9, cited above, where the
period terminates in a conditional clause, which itself
terminates in a participial phrase.

An interesting inversion, or chiastic periodic structure, occurs at the conclusion of the discussion of
astrology:

> scrutatis igitur stellarum motibus, hoc est
> artis opus, totam subvertere religionem,
> dum nullum curare Deum mortalia suadet;
> aut dum posse docet votis elementa moveri,
> innumeram miseris plebem insinuare deorum.
> (716-720)

Here the first dum-clause is to be taken with the preceding
portion of the period, and the second with what follows.

The period may produce the effect of parallelism, too,
as in this example, where the two last verses are in
balance:

> cuius ab effectu firmato cardine rerum,
> ut mala non poterunt sancta probitate repelli,
> sic bona non fugient perversos debita mores
> (710-712)

The poet is supple, too, in adapting the periodic
structure to express various other effects. A series of
short, staccato periods suffices to convey the series of
disasters suffered at the hands of the invading Goths:

---

[4]Valentin, op. cit., 807, citing vv. 114, 175, 253,
316, 392, 398, 515, 600, 616, 735, 740, 745, 790, 829, 947,
and 950. In most of these cases the participial phrase
itself terminates the period. The period may also terminate in an ablative construction, as at v. 155, factore
remoto.

nec querar exstinctam nullo discrimine plebem,
  mors quoque primorum cesset ab invidia,
maiores anni ne forte et nequior aetas
  offenso tulerint quae meruere Deo;
quid pueri insontes, quid commisere puellae,
  nulla quibus dederat crimina vita brevis?
quare templa Dei licuit popularier igni?
  cur violata sacri vasa ministerii?
non honor innuptas devotae virginitatis,
  nec texit viduas religionis amor.
ipsi desertis qui vitam ducere in antris
  suerant, laudantes nocte dieque Deum,
non aliam subiere necem, quam quisque profanus;
  idem turbo bonos sustulit atque malos.
nulla sacerdotes reverentia nominis almi
  discrevit miseri suppliciis populi;
sic duris caesi flagris, sic igne perusti,
  inclusae vinclis sic gemuere manus
                    (39-56).

In the above example, only one period occupies more than
two verses (49-51); two succeeding periods occupy only a
verse each (45, 46).

     But more typical of the author's style is the
longer period, as in these two instances which occur in
succession:[5]

o mersi in tenebras, divinique ignis inanes,
et plus corporeis oculis quam mente videntes!
qui vestrae aeternum naturae et conditioni
audetis conferre Deum, cui si quid amatis
in laudem pravi adicitis, vestrisque beatum
creditis esse bonis, aut ulla incommoda ferre
                    (159-164).
an quia cum magnas urbes populosque tenetis
sub vestro imperio, miserum est insomnibus aegram
partiri curis in multa negotia mentem;
cumque graves trepidis incumbant undique causae,
non fert urgentes industria victa labores;
et si animis aegris depulsa est sollicitudo,
blanda voluptatem requies creat otia nactis;
de Domino hoc sentire pium est, quem semper eumdem
nil gravat, ex toto nil occupat? . . .
                    (165-173).

---

[5] Noted by Valentin, op. cit., 810 n. 5.

In periods of this last type the author's rhetorical training is most apparent; in the second example, particularly,
all of the subordinate clauses lead toward the climax of
the last verse and a half. At other times the longer
periodic structure appears to be used chiefly to convey
additional information; thus the biblical stories of Noe,
of Lot, and of Joseph are each told in a period of some
length (335-40, 351-5, and 356-67, respectively).

3. Rhetorical Figures

a. Antithesis, Anaphora, Chiasmus. Antithesis,
the placement of contrasting terms in opposition one to
another,[6] is found frequently throughout the De providentia.[7] Antithetical figures will often be found to manifest a distinct Christian spirit, or "mentalité nouvelle,"
as Blaise observes.[8] Such, for example, is the contrast

---

[6]Cf. Lausberg, op. cit., 1.389-398, who treats this
figure under the more comprehensive term antitheton and
reserves the word antithesis to denote the substitution
of one letter for another, e.g., as in bobis for bovis.
For further discussion of oxymoron, which Lausberg treats
under antitheton, cf. at nn. 41-44, below.

[7]Cf. Valentin, op. cit., 812 n. 4, who finds antitheses at vv. 190-5, 231, 232, 233, 234, 251, 406, 450,
452, 465, 466, 477, 478, 486, 487, 505, 509, 516ff., 528,
549, 580, 581, 583, 584, 651, 652, 696, 701, 806, 816, 817,
854, 859, 965.

[8]Cf. Blaise, Manuel du latin chrétien 30-31:
"Plus spécialement, toute les figures qui constituent une
antithèse présenteront cette fois une certaine originalité;
car elles ont leur point de départ dans une mentalité
nouvelle. Opposer le corps à l'esprit, c'est déjà dans la
philosophie de Sénèque. Mais il s'établit, dans le latin
des chrétiens, l'habitude constante d'opposer le corps à
l'ame, la chair à l'esprit, l'esprit à la matiére, la vie
du monde, du siècle à la vie chrétienne, la terre au ciel,
ce qui passe à ce qui demeure éternellement. Cette
mentalite est trop connue pour qu'il soit nécessaire de
multiplier les exemples. . . ."

between perishable and enduring things (10), the longer
contrast between man's body and his spirit (229-234), and
that between the attitude of the worldly man and the
spiritual man toward human misfortunes (897-912; cf. 887-
891 and 934-940). Similarly, God's undivided providence
is opposed to man's many and various activities (451 . . .
solidam Domini divisa negotia curam), and a contrast is
made between the living and the dead as recipients of the
fruits of the Incarnation, although the Incarnation itself is the same for all (495-496). Occasionally elements
are opposed which have no specific Christian reference,
as when the poet observes that man desires to exchange his
present condition of life for an opposite one (136-141;
cf. 150). Occasionally, too, a contrast may be repeated
in the poem, as that between the things of God and the
things of man (542-543; 965) or between the wretched man
and the blessed one (704; 857).

Anaphora may be defined as repetition of the same
word or words at the beginning of successive clauses.[9]
Anaphora, too, is effectively used in the De providentia
to point a contrast, e.g., in describing the various fates
ordained for men by the stars:
   'hic,' inquit, 'felix, miser hic erit, hunc rapiet
   mors impubem, hic senio transcendet Nestoris annos'
                   (701-702).
A more complex construction, involving anaphora of
two words, cur and hoc, with chiasmus in the second verse,
represents the pathetic complaining of the sinner as well
as the fact that it was by his own choice that he arrived
at and continues in his present predicament:
   'cur non sum bonus?' hoc non vis. 'cur sum malus?'
               hoc vis.
   'cur volo quae mala sunt, et cur quae sunt bona nolo?'
               (554-555).
Anaphora may, of course, be used without any antithesis intended, as in these verses, where the repeated
hoc stresses the longstanding hope of the Hebrews for a
Messias:

---

[9]Cf. Leumann-Hofmann, Lateinische Grammatik 797
and Lausberg, op. cit., 1.318-320.

hoc etenim lex, hoc veneranda volumina vatum,
hoc patriarcharum spes non incerta tenebat;
ultima cum mundi finem prope curreret aetas,
venturum ad terrena Deum, qui morte perempta
solveret inferni leges, longamque ruinam
humani generis meliore attolleret ortu
                        (467-472)
    Chiasmus,[10] the arrangement of corresponding parts
of a sentence in a crosswise order, is another device used
to express antithesis. In the following instance those
who have turned from God are opposed to those who have
turned toward him:
    aversos revocans et suscipiens conversos (947).
But some sinners are offered the opportunity for repentance and others are not; the poet expresses the pious hope
that he may be numbered among the former:
    meque istis potius societ, quam congreget illis (889).
    A chiasmus involving three terms contrasts the
human and the divine, what is ours and what is Christ's,
but at the same time emphasizes the union of human and
divine in Christ:
    qui dum nostra suis sociat, iunxit sua nostris (965).
    Chiasmus often occurs when several items are men-
tioned in series. Thus there is a certain chiastic
structure in two passages of similar tenor which enumerate various divine operations or instances of divine
providence in the world (191-194; 808-812); in each passage, however, the author seems to avoid chiasmus in
places where it might have been achieved, e.g.,
    exhaurit morbis, cremat ignibus, obruit undis (810).
    Chiastic structure is used also to contrast such
disparate items as speed and delay (187), dense and rarefied elements (127), the hypothetical ability of the
stars to pass decrees but not to change them (706), the
effects of a belief in astrology on those whose horoscopes
are favorable or unfavorable, respectively (704), and
devout as opposed to complaining Christians (20); the
structure of the chiasmus is not perfectly balanced in
all of these cases.[11]

---

    [10]Lausberg, ibid., 1.361 n. 1, observes that the term
chiasmus is a modern one in its application to this figure.

    [11]For an example of chiastic periodic structure,
cf. vv. 716-720, set out at n. 4, above.

The author of the De providentia exploits the possibilities for antithesis inherent in his subject matter,
although the antitheses themselves are quite conventional
on the whole. Chiasmus is not similarly exploited as much
as one might expect; one reason for this may be found in
the poet's preference for simplicity in periodic structure,
as already noted.[12]

b. Aporia. Aporia, or dubitatio, is pretended
uncertainty by the speaker as to how he shall proceed in his
narration. The feigned uncertainty is cast in the form of
a question, and the intended effect is to strengthen the
credibility of the narrative.[13] At one point the poet expresses uncertainty as to how he is to describe the parting
of the waters of the Red Sea:
> quid loquar et trepidis patribus cum incumberet
> hostis,
> divisum pelagus, solidoque rigore ligatas
> instar montis aquas, vacuo cessisse profundo;
> quaque gradum illaesae tulerant tot milia plebis,
> oppressum Aegypti populum coeuntibus undis?
> (400-404).

The question is its own answer and the narrative immediately proceeds to the moral to be derived from the operations
of natural forces in the Hebrews' favor throughout the
period of the exodus and the wanderings of the chosen people
in the desert.

c. Apostrophe. Apostrophe, which is the turn-
ing away from one's usual audience to address a different
audience of the speaker's selection,[14] is a phenomenon
found with some frequency in the De providentia. In most
instances the apostrophe is cast in the form of a rhetorical question directed toward some objector or group of objectors against the doctrine expounded in the poem. Apos-
trophes of this type may be poignant in tone (e.g., 913-918,
addressed to the inhabitant of Gaul who put his trust in
material goods and lost all of them in the Gothic invasion);
they are discussed at greater length below.[15]

---

[12]Cf. 2. Structure of the Period, above.

[13]Cf. Lausberg, op. cit., 1.383-384.

[14]Cf. ibid.,1.377-379.   [15]At nn. 63-67.

INTRODUCTION

An effective apostrophe in the imperative is the following:

error abi, procul error abi (670).[16]

This half-verse and the few succeeding verses (670-672) constitute the poet's brief summation of his case against the astrologers as developed to this point, and a transition to another aspect of the subject, namely the employment of heavenly bodies for holy purposes through divine intervention.

d. Asyndeton. Asyndeton, the omission of the conjunction, serves to give greater point or conciseness to a series of thoughts, often on the same or a closely related theme; the general effect is to quicken or enliven the expression.[17] Asyndeta of series of related terms occur in the De providentia, e.g., at verses 117 (calida, humida, frigida, sicca), 251-252 (coluisse, timere, / ignorare, optare, pati) and 455-456 (vir, femina, servus, / liber, Iudaeus, Graecus, Scytha, barbarus). [18]

Likewise, the poet of the De providentia will sometimes join items in series with a connective only for the last item enumerated, as in the tripartite phrase aqua, lumen, et aura (819, cf. also 574), or in this longer series which explicates the divine operations in regard to man:

dumque inopes ditat, deiectos elevat, auctos
imminuit, solvit vinctos, subigitque superbos
(811-812).

---

[16]Noted by Valentin, op. cit., 810

[17]Cf. Lausberg, op. cit., 1.353-355. Cf. also H. W. Smyth, Greek Grammar, rev. by G. M. Messing (Cambridge, Mass., 1956) 484: "Rhetorical asyndeton generally expresses emotion of some sort, and is a mark of liveliness, rapidity, passion, or impressiveness of thought, each idea being set forth separately and distinctly."

[18] These examples were noted by Manitius, Sitzungsberichte 121 (1890) 7 Abh. 14, as points of contact with other, undoubtedly genuine, works of Prosper.

In this last instance, a perfect asyndeton occurs in the immediately preceding verse:

exhaurit morbis, cremat ignibus, obruit undis (810). In all the above instances, the exigencies of the meter may also play a role in the poet's choice to use or to withhold asyndeton.[19]

e. <u>Dilemma</u>. The poet's rhetorical training is especially evident in his occasional practice of posing dilemmas against objectors to his doctrine.[20] Thus the sinner who wishes to lose the power to sin must in effect desire either to be dead or else devoid of reason (558-560).[21] Astrology must either be false, or else have calamitous effects on man if it is true (698-704),[21] just as the stars themselves must either be able to change decrees or not, with the result that man is free to commit any action heedless of its consequences or else that heavenly bodies have no real power over man in any event (705-715).

An implied dilemma is posed for mankind in general by God's punishment of sinners; either man must accept the punishment as his means to correction of life, or else take his place among the unrepentant, for whom there is no practical hope of salvation (884-896); of course in this case the poet's answer is clear, namely to choose the first alternative. On the other hand, a dilemma concerning the Incarnation, involving an excessive emphasis on either Christ's humanity or his divinity with consequent denial of the one nature or the other, must be avoided to maintain sound doctrine (473-479).

f. <u>Ellipsis</u>. Ellipsis is "the omission of

---

[19]For a more complex situation, where items in series may be subdivided into corresponding pairs, with asyndeton employed in some pairs but withhold in others, cf. vv. 191-194.

[20]Cf. Lausberg, <u>op</u>. <u>cit</u>.,1.217, who notes that the potentialities for creating tension and pathos inherent in this figure cause it to be employed extensively in tragedy, and that it occurs as well in other genres, such as troubador lyric.

[21]These instances are cited by Valentin, <u>op</u>. <u>cit</u>., 809.

words necessary to the grammatical structure of the sentence";[22] ordinarily the words are short, often monosyllabic, and their absence has no effect on the thought. The figure operates by suspending the cohesion which normally exists between semantics and syntax.[23]

Instances of ellipsis of the subject of a period occur at verses 452 (nulla accipitur quae rara videtur), 506, and 669 (hinc vario vitae dominos mercantur honore). In the first instance the subject appears in a different form elsewhere in the period, so that there is little difficulty in supplying cura for verse 452 out of curam, 451. In verse 506 it seems best to postulate res as the subject of the second colon and est as its predicate, so that the verse would read:

non haec vita data est, nulla /res / hic /est / tua,
nec tuus ipse es.

For verse 669 one may understand homines or the like as the subject.

The ellipsis of pronouns likewise occasions little difficulty. Thus eum - Deum may be supplied with intentum in verse 157 (ne curae intentum vigiles durique labores / conficiant), and eum - Omnipotentem with regentem in verse 197 (magna regentem, / curam hominis renuisse putant), the hypothetical eum standing in each case as the object of a finite verb; the same is true of eos - homines in verse 291 (pulsos virtutis ab arce). In verse 654 (ad quod vis extende manum), an accusative form id could be postulated as object of the prepostion ad, and in verse 780 (nec standi vires licuisset sumere lapsis), a hypothetical dative eis could be supplied out of quos, 777; likewise a dative nobis could he supplied in verse 797 (rara facultas / non patitur laesis tempus transire nocendi), from nos, 795, and an accusative form me in the latter half of verse 480 (morsque subactum / detinet), from mihi in the same verse. In none of these instances is the ellipsis particularly harsh.

The ellipsis of an accusative subject of an infinitive in indirect statement is rare. One case occurs

---

[22] C. W. Knapp, Aeneid I-VI (2nd ed., New York, 1928) 97. The arrangement of material in this subsection is suggested in part by Knapp's.

[23] Cf. Lausberg, op. cit., 1.346-347.

at verse 164 (vestrisque beatum // creditis esse bonis),
where eum - Deum may be supplied from Deum, itself the
object of a complementary infinitive, in verse 162; the
presence of the modifier beatum softens the effect of the
ellipsis. In another case, at verse 413 (inter deserta
actos denos quater annos, nec membris nocuisse aevo nec
vestibus usu), a nominal form such as Hebraeos could be
postulated; this ellipsis is made easier by the presence
of the modifying participle actos. In verses 478 (suspicias sine carne Deum), and 479 (hominem sine Numine
credas), respectively, the phrase Christum esse or the
like may be supplied to fill out the period. Finally, a
possible eos might be supplied to act as antecedent for
the quos of verse 693 (nec servire astris vult quos super
astra locavit), although in this instance the ellipsis is
not at all harsh.

Ellipsis of est as the finite verb of the period
is common in prose as well as in poetry. It occurs in
the De providentia once after fas (130), once after
vacuum (407), once in a biblical paraphrase (603, omnia
quae fecit bona valde), and twice in phrases referring
to Christ or to God the Father, viz.,

qui cum Patre Deo semper Deus (463),
solus Deus omnipotens Rex (691).

Either of the two latter phrases would doubtless have
been fixed in Christian prayer forms long since, so that
our author might well think of each of them as a unit.[24]
Perhaps an ellipsis of fuit or erat might be assumed for
the following phrase, also descriptive of Christ:

rex ille, et rerum dominus (516).

Omission of forms such as sum, sumus, es, estis, eram,
eras, eratis, a phenomenon frequent in classical poetry,
seems not to occur in the De providentia. In at least
one case a finite verb is required, but the exact form
to be assumed is not clear, viz.,

non aliter venti spirant, ita nubibus imber (734).

Omission of forms of esse used to denote perfect passive
tenses in the indicative mood is frequent in all Latin;
the author of the De providentia omits only est or

---

[24]For other miscellaneous examples of the ellipsis
of est cf. vv. 408, 458 bis, 565.

sunt.[25] So also the omission of esse itself in indirect
statements in the infinitive mood, either as principal
verb or as auxiliary, is quite conventional and occurs in
the De providentia.[26]

Occasionally an ellipsis appears to be due possibly
to carelessness or haste in composition, e.g.,

terrenamque illapsa domum, dat vivere secum (227).
In this case Deus or the like must be understood as the
subject of dat, and animam, out of anima in verse 224, as
the subject of the infinitive phrase.

The familiar poetic technique of omitting verbs of
saying or speaking does not appear in the poem. The author
is sparing and conservative in his use of ellipsis in
general, and does not even allow himself liberties common
to the classical poets.

g. Enumeratio.[27] Much of the narrative of the
De providentia proceeds by way of enumeration. Thus the
sufferings which ·Gaul incurred through the Gothic invasion are listed in some detail at the opening and again
toward the conclusion of the poem, and within the De
providentia patriarchs of the Old Testament are enumerated, with a recapitulation of the principle activities
of each of them. Similarly, the attributes of God are
noted at some length (172-194), and the effects of external objects are traced on each of the five senses
(587-596).

Enumeration may involve balance, as in this passage:

---

[25]For absence of est cf. vv. 129, 147, 261, 339,
499, 551, 723; of sunt, vv. 259, 433, 896. But notice
also the failure to use ellipsis, e.g., depulsa est
(170), complexa est (497).

[26]Cf. vv. 284, 344, 383, 401, 404, 470, 615, 617,
800 bis, 842, 844, 869.

[27]Cf. Lausberg, op. cit., 1.337-340, and Valentin,
op. cit., 813. /V. cites instances of enumeration at vv.
69, 75, 117, 251, 397, 456, 613, 708, 766, 810, 864, 865,
and 906./ Cf. further Valentin, ibid., 792-793 for
discussion of the technique of enumeration in De prov.

> qui fuerit violentus, atrox, versutus, avarus,
> cuius corde fides cesserit, ore pudor,
> hunc omnes mirantur, amant, reverentur, honorant,
> huic summi fasces, huic tribuuntur opes
> (69-72).

In the first verse four qualities of the unjust man are enumerated, and in the second, two; the third verse contains four honors paid the unjust man, and the fourth, two. A more complex balance is found in the enumeration of the attributes of the pillar of fire which guided the Hebrews in the desert:

> luce tegens et nocte regens, eadem ignis et umbra,
> discutiens flammis tenebras, et nube calores
> (398-399).

The first verse contains two sets of attributes, each set in turn containing two antithetical attributes, while the second contains one set of two attributes.

The poet may model his enumeration very closely on a scriptural passage or passages, as when he lists the peoples of the earth whom Christ came to redeem (455-456).

Likewise, enumeration may be expressed by various syntactical constructions, as when man's lack of the knowledge of evil, and the consequences if man had continued in the state of original justice, are set out prominently by a series of infinitives (251-252, timere, / ignorare, optare, pati), and when various qualities of created things are enumerated by a series of adjectives used substantively (117, calida, humida, frigida, sicca).

Chiastic structure, too, may be employed in enumeration, as in this instance:

> barbatos levesque deos, iuvenesque senesque (766),

where the bearded gods are old, the beardless ones young.

Another technique in enumeration is the use of tripartition. A series of three occurs in this verse descriptive of Christ's manner of life:

> infirmis fortis, rex servis, dives egenis (518).

A particularly effective instance of tripartition is seen in the narration of events surrounding the Crucifixion:

> damnatur iudex, Verbum tacet, inspuitur lux (522).

The familiar division of time into past, present, and future is also expressed in tripartite form:

nam quod ubique agitur, quod gestum est, quodque
    gerendum est (802).[28]

h. <u>Hypallage</u>. Hypallage, the employment of
the transferred epithet, appears chiefly in poetry;[29] a
number of examples occur in the <u>De</u> <u>providentia</u>. Thus
Cain's unsuccessful attempt to deceive God is described
as occurring <u>specie devota religionis</u> (308), when it is
religion, and not Cain's pretense, which is devout, and
the Hebrews in captivity are said to furnish <u>iussos</u>
<u>lateres</u> (380), when in fact it is the Hebrews themselves
who have been ordered (<u>iussi</u>) to furnish the bricks.
Similarly, the poet refers to his <u>maestum ingenium</u> (4),
when it is his grief (<u>dolor</u>) which may properly be described as sorrowful.[30]

i. <u>Hyperbole</u>. Hyperbole, or exaggeration, is
found in the <u>De</u> <u>providentia</u>, as might be expected in a
poem with so rhetorical a tone and dealing with such difficult circumstances.[31] The poet claims that the effects
of the Gothic invasions are worse than if a flood had
submerged all Gaul (27-28), and vividly describes the
universal torment of the just and exaltation of the unjust in this life in the view of complainers (65-82; cf.
860-872). His responses to the complainers are also
hyperbolical in tenor: they have degenerated into the
condition of beasts (200); they are somehow not complete
men (267); if the objectors had their way, the God of
patience and magnanimity would be indistinguishable from
a cruel and merciless tyrant (749-750). Finally, the
poet's own hopes for the future of his work may seem somewhat hyperbolical (970-972).

---

[28]For further examples cf. vv. 75, 574, 578, 810,
838, 865, 906.

[29]Cf. Lausberg, <u>op</u>. <u>cit</u>.,1.344 and the examples
cited there.

[30]A possible hypallage would appear in v. 894 if
<u>turpis</u> were taken with <u>oras</u>, but it seems more satisfac-
tory to take it with <u>vitae</u> and emend <u>extremae</u> to <u>extremas</u>.

[31]For further discussion of the figure cf. Lausberg,
<u>ibid</u>., 1.299-300; 454-455.

j. Hypophora. Hypophora, or subiectio, is
an assumed dialogue--really a monologue--involving questions and answers.[32] It consists in the statement of an
objection by the speaker in the voice of an opponent, or
in his own voice, and the refutation of the objection.[33]
Hypophora is employed to emphasize objections against the
doctrine enunciated in the De providentia, and therefore
to make them more forcible and the refutations more com-
pelling. The principal occurrences of this figure in the
poem may be summarized in the table on page 123.

k. Irony. Valentin remarks on the pervasiveness
of irony in the De providentia.[34] A number of examples
have been noted above,[35] viz., verses 200, 267, and 749-
750. The poet informs us, further, that complainers
against providence may be afraid that God would grow weary
as a man would (155-158); in any case , if they grant to
God the strength to protect man, they deny him the will
to do so (195-198). They do not simply deny providence,
but they actually "remove" it (removent 415) from all
human affairs. Surely ·God's providence should be known
by this point (iam 550), but a new series of objections
arise. Apparently some wish to be good without any effort on their part (624-625) and believe that they could
be so by a change in their birth stars (625-627); therefore they seek the friendship of these "lords of life"
(vitae dominos 669).
Irony of situation arises, too. Men praise the
wealthy man for his goods while neglecting their true
good (854-872), and the people of Gaul grieve over the
loss of their possessions while heedless of the incursions
of the enemy within their own hearts. If they had looked
to their true interior losses, their external possessions
would doubtless have remained safe (913-924). In fact
the denial of providence in the face of so many examples

---

[32]Lausberg, ibid., 1.381-382.

[33]Smyth, op. cit., 679.

[34]Cf. Valentin, op. cit.,798, and his reference to
De ingrat. 309-320. For a full discussion of the figure,
cf. Lausberg, op. cit.,1.302-303; 446-450.

[35]After n. 31.

TABLE 1

HYPOPHORA IN THE DE PROVIDENTIA

Subject	Objection	Voice of Objectors	Refutation
Gothic invasion	23-86	Complainers'	87-94; but in a larger sense the entire De prov. may be viewed as an answer to these complainers.
Comparison of divine to human operations	165-173	Poet's	173-194
Denial of the totality of providence	453-455	Poet's	455-459
Free Will	554-555	Complainers'	556-557
Reliance on the stars to attain deliverance without human effort	624-627	Poet's	627-669; in a larger sense the entire argument against astrology to v. 720.
Astrology; the premise that astrologers might possess some power is assumed for the sake of discussion, and then refuted.	698-703	Poet's	703-715
Denial of the operation of providence over nature and over human affairs in particular.	727-730	Poet's	731-745

123

of providence cited from both the Old and the New Testaments, and in the presence of the sufferings which God had sent as a remedy to his people, may itself be the greatest irony.

1. Litotes. Litotes operates to convey meaning through the denial of the contrary assertion;[36] it has the effect of understatement. Litotes appears twice in the De providentia with a form of incertus, viz., at verses 255 (spes . . . sit non incerta) and 468 (spes non incerta);[37] at verse 839 the phrase non autem dubium est - certum est occurs.[38] Litotes occurs elsewhere with other adjectives, e.g., non aliam . . . necem (51), non aequa facultas (408), non eadem . . . sententia (825); with a prepositional phrase, viz., non sine fasce (58); and with an adverb, viz., non aliter (724).

Each of the following examples illustrates the author's use of litotes in periods:

/mors_/ non uno tantum transfuso errore parentum implicuit /hominem_/ . . . (292-293),

/natura/ non prius a primi vinclo absolvenda parentis, quam . . .

destrueret leti causas et semina Christus (300-302), sed non ista Deo patribus illata remoto, ipse docet . . . (383-384).

Once a litotes occurs which is critical to an understanding of the meaning of the text, viz.,

sic homo, sic Deus es, ut non sis alter et alter (546).

The context is a discussion of the hypostatic union, and the phrase ut non sis alter et alter must be taken to equal ut sis uterque. To take the phrase in its literal meaning would result in a denial of both the divinity

---

[36] Cf. Lausberg, ibid.,1.304-305

[37] One other form of incertus occurs in the De prov. as a substantive, viz., incerta, 208. Forms of certus occur three times, at 149, 180, 742. One form of incertus occurs in De ingrat., viz., incertos, 967; it is a substantive.

[38] Cf. De ingrat. 276, certum est. But non dubium est occurs at De ingrat. 555.

and the humanity of Christ and thus miss the point of the passage.

The double negative construction, equal to an affirmation, appears in the De providentia from time to time, e.g.,

. . . utque nihil non ortum sumpsit ab illo (154),
sed nusquam non esse Dei est . . . (183),
. . . quia summa tenere
non nisi pura potest bonitas (280-281),
nulla tamen placitos Domino non edidit aetas (296),
. . . non est quo vinctus vincere possim,
si non vera Dei virtus mihi consociata est,
aut me non vera Salvator carne recepit (481-483),
non renovat quemquam Christus, nisi corde receptus
(499),
edocti non posse capi nisi de cruce caelum (549).

m. Metonymy. Metonymy may be defined as the substitution for one word of another which stands in substantial relation to it.[39] The figure is employed occasionally in the De providentia, e.g., fletibus (19) is substituted for lacrimis, and armis (661) for bellis. But the poet is sparing in his employment of metonymy, and there are precedents in classical poetry for the instances in which he does make use of it.[40]

n. Oxymoron and Paradox. Oxymoron, the joining of contradictory concepts into a unity,[41] occurs only in an extended sense in the De providentia, i.e., there are no instances of two or more words derived from the same stem in juxtaposition to each other.[42] Instances of

---

[39] Cf. Lausberg, op. cit., 1.292-295.

[40] For fletibus - lacrimis cf., e.g., Verg., Aen. 4.439; Ov., Met. 11.419, 658, 673; for armis - bellis cf., e.g., Verg., Aen. 1.1; Hor., Carm. 4.14.52; Epist. 1.19.7; Ov., Met. 1.126; 5.4; 14.479. But forms of arma are found without metonymy at De prov. 37, 57, 89, and De ingrat. 41, 539.

[41] Cf. Lausberg, op. cit.,1.398.

[42] De prov. thus avoids collocations like sobriam ebrietatem cited by Blaise, Manuel du latin chrétien 32, as an example of a prevalent tendency to the employment of oxymoron among the Fathers of the Church.

oxymoron would include the phrases flagra medentia (896),[43] medicis vulneribus (92),[44] sanctus maledictum / fit Christus (524-525) and sundry expressions pertaining to death, viz., morte perempta (470), pereat mors (487), and exstinctae mortis (534).

All of the above phrases are related to paradoxes in the poem. It is paradoxical that death could be overcome only by Christ's death, that Christ should be considered accursed for the sins of man, and that suffering should have a healing effect in bringing the sinner to repentance. The Incarnation itself results in a paradox:

et vita functos, naturam participando,
edidit, et vivos, vitam mutando, creavit (495-496).

It is paradoxical, too, that Christ, the Lord and King, should live in poverty (516-518), and several of the events surrounding Christ's death are narrated in the form of paradox (519; 522; 523; 524; 528 et medio nox facta die est). The cup which Christ tasted on the Cross, a symbol of death, is the cup of life (calicem crucis ac vitae 875). In the same sense the presence of two natures in the one divine person of Christ is paradoxical (unum / sunt duo 543-544).

Other paradoxes would include the observation that certain elements of creation, taken alone, are injurious, whereas the totality of creation is beneficial (at quae sola nocent, eadem collata mederi 150), the familiar contrast of body and spirit in man (inque unam coeunt contraria vitam 223), and the attitude of the people of Gaul, who ignore their true losses and concentrate their attention on external misfortunes, whereas they might have retained even their external possessions had they repaired their internal deficiencies (913-924).

From the preceding discussion it would appear that paradox is employed in the De providentia not so much as a conscious literary device, but rather because of the intrinsic nature of the subject matter, which is a presentation of points of Christian dogma in their relationship to the doctrine of divine providence.

---

[43] But cf. duris flagris at v. 96.

[44] Contrast medicam curam at v. 880.

o. Parallelism and Balance. The expression of
the same thought twice in adjacent verses is a phenomenon
which appears only occasionally in the De providentia. One
instance occurs in the description of God's special care
for the chosen people of the Old Testament; the point being
stressed is that men of any race were free to come under
the Old Law:

cum tamen et quoscumque eadem sub sacra liceret
ire, nec externos arcerent limina templi (439-440).
At times two closely related but different concepts appear
in adjacent verses, e.g.,

. . . quos aequore toto
iactatos, nimiumque vagis erroribus actos (773-774),
or:

sic pulsata patent redeuntibus atria vitae,
et recipit caeli servatos curia cives. (953-954).
Parallel or balanced expressions also occur; here
the point is one of verbal balance more than of similarity
of thought. A striking instance is the poet's description
of the effects of the Incarnation upon the living and the
dead:[45]

et vita functos naturam participando

edidit, et vivos, vitam mutando, creavit (495-496).

Equally striking, although quite different in form, is
the commencement of these two successive verses concerning the effects of astrology:

ut mala non poterunt . . .

sic bona non fugient . . . (711-712).

But contrary to any impression which might be suggested by the immediately preceding examples, the employment of balanced phrases in the De providentia is

---

[45]In each of the remaining examples set out in this
subsection, the first pair of parallel words or phrases
is underlined once, the second twice, etc.

127

ordinarily quite restrained,[46] as in the following instances:

falsa valent in iudiciis, et vera laborant (78),

at quae sola nocent, eadem collata mederi (150),

amplectenda salus, non exacuenda querela est (886).

A series of balanced expressions may extend over two or more verses, with a different balance in each verse, one or several of the verses being more or less imperfect in its composition. Thus in the following instance neither verse exhibits perfect balance:

hoc operis sectare boni, hoc fuge cautus iniqui

vita beata isto paritur, mors editur illo (651-652).

Similarly, in the following verses descriptive of Christ's manner of life, and of his death, there is perfect balance in the first half-verse, the second verse is partly in chiastic form, and an almost perfect, and restrained, balance appears in the third verse:

. . . nec veste nitens, nec honore superbus

infirmis fortis, rex servis, dives egenis

iustitia iniustis cedit, sapientia brutis (517-519).

p. Paronomasia. In his employment of paronomasia, or the play on words,[47] the author of the De providentia shows that same restraint which he exhibits in the use of such other rhetorical figures as oxymoron

---

[46] In no case does the De prov. show the lack of restraint in the use of this figure which is characteristic of some of the Christian prose writers. Cf. Blaise, Manuel du latin chrétien 30, and the examples cited there.

[47] Cf. Lausberg, op. cit., 1.322-323. The Latin term for this figure is adnominatio.

and parallelism.[48] At one point two verbs of similar
sound are juxtaposed, viz., caedimur et cadimus (16),
while the following tripartite expression involves instances of paranomasia in each of its first two members,
although not in the third:

damnatur iudex, Verbum tacet, inspuitur lux (526).

A play on two meanings of vita, viz., "Christ the
life" and "the life of glory," appears toward the conclusion of the narrative of Christ's life:

. . . dum vita in vita est, in lumine lumen (544).

At several points a play on error - "a straying from the
path" and - "doctrinal error" occurs:

. . . propellat devius error (476),

and

error enim est eius qui cessit limite recti (561),

and once a play on error - "a wandering (at sea)" and -
"doctrinal error":

. . . vagis erroribus actos (774).

q. Personification. Personification consists
in treating an inanimate object or an abstraction as a
person.[49] In the De providentia impersonal objects are
occasionally portrayed acting as subjects, e.g.,

cur mansura pavent, si ruitura cadunt? (10),

si totus Gallos sese effudisset in agros
oceanus . . . (27-28),

/te/ tertia discipulis, Iesu, dedit attonitis lux
(536),

/quaedam/ conciliant varias in mille saporibus escas
(596),

nos, quibus in Christo sunt omnia, non capiant res
occiduae . . . (938-939).

Abstract qualities may be personified in the same

---

[48]For the poet's restraint in the use of oxymoron,
cf. at n. 42, above; on parallelism, cf. at n. 46. Cf.
Blaise, Manuel du latin chrétien 30, for examples of
paronomasia in Aug. and compare e.g., Paul. Nol. Carm.
13.1-2; "Felix, hoc merito quod nomine, nomine et idem
qui merito . . . "; 26: "O felix Felice tuo tibi praesule
Nola." No instances of paronomasia involving proper
names occur in the De prov.

[49]Lausberg, op. cit., 2.932, observes that the term
"personification" is a modern one, dating from the 18th
cent.

manner, e.g.,
>   sed concepta semel facinus crudele peregit
>   impietas, scelere immergens primordia mundi (315-316).

The first instance cited above (10) occurs in the account of the almost universal destruction wrought by the Gothic invasion and is somewhat unusual in that the poet clearly has in mind those persons who will survive the calamity (mansuri), rather than the objects which will remain (mansura), but in this pentameter line mansura is nicely balanced against ruitura. The other instances are quite normal.[50]

    r. Pleonasm. "Pleonasm, or redundancy, is the admission of a word or words which are not necessary to the complete logical expression of the thought. Such words . . . enrich the thought by adding greater definiteness and precision, picturesqueness, vigour, and emphasis; and by expressing subtle shades of feeling otherwise impossible."[51] If this definition is taken in an extended sense to include restatement of thought or the expression of subtle nuances of thought in different phraseology, pleonasms abound in the De providentia. In the following list of examples, shorter pleonasms are those which are contained within a single line of verse; pleonasms of moderate length are contained within portions of two or more verses or comprise an entire single verse, and longer pleonasms extend over two or more verses:[52]

---

[50]Apparent instances involving cura - providentia should not be regarded as true personifications in view of the doctrine that God is his providence, just as he is his mercy, justice, etc.; therefore cura Dei (64), for example, is simply a human attempt to express a divine attribute, whereas God in himself is absolutely simple.

[51]Smyth, Greek Grammar 681; cf. Lausberg, op. cit., 268-269.

[52]Instances noted by Valentin, op. cit., 812 n. 2, are designated by /V_7.

. . . vicina strage ruina (13)
. . . stare regique . . . (24) $\underline{/V\,\underline{7}}$
. . . castam et sine crimine vitam (73) $\underline{/V\,\underline{7}}$
. . . lata . . . strage ruinam (294)
. . . leti causas et semina . . . (302)
. . . vita et tribuenda corona (319)
. . . arcus tenebrarum et spicula mortis (611)
. . . numero . . . visuque . . . (614)
. . . generantque foventque (878)

Pleonasms of Moderate Length

. . . in origine causae
nascendi . . . (235-236)[53]

. . . iam nulla subiret
proelia, nec trepide secum decerneret in se (249-250)
$\underline{/V\,\underline{7}}$ [54]

. . . qua vincere sese
posset, et insanae regnaret fortior irae (313-314)
$\underline{/V\,\underline{7}}$

. . . intus
incisos apices et scripta volumina cordis (419-420)
$\underline{/V\,\underline{7}}$
non superi pariunt ignes, nec ab aethere manat (659)

. . . mortali ex stirpe recisos
. . . nec terrea nectit
progenies . . . (695-697)

. . . quos aequore toto
iactatos, nimiumque vagis erroribus actos (773-774)

at vero aeternum nil effugit, omniaque adsunt
salva Deo . . . (798-799)

---

[53] Cf. Hilar., Trin. 9.7 "dum sibi ipse origo
nascendi est," cited as an example of pleonasm by Blaise,
Manuel du latin chrétien 29.

[54] In this instance, the possibility of conflict in
general is removed by the first member of the pleonastic
expression, and the specific possibility of internal conflict by the second.

. . . excutiamus
peccati servile iugum, ruptisque catenis (941-942)

. . . nemo invitus . . .
fit salvus, nec vi petitur qui sponte recessit
(951-952)

Longer Pleonasms

quamquam et iam gravibus non absint carmina curis
et proprios habeant tristia corda modos (5-6) $\underline{/V\_/}$

ac si te fracti perstringunt vulnera mundi
turbatumque una si rate fert pelagus (7-8) $\underline{/V\_/}$

nec parcunt quidam turbatam incessere mentem,
linguarum et iaculis saucia corda petunt. (21-22)
$\underline{/V\_/}$[55]

et quo promissis adsit fiducia magnis,
ac spes propositae sit non incerta coronae (254-255)
$\underline{/V\_/}$

. . . Adam transfudit in omnes
mortem homines . . .
et transgressoris decurrit causa parentis (489-491)
$\underline{/V\_/}$

at quem nulla viae suscepit linea, nusquam
declinat; nullumque timent non stantia casum. (563-564)

quamvis sollicitis adeas caelestia curis,
et penitus causas rerum scruteris apertas (629-630)

in lucem multos de taetra nocte reversos,
ac posita claros peccati labe videmus (763-764)

quos magni quaestus ditarunt, et quibus amplos
congessit reditus totum res fusa per orbem (862-863)[56]

---

[55] In this pleonasm, the first verse conveys the
thought in a literal way, the second metaphorically. Cf.
n. 56, below.

[56] In this instance, the first member of the pleonasm conveys the idea of enrichment in general, the
second specifies the mode of enrichment. For a similar
transition from the general to the particular, cf. n. 55,
above.

si potius vastata tui penetralia cordis
inspiceres, multaque obtectum sorde decorem,
grassantesque hostes captivae mentis in arce
(916-918)
sic pulsata patent redeuntibus atria vitae,
et recipit caeli servatos curia cives. (953-954)

      s. Prolepsis. Prolepsis may be defined as "the
anticipation of the result of the action of a verb."[57] A
proleptic word or group of words is not really in place
until the action of the verb is completed. Prolepsis appears in a variety of grammatical constructions, as is
evident from the following examples:[58]

    i. In the subject:

tu quoque pulvereus . . .
carpebas . . . viam (57-58)

. . . mentemque adeunt quaecumque videntur,
iudicio censenda hominis . . . (588-589)

et tranquilla fluit cunctorum vita malorum (726)

. . . aliusque resurgens (790)

    ii. In the object:

firma tene cautus vestigia . . . (475)

. . . morsque /me/ subactum
detinet . . . (480-481)

. . . omnipotens te
spiritus umbratum Verbi virtute creavit (501-502)

. . . natalia sidera, quorum
te pravum decursus agit . . . (626-627)

et recipit caeli servatos curia cives (954)

---

[57]Smyth, op. cit., 683, limits this definition to
prolepsis which occurs in the object, but it may be extended to include prolepsis in general. Cf. also
Leumann-Hofmann, op. cit.,620-621. Lausberg uses the
term in a different sense.

[58]In each of the citations, the proleptic word or
group of words is underlined.

iii.   In the separative ablative:

. . . aquas vacuo cessisse profundo (402)

   t. Repetition. There are several surprising
repetitions in such a short poem.[59] Entire passages of
the De providentia are repeated with greater or lesser
variation in content, e.g., the recital of afflictions in
contemporary Gaul stemming from the Gothic invasion (21-62
and 901-933 /V̄ 7), examples of God's Providence in the
Old Testament (303-452, 824-838),[60] remarks on the stabil-
ity of the operations of nature (570-574 and 727-740 /V̄ 7;
cf. 134-150, 816-823).
   Each of the following pairs of examples is illustrative of the author's practice in the repetition of thought
in specific passages of limited length:

187   quam /vim Dei7 non
  effugiant cita nec
  remorantia tardent
	799 . . . nihil est illi
	  /Deo7 tardumve citumve

216 . . . iam pisces
  pontus alebat
	259 . . . pisces quos nutrit
	  pontus et amnes

238-239 sed quia liber
  homo, et sapiens,
  discernere rectis /
  prava potest . . .
	556 liber es; sed cum recta
	  queas discernere pravis

256-257 . . . vitae
  documenta futurae /
  sumit homo . . .
	325-326 . . . documenta
	  minores / propositae in
	  Christo meruerunt sumere
	  vitae

279-280 . . . et alta /
  deiectus regione poli
	619 . . . excelso deiectus
	  Lucifer axe

---

[59] Valentin, op. cit.,802. Instances of repetition
noted by V. are designated /V̄ 7 throughout this subsection.

[60] Specific repetitions in these passages occur as
follows: story of the flood: 335-343, 826; destruction
of Sodom: 350-355, 827; the plagues of Egypt: 387-392,
and the tenth plague: 827-829; crossing of the Red Sea:
400-404, 832.

419-421 ite ipsi in ves-
trae penetralia mentis
. . . / . . . ac scrip-
ta volumina cordis /
inspicite . . .

916-917 si potius vastata
tui penetralia cordis /
inspiceres . . .

427-428 . . . et semine
recti / nemo caret,
similisque omnes
produxit origo
cf. 583-584 . . . unum est / principium servis
et regibus . . .

581-582 . . . numquid non
semine ab uno / venimus,
aut alia est hominum
natura bonorum? /V_7

467 hoc etenim lex, hoc
veneranda volumina
vatum

655 quod legis monitus, et
vatum scripta piorum

488 . . . Christus, qui
se mihi miscuit in se

965 . . . qui /Christus_7
dum nostra suis sociat,
iunxit sua nostris /V_7
cf. 542-543 hactenus in nostris te, Iesu, novimus;
exhinc / in tua nostra abeunt . . .

507 emptus enim es . . .

948 sanguine quos proprio
quaesivit prodigus emptor
/V_7

644 ergo aut aetheriis
nullum est ius ignibus
in nos

689 nullum ergo in nos est
permissum ius elementis

Verbal repetition also abounds, and can be extremely complex, as in this pattern:
292 . . . errore parentum
767 . . . errore parentum
592-593 errores veterum studiorum, et vana
   parentum / dogmata . . .
627-628 . . . quid vana vetusti / perfugia erroris
   Chaldaeis quaeris in astris? /vetusti erroris -
   errores veterum studiorum_7
722 quo captos vanis studiis deduceret error
769-770 . . . et vana secutus / dogmata . . .
The instances of verbal repetition set out below are
classified as internal, internal and final, final, or as
having no correspondence, according to the positions of
the relevant words or phrases in each respective set of
verses:

135

Internal

15 . . . sub tempes-   910 . . . sub tempestate
tate laborum   malorum
cf. 198 . . . sub tempestate relicti

202 aut spem propositam   255 ac spes propositae . . .
in Christo . . .
cf. 326 propositae in Christo . . .

211 . . . Christo   562 . . . Christo
donante . . .   ducente . . .

237 . . . in discrimina   239 . . . discrimina
morum   rerum
cf. 39 . . . nullo discrimine plebem.

381 . . . durus labor   871 . . . durus labor . . .
. . .
cf. 157 . . . durique labores

Internal and Final

207 . . . secum nos de-   250 . . . secum decerneret
ducturus et in se   in se
cf. 111, 488, 493 . . . in se

209 . . . a primis . . .   269 . . . a primis . . .
parentibus   parentibus
cf. 300 . . . a primi vinclo . . . parentis

377 . . . et saevo sus-   944 . . . cum saevo pacta
pecta tyranno (Pharaoh) tyranno (Lucifer)

Final

13 . . . strage ruina   294 . . . strage ruinam
cf. 471 . . . longamque ruinam; 293 . . . prostrata
ruina

534 . . . spicula mortis 611 . . . spicula mortis

No Correspondence

758 . . . promissus   911-912 . . . honoris /
honos . . .   promissi . . .

In terming the use of repetition in the De providentia surprising, Valentin is clearly justified, as both
the number and quality of the repetitions set out above
would suggest. The necessity for repetition of thought
arises from the very structure of the poem;[61] the necessity for the verbal repetitions is derived from the relatively small vocabulary which the author employs in
his composition.[62]

u. Rhetorical Question. The rhetorical question is an interrogation to which no answer is expected,
since the answer is assumed as evident by the speaker in
view of the circumstances which exist.[63] Of the forty-
nine direct questions[64] in the De providentia, all but
seven[65] may be classified as rhetorical; all of the
rhetorical questions are spoken in the voice of the poet
as he appears in the poem, and most are directed to objectors against the doctrine of providence.[66]

---

[61] For criticisms and an appreciation of the structure of the De prov. cf. at nn. 112-120, below.

[62] Approximately 1530 words in the entire poem.

[63] Cf. Lausberg, op. cit., 1.379-381.

[64] Migne also prints 49, but vv. 13-14 and 772-776
are not questions and therefore are not punctuated as
such in this text, while vv. 329-331 and 622-623 are
questions, although not noted as such in Migne.

[65] These seven are posed by objectors to divine
providence. Cf. vv. 23-26, 43-46 (three questions), 554-
555 (three questions).

[66] Viz., at vv. 165-173, 199-202 (two questions),
321-322, 329-331, 346-349, 350-355, 368-371, 422-424,
550-551 (two questions), 565-567 (three questions), 580-
582 (two questions), 606-609, 617-628 (seven questions),
727-730 (three questions), 741-754 (five questions) and
913-918. In addition, one question is directed specifically against objectors who believe in astrology (705-706),

Rhetorical questions often occur in series in the poem, and in any event they may involve a certain complexity. Thus the author directs a general question against those who deny providence (329-332) and follows with specific questions on the same theme dealing with Abraham (346-349), Lot (350-355), and Joseph (368-371), respectively. At one point the poet poses one rhetorical question to himself and almost immediately poses another to the objectors in the course of his reply (317-318; 321-322). The device occurs throughout the De providentia, but only once in the last 200 verses. A few rhetorical questions in indirect statement occur also in the poem.[67]

The principal effect of this device is to impart a distinct polemic tone to the work as a whole; some of the questions also involve irony, e.g.,

an quia cum magnas urbes populosque tenetis
sub vestro imperio, miserum est insomnibus aegram
partiri curis in multa negotia mentem;
cumque graves trepidis incumbant undique causae,
non fert urgentes industria victa labores;
et si animis aegris depulsa est sollicitudo,
blanda voluptatem requies creat otia nactis;
de Domino hoc sentire pium est, quem semper eumdem
nil gravat, ex toto nil occupat? . . . (165-173),

and some strike a mordant note, e.g.,

nam quis erit, modo non pecus agri aut belua ponti,
qui vitiis adeo stolide oblectetur apertis
ut quod agit, velit ipse pati? . . . (422-424)

---

and another against those who crucified Christ (526-527). Rhetorical questions posed by the poet himself to himself and to the reader appear in 3-4 (two questions), 10, 317-318, 400-404 (an instance of aporia), 409-413, and 703. Valentin, op. cit.,810 n. 1, notes that the practice of posing an objection in direct statement is quite Prosperian and occurs in the De ingrat.

[67]At vv. 414-418, 453-455, 698-700. These are posed by the poet, the first two to the objectors in general, the third against believers in astrology.

The author uses the rhetorical question, too, to reveal his impatience at his opponents, who are so slow to comprehend despite the many proofs of God's providence presented to them, as in the following example, where the introductory word, *iamne*, carries great weight:

iamne Dei compertus amor, diffusaque in omnes
cura patet? notum et cunctis astare salutem?
(550-551).

v. *Synecdoche*. Synecdoche is a form of metonymy by which the word employed and the meaning intended are placed in a quantitative relationship, i.e., a word denoting the whole of some object is used for the part or vice versa.[68] The figure occurs from time to time in the De providentia. Thus a word denoting material may be used to indicate a product derived from that material, e.g., vellus = "cord, rope," not "wool, fleece" (830).[69] While the preceding example may be considered as a substitution of the whole for the part, the opposite situation occurs with the term perversi mores = "men of wicked character" (712), where the part, i.e., the moral character, is employed to designate the whole, i.e., the person.[70] Similarly the use of the singular for the plural, e.g., miles = "band of soldiers" (961)[71] may be considered an instance of synecdoche.

w. *Topoi*. Topoi, or loci communes, have their origin in rhetoric. The orator's task is to gain acceptance for some proposition by moving the listener to assent. Topoi began as stock arguments, susceptible of adaptation to diverse occasions and calculated to assist the orator

---

[68]Cf. Lausberg, op. cit.,1.295-298.

[69]Cf. Stat., Silv. 5.3.8. But vellus = "wool" at v. 144.

[70]Cf. Quint., Inst. 2.15.32: "quae si vera essent, pessimorum hominum foret, haec tam perniciosa nocentissimis moribus dare instrumenta."

[71]Cf., e.g., Verg.,Aen. 2.20, 495; 3.400; 9.161; 11.546. Cf. also Lausberg, op. cit.,1.296-297.

in his task of persuasion.[72] Judicial and political oratory ceased to be relevant to the realities of contemporary life after the passing of the Roman Republic, but the topoi gained a renewed lease on life in the rhetorical schools of the Second Sophistic, which flourished in the second and third centuries A.D.[73] Under the influence of the schools, rhetoric, having lost its original purpose, spread into all literary genres. But as rhetoric came to pervade all literature, the topoi assumed a new function; they became clichés, and spread as pervasively as the art which gave them birth. Mediated through the disciplined Asiatic style of the Second Sophistic, and specifically through the schools, with their model authors-- Vergil above all among the Romans--and their books of instruction such as those of Quintilian and Macrobius, topoi descended to the middle ages in great abundance.[74]

The so-called topos of affected modesty, which had its origin in judicial oratory,[75] has its parallel in the De providentia in the poet's explanation that he was kept from composition by the weight of contemporary calamities, but undertook the defense of providence when confronted by complainers (1-20; cf. 407-408).

---

[72] E. C. Curtius, European Literature and the Latin Middle Ages 70; 79. For a comprehensive treatment of all types and subdivisions of the subject, with full quotation from ancient authorities, cf. Lausberg, op. cit., 1.201-220; 224-226. Cf. Lausberg, ibid., 2.740-742 s.v. locus IIIB for an alphabetical listing of topoi.

[73] For a brief history of Greek rhetoric with a survey and assessment of the Second Sophistic cf. J. M. Campbell, The Influence of the Second Sophistic on the Style of St. Basil the Great (CUA Patristic Studies 2; Washington, 1922) 1-19.

[74] L. Arbusow, Colores Rhetorici 92. Cf. ibid., 91-121, and Curtius, op. cit., 79-105, both good surveys of the subject from the perspective of medieval literature.

[75] Curtius, op. cit., 83. Cf. ibid., 83-85 for further treatment.

Under this head, too, might fall the poet's brief, explicit avowal of the metrical difficulties encountered in
expressing his thought in pentameter verse:

at ne sermo moram patiatur ab impare versu,
   heroi numeris porrige pentametrum. (95-96).[76]

     From the ancient consolatory oration came the enum-
eration of famous personages who had to die; in Christian
poetry these persons were not heroes or poets, but the
patriarchs.[77] A reflection of this topos may appear in
the enumeration of the patriarchs in the De providentia
(267-413), although the passage is apologetic rather than
consolatory in tenor. From the consolatory poem, also,
reflections upon the various ages attained by men are derived, as in this brief passage:

'hic,' inquit, 'felix, miser hic erit, hunc rapiet
                   mors
impubem, hic senio transcendet Nestoris annos'
                (701-702).[78]

     The prolonged metaphor of the sea, often found in
patristic literature and especially in the prologues of
various works,[79] appears in the De providentia as a comparison of the poem itself with a brook:

---

[76]Cf. also the metaphor of the sea, vv. 97-103, and
the poet's reference to his work as a parvus libellus
(969).

[77]Curtius, op. cit., 80. For full treatment of
this type of topos cf. ibid., 80-82. On the necessity
for all men to die cf. De prov. 489-491.

[78]For a parallel, cf. Hor., Od. 2.16.30 cited by
Curtius, op. cit. 81. Nestor, proverbial throughout
ancient times for his great age, is the only personage
of classical mythology mentioned by name in the De prov.

[79]Arbusow, op. cit., 108. Variations on the same
theme include the comparison of the task of writing to
a sea voyage, with the hope of a safe return, and the
frequent mention of the harbor or haven. Cf. vv. 772-776.

ista quidem melius divinis edita libris
cognoscenda forent, ubi legis in aequore aperto
promptum esset ventis dare libera vela secundis.
sed quoniam rudibus metus est intrare profundum,
in tenui primum discant procurrere rivo,
qua iacet extremo tellus circumdata ponto,
et qua gens hominum diffusa est corpore mundi
(97-103)

  The representation of nature in its various forms,
amounting at times to an enumeration of the component
parts of the universe, is another favorite topos of
Christian poetry. The topos received its impetus in the
Christian tradition from the Evangelists' account of
natural disturbances accompanying the Crucifixion as well
as from various Old Testament passages, such as the
canticle of the three young men in the fiery furnace.[80]
Several instances of enumeration of constituent elements
in nature which occur in the De providentia are set out
in the following table:

TABLE 2

REPRESENTATIONS OF NATURE IN THE DE PROVIDENTIA

Verses	Subject	Elements of Nature Enumer-ated
111-150	God is the Creator of all things; all created objects serve some useful purpose	Sky, earth, sea (115); warmth, cold, moisture, dryness (117); stationary and slippery objects (125-126); soft and hard, swift and slow, obscure and

[80]Curtius, op. cit.,92-94, citing Matt. 27.51;
Mark 15.33; Luke 23.45; Dan. 3; Ps. 95 (96).11; Ps. 148.
To these may be added the account of the creation in
Gen. 1. Cf. De prov. 516-533 for the account of the
Crucifixion, and also the references at Intro., Biblical
Allusions, ad loc. Cf. Arbusow, op. cit.,111-116, for
additional discussion of topoi relating to nature. For a
brief, clear treatment of the use of nature-imagery in
ancient authors cf. Sister M. Theresa Springer, S.H.N.,
Nature Imagery in the Works of St. Ambrose (CUA Patristic
Studies 30; Washington 1931) xvii-xxii.

clear, bitter and sweet objects (127-129); cold, the sun, heat, frost (136-137); rain (138-139); snakes (140-141); the creatures of the land and sea (147); trees and vegetation (148).

212-217   The creation of the physical universe   The sun (214); the moon and stars, night (215); the earth, cattle, the sea, fishes (216); the air, birds (217).

254-256   Subjection of the universe to man's dominion   Birds and all land animals (258); fishes, the ocean and streams (259); revolution of the sun and moon, the stars (260); measurement of time (261); the powers of herbs (262).

527-533   Disturbances of nature accompanying the Crucifixion   The sun (527); darkness (528); earthquake (528-529).

565-578   Incapacity of nature to exercise free choice, as opposed to man.   Cattle (565); birds (566); creatures of the sea (567); inanimate objects (570-571), specifically plains (571), hills, mountains (572), high mountains, the sea, fields (573), stones, streams, marshes (574), cattle, cliffs, streams (578).

611-616   Subjection of nature to man; natural forces not to be worshipped as gods.   Sea, sky, sun, stars (613).

631-634   God's control over nature   The sea (632), breezes (633), the stars (634).

| 727-740 | The orderly and harmonious operation of nature | Sunrise (731); alternation of night and day (731-732); the orbits of the moon and stars (732); alternation of the seasons (733); winds and rain (734); flowers and their seeds (735-736). |
| 816-820 | Operations of nature the same for the just and the unjust | The sun (817); rain, cold, heat (818); water, light, air (819). |

---

x. _Variety_. A great variety in phraseology appears in the _De providentia_ in the expression of various concepts; the variety and number of the terms used for God and the three Divine Persons is especially noteworthy.[81] Thus God, or specifically God the Father, is termed aeternum,[82] bonus auctor, conditor, creans, factor, genitor, iustus iudex, magnanimus rex, numen, omnipotens, opifex, optimus auctor, parens, pater, perpetuus rex, and sator;[83] Christ is assertor, fons, iudex, lumen, lux, magister, maledictum crucis,[84] ministerium

---

[81] All of the terms set out in this subsection can be controlled through the Index Verborum.

[82] For aeternum as a substantive in the accusative = deum cf. Prud., Apoth. 850, cited at TLL 1.2.1144.47 The nominative aeternus = deus does not seem to appear.

[83] For sator = creator cf., e.g., De ingrat. 891; Paul. Nol., Carm. 10.50; 29.19. For sator mortis = Lucifer cf., e.g., De ingrat. 915.

[84] Cf. Gal. 3.13: "Christus . . . factus pro nobis maledictum."

sibi poenae,[85] Verbum, victor, and the Holy Spirit omnipotens Spiritus or almus Spiritus. Each of these terms
is employed in such a way as to avoid any unpleasant repetitive effect, and likewise none of them seems affected
in its use in the poem.

4. Figurative Language

a. Metaphor. Metaphor, the brief form of comparison, is effected by designating an object in one sphere
in terms of an object in a different sphere.[86] Campbell
has explained the effects of the figure: "The metaphor
is useful in illuminating vividly and suddenly a point
not easily understood by the audience from its subtle or
esoteric nature; for the emphatic expression of emotions;
for effective brevity in any case . . . the pleasure which
the metaphor gives to the audience will be found to rest
partly on the intellectual activity it calls into play in
the effort to establish logical relations between two
ideas; partly on the element of surprise thus invoked;
partly on the originality of connections suddenly revealed."[87]
    While metaphor is a device common to all language,
and occurs perhaps with greater frequency than any other
figure of speech, it underwent a profound realteration in
the schools of the Second Sophistic. The rhetors of the
late Empire turned the use of this figure into a well-
defined technique; most sophistic metaphors are reducible
to four classifications, viz., metaphors of war and related objects, metaphors derived from athletics, metaphors of the hippodrome, and metaphors of the sea;[88] all
four types occur in the De providentia. Among the rhetors
of the Sophistic, the figure tended to be highly elaborated,

---

[85]For ministerium = minister cf., e.g., Itala,
John 7.32: "miserunt ministeria ut eum comprehenderunt."
Cf. also TLL 8.1013.5-11.

[86]Cf. Lausberg, op. cit.,1.285-291, and esp. the
citation, from Quint. 8.6.8: "metaphora brevior est
similitudo."

[87]J. M. Campbell, The Influence of the Second
Sophistic 96.

[88]Ibid.,97.

145

meticulous in detail, theatrical in development, and re-
dundant[89]--in short, it tended to preciosity and excess.
But Christian authors, although trained by the sophistic
rhetors, gave metaphor a new purpose by adapting it to
clarify the abstract terms and precise, but sometimes difficult, content of dogma and theology. In this task the
Christian orators and poets also possessed and made use
of a fund of biblical metaphors drawn from both Testaments.[90]

In the following discussion, metaphors falling
under one or another of the four great sophistic divisions
are treated first, and then metaphors derived primarily
from the Christian tradition.[91]

i. War and Related Objects. Metaphors of this type
appear frequently in the De providentia. The faithful
are under attack by opponents of the doctrine of providence as the poem opens:
nec parcunt quidam turbatam incessere mentem,
    linguarum et iaculis saucia corda petunt (21-22)
The complainers continue their attack as the poem proceeds:
    et tamen, heu! rursus querulis, homo, garrula verbis
    bella moves, iaculisque tuis tua viscera figis
                    (552-553).
But the poet has already called upon God to employ his

---

[89]Ibid.,97

[90]The reader may find the origins of many of the
metaphors set out in this subsection by consulting the
sections on Biblical Allusions and Non-Biblical Parallels.

[91]Brief metaphors of very frequent occurrence are
generally omitted, e.g., references to Christ as lux
(vv. 94, 522, 548, 763), or lumen (459, 544, 586), or the
use of vita = "life in Christ," "the life of grace" (210,
319, 326, 416, 480, 652, 776, 783, 851, 875, 953) or
mors - "spiritual death" (very frequent). Cf. Valentin,
op. cit.,811-812, for discussion of metaphors from the
fields of medicine and warfare, and of metaphors expres-
sive of sin and truth, with reference to the De ingrat.
in each case.

weapons to reduce the enemy to submission:
    prome igitur sanctis caelestia tela pharetris,
    et medicis hostem confice vulneribus! (91-92).
These same weapons will be used in the plan of providence
against all the faithful for two purposes:
    namque eadem cunctos exercent tela fideles
    sub duplici causa, dum quo torquentur iniqui,
    hoc sancti crescunt; et quod poenam attulit illis
    pro culpa, hoc istis dat pro virtute coronam
                    (897-900).
    The theme developed most often in this sphere is
that of the Christian life as a warfare.[92] This theme is
stated in a brief allusion (241,ancipitis caeca inter
proelia vitae) and developed quite vividly in subsequent
passages:
    an tibi caelestes illi, quos protulit orbis
    fertque, viri non haec eadem tolerasse videntur
    quae patimur, motus animi, affectusque rebelles,
    et circumiectis vitia oppugnantia castris?
    sed gladio verbi, fideique umbone potenti,
    vincebant arcus tenebrarum et spicula mortis
                    (606-611),
    nec quia procidimus fusi certamine primo,
    stare, et conflictum vereamur inire secundum.
    cuncta licet variis terroribus impleat hostis,
    et vigili clausas obsidat milite portas,
    cum victo tamen est bellum, si carne vetusta
    exuti, in Christi renovemur corpus, et omnem
    vincendi nobis vim de victore petamus
                    (958-964).
        A subtype of the same theme is the development
of the concept of an interior warfare within the individual Christian. One statement of this concept occurs in
the account of the creation of man:
    dispar conditio est; manet exitus unus utrumque,
    seu potior iuri subdatur posterioris,
    seu se maioris virtuti infirmior aequet.
    est etenim ambarum vinci, est et vincere posse;
    proficere, et minui; regnare, et perdere regnum
                    (230-234).
A restatement, in more forcible terms, appears in the
defense of free will against the astrologers:

---

[92]Cf. Cypr., Mort. 4: "ceterum quid aliud in mundo
quam pugna adversus diabolum cotidie geritur?"

                . . . ipsaque bellum
      libertas movet, et quatimur civilibus armis
                    (660-661).
But the most striking development of the idea is found in
a passage toward the conclusion of the poem which deals
primarily with events in contemporary Gaul:
    nonne magis propriis posses lacrimas dare damnis,
    si potius vastata tui penetralia cordis
    inspiceres, multaque obtectum sorde decorem,
    grassantesque hostes captivae mentis in arce?
    quae nisi per cunctas patuisset dedita portas,
    inque suam cladem facibus fomenta dedisset,
    haec etiam quae facta manu speciosa fuerunt,
    devoti meritum populi testata manerent.
    sed cum deformi iaceant prostrata ruina,
    obiciunt nobis casus nostrosque suosque
                    (915-924).
The latter passage is particularly noteworthy for its
linkage of the metaphorical interior warfare with the actual warfare the poet and many of his contemporaries had
experienced. In keeping with the metaphor of this passage, Satan and his legions have already been described
as castra invidiae . . . et agmina noctis (623).
    ii. Athletics. Several references are made throughout
the De providentia to the athlete's crown, and other references to his prize occur.[93] But the theme of life on
earth as a contest, with heaven the reward, is merely indicated in several short passages and undergoes no further
development in the poem:
    . . . ut superas caperemus in illis,
    hic decertato virtutis agone, coronas (604-605),
    . . . aspera vitam
    dat via, nec campo capitur, sed fine corona
                    (851-852),
    non quantas pariat constans tolerantia palmas,
    nec quo pugna brevis sit processura videmus
                    (873-874).
    iii. The Hippodrome. Metaphors of the hippodrome are
rare in the De providentia; only two occur:
    heu vagus effusis sine lege feratur habenis
                    (599),
    . . . nullis Domini moderantis habenis (727).

---

[93]Corona: vv. 255, 319, 605, 852, 900; bravium:
663; palma: 873.

iv. <u>The Sea.</u> Nautical metaphors are traditional in introductions--Roman poets often compare the composition of a work to a voyage upon the sea.[94] Such a metaphor occurs immediately after the prologue of the De <u>providentia.</u>[95] In the prologue itself the poet allows for the contingency that his voyage may be a troubled one:
ac si . . .
turbatumque una si rate fert pelagus (7-8).

Another metaphor of the sea is closely allied to the first metaphor of the hippodrome cited above; the hippodrome metaphor describes the rash man, the sea metaphor the timid one:
ne nimium trepidus nullum procedat in aequor (598).

A more extensive development of the nautical metaphor occurs in a passage modelled on Vergil and descriptive of those who have reached the haven of faith after enduring a tempestuous journey:
quam multos procul a portu rationis in altum
dedecorum turbo abstulerat, quos aequore toto
iactatos, nimiumque vagis erroribus actos,
nunc reduces iuvat excipere, amplexuque paterno
confotos, nusquam statione abscedere vitae!
(772-776).

But in general metaphors of the sea play only a minor role in the De <u>providentia</u>.

v. <u>Metaphors derived from the Christian Tradition.</u> This class is large and quite diverse in its contents; the inclusion of any given metaphor does not mean that it is never found in non-Christian authors, but rather that it probably receives its development in the De <u>providentia</u> more from the distinctively Christian than from the classical tradition.

Corporeal metaphors are found as early as Plato, and are favored by many authors in both the classical and Christian traditions.[96] Thus the poet of the De <u>providentia</u> can speak of "darts of the tongue" (22),

---

[94] Curtius, <u>op. cit.,</u> 128-129.

[95] At vv. 97-103. For further discussion of this metaphor cf. at n. 79, above.

[96] Cf. Curtius, <u>op. cit.</u>,136-138, who remarks that in metaphors of this type "inner senses are coordinated with the outer."

"eyes of the body" in contrast to the soul (160),[97] "tablets of the heart" (513), "the court of the heart" (926),
"the inner chambers of the heart" (419, 916), and even
"the belly of the heart" (971-972).[98]

Metaphors from various fields of human endeavor, e.g.,
agriculture, medicine, the law, construction, and commerce,
appear a number of times in the poem. In a reference derived from agriculture Adam is termed "rich in the fruit
of the virtues he had cultivated" (277), while sinners are
"rich in the fruit of their crimes" (893).

Medicine provides a reference to the healing property
of nature when it is in harmony with itself:
  at quae sola nocent, eadem collata mederi (150).
References to "healing wounds" (92) and "healing scourges"
(896) also occur. The longest metaphor dealing with any
field of human endeavor concerns the efforts of the Divine
Physician to heal the sinner, whose sould is afflicted
with cancerous sores from Lucifer's poisons:
  sed calicem crucis ac vitae libare verentes,
  vipereum obducto potamus melle venenum.
  dulcia sunt etenim gustu, specieque decora,
  quae morbes mortemque animae generantque foventque,
  canceris et ritu languentia viscera carpunt.
  cumque Deus medicam caelo demittere curam
  dignatur, penitusque putres abscindere fibras,
  incusamus opem teneri, et tabescere morbo
  malumus, antidoti quam vim tolerare severi.
  non igitur mala sunt quae nos mala ducimus, et cum
  ulceribus diris non parcit dextra medentis,
  amplectenda salus, non exacuenda querela est
                    (875-886).[99]

---

[97]Strictly speaking, this is not a metaphor, but
the poet undoubtedly had in mind the "eyes of the soul"
metaphor cited by Curtius, ibid.

[98]Cf. Curtius, op. cit.,137, and the citation there
to Prud., Apoth. 583.

[99]The figure of Christ the Divine Physician is very
frequent in Christian authors. For a treatment of the
figure in Aug. cf. P. Eijkenboom, Het Christus Medicusmotief in de Preken van Sint Augustinus (Nijmegen,1960),
and R. Arbesmann, O.S.A., "The Concept of Christus Medicus

The latter passage is almost an ecphrasis in its vividness and grandeur of description.

From the law come the depiction of the soul as a
defendant liable to the penalty of death (226), the biblical description of the Hebrews as "heirs to the promise"
(438), and a reference to the inability of the stars to
alter the decrees which they supposedly pass:

et quae sideribus danda est reverentia fixis,
si quae ferre queunt, nequeunt decreta movere?
(705-706).

The possibility that the sinner may escape from his
bondage to Satan is also cast in legal terms:

impia non oberunt cum saevo pacta tyranno,
captiva conscripta manu; resolubile Christo est
hoc foedus, quod iure potest subvertere iusto
(944-946).

The promised Redemption is described in terms of a
building operation in which God will raise up the fallen
race (471-472), and God's constant exercise of providence,
with reference to the fate of the world if he should fail
to exercise it, is put in terms taken from the same field:

quae nisi perpetui solers prudentia Regis
astrueret, molemque omnem spirando foveret,
conciderent subita in nihilum redigenda ruina
(738-740).

Business terminology in the De providentia includes
a biblical reference, in the voice of God, to the fact
that there is no profit in the death of the sinner (782),
and a reference to Christ as the purchaser of the race
through his redemptive activity (948), but the most prominent metaphor in relation to this sphere is one which depicts the Redemption itself as a commercial transaction,
with a corresponding obligation on man's part to repay the
debt:

emptus enim es, pretiumque tui resolvere fas est,
quo potes, ut solvens sis ditior, et tibi crescant
quae dederis, cedatque tibi pars ipse Redemptor
(507-509).

References to the Christian life as a road or path

---

in Saint Augustine," Traditio 10 (1954) 1-28. Cf. Valentin, op. cit.,811, for discussion of the metaphor in De
prov. For a similar metaphor cf. De ingrat. 534-537.

are frequent in the poem;[100] reference is made also to God's desire in the Old Testament that the sinner return to the proper path (782-783), and the universe itself is envisioned as proceeding along a path to a fixed goal (742). A notable employment of this metaphor appears in the poet's caution to the reader concerning the great care to be exercised in approaching the mystery of the Incarnation:

> sed tu qui geminam naturam hominisque Deique
> convenisse vides angusti in tramitis ora,
> firma tene cautus vestigia, ne trepidantem
> alterutram in partem, propellat devius error
> (473-476).

Another instance of the metaphor of the path is found in the discussion of free will as implying the potentiality to commit sin:

> error enim est eius qui cessit limite recti,
> quique potest ad iter, Christo ducente, reverti.
> at quem nulla viae suscepit linea, nusquam
> declinat . . . (561-564).

Miscellaneous metaphors in the De providentia include a reference to God as a chastising parent (887-891; cf. 897), the well-worn contrast between darkness and light (e.g., 93-94, 762-764), and the depictions of men as precious vessels (927-930) and of heaven as a court and its inhabitants as citizens (954).

Metaphors are employed throughout the De providentia, although they tend to appear with lesser frequency in the purely narrative portions of the poem,[101] and relatively few of the more striking metaphors occur there. Prolonged metaphors are the exception rather than the rule.[102]

---

[100] Cf. vv. 94, 206, 548, 663, 851.

[101] E.g., in the accounts of the barbarian invasion (1-96), of the events of O.T. history (303-452), and of the Passion and Crucifixion (520-533). An exception to this is the recapitulation of the effects of the Gothic invasion (909-933), which contains the metaphor of warfare (915-924) and also the metaphor of men as vessels of God (927-930).

[102] But cf. 875-886, cited at n. 99, above.

INTRODUCTION

Of the four principal divisions of sophistic metaphor,
only one, that of warfare and related objects, receives
any extended treatment: on the other hand, metaphors of
warfare comprise one of the larger classes of metaphor in
the poem, and at least a few examples of each of the other
three types occur. By far the greater number of metaphors
appear to derive from the Christian and above all the
biblical tradition. In any event, such a division of the
subject into its classical-sophistic and Christian components must always involve some artificiality of treatment
since much that appears in one group could be classified
also in the other.[103]

b. Comparison. "The comparison, like the metaphor, is an expression of a resemblance . . . between two
objects. It draws largely on the same sources and is subject to the same rules. A good comparison may be turned
into a metaphor, and a good metaphor may be turned into
a comparison. Mechanically they differ. A comparison is
a metaphor completed by a grammatical form that calls attention to the resemblance."[104] The comparison clarifies
material treated in a work through its appeal to universal
experience in every sphere of life.[105]

In the sophistic tradition the figure may be divided
into comparisons taken from natural phenomena and those
derived from the technical arts.[106] The author of the
De providentia employs a comparison involving natural
phenomena to show that both the just and the unjust must
endure the same evils in this life:
   utque indiscreta est cunctis aqua, lumen, et aura,
   sic iniustorum iustos mala ferre necesse est
                        (819-820).

---

[103]Campbell, op. cit.,98. This appears particularly
true of the athletic metaphors in the De prov.

[104]Campbell, ibid.,110.

[105]Lausberg, op. cit.,1.419; for a full treatment
cf. ibid., 1.419-422.

[106]Campbell, op. cit.,111.

Falling under the same category of natural phenomena is
the one simile in the poem which deals with animals; the
description of the Gothic invasion is enhanced by noting
that an aged bishop led his people into exile as a shepherd would lead his flock (60).

The technical arts supply two instances of mirror
similes, one an illustration of the operations of the man
in a state of original justice (246), and the other a
longer comparison designed to clarify the point that each
man receives grace according to his capacity and not because of any difference within Christ, the source of grace:

. . . distantia nulla
luminis unius, speculi nisi discrepet usus.
namque velut speculum mens est, quae quo mage tersa
est
expoliente fide, radiisque intenta supernis,
hoc mage confessi resplendet imagine Christi
(458-462).

Another comparison in the poem, namely that of the
calamity of the Gothic invasions to the false conclusions
which some have drawn from the event and have spread among
their neighbors, appears to be inspired by contemporary
events and to have no exact parallel in either the sophistic or Christian traditions:

nec tantus dolor est Scythicis consumier armis,
quantus ab infidis cordibus ista seri
(89-90).

Perhaps the relatively short length of the De providentia, coupled with the poet's extensive use of metaphor, may account for the infrequent appearance of figures
of comparison in the poem.

c. Ecphrasis. Ecphrasis, the detailed description
of a person or object,[107] arose as a natural extension of
the metaphor and the comparison as influenced by that love
of the picturesque, vividness, and amassing of minute detail taught by the rhetors of the Second Sophistic and as-
siduously practiced by their pupils.[108] The development

---

[107] Lausberg, op. cit., 1.544. For a good survey
article on ecphrasis with extensive bibliography cf.
G. Downey, "Ekphrasis," in T. Klauser (ed.), Reallexikon
für Antike und Christentum 4 (Stuttgart, 1959) 921-944.

[108] Cf. Campbell, op. cit., 128-129.

of the figure may be assigned to the second century A.D.; the diction employed was thoroughly poetic, even in oratory.[109] A wide range of subjects lent themselves to ecphrasis, including descriptions of the human body, the sea, nature in its happier aspects, pleasant gardens, and various scenes of dread, e.g., storms, monsters of the sea, and the hideous tortures which later became a feature of Christian hagiography.

Perhaps the most original figure to come out of the Second Sophistic, ecphrasis was destined to have a long and extensive development throughout the Middle Ages and Renaissance.[110] But it had first to be adapted by Christian authors to their purposes; while the ecphrases of the Sophistic were sought for their own sake, Christian authors employed the figure as an aid in their presentation of dogma to a reading public, as in the De providentia, or to enhance the effect of their sermons. To serve these purposes new themes, such as the depiction of biblical scenes or of the grandeur of the universe as God's handiwork, were added to the traditional ones of the schools; thus the province of ecphrasis was enlarged.[111]

An ecphrasis of sophistic tenor appears in the De providentia in the carefully detailed description of the various elements which constitute the universe, with appropriate examples of the harmonious balance which exists between opposite elements for the good of the whole (111-150); naturally the references to God as creator in this passage are distinctly Christian.

Another ecphrasis, which is susceptible of classification under the sophistic heading of scenes of terror, is that on the Gothic invasion, delivered partly in the poet's own voice and partly in the voice of objectors to the doctrine of providence (10-62); but the similar portrait of the same theme toward the conclusion of the De providentia (901-930), with its long metaphor of warfare within the soul (915-924), is more Christian in tenor.

A sketch, rather than a true ecphrasis, appears in

---

[109] Arbusow, op. cit., 93-94.

[110] Cf. Curtius, op. cit., 192-194.

[111] Campbell, op. cit., 129.

155

the description of the wealthy man (860-867); the passage would fall under the sophistic heading of description of persons.

Christian themes yield more instances of this figure than do the sophistic ones. Thus the poet launches into a grand description of God in his powers and operations in this world (172-194; cf. 798-812); earlier he had vividly contrasted the prosperity of the wicked with the misfortunes of the just man, in the voice of complainers against providence (65-86). A number of biblical scenes, too, are developed virtually to the point of ecphrasis, viz., the account of the fall of the first parents (278-294), the account of the exodus and wandering in the desert (377-413), and the narrative of the Crucifixion and Resurrection (516-541), each of which is treated in considerable detail. The portrayal of the return of sinners to God (762-776), as well as the description of temptations from the standpoint of the five senses (587-596), also fail to receive the title of ecphrases only by a small margin. Metaphors, too, may approach ecphrasis in their wealth of detail, as in the metaphors of sin as disease to be cured by the Divine Physician (875-886) or of the life of the Christian as a warfare (958-964).

Ecphrasis in the De providentia appears more in Christian than in sophistic dress; this may be due in part to the fact that the poet already had a firmly rooted tradition of Christian Latin poetry behind him. But occasionally the poet tends to depart from the subject and indulge in the ecphrasis for its own sake, as the rhetors of the Sophistic did; this tendency is perhaps most noticeable in the ecphrasis on the various constitutive elements of the universe (111-150), but then this ecphrasis is itself sophistic in its inspiration.

5. Literary Appreciation. The De providentia abounds in the many and varied devices of traditional and sophistic rhetoric. Indeed, in his employment of rhetorical figures, as well as in his care for metrical correctness, the author may appear at times as more of a technician than a poet. But it is no slight accomplishment to have reduced such refractory material as one would find in a theological tract into verse, and elegant verse

156

at that.[112] For this reason alone, if for no other, the neglect that has been the lot of the De providentia is quite surprising.[113]

The tone of the poem is polemic, and expository rather than strictly logical. Its chief weakness lies in the disposition of the material, which is set out with frequent digression and consequent weakening of the unity of the argument.[114] The author has a plan, and his basic concept of structure is sound, but he fails to execute the plan consistently, primarily because he becomes involved in various sections of the material for their own sake and thus neglects the whole.[115]

Yet the militant spirit and combative tone of the De providentia assures it of a certain grandeur. The poet is intolerant of error and can be quite sarcastic toward those who would lead others into it,[116] but at other times he can be eloquent in his concern for those who have been led astray in their ignorance and inexperience,[117] as he is also in his forceful and persuasive plea for an end to

---

[112]Moricca, Storia 3.1.45-46, considers the De prov. as among the better Christian poems in didactic genre. Manitius, Geschichte 179-180, also remarks on the clarity and graciousness of the style.

[113]Valentin has done work of considerable substance on the poem; Manitius and Moricca supply appreciations, and Manitius some subsidiary material.

[114]Cf. Intro., Outline of Content. The author is quite carried away in his narrative of O.T. history, for example, and appears to lose sight of his purpose. The same criticism would apply to the lengthy prologue on the Gallic invasions, and to the resumés of both topics later in the poem.

[115]Valentin, op. cit., 802.

[116]Cf., e.g., vv. 159-173; 199-200. In this connection it might be noted that the bitter outburst against the Jews at vv. 526-527 is directed in context against those who crucified Christ, and not against the people as a whole.

[117]Cf. vv. 89-90; 969-972.

strife among Christians and a renewal of the great struggle against the forces of evil[118]--an appeal which reads
much like the peroration of a speech. And throughout the
poem the author reveals his great sympathy toward all who
had suffered in the recent calamities, but it is a sympathy tempered by an insight into the causes and true nature of the misfortunes which afflicted so many.[119]

The content of the De providentia is by no means
original. Owing to the nature of the subject, the poet
drew heavily from both the Old and the New Testaments,
and he was indebted to Augustine for much of the theological content. Like all other later poets, he drew heavily
also from the classical poets, and most of all from
Vergil.[120] But despite any lack of originality the poem
is a worthy product of its age.

---

[118]Vv. 955-968.

[119]Cf., e.g., vv. 860-896; 897-933. In reading
these portions of the De prov. one could hardly escape
the conviction that the poet was himself a part of the
events he narrates, an impression confirmed by vv. 57-60.

[120]The author's obligations to Scripture and to the
classical poets have been treated extensively above, in
the sections on Biblical Allusions and Non-Biblical
Parallels, respectively. Cf. Valentin, op. cit.,793-797,
for further discussion of the indebtedness to Aug.

G. OUTLINE OF CONTENT[1]

I. Prologue: 96 verses in elegiac meter.

The author describes conditions in Gaul
which have prevented him from writing and
have led to a questioning of divine pro-
vidence.   (1-96)

    1. He has been prevented from writing
        for a year, but will now express his
        grief in poetic form despite adver-
        sities.   (1-9)

    2. Happy is the man unmoved by afflic-
        tions, who puts his trust in im-
        perishable things.   (10-14)

    3. But we are weak, and tearfully give
        way before the destruction all around
        us. Even as we attempt to give some
        encouragement to the faithful, we
        meet with complainers. /The com-
        plainers speak:/   (15-20)

        a. "You believe that everything is
            governed by God's /providential/
            will. Why then have the innocent
            suffered the destruction of their
            cities and other great evils?   (21-26)

        b. "The calamity is more severe than
            if all Gaul had been overwhelmed
            by flood, for flocks, plants,
            trees, vines, and buildings are
            destroyed, and other buildings
            abandoned.   (27-32)

---

[1] The section divisions, marked by Roman numerals
are those of the Maurist edition of 1711, retained in
the Migne reprint; the division into subsections is my
own. Words or phrases in brackets have been inserted to
clarify the content of the poem; verse numbers are placed
within parenthesis in their appropriate positions.

c. "For ten years now we have
   suffered from the ravages of
   the Goths and Vandals, and none
   of our defenses has been able
   to withstand them. Our loss
   has been total.   (33-38)

d. "But our complaint is not even
   against the indiscriminate taking
   of human life or the slaying of
   prominent persons, since adults
   at least may have suffered a just
   punishment for offending God.   (39-42)

e. "Innocent children committed no
   crimes /and yet were killed/.
   Churches were destroyed, virgins
   and widows harmed, even pious her-
   mits suffered death, and priests
   endured all the torments of their
   people. The good and the wicked
   alike met the same fate. You
   yourself were driven out of your
   city with your bishop when the
   Goths put it to the torch. Evils
   were so compounded, there is no
   order in which to describe them.   (43-62)

f. "But God may decree a time of
   peace. If we recall both the
   recent and more distant past, we
   find that first place has always
   gone to the unjust, while the just
   have gotten virtually nothing. The
   wicked man receives the love,
   honor, and admiration of all; the
   virtuous man lives unhonored,
   scorned, an exile in every land.   (63-76)

g. /Further examples of the prosperity of the wicked:/ "The evil
   man enjoys good health; the virtuous one suffers diseases.
   Falsehood overwhelms truth. The
   innocent are punished, the guilty
   freed. The adulteress and the
   blasphemer are free to violate
   sacred things.   (77-82)

    h. "But if God exercised his provi-
dence over us, crimes would be
punished, or else all men would
be virtuous."   (83-86)

4. These thoughts, spread by unbelievers,
harm many who are not properly instructed; this is a worse affliction
than the attack of the Goths.   (87-90)

5. Destroy the enemies /who spread such
teachings7, O Lord, with healing
wounds, so that some of them at least
may escape their darkness and return
to your light.   (91-94)

6. The pentameter will now be extended
to epic meter.   (95-96)

II. All men believe that God exists, and is
the creator of all things. He disposes
everything as he sees fit in his wisdom.   (97-150)

1. The uninstructed could understand
sacred truths better in Scripture,
but are afraid to do so. Let them
learn then from this poem. /The
point is conveyed through an extended metaphor of the sea, land,
and streams.7   (97-103)

2. All men have believed that there is a
God; even though their error led some
to believe in many gods, it is innate
in all men to acknowledge their creator.   (104-108)

3. God is eternal, immutable, uncreated,
omnipresent, and the creator of the
universe and of the existences and
accidents of all beings.   (109-114)

4. Therefore whatever exists has God as
its creator, who by his Word produced
all things, both the great and the
small.   (115-120)

161

5. God sustains his creation through the
   contrariety or opposition of objects
   one to another. /Specific examples
   follow:/ soft and hard, dense and rarefied, solid and liquid, swift and slow,
   obscure and clear, bitter and sweet. (121-129)

6. All things have been created properly,
   and the creator regulates all his works
   for the good of the whole.   (130-133)

7. Therefore all things may constitute a
   good or an evil for man according to
   the circumstances--cold and heat, the
   rain, serpents and other animals.   (134-145)

8. All things exist for definite reasons
   and give glory to God their creator,
   and all are beneficial through the
   opposition of contraries.   (146-150)

III. God, who created the world, also exercises his providence over it. His actions are not to be judged as are the
   actions of men.   (151-194)

1. God exists, and he is perfect. /A brief
   recapitulation of the principal point
   made in the preceding section/.   (151-152)

2. God governs the universe he created,
   and without him nothing could continue
   in existence.   (153-155)

3. God is not wearied through the exercise of his providence.   (156-158)

4. /The argument of those who hold the
   contrary opinion is refuted/. They
   err who reduce God to their own /un-
   happy/ condition, and imagine that he
   suffers their own various anxieties
   and needs a respite as they do. To
   think this of God is an impiety.   (159-173)

5. /On the contrary,7 God is eternal and
   controls all things past, present,
   and future, being himself the author
   of time.   (173-177)

6. Likewise God is omnipresent, and unlike all created things he is without
   limit or boundary. "Nowhere is there
   question of God's non-existence."2   (178-184)

7. Therefore only a power such as God
   enjoys could rule the universe without
   weariness. This power encompasses all
   things, and is both omniscient and
   omnipresent. It does not need instruction on anything knowable, but
   itself perceives everything and acts
   in many diverse ways.   (185-194)

IV. God does in fact choose to exercise his
    omnipotence by caring for man in a pro-
    vidential manner. The beginnings of
    God's providence over man in /salvation7
    history: the original condition of the
    created universe, the special creation
    of man.   (195-266)

1. Some men may suppose that God has refused to exercise his providence over
   man, in view of man's short life and
   the misfortunes he must endure.   (195-198)

2. But they /who hold the foregoing view7
   have forgotten God the Father and thus
   have fallen into the condition of savage brutes by their own volition,
   either because of their ignorance of
   the origins of human nature or because
   they are overwhelmed by present

2De prov. 183: "sed nusquam non esse Dei est."

conditions.[3] Let them overcome their
fears and gain eternal glory through
Christ.   (199-207)

3. /To meet the difficulties of such men7
    the author will describe the origin of
    man, his loss of grace, and its re-
    storation through Christ: (208-211)

    a. God made the universe and every-
        thing in it--sun, moon, stars,
        land, sea, birds, beasts, fishes. (212-217)

    b. /The special creation of man:7
        Man was created from the hand of
        God as the only creature capable
        of receiving the power of reason;
        this power is his special glory. (218-222)

    c. Man was formed of contrary ele-
        ments, soul and body. The pro-
        perties of the soul: its creation
        from nothing, it immortality,
        its capacity for suffering and
        for glory.   (222-228)

    d. /The conflict of the two con-
        traries in man:7 Either element
        may gain the victory or suffer
        defeat, may increase or be di-
        minished.   (229-234)

    e. Neither condition of birth nor
        any external force determines
        which element will gain the vic-
        tory. Man is free, and possesses
        the power to choose, but he must
        remember that he has received
        even the power of choice from
        God.   (235-243)

---

[3]The author does not immediately answer those who
have been overcome by present circumstances /but cf. 1-96,
above7. The answer to the first group, those who do not
realize their origins, follows immediately.

f. Under these circumstances, man received original virtue. Had he cultivated it in justice, he would have shone as a mirror of God's light and received an eternal reward /without death/. (244-248)

g. God's work would then have been brought to completion in man without conflict or internal struggle or any incorrect choice, for it was unimpeded by fear, ignorance, desire or suffering and lacked nothing to further its growth. (249-253)

h. To assure man of the future gifts that were promised him, God granted many gifts to him in the present life, including dominion over the lesser creatures, knowledge of the sky and heavenly bodies, the power to enumerate periods of time, knowledge of herbs, the right to assign names to things and the power to increase his own abilities. (254-263)

i. Man was therefore more powerful than all living creatures, and bound only to serve God; he exercised his rule over lesser creatures through his power of reason.(263-266)

V. The condition of man after the fall. The continuation of God's providence over man as exemplified in the just men of the Old Testament before the giving of the Law to Moses. (267-413)

1. Man may not recognize himself in the description of the state of his first parents, because he is much weakened by the effects of sin. (267-271)

2. To learn his own nature, he must therefore return to his origins, and consider himself as Adam was before the fall.(272-277)

3. But Satan, who had already been driven
   from heaven, envied Adam, and drove him
   to pluck the fruit from the branches
   of the tree of the knowledge of good
   and evil /i.e., to commit the first
   sin7.   (278-288)

4. As a result of Adam's sin, death overcame all men and spread its evils everywhere, for succeeding generations added
   their own sins to the original sin.   (289-294)

5. Still each generation produced at least
   some just men who were pleasing to God;
   but even they suffered death, for human nature would be freed from the bonds
   of original sin only through Christ,
   who would overcome death.   (295-302)

6. "But through examples derived from
   man's origins we can readily understand that God's providence is present
   to aid all men, always and everywhere."   (303-304)

   a. The story of Abel and Cain. The
      story proves, not that God was
      unable to protect Abel, but that
      the glory of the future life sur-
      passed the calamity of Abel's
      death.   (305-320)

   b. God took Henoch alive from the
      earth to remove the fear of death
      from men and to give them hope.   (321-324)

   c. God took Elias up in the fiery
      chariot as further proof of the
      /eternal7 life that Christ would
      set before them.   (325-328)

   d. God did not abandon his providence
      over man even when men indulged in
      every kind of sin and begot the
      abominable giants.   (329-331)

166

e. God gave men ample time for repentance, and at last destroyed their
sins through the flood, but spared
Noe and his household. /An account
of the flood follows. The moral:/
God spared Noe's family in his providence so that man might be reborn
in the Body of Christ, and might see
the justice of God toward the good
and the wicked.   (332-345)

f. God's love for man extended to our
posterity when he made his Covenant with Abraham.   (346-349)

g. God destroyed Sodom only after a
considerable delay and when he
could find no possible reason to
spare it;[4] even then, the innocent
Lot was allowed to depart and given
a small city nearby to rule.   (350-355)

h. God prepared a place in Egypt to
sustain the patriarchs and their
descendants in the time of famine;
the story of Joseph. /The moral:/
Joseph did not complain against
God, for "he knew that all things
happen for mysterious reasons under
the judgment of a just God."[5]   (356-371)

i. Thus in this world just men must
endure the wicked, for God has
given the unjust full freedom for
a short time by withholding his
wrath from them.   (372-376)

---

[4] The author of the De prov. is writing of God in
human terms, as the O.T. narrator did; there is no impli-
cation of any indecisiveness or lack of foreknowledge in
God himself.

[5] De prov. 370-1.

167

j. /As an example of the truth of
the last statement/ the Hebrews
suffered various oppressions from
the Egyptians, but God showed his
providence over them by raising up
Moses and commanding him to order
Pharaoh to release the /Hebrew/
people, else Pharaoh would suffer
God's wrath.   (377-388)

k. Pharaoh pretended compliance with
the Lord's command, but his hardening of heart led in the end to his
own destruction.   (389-392)

l. The exodus from Egypt, the fiery
column over the Hebrew camp, the
parting of the Red Sea to allow
the Hebrews to pass through, and
the subsequent coming together of
the waters over the Egyptians.
/The moral:/ Nature is at the service of God; just as it may benefit man, so may it execute God's
anger.   (393-406)

m. /Various examples of God's providence toward the Hebrews in the
desert:/ The manna; water from the
dry rock /of Horeb/; bitter water
turned to sweet /at Mara/; the
Hebrews suffered no injury to their
limbs or harm to their clothing in
the forty-years' wandering.   (407-413)

VI. The giving of the Law; natural law; God's
providence manifested toward all nations
after the giving of the Law; God's universal salvific will and our union in
Christ; the Incarnation, foretold by
the Law and the prophets.   (414-472)

1. Did God begin to fashion men's hearts
only when he gave the Law /to Moses/?
/If so, this would be a point in support
of those who maintain that God does not
constantly exercise his providence

168

over man_7.   (414-418)

2. Look into your heart, and see the
    /natural_7 law written there. /As
    proof for the existence of natural
    law,_7 no one would desire to suffer his
    own evil deeds; thus each man condemns
    in others the very crimes to which he
    is prone himself.   (419-426)

3. /As a further proof for the existence
    of natural law,_7 all men have God as
    their Father, and because of this
    common origin all are born with the
    potency to perform virtuous acts ("the
    seed of virtue"6). Some men did in
    fact live virtuously before the giving
    of the Law, for they knew God the
    Father and the /natural_7 law; all men
    receive God's law engraved in the
    heart upon their creation into this
    life.   (427-433)

4. The effect of the law given to Moses
    was not to manifest God's providence
    over man for the first time--/for that
    had been done already_7--but to give
    the Hebrews an additional support in
    keeping their faith /in Yahweh_7 so
    that they might become heirs to the
    promise /made to Abraham_7.   (434-438)

5. Any person could come under the Law and
    promises; the prophets in turn often
    spoke to other peoples. /As an example
    of the first point,_7 the Queen of Saba
    received the word of the Lord from
    Solomon; /as an example of the second,_7
    Ninive accepted Jona's prophecy and re-
    pented of its sins.   (439-447)

6De prov. 427-8: "et semine recti / nemo caret."

169

6. But enough of these separate occur-
    rences; God's providence is one, and
    no manifestation of it stands in iso-
    lation from the totality. (448-452)

7. /As evidence of the foregoing state-
    ment,/ God has willed salvation for
    all peoples of every race and condi-
    tion of civilization without any par-
    tiality toward persons--all are one
    in Christ. (453-457)

8. /A restatement and expansion of the
    preceding point in metaphorical terms:/
    Christ is the one Light for all men;
    the only differences exist in the
    mirrors that reflect the Light. The
    mirror is the soul, which may be po-
    lished by faith to reflect Christ's
    image with greater brightness.[7] (457-462)

9. Christ is God, together with the Father;
    without diminution of his divine maj-
    esty, he became incarnate, as the Law,
    the prophets, and the patriarchs had
    foretold, to destroy death and bring
    humanity to a new birth. (463-472)

VII. The Incarnation and the two natures of
    Christ; man's response to Christ; Christ's
    example; the Crucifixion and Resurrection;
    the hypostatic union. (473-549)

1. You must be careful now to avoid two
    errors concerning the nature of Christ--
    the denial of his humanity or else the
    denial of his divinity. (473-479)

2. Man can overcome the dominion of death
    only through union with Christ, who is
    true man /and who therefore alone can

---

[7]The mirror of the metaphor is a mirror of metal,
not the modern one of glass; polishing would therefore
improve its reflective powers.

make adequate atonement as a representative of the human race⁊. Further,
Christ's assumption of human nature is
in no way an insult or diminution to
his divinity; he, being Life, became
true man to overcome death, and has in
fact joined himself to man so that man
might have life in him.   (480-488)

3. ⟦An expansion of the preceding point in
    terms of salvation history:⟧ Adam's sin
    passed to all his descendants; Christ,
    the new man born of the Virgin Mary,
    and being wholly without sin, brought
    man from death to life. He will grant
    that new life to those who receive him
    in their hearts, just as he granted
    grace to the patriarchs of the Old Testa-
    ment who saw him through faith.   (489-499)

4. ⟦Man's response to Christ:⟧ How great
    is the gift granted to man! He may be-
    come a son of God! Destroy the old
    life of the flesh that has come down
    from our forefathers, for the Christian
    has nothing in this world, not even
    himself; he has been redeemed and must
    pay the price of his redemption ⟦i.e.,
    share in Christ's redemptive work insofar
    as he can⟧ so that he may gain Christ as
    his reward.   (500-509)

5. ⟦Man's response, based on Christ's exam-
    ple:⟧ Christ's yoke is easy, not harsh
    like that of the Old Law. Let men offer
    a ready obedience to it, for Christ has
    given us the example in his own life.(510-519)

6. ⟦Christ's example in the Passion and
    Crucifixion:⟧ Christ submitted humbly
    to his passion and death, and became
    the curse of the Cross, while Barabbas
    was spared.   (520-525)

7. Upon Christ's death, the world of nature
    showed its displeasures: the sun disap-
    peared from the sky, the earth quaked,

171

the bodies of the saints rose from
their tombs, and the veil of the temple
was torn in condemnation of the terrible sacrilege.   (526-533)

8. In his death and Resurrection Christ
    won a victory over the flesh; his
    many appearances between the Resur-
    rection and Ascension to the Apostles
    and disciples, and other proofs of
    his Resurrection.   (534-541)

9. The human nature of Christ, far from
    being destroyed, is now magnified, so
    that Christ in his glory retains both
    the human and the divine natures /the
    hypostatic union/. Man must share in
    Christ's glory, but can do so only
    by sharing as well in Christ's cross.(542-549)

VIII. Providence and man's free will; /the
      right exercise of free will:/ abuses
      which man must avoid; the proper use
      of temporal goods; the example of the
      saints of all ages.   (550-623)

  1. All men should now understand God's
      love and providential plan of salva-
      tion for all.   (550-551)

  2. But man still complains. "Why do I
      choose the evil and not the good?"
      he laments. But man is free, and
      he himself has improvidently em-
      braced the worse course.   (552-557)

  3. /Man replies:/ "Would I were not able
      to sin!" But in reality to wish this
      is to wish to be dead or else devoid
      of reason. Besides, the sinner can
      repent and return to Christ; pity the
      man who has no path to return to more
      than the one who has lost the path and
      can find it again!   (558-564)

  4. /A further argument for the value of
      man's free will, against those who

172

would wish to surrender it:⦎ God does
not manifest his ⦏special⦎ providence
or his law for the benefit of lower
animals, all of which are bound by
instinct and self-interest; inanimate
objects, too, have no power to change
their manner of existence.   (565-574)

5. For their activities all lesser
    creatures receive no reward; they
    are ordered toward man, without
    really understanding what they do.
    Would a man wish to exchange his
    nature for theirs?   (575-578)

6. Still you complain: "But I want to
    be better!" Look to the example of
    the saints--have they brought unhappiness
    upon themselves? All men spring from
    the same origin and all receive the
    same nature ⦏and therefore you can do
    what the saints have done, if you will
    to do so⦎.   (579-586)

7. Differences among men occur after they
    have entered the world. Man must dis-
    tinguish among all the objects that
    assail his five senses, and stear a
    course set to avoid both scrupulosity
    and license.   (587-599)

8. Therefore man must strike a balance and
    use all things in moderation so as to
    glorify God, for God made all things
    good for our salvation and not for our
    temptation.   (600-605)

9. Moreover, the saints have suffered all
    the evils and disorders of human nature
    that we suffer; but with the word of
    God and with faith they overcame (606-611)
    death.

10. And when the saints saw God's world,
    they did not worship created objects,
    which are inferior to man ⦏a reference
    to idolatry and astrology⦎, but with

reason as to their guide gave true worship to the author of creation.   (612-616)

11.   The truth is, you would have complained
even had you been created as angels;
would you then have followed God or
Lucifer, I wonder?   (617-623)

IX.   /The discussion of free will continued:/
Those who would seek an excuse for their
sins in the power of the stars are refuted:
man is not subject to the stars, but the
stars are sometimes subject to him, as
is shown by examples from the Old Testament; other arguments against astrology.   (624-720)

1.   You apparently believe that you could
be good if your birth stars were only
different, and thus you indulge in the
practice of astrology.   (624-628)

2.   With all your care for celestial and
other natural phenomena, you do admit
that God controls all the various elements in his creation.   (629-634)

3.   But the all just God has prescribed a
monstrous injustice if man's conduct
is governed by the stars, for /on the
one hand/ he commands men to act vir-
tuously and punishes their offenses,
whereas /on the other / he hobbles
each man with a star that does not
leave him free to choose between good
and evil. Truly the star itself is
both man's sin and his virtue!   (635-643)

4.   /But this is absurd, and/ therefore
the stars possess no enduring power
over us. /On the contrary,/ man
receives God's commandments, his rewards and his punishments.   (644-648)

5.   /The principal commandments are speci-
fied:/ "Worship God alone, and serve
only him." "Do the good and avoid the
evil; the good leads to life, the evil

to death--yours is the choice." But
all the commandments and holy writings
and even God's own words are futile
if man is controlled by a force external to himself.   (649-657)

6. In fact man is not harmed by the stars;
rather his evil arises from within.
His very liberty is the cause of his
inner turmoil; when he is weak or
weary of the struggle, Satan uses the
opportunity to seize power over him by
persuading him that his fate lies in
the stars /and not in his own will/.(658-669)

7. Error, begone! We know the old snares
well, for God has warned us and seeks
to free us from them.   (670-672)

8. /In the Old Testament/ the adoration
of Rempha and other celestial bodies
brought great misfortunes on men. /On
the other hand, men were sometimes
given control of celestial bodies/.
Josue delayed the setting of the sun
at Jericho; Elias kept the heavens
from raining for a time, and on other
occasions brought fire down from the
sky. The same power would have passed
to Christ's disciples but for the
Lord's mercy and forbearance.   (673-688)

9. Therefore none of the elements has
power over man, /and it would not be
fitting for them to have it,/ since
God wills that man, whom he has
created superior to the stars, should
not be subject to them. And when men
have been renewed in baptism, they are
not bound by their earthly origin,
but live in the temple and body of the
Lord /which is all the more reason why
it would be unfitting for them to be
subject to the stars, since the baptized
are so clearly elevated above the level
of nature/.   (689-697)

175

10. But if anyone persists in believing
that man's fate is determined by the
stars, does he give any benefit to
man through his belief? /On the contrary,7 he takes hope from the unlucky
man, and /salutary7 fear from the
lucky one. (698-704)

11. And if the stars can decree man's fate,
but cannot change it, why should man
not abandon himself to every sort of
action? The star will be the same;
goodness will not deliver a man from
evils, while the wicked will still receive their appointed benefits. But
on the other hand man's destiny may
be subject to change. In either event,
the power of fate is destroyed. (705-715)

12. Thus astrology ends either by denying
divine providence or else by substi-
tuting for it a host of gods, the
elements, and teaching that these can
be moved by prayer. (716-720)

X. The fact that the good suffer adversities
and the wicked are rewarded in this life is
not an argument against providence; God's
reasons for acting in this manner. (721-804)

1. /Transition:7 Having exposed the astrologers, we must answer those who complain that God does not exercise his
providence over the world, because the
good suffer hardships and the wicked
remain unharmed. (721-726)

2. Let those who make this complaint look
at the order and harmony of nature--
the regularity of day and night, the
unvarying paths of moon and stars, the
alternation of seasons, the unchanging
operations of the wind, clouds, and
rain, the fact that each flower reproduces only its own species, /in short7
the abiding order of the universe, and
all providentially sustained in being
by the creator. (727-740)

3. All the aforementioned operations of
    nature take place under God's provi-
    dence; but God, out of his special love
    for man, has made us in his own image
    and given us a share in his everlast-
    ing life.   (741-745)

4. The complainers protest that rewards
    and punishments are not given in this
    present life. But if God punished all
    faults now, he would be a cruel tyrant
    rather than a merciful Lord, and no
    part of the human race would be left
    to possess the earth, since none are
    free of all sin. Besides, there would
    be no opportunity for the practice of
    virtue--the virtuous man would already
    have received his reward in heaven.
    Truly this world would have reached its
    end, and no one would remain to con-
    tinue the human race.   (746-758)

5. But see how the race has proceeded
    from one generation to the next! And
    see the new race, reborn from Christ
    in baptism! The Lord in his patience
    has given many men the opportunity to
    attain to glory by repenting of their
    former evil way of life.   (759-764)

6. /Examples of the last statement:/ The
    idolater now worships the one God; the
    seeker after worldly wisdom now seeks
    the wisdom of Christ that is foolish-
    ness to the world.   (765-771)

7. /A further example, cast in the form
    of a metaphor of the tempest:/ Many
    persons have been swept out to sea by
    a storm of errors; now they have re-
    turned to the harbor of life amid
    great rejoicing. But had God punished
    them in their former life, they could
    not have repented and led a better
    life.   (772-780)

177

8. God does not wish the sinner to die,
therefore, but to repent and live;
vengeance on the sinner belongs to God
alone. /The point is bolstered by quotations from Scripture/. This is the
reason the punishment of the wicked is
postponed, so that they may return to
the path of virtue; but those who persist in their evil will meet a terrible end, without hope of mercy. (781-794)

9. It is characteristic of men to seize
the opportunity for vengeance while
they can; but God is eternal, and acts
outside our context of time. All
things are present before him in a
single moment /and therefore he has no
need of a quick vengeance, such as we
think of it/. (795-804)

XI. Misfortunes that befall both the good and
the wicked /are not an argument against
providence/; examples of God's providence
in the Old Testament; man's failure to
recognize God's providence in events
because of his erring sense of values. (805-896)

1. God will reveal what is now hidden at
the general judgment; meanwhile, he
has given proof of his justice in
every age. /Examples, cast in general
terms, of God's punishment of the
wicked and mercy to those in need/.(805-812)

2. Whenever God punishes the unjust, the
just appear to suffer with them, and
for some good reason. /By analogy
with nature we see that/ all men, just
and unjust, share the sun and rain and
other elements; moreover, the sufferings
of the innocent may bring about the conversion of sinners and serve them as an
example of virtue. (813-823)

3. /And it is not always true that the
   just suffer with the unjust7. When the
   damned approach their end, the just are
   spared, as in the flood, the destruction
   of Sodom, the killing of the first-born
   of Egypt, and the deliverance of Rahab
   the harlot.   (824-831)

4. /Further examples of God's providence
   toward just persons, which do not involve the unjust:7 The crossing of the
   Red Sea and of the Jordan; the story of
   Habacuc; Peter's release from prison;
   Daniel in the lions' den. /The references at this point are cast in very
   general terms, and no names are mentioned in the text7.   (832-838)

5. It is true that young children perished
   in the flood because of the sins of
   others; but this may be viewed as a
   mercy to them, becuase they perished
   before they could themselves share in
   the /universal7 wickedness.   (839-847)

6. No form of death is an evil to the good
   man; it does not matter exactly how he
   attains the crown of glory.   (848-852)

7. But we do not view good and evil correctly. Neglecting our true good, we do not
   consider others from the standpoint of
   virtue or vice, but associate both good
   and evil with material things. "We are
   citizens of heaven, but we love the
   things of earth."8   (853-859)

8. /A specification of the last statement:7
   We consider men happy because of their

8De prov. 859: "caelo ascripti terrena fovemus."
In this and the following vv., the author may have in
mind conditions in Gaul; he returns explicitly to that
theme at vv. 901 ff.

honors and various manifestations of
wealth, all of which they may lose in
an instant. Ignoring man's true good,
we consider men without material goods
to be unhappy and regard their misfortunes as an argument against /God's/
justice.   (860-872)

9. Not considering the reward, and disre-
    garding our one goal in life, we reject
    the Cross and embrace the allurements
    of sin. /A metaphorical description
    of sin as a disease, specifically a
    cancer, follows:/ God sends his remedy,
    suffering, to heal our wounds, but we
    prefer the disease to the cure, and
    choose to complain the more rather than
    to seek our true health.   (873-886)

10. In truth, God punishes sinners out of
    love for them. May we be numbered
    among them rather than among those
    whom God has abandoned to their own
    devices; the latter prosper materially
    to the end of their lives, and bring
    great afflictions on the just and
    healing remedies on the mediocre. (887-896)

XII. The role of suffering /in the plan of
     providence;/ the sufferings of contem-
     porary Gaul; man's triumph over Satan
     comes /in God's providential plan for
     our salvation/ only through Christ;
     conclusion.   (897-972)

1. There are two reasons for suffering, to
    punish the wicked and to enable the
    good to increase in virtue.   (897-900)

2. The servants of God are unmoved by
    contemporary sufferings, /examples of
    which follow,/ because they have lost
    nothing of any enduring value; their
    true wealth is in heaven, and they face
    present misfortunes with the firm hope
    of eternal glory.   (901-912)

3. But the complainers grieve over their
   material losses, rather than over the
   inroads and ravages of sin in their
   own hearts. Had they not fallen into
   such interior evils, /perhaps/ their
   external possessions would have remained intact as well. As it is, they
   have lost both.   (913-924)

4. Let us then weep in the ruins of our
   hearts for the ruin all around us. Once
   we were vessels of God, sanctuaries of
   Christ, adorned with spiritual orna-
   ments; let us not complain now at
   God's providential judgments which
   far surpass our power to understand. (925-933)

5. Proud sinners enjoy material success,
   but the true Christian is not a slave
   to any possession. Let us break the
   bonds of sin and return to Christ; he
   can dissolve our servitude to sin and
   covenants with Satan.   (934-947)

6. Christ redeemed us with his blood. We
   can be saved, if we choose salvation;
   we have only to knock at the gate, and
   heaven is open to us.   (948-954)

7. Therefore let us give up our petty dis-
   putes and enter into the great struggle
   with the forces of evil. Satan has
   been conquered, and we too can conquer
   him by putting off the old man and
   seeking our triumph through Christ. (955-964)

8. For Christ has united himself to our
   humanity and united us to his divinity
   so that we may be one with him. He
   gathers those who have scattered and
   raises up those who have fallen; without him we cannot stand /against the
   forces of evil/.   (965-968)

9. /Conclusion:/ These thoughts have been
set down for the uninstructed. Once
they have tasted the living waters,
they will pour forth abundant streams
for their brethren.   (969-972)

H. METRICS

Introduction. In the discussion which follows,
attention has been given to the De ingratis as well as
to the De providentia, because of the traditional relationship between the two poems. At least a few parallels with
the elegiac poets, or with Horace or Vergil, have been
cited wherever possible. The term "closed" refers to a
syllable ending with a consonant, "open," to one terminating in a vowel or diphthong; "arsis" will apply to the
syllable receiving the metrical ictus, and "thesis" to
the remainder of the foot. The term "elegists" and the term
"elegiac poets" refer to Tibullus, Propertius, and Ovid.

1. Quantity: a. Closed and open syllables:
There are three cases in which the final consonant of a
word is allowed to close the ultima, which receives the
ictus, even though the following word begins with a
vowel (with or without h),[1] viz., an, 329;[2] patribus,

---

[1] Cf. R. G. Kent in Mélanges J. Marouzeau, who finds
54 cases in Verg. of a closed final syllable before a
word beginning with a vowel or h. Kent's comment on this
phenomenon is: ". . . the simple explanation of our long
final syllables with short vowel and single final consonant as long before an initial vowel, is that the poet
holds the consonant with the word which it ends, instead
of carrying it over to the next word--the syllable is
then a closed syllable, and long 'by position'".

[2] an: Cf. TLL 2.1.23: "An pro longa syllaba passim
poetae christiani ponunt, velut Iuvenc. 2.515 (anne codd.
recc.); 3.326; 4.526." --- The same usage of an occurs
at De ingrat. 90. Huegelmeyer, Carmen de Ingratis 130,
notes than an is in the initial position in nine of its
ten appearances in the De ingrat. It is in the same position in five of six occurrences in the De prov.

383;[3] credis, 625.[4] At ope, 266, advantage is taken of
the Vergilian freedom of allowing the initial consonant
of a word beginning with a mute and liquid to form in
conjunction with the ultima of the preceding word a closed
syllable receiving the ictus.[5] A more difficult case is
the ictus allowed to fall on the ultima of ignara, 188
(nom. sg.),[6] before a caesura, but this phenomenon is
paralleled in Vergil,[7] and appears as well in medieval
poets.[8] The poet's treatment of the first syllable of

---

[3] patribus: cf., e.g., Verg., Aen. 4.64, pectori-
bus; 2.563, domus. Cf. also Cooper, Introduction to the
Latin Hexameter 51-52.

[4] credis: cf. J. Marouzeau, "Quelques traces de
l'aspiration initiale," in Recueil Max Neidermann
(Neuchâtel 1954) 238ff.

[5] ope: Huegelmeyer, op. cit.,25, notes a similar
instance at petere (De ingrat. 462).

[6] There is another instance if the reading illaesa
is accepted in 403, as in the Maurist text. The present
text restores the reading illaesae, found in the Lyons
edition.

[7] ignara: cf Aen. 3.464, gravia. Cf. further
A. E. Housman, Classical Quarterly 21 (1927) 2-11, cited
by Platnauer, Latin Elegiac Verse 59 n. 3. Housman
demonstrated that one line of Tib., three of Prop., and
one in the Am. of Ov., all of which showed the same
phenomenon, were defective and in need of correction.

[8] Cf. Strecker, Introduction to Medieval Latin 72,
who cites the following example: "sit tibi potus aqua,
sit magnus carduus esca." The verse is from Nigellus
Wireker, Speculum Stultorum, and may be found in context
in T. Wright, The Anglo-Latin Satirical Poets 1 (Chroni-
cles and Memorials of Great Britain and Ireland 59;
London 1872) 35. Cf. also Speculum Stultorum ed. by
J. H. Mozley and R. R. Raymo (U. of California English
Studies 18; Berkeley 1960).

neque, 756, as closed, appears to be unexampled.[9] Two or three other apparent cases can be explained satisfactorily.[10]

When a mute precedes a liquid, the mute may either close a preceding syllable, or may be taken with the following liquid, in which case the preceding syllable is open and its quantity depends upon the quantity of its vowel.[11] The poet's choice here is not so wide as it might seem, however, for certain syllables must be open to avoid a Cretic sequence, e.g., the first syllable of most oblique forms of proprius or the second syllable of most oblique forms of arbitrium. In fact there are six occurrences of forms of proprius and four of forms of arbitrium in the De providentia, and all the variable syllables are open.[12] Variations in quantity are found

---

[9] Contrast the normal treatment of the first syllable of neque as open at De prov. 485; De ingrat. 10, 345, 476. An alternative explanation for the quantity would be to assume an hiatus in the line.

[10] For resolvere, 507, and profunda, 759, cf. at nn. 36-38, below. Quibus, the reading of the Maurists at 850, seems unexampled, but the difficulty is removed by adopting the Lyons reading quibus e, as is done in this text.

[11] Cf. Cooper, Introduction to the Latin Hexameter 7-9. In certain syllables where the mute and liquid combination occurs there is no question of a poet's option, for the vowel is long and the syllable must therefore be long. Examples in the De prov. include: atria (914, 953), forms of frater in the oblique cases (five times), declinat (564), declinare (714), decreta (706), lubrica (125), matrum (379), nutrit (259), servatrix (653).

[12] The figures for the De ingrat. are even more striking: thirteen occurrences of proprius, twenty-eight of arbitrium, all treated as open.

in the De providentia only in the word atrox[13] (where the
variable syllable is closed once, and open once), the
word duplex[14] (closed once, open twice), and in oblique
forms of pater (closed three times, open four), and of
sacer (closed seven times, open twice).[15] A few such
syllables are treated as invariably closed or open throughout both the De providentia and the De ingratis, but the
number of instances is too small to suggest any meaning-
ful judgment about the relationship of the two poems.[16]

     b. Long and short vowels:
          i. Vowels regularly treated as long: There
are two instances in the De providentia in which vowels
regularly treated as long appear as short,[17] viz., the i

---

[13]The first syllable of atrox is open in Verg.,
Culex, Hor., Ov., Luc., Val. Flac., Stat., Mart. It is
closed in Sen., Sil. Ital., Juv., Claud. Cf. TLL 2.2.1108.

[14]But only in one of the three cases is there a
real choice, as the two open syllables occur in oblique
cases, where the poets virtually always employ an open
syllable. Cf. TLL 5.1.2258.

[15]atrox, duplex, and pater do not occur in the
De ingrat. The variable syllable in forms of sacer is
closed four times there, and open once. Other variable
syllables in the De ingrat. occur in forms of utrumque
(closed once, open once), and tenebrae (closed twice,
open six times). The variable syllable in utrumque appears twice as open in De prov., and that in tenebrae
three times as open.

[16]For example, the variable syllable in oblique
cases of ager is closed six times in the De prov., once
in the De ingrat.; of liber - "book", closed twice in
each poem. The variable syllable of petra is open once
in each poem; that of lacrimas open once in De prov.,
and of its cognate lacrimosis open once in De ingrat.

[17]If the Maurist and Migne reading promat (237)
is allowed to stand, there is a third instance, as the
o of promat must be short. Forms of this verb appear

of bravio, 663,[18] and the a of squalidos, 913.[19] In both
cases the syllable concerned is treated as open.

    ii. Final o: The practice of shortening a
final o appears in Latin poetry in the elegiac poets of
the Golden Age in third-declension nominative formations
terminating in o, including the pronominal form nemo; in
the first person singular present active indicative of
verbs; in adverbial forms such as ergo; and in certain
miscellaneous forms, e.g., ego, duo. Poets of the Silver
Age extend the same treatment to ablative singular forms
of the gerund and gerundive; the o of the second-declension
dative and ablative singular endings is not shortened.[20]
In medieval verse the option of shortening final o tends

---

twice in Verg.: Aen. 2.260, promunt; 5.191, promite;
once in De prov.: 656, promeret; and twice in De ingrat:
xix, promat; 823, promunt. In all of these instances the
o is long. The difficulty is resolved by the adoption of
the Lyons reading premat. The situation here is the re-
verse of that which prevails at De ingrat. 144, where the
Lyons reading promis is rejected by Huegelmeyer in favor
of the metrically preferable reading premis of other editions.

[18]bravio: The i of this word is shortened also
at Ambr., Hymn. 2.72.5. The shortening in each instance
is incorrect. Cf. TLL 2.2.2153.29-30.

[19]So at De ingrat. 803 the first a of squalida
is shortened. Cf. Huegelmeyer, op. cit.,25. In each
of the two instances shortening occurs in the same metrical position, viz., in the thesis of the second foot.
The only other appearance of the stem in either poem,
De ingrat. 677, squalenti, shows the long a. For the
normal form with the a long, cf. also Ciris 506; Culex
333.

[20]Cf. F. Vollmer,"Römische Metrik," in Gercke-
Norden, Einleitung in die Altertumswissenschaft 1.8.
Vollmer notes that the shortening of o assumes practical
importance in the dating of verse of uncertain provenance.
Lucr. shortens the final o of homo; the o of nemo is first
shortened in Ov.; the o of nescio and nolo first in Catull.
Ablative forms of the gerundive are shortened first in
Sen., e.g., Tro. 264, vincendo.

to become a requirement in certain forms.[21] The table on
page 188 would suggest that the process of shortening is
already well-advanced in the De providentia.

Final o is clearly long only in nolo, 781,[22] and
the adverbs modō, 376,[23] and adeo, 423.[24] Miscellaneous
instances of short o are ego, 487, and duo, 544;[25] appearing in the syllaba anceps are the imperative memento, 649,
and gerundive vocando, 794.[26]

A similar table (see page 189) for the principal
forms occuring in the De ingratis yields comparable results.

The preference for short o in both the De ingratis and the De providentia is apparent; a similar

---

[21] Cf. Strecker, Introduction to Medieval Latin
72: "Final o, which was already often short in the time
of Augustus, is short. This is especially the case with
the ablative of the gerundive construction which is so
often used for the present participle: expergiscendo
saporem (almost always short). Otherwise the ablative in
o is always long." Cf. also Norberg, Introduction à
l'étude de la versification latine médiévale 9-10.

[22] nolo: This word appears one other time in the
De prov. (555) where the final o is syllaba anceps. It
does not appear in the De ingrat.

[23] modo: The final o is shortened, however, at
De prov. 422 and De ingrat. 555, its only other occurrences
in either poem.

[24] adeo: The o appears in prodelision at De
prov. 180; the o is long at De ingrat. 410.

[25] Platnauer, Latin Elegiac Verse 50-51, reports
that ego is scanned short in classical poetry with the
possible exception of Prop. 4.2.3. The o of duo is
always short in the elegiac poets.

[26] For discussion of the treatment of o in speci-
fic words cf. Platnauer, ibid., 50-53; Siefert, Meter and
Case 12 n. 16 /nemo, homo/, and G. B. Townend, "Oxytone
Accentuation in Latin Elegiacs," American Journal of
Philology 71 (1950) 22-39 /ergo/.

TABLE 1

METRICAL TREATMENT OF FINAL O̲ IN THE DE PROVIDENTIA

Form	Short o̲	Long o̲	Elision	Prodelision	Syllaba Anceps
Substantives	13	0	5	4	4
Verbs	3	1	2	0	1
Adverbs	1	2	11	1	0
Gerunds	5	0	0	0	1
Other Forms	2	0	0	0	2
Total	24	3	18	5	8

TABLE 2

METRICAL TREATMENT OF FINAL O IN THE DE INGRATIS

Form	Short o	Long o	Elision	Prodelision	Syllaba Anceps
Substantives	6	1	4	0	6
Gerunds	13	0	0	1	4
Adverbs	10	4	13	0	0
Total	29	5	17	1	10

preference in the prose works of Prosper is reported by Young for the De vocatione omnium genitium, while Young's investigation of the Contra collatorem has yielded no significant results.[27]

iii. Greek accusative endings in -as: This termination is found in the accusative of certain third-declension nouns, and the vowel a was probably felt to be short; at least Ovid generally treats it as short.[28] There are two occurrences in the De providentia, lyncasque, 142, where the syllable is closed,[29] and gigantas 331, where the -as is the syllaba anceps of the verse.[30] There are no comparable instances in the De ingratis.

iv. hic. hoc: The vowel of the nominative singular masculine and nominative and accusative singular neuter of this demonstrative pronoun is always short, but hic is generally scanned as a closed syllable, and hoc invariably so.[31] These forms tend to appear in both the De providentia and the De ingratis either at the opening of a verse or under another metrical ictus;[32] the syllable is treated as closed in both poems.

---

[27]Young, Studies on the Style of the 'De vocatione' 156. The De vocat. does perfer long o in the nominative terminations tio, sio, cio. Only one such termination is found in De prov., conditio (230), in prodelision.

[28]Siefert, Meter and Case 56 n. 84. But it is long at Ov., Fast. 3.105.

[29]The a of lyncas is short at Hor., Od. 4.6.34.

[30]Ov. treats the -as of gigantas as a syllaba anceps three times: Fast. 5.35; Met. 1.152; 5.319. It is treated in the same way at Mart. 11.52.17; Sil. Ital. 12.143.

[31]Cf. Cooper, op. cit., 16, for a good discussion of this phenomenon. For hoc also Seifert, op. cit., 45 n. 5.

[32]The only exceptions are: De prov. 625, 703 (hoc); De ingrat. 924 (hoc).

v. istius type: This type includes the
genitives istius, ipsius, and illius, where the medial i
is sometimes long, sometimes short. These words do not
occur in the De providentia; the sole example in the De
ingratis, istius, 99, shows the i as short.

vi. utrius type: This type includes the -ius
genitive endings of nine adjectives. The only example in
the De providentia is unius, 459, where the i is long; in
the De ingratis, unius, 900, where the i is short.[33]

vii. sibi type: This type includes the dative
forms mihi, tibi, sibi, where the final i may be either
long or short. The following table indicates the distribution of quantity for words of this type in the De providentia.

TABLE 3

QUANTITY OF FINAL I IN MIHI, TIBI, SIBI
IN THE DE PROVIDENTIA

Word	Long	Short	Prodelision
mihi	0	8	0
tibi	3	4	1
sibi	5	3	0
Total	8	15	1

The number of instances is too few to suggest
much comparison with other works.[34] In the De ingratis,

---

[33]Ov. treats the i of unius as long at A.A.
1.688, but as short at Am. 1.13.20. Cf. Platnauer, op.
cit., 54.

[34]Young, op. cit., 179, notes that final i in
words of this type is ordinarily long in Vocat. gent.

the final i of sibi is long four times, short three, and
is found once in predelision; mihi appears but once, and
the final i is short; tibi appears three times, twice
with the final i short and·once with the final syllable
elided.

viii. -eris, -eritis: The quantity of the i
in the -eris termination of the perfect subjunctive and
the future perfect indicative, and of the penultimate i
in the -eritis termination of the same tenses, is thoroughly confounded even in the elegiac poets.[35] Only one
example occurs in the De providentia, dederis, 509, and
there the quantity of the i is uncertain as the syllable
is closed. No instances are found in the De ingratis.

ix. Prefixes re- and pro-: In words compounded with the prefix re-, the vowel of the prefix ordinarily appears in the De providentia and the De ingratis
as short. The exceptions are: De prov. 507, resolvere;
De ingrat. 105, reperientibus; 947, reperiantur.[36] The
vowel of the prefix pro- is long at profunda, De prov.
750, while forms of the same word appear four other times

---

[35] Platnauer, op. cit.,56.

[36] The seeming exception involving the first syllable of religio (De prov. 48, 308, 650, 717; De ingrat.
42, 878) is not real, as the l is doubled and thus closes
the first syllable of the word, whereas the vowel remains
short. Cf. Siefert, op. cit.,10 n. 5. But resolvere is
a genuine exception, as is shown by the fact that Verg.
uses forms of resolvere thirteen times, always with the
e of the prefix short. The cognate resolubile appears
with the e short at De prov. 945, a metrical necessity
for this word. The long first e in the forms of reperio
is a metrical necessity if the word is to be used in
dactylic verse. Cf. also Ernout-Meillet, Dictionnaire
étymologique 856: "la forme tardive repperio a été
influencée par le parfait," which suggests that the first
syllable may be closed as in religio.

in the De providentia with the vowel of this prefix
short.[37] The vowel of the prefix appears as short at propago, De prov. 759.[38]

     x. Miscellaneous forms: The i of excitus
may be either long or short.[39] It appears as long once
in the De providentia (388), short twice in the De providentia (530-896) and once in the De ingratis (363). The
same option applies to the second i of ibi,[40] which is
treated as short at De prov. 793, its only appearance in
either poem, and to the i of ubi, which appears as short
at De prov. 98 and De ingrat. 283.[41]

     xi. Biblical proper names: Perhaps in no
other area does poetic practice vary so widely as in the
treatment of biblical names. Thus the first a of Adam
tended to be long when the word filled the sixth foot of
a verse, but short elsewhere.[42] At De prov. 275, 489, the
first a is short, but at De ingrat. 162, where the word
closes a verse, the first a is long. The a of Abel is

---

[37] De prov. 100, 182, 370, 402. The quantity is
short in all eight appearances of the word in Verg., e.g.,
Georg. 2.391, and in the one appearance in De ingrat.
(889). But cf. Ernout-Meillet, op. cit., 949: "les poètes
usent suivant leur commodité de cette double quantité,"
i.e., with reference to words beginning with pro. Note
also that forms of the cognate verb profundere show the
long o, e.g., De prov. 971, but occasionally the short o,
e.g., Verg., Aen. 12.154.

[38] It is short at Aen. 6.870; 12.827; long at
Georg. 2.26, 63.

[39] TLL 5.2.1245.   [40] TLL 7.1.140.

[41] The quantity of the e in ubique and the second
e in denique is short. Lewis and Short is deceptive on
this point. Cf. De prov. 134, 181, 901, denique; 18,
ubique; cf. also, e.g., Aen. 2.70, denique; 2.369,
ubique.

[42] TLL 1.1.564.

ordinarily long, but at De prov. 306 it is short.[43] Cain, a dissyllabic word, appears to be treated like Adam, in that the first vowel is found short within a verse more often than not, but is long when it appears in the sixth foot;[44] it appears as short within the verse at De prov. 309. The o of Noe, De prov. 337, is short, and indeed the Latin poet seems free to treat the first vowel as variable in quantity, despite the fact that in both Greek and Hebrew it is regularly long.[45] The variation in Ninive is even greater, for either i may be long or short, or the word may be spelt Nineve, with the i and penultimate e short.[46] It appears at De prov. 455 as Ninive, with the i short in both the first and second syllables. On the other hand, Abram invariably appears with the a long,[47] as at De prov. 347, and Moses with both vowels long,[48] as at De prov. 434, Mosi, and 385, Mosen.

c. Variable forms: The poet has at his disposal forms of certain words and inflectional terminations; since the use of these affects the scansion of a verse by providing different quantities as required, a consideration of the more common types follows.
i. Syncope: "By syncope is meant the contraction of a word due to the loss of a medial letter."[49]

---

[43]For the a as long cf., e.g., Prud., Peri. 5.372; 10.829; Ditt. 7.

[44]TLL, Onom. 2.61.19-22.

[45]Forcellini 6 (Onom. 2) 346.

[46]Forcellini 6 (Onom.2) 343. [47]TLL 1.1.130.

[48]Souter, s.v. The treatment of biblical names is arbitrary in medieval verse. Cf. Strecker, op. cit., 58, and Norberg, op. cit.,18-19.

[49]Platnauer, op. cit.,69. When, as a result of syncope, two vowels appear together, they tend to coalesce--this is synizesis. Thus the form nil in the above paragraph is an example of synizesis. Other instances of synizesis occur at De prov. 50, suerant; De ingrat. 597,

Syncope is found as early as Ennius[50] and is frequent in
the elegiac poets. Syncopated forms which occur more
than once in the De providentia, with the number of instances in parenthesis, are: periclo (3), vinclo, vinclis
(2), subiit (2), nosse (4), nil (6) and ni (2). The
author seems especially fond of syncopated forms of the
verb noscere, for in addition to nosse, nossemus occurs
once and norat once. The forms dites, ditia, ditior and
ditarunt occur also once each. In all there are approximately forty examples of syncope in the poem.

In the De ingratis syncopated forms which appear
more than once are apprendere (2), nosse (3), and nil
(5). Another form of noscere, norit, appears once. Approximately twenty-five examples of the phenomenon occur
in that poem. Besides the words noted above, words which
appear in syncopated form once each in both poems are:
dextram, saeclis, tolerasse, transisse, and valde.

ii. -erunt, -ere: The third person plural
of the perfect active indicative may end in either -erunt
or -ere. The De providentia shows thirteen occurrences
of -erunt (two of these in subordinate clauses) and seven
of -ere (three in subordinate clauses). The De ingratis
has fewer total instances, containing only two examples
of the -erunt termination (one in a subordinate clause)
but eight of -ere (four in subordinate clauses).[51] The
practice of shortening the e in the -erunt endings, found
occasionally in the elegiac poets, does not occur in
either poem.

iii. Miscellaneous forms: The old form
honos, with the second o long, appears twice in the De
providentia (758, 846), as against only one appearance
of honor (47); honor appears once in the De ingratis (96)

---

desuescere; 674, sueta. Cf. further Cooper, op. cit.,
57-58.

[50]Cordier, Les débuts de l'hexamètre latin 75,
lists mi, di, dis, isdem, as syncopated forms occuring
in Enn.

[51]Verg. prefers -ere, using it 231 times in his
works as against only 29 instances of -erunt; Juv. uses
-erunt 21 times, and -ere only thirteen. Cf. J. Marouzeau,
Traité de stylistique (Collection d'études latines 12;
Paris 1935).

and honos once (16).[52]

The archaic form of the present passive infinitive in -ier occurs twice in the De providentia: popularier, 45; consumier, 89.[53]

here is found in the elegiac poets, but its form changes to heri at the end of a pentameter line.[54] here, the more recent form, proceeded to displace the older heri, and it is not surprising that here should appear the preferred form at De prov. 804. There are no other instances in either poem.

d. Hypermetron and semi-hiatus: No instances of semi-hiatus are found in either the De providentia or the De ingratis, nor are there any hypermetric verses.

Conclusion: In virtually every instance the De providentia follows classical norms for quantitatively correct verse; its exceptions are exceptions normal to classical usage. In shortening the final o the poet simply extends a tradition reaching back through Seneca and Vergil to the elegiac poets and to Catullus. There is little of the uncertainty about correct quantities

---

[52] Cf. Ernout-Meillet, op. cit.,531: "Honos est usité jusquà l'époque impériale, ou honor prend le dessus; du temps de Quintilien, honos était vieilli, cf. Inst. Or. 1.4.13." Cf. also C.D.Buck, Comparative Grammar of Greek and Latin (Chicago 1932) 192: "In general the nom. sg. -or is usual from Plautus on, but the older forms in os appear occasionally even in later writers, especially honos."

[53] The same form is found at Enn., Frag. 56, laudarier; Plaut., Bacc. 396, dicier; Verg., Aen. 4.493, accingier. There are four other occurrences in Verg. Cf. Cordier, op. cit.,73. popularier is cited in Neue-Wagener, Formenlehre der lateinischen Sprache 3.231 for Prud., Psych. 214; Anth. Lat. 859.3. Consumier is cited exclusively for the De prov. in TLL 4.605.75; Neue-Wagener does not cite the form.

[54] Cf. Platnauer, op. cit.,55, and the references to Quint. cited there (Inst. 1.4.8, 7.22).

which characterizes medieval poets;[55] in fact, the only
uncertainty would appear in the handling of biblical
names, and even the classical poets show variations in
bringing foreign words into Latin.[56]
There are certain similarities in the treatment
of quantity between the De providentia and the De ingratis,
but hardly enough cases appear to warrant even a tentative
judgment on the relationship between the two poems.

2. Elision: Among the classical poets, elision
is found most often in Vergil and Persius and relatively
infrequently in Lucan; in later Latin poetry it occurs
very rarely in Claudian.[57] Midway between these extremes
in frequency of elision stand Catullus, Juvenal, Horace,
and Ovid, although Catullus allows elision of monosyllables
more frequently than the other elegiac poets, and Ovid is
the most careful of the elegists in avoiding elisions.[58]
Huegelmeyer observes that, while the frequency of elision
appears to decrease in the later classical poets, such is
not the case with the Christian poets.[59] The following
table shows that the incidence of elision in the hexameter
verses[60] of the De providentia approaches that in Vergil
and in the De ingratis, and is almost identical with that
in Persius.

---

[55] But many of the seemingly "incorrect" quantities in medieval verse reflect differences in orthography
and pronunciation. Cf. Strecker, op. cit., 58-77, for a
complete discussion of the problem.

[56] Cf., e.g., the differing treatment of the first
a of Atlas at Ov., Met. 2.296; 15.149.

[57] Cf. Huegelmeyer, op. cit. 25, who reports the
ratios: Verg. and Pers., one in every two lines; Hor.
in his hexameter verses, one in three; Ov., one in four;
Lucan, one in six; Claud., one in eighteen.

[58] K. P. Harrington, The Roman Elegiac Poets
(New York 1914) 66.

[59] Huegelmeyer, op. cit., 25.

[60] For the pentameters cf. at nn. 169-171, below.

TABLE 4[a]

PERCENTAGE OF ELISION IN THE VERSE
OF REPRESENTATIVE POETS

	Number of Verses	Number of Elisions	Percentage
Vergil	3231	1775	55
Horace	4141	1350	35
Ovid	3075	796	26
Persius	650	331	51
De ingratis	1018	552	54
De providentia	924	463	50

[a]This table is adapted from Huegelmeyer, op. cit.,
26.

Four verses of the De providentia (506, 802, 848,
904) have three elisions, and sixty-one verses have two
elisions. The percentage of verses with multiple elisions is 7%, as against 7.6% in the De ingratis.[61]
Elision in the classical poets is distributed
within the verse in the following descending order of
frequency: arsis of the second foot; thesis of the fourth
foot; thesis of the first foot; arsis of the third foot.[62]
Strikingly enough, the order of frequency in the De providentia is precisely the same, as indicated by table 5.

[61]Huegelmeyer, op. cit.,26, reports five verses
of three elisions and seventy-two of two elisions for the
De ingrat.

[62]B. L. Gildersleeve and G. Lodge, Latin Grammar
(Boston 1894) 473. 784 n. 5. The terms "arsis" and
"thesis", as used in Gildersleeve-Lodge, have been reversed
to conform to the usage in this dissertation.

TABLE 5

DISTRIBUTION OF ELISIONS ACCORDING TO METRICAL FEET AND
POSITION IN ARSIS AND THESIS IN THE DE PROVIDENTIA

Metrical Foot	Arsis	Percentage	Thesis	Percentage	Total	Percentage
1	1	0.2	66	14.2	67	14.4
2	99	21.4	23	5.0	122	26.4
3	61	13.2	21	4.5	82	17.7
4	60	13.0	83	17.9	143	30.9
5	12	2.6	18	3.9	30	6.5
6	3	0.6	16	3.5	19	4.1
Total	236	51.0	227	49.0	463	100.0

Considering the four most common positions for elision noted in the discussion preceding table 5, and adding to them the arsis of the fourth foot, it will be noted that 79.7% of the elisions in the De providentia occur in one or another of these five positions; the similar table of Huegelmeyer indicates that 79.5% of the elisions in the De ingratis occur in one or another of the five favored positions.[63]

The poet of the De providentia observes not only the frequency of elision of the classical poets, but also a number of finer points applicable to one or another specific metrical position. For example, in the fifth foot of the verse, elision following the first syllable of the dactyl is rare in the classical poets, whereas they frequently elide between the second and third syllables.[64] Examining the eighteen occurrences of elision noted above for the thesis of the fifth foot, we find that thirteen of them occur between the second and third syllables of the dactyl (e.g., ducere in antris, 49; in aequore aperto, 98), and only five following the first syllable of the dactyl.[65] Again, elision between the fifth and sixth feet of the hexameter is rare among the classical poets,[66] and occurs only three times in the De providentia (338, 487, 798).

As in the De ingratis, so in the De providentia there is virtually no discernible preference as between the elision of a short vowel or of a long one (diphthongs

---

[63]Huegelmeyer, op. cit.,27.

[64]Rare would be the type ergo age terrae (Verg., Georg. 1.63); the moenia habetis type (Verg., Aen. 9.782) would occur frequently. Cf. Nougaret, Traité de métrique latine classique 50.

[65]In four of the five instances, elision of -que is involved. The cases are: sive animatum, 116; atque elementa, 119; felque et acetum, 523; cuique elemento, 631; atque here, 804.

[66]Nougaret, Traité de métrique latine classique 50, cites as an example Verg., Aen. 1.99 Hector ubi ingens.

being included with long vowels).[67] The following table
sets the poet's practice in the De providentia against
that of several Augustan poets and of Prosper in the De
ingratis. The symbols used in the table are: T, for the
prodelision of est;[68] Q, for the elision of -que; M, for
the ecthlipsis of a final syllable in -m; S, for the elision of a short vowel; L, for the elision of a long vowel
or diphthong.[69]

TABLE 6[a]

QUALITY OF ELISION BY PERCENTAGE IN THE
VERSE OF REPRESENTATIVE POETS

	T	Q	M	S	L
Vergil	3	24	27	23	22
Horace	12	8	32	27	21
Ovid	22	42	10	22	4
Persius	9	11	21	37	21
De ingratis	9	9	30	31	21
De providentia	11	13	26	27	22

[a]This table is adapted from Huegelmeyer, op. cit.,
20.

[67]The situation is quite different among the elegiac poets, who consistently prefer to elide a short vowel
rather than a long one. Cf. Platnauer, op. cit.,72, who
finds twenty elisions of short vowels and only three of
long ones in an examination of two hundred lines of Tib.
His figures for Prop. and Ov. are similar.

[68]Or of es; there is only one case of the latter
(De prov. 507).

[69]In order to make the table as accurate as possible, seventeen doubtful cases were excluded from the

The treatment of est in the De providentia is very close to that of Horace; -que is elided slightly more often than in Persius. The figures for both est and -que in the De providentia are somewhat higher than the corresponding figures for the De ingratis. The incidence of ecthlipsis of -m in the De providentia is very close to Vergil's practice; the percentage of elision of long vowels is exactly that of Vergil, and accords generally with that of all the poets except Ovid. Short vowels are elided in the same ratio as in Horace; the figures for both short vowels and ecthlipsis of -m are somewhat lower in the De providentia than in the De ingratis, while the ratio of elision of long vowels in the two poems is almost identical.

Elision involving monosyllabic words takes place thirteen times in the De providentia: cum occurs in elisions six times (329, 350, 400, 619, 741, 842); iam, twice (487, 767); si, four times (106, 170, 577, 848); nam once (951).[70] The six elisions involving cum are elisions of the conjunction; conforming to classical practice (and to the practice of the De ingrat.), the preposition cum is not elided. All of these words except perhaps nam are susceptible to elision in the elegiac poets. But the De providentia differs strikingly from the works of the elegists in that it shows no cases of elision involving the monosyllabic pronouns me, te, and se, which form over half the elided monosyllables of Tibullus, Propertius, and Ovid.[71] Vergil sometimes

---

De prov., i.e., such words as vero (121), homo (238), ergo (432), erro (558). Discussion of these types will be found at nn. 20-21, above. The abbreviations are taken from R. G. Kent, "Likes and Dislikes in Elision," Transactions of the American Philological Association 54 (1923) 86-97, and conform to those in Huegelmeyer's study.

[70]Huegelmeyer, op. cit.,28, reports twenty monosyllabic elisions in the De ingrat. There cum is also elided six times, iam twice, but si only once, and nam is not found in elision.

[71]Platnauer, op. cit.,78. A total of forty-nine elisions of me, te, and se is reported, as against only forty-four elisions of other monosyllables.

elides these three pronouns;[72] Prudentius elides them only occasionally.[73] As in the De providentia, so in the De ingratis there are no instances of such elision.

Rarely does the first foot of a verse commence with monosyllabic elision; only one such elision is found in the De providentia, nam, 951.[74] The favorite position for elision of a monosyllable is the thesis of the first foot, with seven instances (170, 350, 577, 619, 741, 842, 848); monosyllabic elision is found three times in the thesis of the fourth foot (329, 400, 767), and once in the arses of the fifth (106) and sixth (487) feet.

atque is elided six times in the De providentia (37, 119, 122, 466, 804, 904), and fails to be elided three times (52--prodelision of est, 152, 757). The number of cases is too small to make any conclusions, but it might be observed that the 2:1 ratio in favor of elision is approximately the same as that for Juvenal, and does not vary greatly from that for Lucretius.[75] The elegists

---

[72]In the Ecl., me is found in elision six times (1.40; 2.25, 43; 3.10, 74; 10.56) and once in prodelision (5.4); but there are twenty-five cases of non-elision. te is elided twice (2.73; 9.22); thirty other times elision fails to occur. se is not elided in the Ecl., where it occurs eight times. For elision of se, cf. e.g., Aen. 11.815.

[73]For example, in Symm. monosyllabic me occurs ten times without elision, one of these times with hiatus (2.159); te occurs twelve times with no elision; se occurs seventeen times and is elided only twice (1.290; 2.394).

[74]Cf. Nougaret, op. cit.,50, and the examples cited there: Lucr. 4.1204, cum interea; Verg., Ecl. 3.48, si ad vitulam; Hor., Serm. 1.1.52, dum ex parvo.

[75]Juv. 65.6% elided; 34.4% non-elided. Lucr. 68.3% elided; 31.7% non-elided. For these and other figures on elision of atque cf. Platnauer, "Elision of atque in Roman Poetry," Classical Quarterly 42 (1948) 91-93. In the De ingrat. there are only two occurrences of atque, one elided (815) the other not (xiii).

almost invariably elided atque; of nineteen possible cases of unelided atque in elegiac poetry, only four fail to yield to emendation.[76] The practice of the medieval poets in regard to elision of atque varies; some avoid it entirely.[77]

Elision may produce certain special effects; the description of these is necessarily subjective. For example, perhaps the missing vowels at De prov. 904, argenti atque auri amissis, suggest the loss of gold and silver itself or the rapidity of the loss, with three elisions occurring in quick succession.

In certain passages elision disappears for several verses, e.g., 173-176 (the omnipresence of God), 212-217 (the works of Creation), 296-299 (the just men of the Old Testament, who nevertheless fell under the penalty of original sin), and 965-968 (the effect of the Redemption, man's dependence on Christ, Christ's activity exercised on man).

3. Hiatus: Hiatus may be defined as "failure to elide, when the conditions for elision are present."[78] The phenomenon occurs occasionally in Catullus, Horace, and Propertius, and with somewhat greater frequency, although still not commonly, in Vergil.[79] There is only one example of hiatus in the De providentia, at verse 343

---

[76] Platnauer, Latin Elegiac Verse 78-82.

[77] Strecker, op. cit., 72; cf. Norberg, op. cit., 32-36.

[78] Cooper, op. cit., 48.

[79] Gildersleeve-Lodge, op. cit., 473. 784 n. 6, cite two cases in the hexameter of the elegiac distich for Catull. (66.11; 107.1); two cases for Hor. (Sat. 1.1.108; Epod. 13.3); and one case for Prop. (3.7.49). Platnauer, Latin Elegiac Verse 57-59, reports that hiatus is frequent in the elegists after the interjections o, heu, and a, and finds also nine instances of Greek hiatus in Ov. He notes that "instances of caesural hiatus are almost always confused by textual considerations." Most of the approximately forty cases in Verg. are conveniently set out in Cooper, op. cit., 48-50. For a good discussion of the subject, with many references to Verg., cf.

in the thesis of the first foot:
 idem homo in Christi corpus nascendo veniret.
 The poet's intent appears to be to separate idem
homo from the rest of the verse and join it more closely
to the ending semine ab ipso of the preceding verse (342),
in order to emphasize that man is truly "the same from
his very seed", i.e., essentially good despite the effects
of original sin.
 Hiatus occurs once in the De ingratis (222);
usually the medieval poets avoid it.[80]

 4. Diaeresis: Diaeresis may be defined as the
simultaneous ending of a word and a metrical foot, i.e.,
coincidence between word ending and metrical ending.[81]
Thus, like caesura, but unlike diaeresis-pause and caesura-
pause, diaeresis as treated here is a purely metrical concept; the incidence of diaeresis depends only on one's
definition of what constitutes a word. Pauses, on the
other hand, depend upon the content of the poem and the
way in which one reads the verse.
 There is ample warrant for considering a preposition and its object as one word when the object follows
the preposition immediately (e.g., sub tempestate, De
prov. 15; in agros, 27; in antris, 49; ab urbe, 59, etc.)[82]

R. G. Kent, "A problem of Latin prosody," in Mélanges J.
Marouzeau (Paris 1948) 303-308.

 [80]Strecker, op. cit.,72, suggesting that hiatus in
a well-written poem occurs chiefly as the result of verbal
quotation, especially from the Bible. Cf. Norberg, op.
cit.,36-37.

 [81]Cooper, op. cit. 21. Cf. Siefert, "Reading Latin
Verse" 93; "If word and foot terminate together, we have
what is called a diaeresis."

 [82]Cf. Cooper, op. cit.,4-5: "Preposition and word
governed by preposition were felt, accented, and sometimes
written, as one word." Cf. Nougaret, op. cit.,5, for a
similar statement. An earlier statement, less inclusive
than the foregoing, is that of A. G. Harkness, in "Final
Monosyllables in Latin Prose and Poetry," American Journal
of Philology 31 (1910) 173: "Verse employs the preposition followed by the pronoun, as inter se, as one word,

An indefinite pronoun preceded by si may also be considered as forming a single word, as may cases of prodelision.[83]
Accordingly, diaeresis is not considered as occurring between the components of any of the above-mentioned compounds.

The following table indicates the incidence of
diaeresis by metrical feet in representative classical
poets and in the De providentia:

TABLE 7[a]

PERCENTAGE OF DIAERESIS BY METRICAL FEET
IN REPRESENTATIVE POETS

	I	II	III	IV	V
Catullus	49.7	7.0	11.3	73.0	58.3
Lucretius	43.0	18.7	17.0	57.0	44.3
Vergil	42.8	16.4	15.0	51.1	60.6
De providentia	42.1	12.7	20.8	47.0	47.3

[a]This table is adapted from E. H. Sturtevant,
"The Doctrine of Caesura, A Philological Ghost," American Journal of Philology 55 (1924) 329-350. Sturtevant's
sample is based on 500 verses of the Aen. and 300 verses
each of Catull. and Lucr.; the figures for the De prov.
include all 924 hexameter lines of the poem. In his
article, Sturtevant opposes the concept that verse tends
to fall apart through too much diaeresis.

but this principle does not apply at the close of the
sentence in prose." Harkness speculates that the poets
have adopted colloquial usage in this regard.

[83]Cf. Nougaret, op. cit.,5. Cases involving si
and its compound nisi in the De prov. are: si quis (73,
267, 698, 941), si quid (645), nisi quem (679). For examples of prodelision, cf. innatum est (108), quocumque
est (116), effectum est (152).

INTRODUCTION

The De providentia is closest to Vergil in the
matter of first-foot diaeresis; diaeresis occurs more frequently at the end of the second foot than in Catullus,
less frequently than in Vergil or Lucretius. Third-foot
diaeresis occurs more frequently, and fourth-foot diaeresis
less frequently, than in any of the classical poets considered. The ratio for diaeresis at the end of the fifth
foot approximates that in Lucretius.[84]
 The following table indicates the number of diaeresis in the De providentia by foot, and the percentage
of total diaeresis (100%) for each foot:

TABLE 8

PLACEMENT OF DIAERESES BY METRICAL FEET
IN THE DE PROVIDENTIA

	Number	Percent
I	389	24.8
II	117	7.5
III	192	12.2
IV	434	27.7
V	437	27.8
Total	1569	100.0

The table indicates that diaeresis occurs most
often at the end of the first, fourth, and fifth feet of
verse, and with considerably less frequency at the conclusion of the second and third feet, as would be expected from the preceding discussion. Considering the total

[84]Diaeresis occurs comparatively infrequently at the second foot of the hexameter verses in the elegists also.
The percentages are: Tib. I-II 9%; Lygd. 1%; Corp. Tib.
14%; Prop. 4.5%; Ov. 2.5%. But about 50% of the hexameter
verses in the elegiac poets show diaeresis at the conclusion of the first and fifth feet, a somewhat higher

number of diaereses theoretically possible in the De providentia as 4620 (924 x 5), the percentage of actual occurrence of the phenomenon is 34.0%; the percentage in the De ingratis is 33.8%.[85] In the De providentia there are only four verses (481, 546, 554, 555, or only .4% of the total number of verses) with as many as five diaereses; thirty (3.2% of the total) with four diaereses; 165 (17.9%) with three diaereses; 315 (34.1%) with two; 305 (33.0%) with one; and 105 (11.4%) with no instances of diaeresis.[86]

5. Caesura: Platnauer defines caesura as "the division of a metrical foot between two words"; as a metrical term, it does not imply sense-pause.[87] The principal function of caesura, as Cooper notes, is to bind the verse together by affording a closer linkage from foot to foot.[88]

---

percentage than that of the De prov. The Roman elegists do not seek to avoid diaeresis at the close of the fourth foot, the so-called "bucolic diaeresis." The percentages range from 43% (Ov., Fast.) to 52% (Tib. I-II; Prop. IV). Cf. Platnauer, Latin Elegiac Verse 18-22.

[85] That is, 1702 diaereses, as reported by Huegelmeyer, op. cit., 29, out of a possible total of 5090 (1018 x 5).

[86] Cf. Sturtevant, "The Doctrine of Caesura, A Philological Ghost," who cites Lucr. 1.662; Verg., Ecl. 8.83; Georg. 3.213, among others, as examples of verses with five diaereses. He maintains that "lines in which all feet except one close with a word end are common at all periods," and notes twelve examples in Aen. 1.

[87] Platnauer, Latin Elegiac Verse 4 and n. 1. On caesura as a purely metrical term, cf. also Siefert, "Reading Latin Verse" 93: "There are as many caesurae as there are word divisions occurring within feet; their weakness or their strength depends entirely on one's estimate of their importance in the articulation of the sense and upon the rhetorical impetus of the passage."

[88] Cooper, op. cit., 21. Another viewpoint is expressed in general terms by S. Basset, "Caesura. A Modern Chimaera," Classical Weekly 18 (1925) 76: "The phenomenon

INTRODUCTION

Caesura after the first long syllable, in either a dactylic or a spondaic foot, is termed masculine; after the
first short syllable of a dactylic foot, feminine. Most
cases of so-called "double" caesura, i.e., the appearance
of more than one caesura in a foot, can be resolved into
a normal caesural pattern by considering one or the other
of the monosyllables involved as proclitic or enclitic, or
else by further reference to the content of the poem; all
such cases have been resolved in preparing this study of
the De providentia.[89]

The following table indicates the number of occurrences of masculine and feminine caesura in the De providentia and the percentage of total hexameter lines (924
or 100%), in which caesura occurs in each of the first
four metrical feet.[90] In preparing the table, the criteria

TABLE 9

PLACEMENT OF CAESURAE BY METRICAL FEET
IN THE DE PROVIDENTIA

Foot	Masculine	Feminine	Percentage
1	437	109	59.1
2	589	98	74.4
3	761	119	95.2
4	601	42	69.6

of caesura is nothing but the beautiful adjustment of the
conflict between the language and the rigid scheme of six
dactylic or spondaic feet." On the relationship of caesura to ictus and accent cf. at nn. 121-129, below.

[89]Cf. Platnauer, Latin Elegiac Verse 4-5 on
"double" caesurae and their resolution. Cases in the De
prov. include 175, tenens et agenda; 422, nam quis erit;
424, ut quod agit; 523, felque et acetum; 659, ignes, nec
ab aethere; 728, putas, quid ab ordine; 736 suum, nec
abest; 802, nam quod ubique; 849, Deo, nec enim; 969, haec
sat erit, all considered masculine, and 531, ne quid
opertum, regarded as feminine.

[90]For the percentages of occurrence of caesura in
the fifth and sixth feet of the De prov., cf. n. 155, below.

for judging what constitutes a word outlined in the preceding section on diaeresis were followed, except for the resolution of "double" caesurae explained above.

There is a decided preponderance of masculine over feminine caesura; caesura occurs regularly in the second and fourth feet, commonly in the first, and almost always in the third.[91] Only forty-four hexameter lines, or 3.8%, in the De providentia have no caesura in the third foot; the elegists are even more careful in this regard. The percentage of non-caesura in the third foot ranges around 2% for Tibullus and Propertius, and drops to a low figure of .1% in Ovid.[92] More than 85% of the verses of Ennius, Lucretius, and Vergil show caesura in the third foot.[93]

The percentage of feminine caesura as compared with total caesura in the third foot ranges from a high of 20% in Tibullus I-II to a low of 1.5% in Lygdamus, the overall average of the elegists being 8%.[94] The percentage in the De ingratis, as derived from Huegelmeyer, is 10%;[95] in the

---

[91]Cf. E. H. Sturtevant, "The Doctrine of Caesura, A Philological Ghost," American Journal of Philology 55 (1924) 333: "The striking feature in the arrangement of word ends in the Latin hexameter is that masculine caesura is rare in the fifth and sixth feet, fairly common in the first foot, and very common in the second, third, and fourth. Many Latin hexameters have masculine caesura in all three of the middle group of feet, and a very large majority have masculine caesurae in two of them. There are very few lines, like Vergil Ecl. 5.52, with no masculine caesura in second, third, or fourth foot." In the De prov. every verse contains a masculine caesura in either second, third, or fourth foot; for verses with masculine caesura in all three feet, cf. e.g., 1, 480, 950. On the prevalence of caesura in the third foot in general, cf. Platnauer, Latin Elegiac Verse 6: "In other feet a caesura is optional; here it may be regarded as obligatory."

[92]Platnauer, ibid.,7-8.   [93]Nougaret, op. cit.,30.

[94]Platnauer, Latin Elegiac Verse 9.

[95]Huegelmeyer, op. cit.,30, table 4.

De providentia the corresponding figure is 13.5%. In the
fourth foot the percentage of feminine caesura varies from
1.4% in Propertius I to a high of 6.4% in the Fasti
of Ovid;[96] Lucretius shows a much higher percentage (14%,
or 106 verses).[97] The percentage for the De providentia
is 6.5%; for the De ingratis, as derived from Huegelmeyer,
2.8%.[98]

6. Pause: Pause is determined by the way in which
one reads a given verse or series of verses, and is therefore to some extent a subjective phenomenon. Ordinarily
a hexameter line will require one or more pauses by its
very length. Pauses are termed diaeresis-pauses, or
caesura-pauses; the two types differ in their effects, and
masculine caesura-pause differs from feminine caesura-
pause.[99]

Diaeresis-pause marks a very clear division of the
verse. Diaeresis pause after the first foot often conveys
an element of fulfillment or relief; the suspense aroused
in reading the preceding verse has been satisfied. The
poet of the De providentia employs this device to throw
into sharp relief the creative activity of God:
                          . . . qui divite Verbo,
     quod Deus est, rerum naturas atque elementa
     protulit,/et summis opifex intentus et imis
                          (118-120),
and to indicate Nineveh's acceptance of Jona's prophecy:
     sec Ninive monitis Ionae sub tempore cladis
     credidit / . . .   (445-446).
Diaeresis-pause after the first foot can be used
effectively in successive verses:
     quod si forte lupos, lyncasque ursosque creatos
     displicet, / ad Scythiae proceres regesque Getarum
     respice / . . .   (142-144).

---

[96]Platnauer, Latin Elegiac Verse 10.

[97]Nougaret, op. cit., 30.

[98]Huegelmeyer, op. cit., 30, reports 618 masculine
and only 18 feminine caesurae in this position.

[99]For numerous examples of diaeresis-pause and of
caesura-pause, both masculine and feminine, esp. in Verg.,
cf. Cooper, op. cit., 22-27.

Diaeresis-pause after the second foot occurs in the
narrative of the Old Testament patriarchs:

. . . /Abram/ genitor populorum,
promissum genus / innumeris censebat in astris
(348-349).

After the third foot, diaeresis-pause may mark a
contrast of some kind, e.g., as between "swift" and "slow",
neither of which affect God's power in the slightest:

/vis/ quam non effugiant cita, / nec remorantia
tardent (187),

or between the world's judgment of men as "wretched" or
"happy," a judgment based in either case on a false sense
of values:

nec quemquam vitiis miserum, / aut virtute beatum
censentes . . .   (857-858),

or simply between good and evil:

hoc operis sectare boni, / hoc fuge cautus iniqui
(651).

It may operate in the same position to distinguish
alternatives, neither of which is desirable:

aut esse exanimum cupis, / aut rationis egenum
(560).

Diaeresis-pause after the fourth foot--"bucolic"
diaeresis--combines with alliteration and concord between
ictus and accent to produce a fine effect in the poet's
description of the absence of time before God:

. . . sine tempore / tempora condens (177).

A similar effect appears in the account of the destruction of Sodom and Gomorrah:

. . . descenderet / igneus imber (350).

In another verse describing the timelessness of
God, diaeresis-pause is used effectively after each of
the three concluding feet:

nec dilata umquam, nec festinata putemus
quae veniunt, nostris mutantur / tempora / rebus /
(800-801).

Diaeresis-pause is used in the same way to distinguish
items in a series:[100]

---

[100]Pause, ordinarily optional with the poet, is
required in one circumstance, viz., when the syllaba
anceps of the verse is short, thus producing a trochaic
ending. The trochee and pause together make up the time-
equivalent of a spondee. Cf. Cooper, op. cit., 18, 26.

. . . humida, / frigida, / sicca / (117).

The masculine and feminine caesural pauses are not so abrupt as diaeresis-pause; the word and the sense are completed, but the metrical foot remains incomplete.[101] Considering the normal dactylic or spondaic foot as consisting of four beats, and a long syllable as having two beats, while a short syllable contains but one, masculine caesura pause occurs at the exact middle of the foot, after the first syllable has received its value and before the remaining beats. Thus masculine caesura-pause is characterized above all by balance. The following examples illustrate this phenomenon in each foot of verse:

First foot:
    hic / nullis mundi causis exstantibus, in se (111).
Second foot:
    non latet hanc / sanctis onerans altaria sacris
    iustus Abel, / qui primitiis ovium grege lectis
                        (305-306).
Third foot:
    deteriora legis,[102] / placitisque improvidus haeres
                        (557).
Fourth foot:
    iustitia iniustis cedit, / sapientia brutis
                        (519).
Fifth foot:
    dulcius ille favis haurit; sanctus / maledictum
                        (524).

Sixth foot:
    iusque voluntatis, quo temperat arbitrium / mens
                        (240).

Feminine caesura-pause occurs after three-quarters of the foot has been enunciated, and conveys, not a sense of balance, but a faltering or falling in the verse. In the classical poets it conveys such diverse effects as the attempt of a soldier to rise after losing a leg in

---

[101]Cf. Cooper, op. cit., 24: "There is no abrupt halt, but a moment of rest which carries in itself a sure promise of resumption."

[102]This phrase recalls the famous deteriora sequor (Ov., Met. 7.21) in the same metrical position.

battle or the boiling-over of a cauldron.[103] Examples
from the De providentia of the effects of feminine caesura-
pause in each of the five feet in which it may occur are:
First foot:

  scire / potestates herbarum, et nomina rebus
  indere, / et ingenium varias augere per artes
                    (262-263).

This is a very compressed description of man's
tasks upon earth; it is as if the poet could not wait, but
must move ahead into the verse as quickly as possible,
since the tasks are so many. The pause after indere (263)
conveys some of the effect of fulfillment or release of
suspense expressed in diaeresis-pause in the first foot.
Second foot:

  quos Deus ipse / modo dilata sustinet ira
                    (376).

Expanding upon the state of human affairs, the
poet points out that just persons must endure unjust
persons in this world, where the advantage seems often to
lie on the side of injustice. There is at least a brief
moment of suspense here--how will God treat the unjust?
Third foot:

  ignorare, optare, / pati iam nescia, nullis
                    (252).

The series of infinitives in this and the preceding verse describe human experiences, such as fear, ignorance, desire, and suffering, which man would not have to
undergo if Adam had not sinned. As these experiences are
unpleasant and disturbing for the most part, so the caesura here appears to convey some disturbance in the verse
itself.
Fourth foot:

  cum raptum ignitis per inane / iugalibus Helim
                    (327).

This example of the least frequent of feminine
caesurae may suggest the movement of Elias' chariot
through the air; one could imagine that such a steep ascent was not likely to be smooth.

---

[103]Lucr. 3.652 and Verg., Aen. 7.466 respectively.
The definition and examples of feminine caesura-pause are
taken from Cooper, op. cit.,25.

Fifth foot:
    exuti, in Christo renovemur corpus, / et omnem
                      (963).

    Here the caesura appears to mark a distinction be-
tween two similar actions, renewal into the body of Christ
and what should follow as its natural effect, complete
reliance on Christ for all power to conquer the enemy,
Satan. Caesura in this position is of such frequent occurrence, however, that its impact is largely diminished.

    Pauses do not exist in isolation, but in combina-
tions. A mark of a good poet is his skill in the combination of pauses, and the poet of the De providentia is not
lacking in this regard, as witnessed by his description
of the Lord's attempt to prevent Cain from killing his
brother:
    nec revocare ferum / Dominus / sermone benigno
    abstinuit: / quantumque nefas strueretur ab ipso /
    ingessit, / formamque dedit / qua vincere sese
    posset, / et insanae / regnaret fortior / irae /
                  (311-314).

The pauses here are:
    311: Masculine caesura pause in third foot,
           Masculine caesura pause in fourth foot.

    312: Masculine caesura pause in second foot,
           Diaeresis pause at end of verse.

    313: Masculine caesura pause in second and fourth foot.

    314: Feminine caesura pause in first foot,
           Masculine caesura pause in third foot,
           Diaeresis pause after fifth foot,
           Diaeresis pause at end of verse.

    7. Verse structure: The employment of spondees
and dactyls in given matrical patterns in the De providentia is treated in this section. In accordance with the
practice in the preceding metrical sections, only the 924
continuous hexameter verses of the poem are considered
here.

    The following table shows the poet's preferences
among the sixteen possible permutations of dactyls and
spondees in the first four feet of the hexameter lines:[104]

---

    [104]For the pentameters, cf. table 21, after n.
171, below.

TABLE 10

VERSE PATTERNS IN THE DE PROVIDENTIA

Pattern		Number	Percentage
1.	DDDD	23	2.5
2.	DDDS	53	5.7
3.	DDSS	92	10.0
4.	DSSS	122	13.2
5.	DSDS	98	10.6
6.	DSSD	44	4.8
7.	DDSD	31	3.4
8.	DSDD	37	4.0
9.	SSSS	76	8.2
10.	SSSD	39	4.2
11.	SSDD	41	4.4
12.	SDDD	26	2.8
13.	SDSD	35	3.8
14.	SDDS	53	5.7
15.	SSDS	70	7.6
16.	SDSS	84	9.1

The most frequent pattern in the De providentia, as in Vergil and in the De ingratis, is DSSSDS, which conveys a "subtle symmetry," as Cooper remarks.[105] Such symmetry, suggesting as it does complexity and involvement, is used appropriately in the first, second, and last verses of the following passage describing the effects of original sin:

mors hominem, culpa in cunctos manante minores;
quae semel antiqua pulsos virtutis ab arce,
non uno tantum transfuso errore parentum
implicuit, sed cum populis nascentibus aucta,
multiplicem lata porrexit strage ruinam
(290-294).

The clear balance of DSDSDS affords a pattern which appears especially useful in pointing a contrast, as for example between the old and the new, this world and

[105] For further discussion of the effects of this and other specific verse patterns cf. Cooper, op. cit., 28-31, and K. B. Steele, "Variations in Latin Dactylic Hexameter," Philological Quarterly 5 (1926) 212-225.

the next:
    nil veteris coniunge novo, non hic tibi mundus
                (505),
or between night and day:
    et medio nox facta die est; concussaque tellus
                (528),
and also for listing items in a series:
    quae patimur, motus animi, affectusque rebelles
                (608).

    One of the less frequently used patterns, DDSDDS,
which has a certain symmetry of its own,[106] appears in
this succinct description of the Resurrection:
    tertia discipulis, Iesu, dedit attonitis lux
                (536).
The same pattern is used to express the conclusion that
heavenly bodies do not affect man's free exercise of virtue:

            . . . si quid obest virtuti . . .
    non superi pariunt ignes, nec ab aethere manat
                (658-659),
and to raise a pointed question concerning the benefits
to be derived from astrology:
    quaero quid hac trepidis mortalibus afferat arte?
                (700).

    At opposite extremes to each other are the swift
pattern DDDDDS and the slow SSSSDS.[107] The rapid dactylic
pattern conveys the eagerness with which the Queen of Saba

---

[106] Verg. recognized the particular value of this
pattern in _Ecl._ 8, in the repetitive verse: incipe,
Maenalios, mecum, mea tibia, versus (21, 25, 28a, 31, 36,
42, 46, 51, 57) and its mate, desine, Maenalios, iam desine,
tibia, versus (61), as well as in the concluding verse:
parcite, ab urbe venit, iam parcite carmina, Daphnis (109).

[107] The pattern SSSSSS is extremely rare, and does
not occur in the _De prov._, where the only two spondaic
verses (477, 947) follow the pattern SDSDSS. The pattern
DDDDDS is used by Verg., e.g., to reproduce the sound of
galloping hoofs: quadrupedante putrem sonitu quatit ungula
campum (_Aen._ 8.596). Juv. is fond of the SSSSDS pattern,
and uses it in citing Cicero's unfortunate verse in the
same pattern: o fortunatam natam me consule Romam (_Sat._
10.122).

heard the word of God from Solomon on her famous visit to Jerusalem:

auribus eloquium Domini venerata trahebat
(444),

and depicts the sudden destruction that would befall the universe if the divine sustenance were removed:

conciderent subita in nihilum redigenda ruina
(740).

The more frequent spondaic pattern, with a dactyl only in the fifth foot, portrays the momentous struggle between all created things which, in the poet's view, maintains them in balance:

quod vero adversis compugnant condita causis
(121),

obscurum obiectum, et dulci contendit amarum
(129),

and emphasizes the massiveness of the universe itself:

omnem autem hanc molem mundi qui condidit, ipse
(153).

In the immediately preceding verse alliteration also performs the same function.

The table on page 219 presents the sixteen possible verse patterns ranked according to frequency of use in selected classical poets, the De ingratis, and the De providentia. The most frequently used pattern is numbered 1, the next most frequently used 2, and so on.

The table reveals that both the De providentia and the De ingratis show no striking divergences from classical norms in verse patterning. As in all the classical poets considered, the DSSS pattern is the most frequent one in both later poems. The symmetrical DSDS does appear more often in the De providentia and the De ingratis, however, than in the classical poets. Less significantly, because much smaller percentages are involved, the SSDD pattern appears also in both poems more frequently than in the classical poets. Patterns which appear with lesser frequency in the De providentia than in the classical poets are DSSD, DDSD, and SDSD; the percentages involved would not seem to be very significant.

Table 12, on page 220, illustrates the number of verses in the Aeneid, the De ingratis, and the De providentia which fall under each of the five different combinations normally possible.

TABLE 11[a]

VERSE PATTERNS RANKED BY FREQUENCY OF USE IN REPRESENTATIVE POETS

Pattern	Lucretius	Aeneid	Horace	Juvenal	Persius	De ingratis	De providentia
DDDD	13	15	16	15	13	15	16
DDDS	5	6	8	9	6	8	7-8
DDSS	2	2	4	2	2	5	3
DSSS	1	1	1	1	1	1	1
DSDS	3	3	3	3	4	2	2
DSSD	6	8	6	5	5	7	9
DDSD	8	10	12	10	9	14	14
DSDD	10	12	13	12	8	12-13	12
SSSS	7	5	5	11	7	4	5
SSSD	14	13	11	13	14	9	11
SSDD	16	14	14	16	16	12-13	10
SDDD	15	16	15	14	15	16	15
SDSD	11	11	10	7	10	10	13
SDDS	9	9	9	8	12	11	7-8
SSDS	12	7	7	6	11	6	6
SDSS	4	4	2	4	3	3	4

[a]Figures for the classical poets in this table are adapted from Steele, op. cit.,224. Figures for the De ingrat. have been derived from Huegelmeyer, op. cit.,33, Table 5. Where the number of verses in different patterns was found to be equal, two figures are given.

219

TABLE 12[a]

COMBINATIONS OF DACTYLS AND SPONDEES IN SELECTED POETS

Combination	Aeneid		De ingratis		De providentia	
	Number	Percentage	Number	Percentage	Number	Percentage
5S, 1D	701	7.1	89	9.0	76	8.2
4S, 2D	3238	32.9	373	36.6	313	34.1
3S, 3D	4011	40.7	375	36.7	363	39.3
2S, 4D	1680	17.0	150	15.0	147	15.9
1S, 5D	209	2.1	27	2.7	23	2.5

[a] The figures for the Aen. are taken from Cordier, Les débuts de l'hexamètre latin 67; those for the De ingrat. are derived from Huegelmeyer.

INTRODUCTION

It is obvious, considering the structure of the sixth foot, that 6D is an impossible figure for a hexameter line. 6S is theoretically possible, but extremely rare, and is not found in the De providentia or the De ingratis.[108] Table 12 suggests a reasonably close correspondence between the two later poems and the Vergilian norm. In the combinations 4S, 2D and 3S, 3D the De providentia is closer to the Aeneid; in the other combinations it is nearer the De ingratis.

Table 13 indicates the numbers and percentages of dactyls and spondees, respectively, in each of the first four feet of the De providentia:

TABLE 13

PERCENTAGES OF DACTYLS AND SPONDEES
IN THE DE PROVIDENTIA

Foot	Dactyls		Spondees	
	Number	Percentage	Number	Percentage
1	500	54.1	424	45.9
2	397	43.0	527	57.0
3	401	43.4	523	56.6
4	276	29.9	648	70.1
Total	1574	42.6	2122	57.4

The higher total percentage of spondees is normal, since it is easier to form spondees than dactyls in the Latin language; as Steele remarks, "the heavier foot is predominant in most Latin dactylic poetry."[109]

The following table, derived primarily from Steele's study, gives the percentage of dactyls in the first four

[108]Cooper, op. cit.,28, cites two problematical instances from Enn.

[109]Steele, op. cit., 212.

221

feet of hexameters in representative Latin poets:

TABLE 14

PERCENTAGE OF DACTYLS IN REPRESENTATIVE LATIN POETS

Poet	Percentage
Ennius	39.8[a]
Catullus 64	35.6
Lucretius	44.5
Vergil: Eclogues	48.4
Georgics	44.1
Aeneid	44.1
Horace	45.1
Ovid: Metamorphoses	54.6
Fasti	54.2[b]
Juvenal	44.1
Persius	44.1
Valerius Flaccus	53.4
De ingratis	41.1[c]
De providentia	42.6

[a]But Cordier, op. cit., 65, reports a percentage of 40.3% dactyls for Enn.

[b]This figure was derived from Siefert, Meter and Case 16 n. 12.

[c]This figure was derived from Huegelmeyer, op. cit. 34, Table 6.

INTRODUCTION

The percentage for the De providentia approximates
those reported for Lucretius, the Georgics and Aeneid of
Vergil, Horace, Juvenal, Persius, and the De ingratis.
    It may be instructive to compare the early poet
Ennius, Vergil in his Aeneid, and the De ingratis and De
providentia in regard to percentages of dactyls by individual feet in the hexameter. In each instance the percentage of spondees may be derived by subtraction of the given
figure from 100.0%.

TABLE 15[a]

PERCENTAGE OF DACTYLS BY FEET IN SELECT LATIN POETS

Foot	Ennius	Aeneid	De ingratis	De providentia
1	42.5	60.8	55.5	54.1
2	42.9	48.2	39.7	43.0
3	39.0	39.9	39.8	43.4
4	36.6	25.6	30.3	29.9

[a]The percentages for Enn. and Aen. were derived
from Cordier, op. cit.,68; for De ingrat., from Huegelmeyer, op. cit.,34, Table 6.

    The percentages for the first and fourth feet show
clear similarities between the Aeneid and the two later
poems, as contrasted with Ennius; the figures for the third
foot are higher for the De providentia than for the other
poems considered; surprisingly, the affinities of the third
foot appear to lie among Ennius and the two later poems
as against the Aeneid.[110]

___

[110]But variation is the rule in this matter among
Latin poets. Cf. Steele, op. cit.,219: "Not only are
the works of Vergil different in the use of the schemata,
but different books of the same work, and different sections of the same book show equal divergences. Given the
data in any work, book, or section, we cannot by multipli-
cation get the schemata for larger units, nor can we by

Table 15 reveals a clear tendency in the Aeneid, De ingratis, and De providentia to make the first foot of the hexameter verse a dactyl. This same tendency appears in all the Latin hexameter poets after Catullus.[111]

Platnauer has calculated the percentage of hexameters opening with spondees in the elegiac poets. Table 16 compares some of Platnauer's figures with those for the poems treated in Table 15:[112]

TABLE 16

PERCENTAGE OF SPONDEES IN FIRST FOOT OF HEXAMETER
VERSES IN REPRESENTATIVE LATIN POETS

Poet	Percentage
Ennius	57.5
Tibullus I-II	23.0
Lygdamus	44.5
Propertius I-II (average)	42.0
Propertius III	36.5
Propertius IV	27.0
Ovid: Amores	20.0
Fasti	10.7[a]
Vergil: Aeneid	39.2
De ingratis	44.5
De providentia	45.9

[a]The exceptionally low percentage of spondees here is in accord with the high percentage of dactyls (54.2%) in the Fast. as a whole.

division of the larger get the facts for the smaller." Steele offers a number of illustrative examples of the point, e.g., in Verg. the spondee is predominant, but in Ecl. 8 and 9 it ranges below half.

[111]Steele, op. cit.,212.

[112] Platnauer, Latin Elegiac Verse 38.

INTRODUCTION

The percentage of dactyls in the first foot of the
De providentia is only slightly higher than the percentages for the elegiac poets, the Aeneid, and the De ingratis;
not surprisingly, it is far below that for Ennius. The
percentage for the De ingratis stands in virtually the same
position, being higher than that of the Aeneid and all the
elegiac poets except Lygdamus, whom it equals, and being
also substantially below that of Ennius.

The data in the foregoing section, when considered
in the aggregate, emphasize the considerable extent to
which the poet of the De providentia, like Prosper in the
De ingratis, adhered to the classical norms. There are
similarities in percentages between the De providentia
and the De ingratis at many points, but these are not
necessarily greater, and are sometimes slightly less, than
the similarities that exist between each work and the
works of the classical poets of the Golden and Silver Ages.

8. Spondaic verses: A spondaic verse is one in
which the fifth foot, normally dactylic, appears as a
spondee. While exceptional, such verses do appear in
Ennius' Annals once in every 48 lines on the average;[113]
they are found with greater frequency in Catullus.[114]
The elegists seldom use the spondaic verse; Tibullus never
does.[115] There are only thirty-one spondaic verses in

---

[113]O. J. Todd, "Caesura Rediviva," Classical Philology 37 (1942) 22-37.

[114]Siefert, Meter and Case 11 n. 9, reports 42
spondaic verses for Catull. in 794 hexameters (5.3%);
Steele, op. cit.,213, reports the same number. Nougaret,
op. cit.,45-46, finds thirty cases in the 408 hexameters
of Catull. 64, a figure which leads him to conclude that
Catull. uses spondaic verses as an affectation. But Platnauer, Latin Elegiac Verse 38-39, notes that only two
spondaic hexameters are found in the elegiac verses of
Catull., who there follows the general tendency among the
elegists to avoid them; the exceptions are 68.87 and the
SSSSSS verse 116.3.

[115]Platnauer, Latin Elegiac Verse 39, cites seven
cases in Prop., six of them ending in Greek words; eighteen
cases in Ov., two of them only with Latin terminations
and a third certainly spurious. Todd, op. cit.,27 n. 15,

Lucretius, and thirty-two (.25%, or about one in each 403 lines) in all of Vergil.[116]

In the De providentia there are only two spondaic verses (.22%, or one in each 462 lines); there are four in the De ingratis (.39%, or one in about 254 lines).[117] Spondaic verses are seldom found in the medieval poets.[118]

The spondaic verse is slow and solemn in pace. One such verse in the De providentia is found in the poet's cautionary description of the heresy which held that Christ was true God, but not truly a man:

si cernens operum miracula divinorum (477).

The other spondaic verse appears as part of a description of the majestic redemptive work of Christ:

aversos revocans et suscipiens conversos (947).

Even in their treatment of this minor phenomenon, the classical poets observe certain rules--the verse generally ends in a word of three or four syllables,[119] and the

---

reports an average of one in each 307 lines in Ov., Met. Cf., e.g., Prop. 1.13.31; Ov.,Am. 1.6.53; Fast. 2.787; 5.83.

[116] For the number of verses cf. Steele, op. cit. 213; for the ratio 1 - 403, Todd, op. cit.,27 n.15. For a brief, illuminating discussion of the spondaic verse with special application to Verg., cf. Cooper, op. cit.,30. Cf., e.g., Ecl. 5.38; 7.53 (the latter a verse with two instances of hiatus also); Georg. 4.270; Aen. 12.83.

[117] Huegelmeyer, op. cit.,34 and n.1.

[118] Strecker, op. cit.,73; Norberg, op. cit.,64-65.

[119] Todd, op. cit., reports thirteen trisyllabic and seventeen quadrisyllabic endings in the 32 spondaic verses of Verg. Cf., e.g., Aen. 12.863, culminibus desertis; 5.320, intervallo, cited by Nougaret, op. cit.,45-46. The only exception in Verg. is Ennius' tagphrase magnis dis, repeated Aen. 3.12; 8.697.

fourth foot is most often a dactyl.[120] The two spondaic
verses in the De providentia conform to these criteria;
in the De ingratis the four spondaic verses (83, 392, 474,
788) also follow the same classical norms.

9. Concord of ictus and accent: It is usual in
hexameter verse to stress the first syllable of each foot
as an indication of rhythm, whether the foot is dactylic
or spondaic; this stress is termed ictus.[121] But each
Latin word, in poetry or prose, has its own stress accent,
determined by the rule of penultimate accentuation.[122]
Conflict occurs when the ictus and the word accent fall
on two different syllables of a metrical foot; coincidence
of ictus and word accent produces concord.[123] In view of
the rule of penultimate accentuation, diaeresis and feminine caesura will result in concord, unless a monosyllabic
word is involved.[124] Conversely, a frequent incidence of
concord between ictus and accent tends to result in excessive diaeresis, although diaeresis can be avoided by

---

[120]Cordier, op. cit.,67, reports that the fourth
foot is always a dactyl in Lucr., and is dactylic in Verg.
with three exceptions, viz., Georg. 3.276; Aen. 3.74;
7.634.

[121]For a more extended treatment of ictus, cf.
Cooper, op. cit.,35-36.

[122]That is, the penult is accented, if it is long;
if it is short, the accent recedes to the antepenult.
Cf. Cooper, op. cit.,2-3.

[123]Conflict is an impossibility in Greek verse,
which used pitch accent as the normal word accent, and
stress only to mark rhythm. For the relationships between concord and conflict in the hexameter, with several
apt examples, cf. Siefert, "Reading Latin Verse" 94-97;
Cooper, op. cit.,37-40. For a brief summary of the matter
with special reference to the De ingrat., cf. Huegelmeyer,
op. cit.,34-36.

[124]Siefert, "Reading Latin Verse" 94.

special contrivance in such a situation.[125]

If complete concord led to excessive diaeresis, complete conflict between ictus and accent produced equally harsh effects.[126] The Latin poets resolved the difficulty in practice by seeking concord more often than not at the opening of a verse, and almost invariably at the conclusion, where reassertion of the rhythm was considered especially desirable; this compromise, developed after considerable experimentation, became the pattern chosen by Vergil and his successors.[127]

Siefert's description of the Vergilian pattern clarifies the matter further: "Vergil's practice, in the Aeneid more especially, may with some over-simplification be analyzed as follows. Of the six ictuses in every line, the first two may or may not coincide with the word accent; the second or middle two will ordinarily be in conflict with the word accent; the last two will almost always be in concord with it . . . the middle of the line, or even

---

[125]E.g., Hor., Epist. 1.9.4.: dignum mente domoque legentis honesta Neronis. Hor. avoids excessive diaeresis here only by employing four feminine caesurae in the line; but feminine caesura itself, especially when pause is present, has its own special function to perform, and excessive use of the feminine caesura can be as undesirable as excessive diaereses. Cf. Siefert, "Reading Latin Verse" 96 and the verses cited there, viz., Hor. Epist. 1.11.29; Lucr. 1.217, 236. Siefert does not find any verses of this type in Verg.; he notes that they occur frequently in the prosaic passages of Lucr. A verse that shows almost complete concord in the De prov. is 411: siccae rupis aquam et dulcorem fontis amari.

[126]For examples of the undesirable effects of both complete concord and complete conflict, cf. Cooper, op. cit., 38-39.

[127]Cooper, op. cit. 39. An example of the earlier experimentation is the practice of Catull., who appears to extend the rule of concord to the fourth foot, and crowds words requiring conflict into the second and third foot. Cf. Sturtevant, "Harmony and Clash of Accent and Ictus in the Latin Hexameter" 51-73, and Table 17, below.

the first two-thirds, if the conflict has begun so early,
are raised above the tone of normal prose by reason of
the fact that every syllable, if the rhythm is spondaic,
or almost every syllable, if the rhythm is dactylic, is
sustained either by word accent or by metrical stress."[128]
The basic Vergilian pattern is therefore one of Freedom-
Conflict-Concord; concord is more frequent than conflict
in the first foot, almost universal in the fifth and sixth
feet, more frequent in the fourth foot than in the second,
and least common in the third foot.[129]

The following table compares the frequency of concord between ictus and accent in the first four feet of
hexameter verses of representative Latin poets with that
of the De providentia.[130] We are dealing here with accented words; but what constitutes an accented word? The
problem becomes particularly acute in regard to the treatment of monosyllables, and can affect the percentages substantially, particularly in the first foot.[131] Monosyllabic nouns, adjectives, adverbs and interjections have
been counted as accented (e.g., lux, 522, 536, 578; hanc,
287; heu, 33, 552); monosyllabic verb forms have been

---

[128]Siefert, "Reading Latin Verse" 94.

[129]Sturtevant, "Harmony and Clash of Accent and
Ictus," supplies the following table of preference for
concord, in which the Roman numerals represent feet and
the Arabic ones preferences:

I	II	III	IV	V-VI
2	4	5	3	1

[130]For data on the fifth and sixth feet cf. at
Table 22, after n. 175, below.

[131]This is true because of a pronounced tendency
in Latin poetry to place monosyllables at or near the
opening of the verse. As an illustration, the following
figures would apply in the De prov., depending on whether
all doubtful monosyllables were counted (inclusive figure)
or none were (exclusive figure):

Foot	Inclusive	Exclusive	Difference
1	73.2%	40.0%	23.2%
2	26.7%	16.7%	10.0%
3	19.9%	16.0%	3.9%
4	43.1%	39.4%	3.7%

considered accented (e.g., dant, 156) except for certain forms of sum, which have been considered on their merits and generally resolved as unaccented. Monosyllabic prepositions (e.g., ab, de, ex, in) are counted as unaccented, whereas dissyllabic ones are considered to receive an accent (e.g., inter). Conjunctions (e.g., et, at, ac, nec, aut) are generally treated as unaccented. Relative and indefinite pronouns are generally counted as unaccented, but personal pronouns as receiving the accent.

TABLE 17[a]

PERCENTAGE OF CONCORD BETWEEN ACCENT AND ICTUS
IN REPRESENTATIVE LATIN POETS

Foot	1	2	3	4	Average
Lucretius	63.0	23.5	12.4	44.4	38.0
Catullus 64	65.8	14.0	9.3	67.0[b]	40.0
Vergil Aeneid	57.7	22.5	18.6	33.5	36.0
Horace Satires 1	60.9	17.2	12.7	38.2	36.0
Ovid Metamorphoses 1	80.0	24.8	12.6	45.3	40.0
De ingratis	73.8	22.3	16.2	38.6	38.0
De providentia	53.8	18.2	16.4	40.7	32.0

[a]This table is adapted from Sturtevant, "Harmony and Clash of Accent and Ictus" 58. The figures for the De ingrat. are from Huegelmeyer, op. cit., 36, Table 7.

[b]Readers of Huegelmeyer's study may correct the misprint 6.7 which appears in his table at this point.

This table reveals that the pattern in the De providentia is essentially the same as that in the De ingratis and in all the classical poets considered, i.e., concord in the first foot, decreasing in the second foot and still

230

further in the third, but increasing in the fourth.[132]

Concord in the last four feet of the verse is rare in Vergil; it may indicate the rhythm of tramping feet on a swaying bridge, may produce a rocking effect, or may describe majestic Fury seated upon armor and bound with a hundred chains of bronze.[133] In the De providentia such a verse is used to enhance the majesty of the law and the prophets, and, with the repeated hoc, to indicate the concord that exists between the two:

hoc etenim lex, hóc veneránda volúmina vátum (467).

Concord in the last three feet of the verse is more frequent in both Vergil and the De providentia. As Jackson-Knight observes, "stress accent at the beginning of the fourth foot is one of the most powerful means of distinguishing one verse from another verse, and even, as it is used by Vergil with infinite delicacy, paragraphs, long passages, and even whole books, from each other."[134] Examination of the last verse of each of the eleven divisions of the poem proper[135] in the Maurist text reveals that no less than six of them terminate with concord of ictus and accent in the fourth, fifth, and sixth feet (266, 472, 623, 720, 896, 972), including the last verse

---

[132]The only irregularity is the higher percentage of concord in the fourth foot than in the first noted for Catull. Cf. n. 127, above.

[133]Georg. 1.357; Aen. 2.9; 1.195, respectively. The first two examples are cited from Siefert, "Reading Latin Verse" 95; the last from Todd, "Caesura Rediviva" 28 n.18.

[134]W. F. Jackson-Knight, Accentual Symmetry in Vergil 9-10. Jackson-Knight's discussion gives special emphasis to concord and conflict in the fourth foot. Cf. also Todd, op. cit.,28 n. 18 for several examples of harmony in the last three feet in the Aen. (viz., Aen. 1.4, 6, 9; 4.2). Siefert, "Reading Latin Verse" 95, notes substantially the same effect of concord in the last three feet as does Jackson-Knight.

[135]Not counted among the eleven is the prologue, in elegiacs.

of the poem (972), while a seventh case might be considered doubtful (et, 194); only four clearly do not have this termination (150, 413, 549, 804).

Periods often terminate with such concord in the De providentia:

et qua gens hominum diffusa est corpore mundi (103),
innatum est cunctis genitorem agnoscere verum (108),

as do subordinate clauses:

seu nostros annos, seu tempora prisca revolvas (104),
quod vero adversis compugnant condita causis (121),

or even items in series:

sive expers animae, calida, humida, frigida, sicca
(117).

There are only twenty-six cases of conflict between ictus and accent in the fifth and sixth feet of hexameter verses in the De providentia--fourteen (1.5%) in the fifth foot and twelve (1.3%) in the sixth.[136] The number of instances reported by Huegelmeyer for the De ingratis is eight and two respectively;[137] the totals involved are too small to permit any conclusions.

In every measurable factor, then, the verse of the De providentia conforms to classical canons regulating the concord and conflict of ictus and accent.

10. Verse-endings: The following table compares Vergilian practice in regard to verse endings, as illustrated by Aeneid 11, with the practice of Prosper in the De ingratis and with that of the author of the De providentia. The eleventh Aeneid, the second longest book of Vergil's epic, was chosen for comparison because its 915 hexameter verses closely approximate in number the 924

---

[136] In the fifth foot, vv. 180, 273, 306, 348, 391, 412, 524, 579, 587, 786, 849, 915, 947, 965. 947 is spondaic. In the sixth foot, vv. 240, 265, 355, 501, 522, 536, 559, 671, 691, 701, 868, 938. There is secondary stress accent in the fifth foot of oppiduli Loth (355) which makes for concord in that foot, but not of course in the sixth; etiam nunc (887) may be considered as one word, thus producing concord in the sixth foot of its verse.

[137] Huegelmeyer, op. cit., 36 and n. 30.

continuous hexameter verses of the De providentia.[138]

The definition of what constitutes a word as given
by Cooper is employed in the table.[139] Thus omnibus idem
est (De prov. 817), for example, is counted as constitut-
ing a 3-2 pattern of verse-ending and idem est is itself
considered a dissyllabic ending; similarly, spargantur in
aures, with its monosyllabic preposition, (87), is counted
a 3-3 ending and in aures is considered a trisyllable.
Cooper's principles are applied without regard to the
position of a word in any given foot or feet, so that a
sanguine plagam (829), for example, is treated as a case
of the 4-2 pattern. Elided vowels had no appreciable effect on verse pattern, and are not counted here; thus
ducere in antris (49) constitutes a 2-3 pattern.

Table 18 indicates that the three works in question
show a preponderance of dissyllabic and trisyllabic endings. While Vergil prefers the **dissyllabic ending**, both
of the later poems show a slight preference for terminating a line of verse with a trisyllable.[140] The reason

---

[138]The version of Aen. 11 used throughout is the
Oxford text edited by F. A. Hirtzel (Oxford, 1900, with
many reprints); of the De ingrat., Huegelmeyer's text.
Only 912 lines of Aen. 11 are actually included in the
table. Two half verses (375, 391) had of necessity to
be excluded, and in order to insure as accurate a comparison as possible one verse (404) which is bracketed in
the Oxford text is excluded. Of the 1018 hexameter verses
of the De ingrat., one (911), which is bracketed by
Huegelmeyer, was likewise excluded. There are no exclu-
sions in the De prov.

[139]Cf. at nn. 82-83 above. Cf. Cooper, op. cit.,
40-41 for the treatment of prepositions and their objects,
the si quid construction, and cases of prodelision.

[140]Huegelmeyer, op. cit.,37, concludes that the
De ingrat.contains more dissyllabic than trisyllabic
endings, but his method of counting prepositions and the
words governed by them is different. Had Huegelmeyer's
method been adopted in the present study, the De prov.
too would doubtless have shown a slight predominance of
dissyllabic endings, and the predominance of dissyllabic
endings in Aen. 11 would be somewhat larger than it appears here.

TABLE 18

NUMBER OF SYLLABLES IN TERMINAL WORDS IN SELECT LATIN POETS

Number of Syllables	Aeneid 11 (912 verses)		De ingratis (1017 verses)		De providentia (924 verses)	
	Number of Verses	%	Number of Verses	%	Number of Verses	%
1	7	.8	16	1.6	22	2.4
2	476	52.3	442	43.4	427	46.2
3	422	46.2	464	45.7	434	47.0
4	6	.6	39	3.8	21	2.3
5	1	.1	56	5.5	20	2.1

for this preference for the dissyllabic and trisyllabic terminations is that the classical poets--and their later imitators--sought to achieve concord of ictus and accent in the last two feet of the verse. But as Siefert observes, "concord in the last two feet required either a feminine caesura in the fifth foot or a diaeresis at the end of it."[141] In a normal dactylic line, only the dissyllabic ending will produce diaeresis at the close of the fifth foot while retaining concord in the sixth; only a trisyllable will give feminine caesura in the fifth foot. The monosyllabic termination would result ordinarily in conflict in the last foot, even while it allowed for the possibility of feminine caesura in the fifth foot, and pentasyllabic endings would make any caesura or diaeresis an impossibility in either of the two final feet.

As early as Ennius, Latin verse shows a tendency to avoid the accented monosyllabic termination; a similar tendency is observable among prose stylists. Historians use the monosyllabic ending sparingly, although it appears with somewhat greater frequency in oratorical and epistolary style.[142] The elegists apparently end many hexameters with a monosyllable, but in only four instances is there

---

[141] Siefert, "Reading Latin Verse" 97. The truth of the statement derives from the rule of penultimate accentuation in Latin. The spondaic hexameter presents a different situation; both spondaic hexameters in the De providentia (477, 947) achieve concord of ictus and accent in the last foot, and concord of ictus with secondary accent in the fifth foot, through the use of tetrasyllabic endings. The same is true of the four spondaic hexameters of the De ingrat. (83, 392, 474, 788).

[142] A. G. Harkness, "Final Monosyllables in Latin Prose and Poetry," American Journal of Philology 31 (1910) 170-174, who observes that "the usage of the hexameter and the pentameter is due to the relation of accent and ictus." (p. 173). At least nine of the twenty-two cases of monosyllabic endings in the De prov. involve conflict of ictus and accent (240, 355, 501, 522, 536, 671, 701, 868, 938).

a real caesura in the sixth foot;[143] in the other cases
the final monosyllable may often be regarded as forming
a unit with a preceding monosyllable or polysyllable, e.g.,
fas est, nil est, non est, et qui, ad os est. Vergil and
Horace occasionally use the monosyllabic ending for special effect; when the effect intended is comic, there may
be an element of rhyme.[144]

The De providentia is quite conventional in its use
of monosyllabic endings. Both ac si (870) and et cum
(884) can be considered as forming unitary compounds and
thus avoiding caesura in the final foot of the verse; hoc
vis (554) at least avoids caesura-pause. The unemphatic
est appears three times (507, 716, 849); short pronouns
are found six times (me,647; te, 501, 559; se, 273; nos,
671; quos,826). Forms of vis (vi 265; vim 273, 868) as
well as the nominative form res (938) and rex (691) are
paralleled in the Aeneid, while lux (522, 536) finds its
parallel as early as Ennius.[145] The only monosyllabic word
which would clearly not be exemplified in classical verse
is Loth (355); the principal classical effect which is

---

[143]Platnauer, Latin Elegiac Verse 13. Platnauer's
four "intractable examples" are amor qui (Prop. 2.25.17),
quibus nos (Ov., Pont. 4.9.101), Aeonius fons (Pont.
4.2.27) and Cupido, est (Am. 2.9.47; apparently prodelision of est over a comma).

[144]E.g., exiguus mus (Verg., Georg. 1.181); ridi-
culus mus (Hor., A.P. 139). A more weighty effect is
given by praeruptus aquae mons (Aen. 1.105). For a full
discussion of the special effects of short verse terminations with many examples from Verg. especially, cf. J.
Marouzeau, "Mots longs et mots courts," Revue de philologie
48 (1924) 31-43.

[145]Compare opum vi (Aen. 9.532; 12.849) with
corporea vi (De prov. 265); vetat res (Aen. 7.592) and
capiant res (De prov. 938); hominum rex (Aen. 2.648;
10.2, 473) and omnipotens rex (De prov. 691). For lux
cf. Enn., Ann. 90, foras lux. These examples are derived
from Marouzeau, "Mots longs et mots courts." Marouzeau
notes that autonomous words tend to be polysyllables,
whereas accessory words are monosyllables.

lacking in the monosyllabic usage of the De providentia
is the comic.

The dismal word mors produces its effect in the description of the various fates which await different men
according to the astrologer:

 'hic,' inquit, 'felix, miser hic erit, hunc rapiet
        mors' (701).

The reader is told emphatically that it is the mind (mens)
which must control the will:

 iusque voluntatis, quo temperat arbitrium mens
       (240).

The perishable things of this world (res) literally tumble down from one verse to the next:

 nos, quibus in Christo sunt omnia, non capiant res
 occiduae . . .   (938-939),

but the monosyllabic termination gives a different kind
of emphasis to Christ, the light (lux):

 damnatur iudex, Verbum tacet, inspuitur lux (522).

The tetrasyllabic ending is found with some frequency in Ennius, who uses it approximately once in every
fifteen verses; the ratio drops to one in 43.6 verses in
Lucretius, and one in 257.1 in all of Vergil.[146] Vergil
differs from the two earlier poets, too, in that almost
all of his tetrasyllabic verse endings involve Greek
words.[147]

The ratio of one tetrasyllabic ending to every 44.0
lines in the De providentia is similar to that in Lucretius, and the ratio of one to 26.1 lines in the De ingratis is actually somewhat closer to Ennian than to
Lucretian practice. Both later poems also resemble the
works of Ennius and Lucretius in that almost all their
tetrasyllabic endings are words of Latin origin. In the
De providentia only three of the twenty-one instances

---

[146]Todd, "Caesura Ridiviva" 27.

[147]Nougaret,Traité de métrique latine classique,
reports forty-nine tetrasyllabic endings involving Greek
words for Verg., e.g., hyacinthus (Ecl. 3.63), Meliboei
(Ecl. 5.87), and only four Latin ones, e.g., semiviro
comitatu (Aen. 4.215), the other instances being Aen.
4.667; 6.11; 10.505. In contrast, Todd reports 36 tetrasyllabic endings for Enn., including only two Greek words,
and 170 for Lucr., including only four words that are
Greek in origin.

comprise words of Greek derivation, in each case a form of elementum (elementa, 119; elemento, 631; elementis, 689), while the others are such normal Latin words as miserentis, 346; populorum, 348; pereundi, 391; and violatur, 484.

Just as Ennius and other early Latin poets use the tetrasyllabic ending with no apparent restriction, they employ pentasyllabic terminations with the same freedom.[148] Lucretius evidently does not hesitate to use such verse terminations as exoriuntur, 1.869; purpureai, 2.52; principiorum, 2.135, and many others, as the occasion demands. The elegiac poets, on the contrary, almost never allow such license.[149] Vergil's practice is close to that of the elegists; of eighteen possible pentasyllabic endings in the Aeneid, as reported by Nougaret, only one is a pure Latin form (quadrupedantum, 11.614).[150]

A glance at Table 18, however, reveals that the De providentia contains a substantially higher percentage of pentasyllabic endings than that found in Vergil; in fact, the De providentia alone contains more pentasyllabic terminations than all of Vergil. Such endings as sollicitudo, 170; religiones, 650; conditionis, 454; deliciarum, 283; and insinuavit, 514, have a distinctly Lucretian ring; not a single one of the twenty pentasyllabic endings of the De providentia is derived from the Greek, and only three at most are distinctly Christian usages (glorificato, 345, and perhaps omnipotenti, 195, and omnipotentis, 567). The figures for the De ingratis are still more striking.

---

[148] Marouzeau, "Mots longs et mots courts" 33. After discussing the monosyllabic ending, Marouzeau proceeds to delineate the use of long words, i.e., for the most part words of five or more syllables, with special reference to the poets, and then considers the possible effects of such words.

[149] Platnauer, Latin Elegiac Verse 13, reports one Greek pentasyllabic ending in Prop., three pentasyllabic proper nouns in Ov., and one Latin pentasyllabic termination in Prop. (increpitarent, 2.26.15); he reports none for Tib.

[150] Nougaret, op. cit.,45.

INTRODUCTION

A long word can be exploited to convey a sense of solemnity and majesty, particularly if it is strengthened by another long word nearby.[151]   Many of the pentasyllabic endings of the De providentia are of this type, e.g., devotae virginitatis, 47; concedunt omnipotenti, 195; praefortibus imperitare, 266; possessorem tantarum deliciarum, 283. But long words can give the impression of haste and rapidity as well;[152] the only certain instance of this effect in the De providentia is the termination excutiamus, 941.

Medieval poets do not appear to employ tetrasyllabic or pentasyllabic endings with any great frequency, but the question is open to further study.[153]

Table 19 indicates the word-sequences most frequently used to close the hexameter by Vergil in the eleventh Aeneid, by Prosper in the De ingratis, and by the poet of the De providentia. The same criteria were used to determine what constitutes a word as in the preparation of Table 18.

Table 19A, derived from Table 19, indicates at a glance the order of preference (1, 2, 3, or 4) in the three works in regard to the four word-sequences which range substantially above 10%.

The pattern 3 - 2 is most frequent in the three works considered; in accordance with a general tendency in Latin poetry, however, the percentage of its use decreases after Vergil.[154] The 3 - 2 combination preserves concord of ictus and accent and avoids caesura, for both the dactylic and the spondaic foot can be formed by a metrical word, e.g., abdidit altos, Aen. 11.810; atria vitae, De ingrat. 687; vinea fallat, De prov. 936. The sequence of two trisyllables holds second place in Aeneid

---

[151]Marouzeau, "Mots longs et mots courts" 37.

[152]Marouzeau, ibid.

[153]Strecker, op. cit.,73. But the medieval poets would occasionally use such endings in paronomasia, just as they would employ monosyllabic terminations for the same purpose. Cf. Norberg, op. cit.,60.

[154]Nougaret, op. cit.,42.

TABLE 19[a]

NUMBER OF SYLLABLES IN VERSE-ENDINGS IN SELECT LATIN POETS

Number of Syllables	Aeneid 11		De ingratis		De providentia	
	Number of Verses	%	Number of Verses	%	Number of Verses	%
3 - 2	260	28.5	213	20.9	193	20.9
4 - 2	177	19.4	134	13.2	145	15.7
5 - 2	17	1.9	27	2.7	33	3.6
1 - 2 - 2	6	.7	26	2.6	18	1.9
2 - 1 - 2	7	.8	11	1.1	16	1.7
3 - 1 - 2	6	.7	8	.8	8	.9
2 - 3	151	16.6	186	18.3	152	16.4
3 - 3	202	22.1	184	18.1	178	19.3
4 - 3	62	6.8	82	8.1	95	10.3
5 - 3	6	.7	12	1.2	8	.9

[a] The table, as indicated above, includes only the more frequent verse-endings in the works considered; percentages indicate per cent of total lines. Huegelmeyer's results for the De ingrat. /op. cit.,38,Table 9/ have been adapted to conform to Cooper's criteria.

TABLE 19A

Pattern	Aeneid 11	De ingratis	De providentia
3 - 2	1	1	1
4 - 2	3	4	4
2 - 3	4	2/3	3
3 - 3	2	2/3	2

11 and in the De providentia, and almost so in the De
ingratis. This sequence produces feminine caesura in the
fifth foot, and therefore a high percentage of two successive trisyllables is to be expected in the three poems
in view of the frequent occurrence of feminine caesura in
this position in the verse.[155] It is clear that Vergil
prefers to conclude a verse with a dissyllable preceded
by a word of three or more syllables, or a trisyllable
preceded by a word of two or more syllables;[156] it is
equally clear that the preferences reflected in both the
De providentia and the De ingratis are distinctly in Vergil's manner.

The classical hexameter ordinarily closed with a
regularly accented word; pronouns, prepositions, conjunctions, interjections, and enclitics in effect, such
as meus or fuit, were generally avoided.[157] The elegiac
poets conclude more than 80% of their hexameter lines with

---

[155]In the De prov., e.g., the percentages of caesura in the last two feet are:

	Masculine		Feminine		Total	
	Number	%	Number	%	Number	%
5th foot	49	5.3	459	49.7	508	55.0
6th foot	22	2.4	. .	. .	22	2.4

[156]Cooper, op. cit., 40-41.

[157]A. G. Harkness, "The Word-Group Accent in Latin Hexameters," Classical Philology 3 (1908) 43, notes that
Catull. 64 shows 402 of 408 hexameter lines closing in

substantives or verbs, and another 2% only with adjectives;[158] Vergil's practice is similar. When a noun in the final position is modified by an adjective, homoioteleuton may occur between the last syllables of noun and adjective if they are in the same declension:

    stare, et conflictum vereamur inire secundum
                    (De prov. 959).

Occasionally homoioteleuton is avoided--and there is no evidence that it was deliberately sought very often--by eliding the final syllable of the adjective which is taken up, as it were, by the final syllable of the noun, which is itself the final syllable of the verse:

    quae mundi rebus divinam absistere curam
                    (De prov. 724).

    Table 20 indicates the various parts of speech of the final words in each verse of the De providentia and the percentages of each:

TABLE 20

PARTS OF SPEECH OF TERMINAL WORDS
IN THE DE PROVIDENTIA

Parts of Speech	Number	Percentage
Nouns	436	47.2
Pronouns[a]	78	8.4
Other Substantives [b]	74	8.0
Adjectives	86	9.3
Verbs[c]	175	19.0
Participles	66	7.2
Adverbs	7	.7
Conjunctions	2	.2

[a]Twelve pronominal adjectives are included here.

[b]These include adjectives and participles which are used as substantives and five gerunds.

[c]Included are all verb forms not otherwise accounted for.

---

noun, verb, or adjective, whereas pentameter lines frequently close with enclitics.

[158]Platnauer, Latin Elegiac Verse 40-48.

The poet of the De providentia shares the preference of the classical poets for terminating a verse with
a noun or a verb, although the "weak" pronominal ending
is better represented than one might expect from the classical norm. The most obvious point of divergence from
the classical poets, however, lies in the comparatively
high percentage of adjectives and also of participles,
many of which are really adjectival in usage. The incidence of conjunctions and adverbs is normal by classical standards. Similarly, Huegelmeyer reports that the
number of terminal pronouns, adjectives, and participles
in the De ingratis is higher than that found in the classical poets.[159]

The increased preference shown in both later poems
for adjectival endings, the decreased percentage of verses
terminating in the 3 - 2 pattern (although they still
constitute the greatest percentage), and the somewhat
greater willingness to use terminal endings of one, four,
or five syllables are the most noticeable characteristics
that distinguish the verse endings of the De providentia
and the De ingratis from those of Vergil, and the two latter variations, at least, have some precedent in earlier
Latin poetry.

11. Alliteration and Assonance: Alliteration,
both initial and internal, occurs frequently in the De
providentia.[160] Initial alliteration appears in a cir-
cumlocution for the prophetic books of the Old Testament:
. . . veneranda volumina vatum (462),
and, with repetition, in a verse stressing man's inability
to renounce sin without the help of grace:
. . . non est quo victus vincere possim (481).
Occasionally two sequences of initial alliteration are
found, as in this description of the sun standing still
in the heavens:
. . . cum lux famulata
nesciret nisi quem faceret victoria finem (678-679).

---

[159]Huegelmeyer, op. cit.,39.

[160]For a concise discussion of alliterative effects with special reference to Verg., cf. Cooper, op.
cit.,31-34. Cf. Huegelmeyer, op. cit.,39, for several
examples in the De ingrat.

Initial and internal alliteration may be combined to good effect; the preponderance of the liquids m and n in the following example is intended to suggest the severity of Adam's condemnation to the earth:

qualis Adam nondum terram damnatus in istam (275). The strong c, l, and t sounds, as well as the gentler s, are employed to good effect in the following brief depiction of Christ's triumph over death:

te vero exstinctae calcantem spicula mortis (535).

Alliteration, along with assonance, performs a subsidiary metrical function in binding verse together.[161] For example, words at the opening or closing of a verse, or in both positions, may have their own alliteration or assonance:

quidquid quocumque est in corpore, sive animatum
(116),

quod vero adversis compugnant condita causis (121), atque aliis alia obsistunt, contraria discors (122), quaero quid hac trepidis mortalibus afferat arte
(700).

12. Rhyme and homoioteleuton: There are many instances of homoioteleuton, or similarity of endings within a verse, in the De providentia, e.g.:

nec summi patris ignari, nec iuris egeni (431), venimus, et fibris gerimus, quae condita libris
(433),

littera praesenti damnaret crimina poena (435), neu vagus effusis sine lege feratur habenis (599). But a more remarkable example extends over two verses:

infirmis fortis, rex servis, dives egenis; iustitia iniustis cedit, sapientia brutis (518-519).

Rhyme in the strict sense, as Herescu points out, involves not only correspondence of terminal syllables, but comprises also correspondence of syllables supporting the metrical ictus, i.e., Herescu would consider fléntes--plorántes as homoioteleuton, but plorántes--lacrimántes

---

[161] Verse is bound together principally by the careful arrangement of concord and conflict in ictus and accent and the skillful placement of caesurae. For further examples of this use of alliteration, with special reference to Prop., cf. B. O. Foster, "On certain euphonic embellishments in the verse of Propertius," Transactions of the American Philological Association 40 (1909) 31-62.

as true rhyme.[162]

There are very few instances of such rhyme in the De providentia, e.g.:

> displicet, ad Scythiae proceres regesque Getarum
> eximius decor est tergis horrere ferarum (143, 145),

or the repetitive verse-endings:

> quae numquam ignara, numquam longinqua, nec ullis
> translata accedens regionibus, absit ab ullis
>   (188-189).

There appear to be no examples at all of rhyme in this sense between successive hexameter verses of the De providentia, other than the repetitive verse-ending cited above. Instances of rhyme within a verse occur, often involving the enclitic -que:

> condidit ut voluit, formas, numerosque, modosque (113),
> barbatos levesque deos, iuvenesque senesque (766).

Considering rhyme in a more general sense as correspondence of terminal endings (e.g., potitos - iniquos, 374-375; verso - periclo, 134-135), and requiring neither perfect correspondence between terminal syllables nor between syllables receiving the metrical ictus, there are forty-eight cases of end-rhyme between successive verses; five of these involve rhyme between three successive verses in each case (143-145, 252-254, 304-306, 754-756, 954-956).[163]

---

[162] N. I. Herescu, La poésie latine: Étude des structures phoniques (Paris, 1960) 136. There are about thirty examples of rhyme of this type in the Aen., e.g., subisset - fuisset, 9.957, 959; orator - ciator, 10.804-805. In all there are some fifty examples in the Aen. if repetitions of the same word are counted. /Herescu, op. cit.,173-174/. Heugelmeyer, op. cit.,39, sets out two examples from the De ingrat.: negare - violare, 179-180; vitescunt - valescunt, 396-397.

[163] It is doubtful whether rhyme was a deliberate feature of classical verse. For an incisive discussion of rhyme with special reference to elegiac verse, cf. Siefert, Meter and Case 39-43. For a discussion of rhyme in medieval poetry cf. Norberg, op. cit.,38-53. For a brief history of rhyme patterns, with special attention to the development of rhyme in medieval verse, cf. R. A. Browne, British Latin (Oxford,1954) xli-l. For information on Leonine rhyme cf. Strecker, op. cit.,73-74, and the numerous references cited there.

13. Repetition and variety:[164] In the De providentia repetition, both of words and of concepts, is not uncommon. In order to avoid any monotonous effect that might ensue, the poet will often use the same word with a variation in metrical ictus, i.e., the word will receive the ictus at one point but not at another:

sic duris caesi flagris, sic igne perusti (55), and:
error enim est eius qui cessit limite recti,
quique potest ad iter, Christo ducente, reverti
(561-562).

If the word is susceptible of inflection, a change in termination may accompany the change in accent:

'solum,' inquit, 'venerare Deum, solique memento'
(604),

or there may be a change from passive to active form in the verb:

est etenim ambarum vinci, est et vincere posse
(233).

In the case of adjectives particularly, a prefix may turn a positive form into a negative one:

aut cursu instabili, stabili aut torpore perirent
(126).

A verb and its cognate noun may be coupled:

proficere, et minui; regnare, et perdere regnum
(234).

The same concept may be expressed in the De providentia by different words, e.g., the sea appears as mare, aequor, or pontus, fire is flamma or ignis, night nox or umbra, and the earth terra, mundus, or tellus.

Apart from such familiar poetic terminology, the principle variations in the poem center around Christian persons and concepts, e.g., Adam is referred to as summum sancti generis . . . caput, 273; Adam, 275, and possessorem tantarum deliciarum, 283; Joseph is Ioseph, 361, but he also appears, according to the particular part of his story being narrated, as castum, 363; vatem, 365, and fratrem, 367. Since it would be a metrical impossibility for the very subject of the poem, providentia, to appear

---

164
For a thorough discussion of repetition with special reference to Verg., cf. Herescu, op. cit.,182f.

as a word in the poem itself, the concept of providence
is generally conveyed by cura or cura Dei, or else by a
periphrasis describing God as operating in a providential
manner:

> haec igitur vis sola potest moderamina rerum
> dividere, et placidis eadem persistere curis
> (185-186).

A particular problem was presented by the necessity to refer to the Deity almost constantly throughout
the De providentia. The difficulty is surmounted in
various ways, e.g., in verses 98-198, the first hundred
successive hexameter lines, God is termed Deus (105, 119,
151, 183), auctor (106, 118), opifex (120), sator ille
(132), factor (155), Dominus (172), omnipotens (195),
magna regens (196), qui condidit, ipse (153), unus (158),
ille (175), and, with reference to his attributes, haec
vis (185) and haec testis rerum (191). Often a further
qualifying phrase will appear:

> de Domino . . . quem semper eumdem
> nil gravat, ex toto nil occupat . . . (172-173)

and:

> . . . qui totus ubique,
> penetrat mundi membra omnia liber et ambit
> (183-184).

14. Miscellaneous metrical devices: Tmesis is
the resolution of a compound word into its original elements with the insertion of an intervening word or words;
for the most part, the classical poets use the device as
nothing more than a metrical convenience.[165] There are
two examples in the De providentia:

> non prius a primi vinclo absolvenda parentis,
> quam maiestate incolumi generatus in ipsa,
> destrueret leti causas et semina Christus
> (300-302);
> occidit ante sua caderet quam noxia culpa (847).

Platnauer considers tmesis in a wider sense as occuring between a substantive and the preposition gavern-
ing it.[166] In this connection the use of the preposition
inter is of some interest. Only three times in eight

---

[165]Cooper, op. cit.,60-61.

[166]Platnauer, Latin Elegiac Verse 97 and n. 1.
Cf. ibid.,97-103.

occurrences in the De providentia does inter completely
avoid tmesis in Platnauer's use of the term (caeca inter
proelia, 241; inter deserta, 412; inter crimina, 492).
A listing of the five remaining cases follows:

    flammas inter et inter aquas (14)
    plaustra inter et arma (57)
    inter hyperboreas . . . pruinas (137)
    externos inter (359)
    multa inter morum delicta (777).

    It seems appropriate that inter, which means "be-
tween," should literally appear between its constituent
elements in three of the five cases set out above, as it
does also at caeca inter proelia, 241.

    Hexameter verses of five or only four words express
a certain gravity or sonority of feeling.[167] There are
two verses of only four words in the De providentia;[168]
one of these is a periphrasis for the name Adam, but at
the same time it conveys more than a hint of the grave
responsibilities that Adam bore:

    qui possessorem tantarum deliciarum (283).

The other (464) aptly describes the Incarnation:

        /Christus/ . . . inque paterna
  maiestate manens, miscetur conditioni
  humanae . . .   (463-465).

    Verses of five words are much more frequent, and
their effects are similar. The two spondaic hexameters
of the De providentia each contain only five words, of
which only four in each case are really significant:

  si cernens operum miracula divinorum (477),
  aversos revocans et suscipiens conversos (947).

    15. Elegiac distich: The first ninety-six verses
of the De providentia consist of elegiac distichs, or
dactylic hexameter verses followed alternately by pentameters, so that there are in all forty-eight pentameters.
This number of verses would not provide sufficient material for an extensive metrical study, but several observations of metrical phenomena can be made.

---

  [167]Cooper, op. cit.,45.

  [168]The De ingrat. contains four such verses (63,
436, 894, 935).

INTRODUCTION

The pentameter must always have a caesura at the mid-point of the verse, and elision at this point is virtually never allowed by the elegiac poets;[169] likewise, there is no elision at this principal caesura in the De providentia. Elision of an initial monosyllable is avoided,[170] and elision of any kind is rare in the second hemistich of the verse; no examples of either type of elision are found in the pentameters of the De providentia, where, in fact, elision occurs in the first hemistich in only eight verses (16.6%).[171]

Table 21 compares the practice of the poet of the De providentia with that of Catullus and the elegiac poets in regard to the use of each of the four verse patterns possible in the first hemistich of the pentameter.

TABLE 21[a]

VERSE PATTERN IN FIRST HEMISTICH OF THE
PENTAMETER IN THE DE PROVIDENTIA

	DD	DS	SD	SS
Catullus	10.4	35.9	16.0	37.7
Tibullus	24.0	58.6	5.2	12.2
Propertius	24.1	43.0	16.5	16.4
Ovid	30.9	52.4	8.3	8.4
De providentia	16.6	33.4	29.2	20.8

[a]The percentages for the elegists are taken from Platnauer, Latin Elegiac Verse 37, and are based on an examination of Ov., A.A. (746 verses) and a similar number of verses from Tib. I and Prop. II. The percentages for Catull. are supplied by Siefert, Meter and Case 92, Table 20.

---

[169]Platnauer, Latin Elegiac Verse 13-14. But 18 cases of elision at this point are reported for Catull. by Harrington, op. cit.,65. Cf. e.g., Catull. 68.10.

[170]Nougaret, op. cit. 57.

[171]De prov. 2 (prodelision), 8, 18, 22, 32, 38, 84.

Granting that the total number of verses involved is small,[172] the poet of the De providentia shows a preference for opening the verse with a spondee (50%, or SD plus SS) that is exceeded only by Catullus (53.7%) and remotely approached by Propertius (32.9%).[173] The percentage for the DS pattern in the De providentia is also close to that of Catullus. The second hemistich invariably follows the DD pattern in all writers of elegiac verse.

The percentages of concord between metrical ictus and primary stress accent in the four feet[174] of the pentameter are as follows: first foot, 58.3% (28 verses); second, 25.0% (12 verses); third, 93.8% (45 verses);[175] fourth 77.1% (37 verses). Table 22 compares the usage of the De providentia with that of selected works of the elegiac poets in regard to concord of ictus and accent in the two hemistichs of the pentameter.

The De providentia appears to be quite normal in the first hemistich, but shows a somewhat smaller percentage of concord in the second hemistich than the elegiac poets and Martial, mainly because of a smaller percentage of concord in the fourth foot.

---

[172] The number of verses in each pattern is: DD 8; DS 16; SD 14; SS 10.

[173] Cf. Wheeler, Catullus and the Traditions of Ancient Poetry 168-169, who views the history of the elegiac distich as involving a struggle to secure dactylic movement, and Ov. as the first Roman to achieve success in this endeavor, while the verses of Catull. are heavy with spondees.

[174] The pentameter is considered here as having four feet, two preceding and two following the principal caesura. The final syllable of each hemistich is not counted as belonging to any metrical foot.

[175] If secondary stress accents were included, there would be two additional verses (48, 84), leaving only one exception (54).

TABLE 22[a]

PERCENTAGE OF CONCORD IN THE PENTAMETER
IN REPRESENTATIVE LATIN POETS

	I - II	III - IV
Catullus	45.3	68.8
Tibullus	41.1	95.7
Propertius	44.4	93.6
Ovid	40.8	99.4
Martial	40.5	95.6
De providentia	41.7[b] ⟨58.3/25.0⟩	85.5 ⟨93.8/77.1⟩

[a]This table is adapted from figures supplied by Sturtevant, "Harmony and Clash of Accent and Ictus" 76.

[b]The bracketed percentages represent the situation in the first and second, and third and fourth feet, respectively.

The most convenient way of increasing the concord in the last two feet of the pentameter is, as Sturtevant noted, to put a dissyllable at the conclusion of the verse.[176] Such a terminal dissyllable resulted in feminine caesura in the fourth foot, and thus ordinarily necessitated a long penultimate syllable at the ictus of that foot, according to the law of penultimate accentuation.[177]

---

[176]Sturtevant, "Harmony and Clash of Accent and Ictus" 80.

[177]The only other possibilities would be the intervention of a monosyllable or an elided ultima, both of which were avoided in this position; concord in the fourth foot, however achieved, regularly resulted in concord in the third. Cf. Sturtevant, ibid.

251

The successors of Catullus elevated the use of the dissyllable from a convenience into the so-called law of the dissyllabic ending, by which the verse was required to terminate in a dissyllabic word of iambic form.[178]

We may agree with Siefert that the pentameter gained a greater measure of concord between ictus and accent through the dissyllabic law;[179] conversely, the dissyllabic law, itself developed as the result of a conscious striving for concord in the second hemistich of the verse.[180]

The percentage of terminal dissyllables in the pentameters of the De providentia is 66.7% (32 verses); of trisyllables, 12.5% (6 verses); of tetrasyllables 16.7% (8 verses); of pentasyllables 4.1% (2 verses). In view of the smaller percentage of concord of ictus and accent reported for the second hemistich of the pentameter in the De providentia in Table 22, above, as compared with the figures for the elegists, it is to be expected that the percentage of dissyllabic endings (66.7%) in the later poem should not approach the 90% and more found in Tibullus and Ovid; it is, however, about the same as the percentage of dissyllabic endings in Propertius I (63.5%) and

---

[178] Neither the Greek elegists nor Catull. appear to have known of this law. Cf. Wheeler, op. cit.,168-169. The verse of Prop. reflects the development of the dissyllabic law. In Book I the proportion of iambic word endings is 63.2%, but by Book IV it has increased to 98.3%, thus approaching closely the 100% of Ov. in Book II of the Fast. Cf. Sturtevant, "Harmony and Clash of Ictus and Accent" 76ff.

[179] Siefert, Meter and Case 66-67.

[180] Cf. Harkness, "Final Monosyllables in Latin Prose and Poetry" 171-172: "The regular ending is the iambic word and the reason for this is that the norm of the verse is harmony of accent and ictus in the fourth and fifth /i.e., third and fourth/ feet and a final syllable without a sentence accent. This form can only be obtained by ending with an iambic word."

considerably higher than that in Catullus (38.4%).[181]

No monosyllabic endings occur in the De providentia.[182] Of the six trisyllabic endings reported in the
poem, four may by another definition be regarded as tetrasyllabic (et cadimus, 16; aut oleis, 30; est vacuas, 32;
et Geticis, 34). Platnauer suggests that the trisyllabic
ending may have been avoided by the elegists in order to
keep the rhythm from becoming anapestic.[183] The two in-
disputable cases of trisyllabic termination in the De providentia result in masculine caesura in the fourth foot
(fert pelagus, 8; suppliciis populi, 54). The eight tetrasyllabic terminations include one dissyllabic preposition
followed by a dissyllable (inter aquas, 14) and one monosyllabic preposition followed by a trisyllable (in querulos,
20); one of the two pentasyllabic endings involves a monosyllabic preposition followed by a tetrasyllable (ab invidia, 40). Terminations of four or more syllables are comparatively rare in the elegists.[184]

Twenty-five (52.7%) of the pentameter verses of
the De providentia conclude with a noun, and six more
(12.5%) with another substantive; twelve (25.0%) terminate with a verb, and only three (6.3%) with an adjective,
and two (3.5%) with a pronominal adjective. The total
percentage of 91.2% of terminations in substantives or
verbs is higher than the more than 80% termination in
these forms reported for the elegists,[185] but the number

---

[181] These percentages are derived from Siefert,
Meter and Case 123, Table 48. The discrepancies between
Siefert's figures and Sturtevant's for the same phenome-
non are insignificant.

[182] Monosyllabic endings in this position are extremely rare among the elegists. In his Table 48, cited
above, Siefert reports only one for Catull., ten for
Prop., six for Ov., and none for Tib.

[183] Platnauer, Latin Elegiac Verse 15-16; he finds
only three in some 10,000 Ovidian pentameters.

[184] Platnauer, ibid.,17, counts 22 tetrasyllables
for Tib., 166 for Prop., 31 for Ov. exclusive of the Her.;
eight pentasyllables for Tib., 21 for Prop., 12 for Ov.

[185] Platnauer, ibid.,40.

of verses involved is too small to make any conclusions.

A kind of metrical repetition occurs when feminine caesura in the second foot of a pentameter is preceded by a dactyl; the two hemistichs of the pentameter are then interchangeable.[186] Although such reversible pentameters are generally avoided by the elegists, there are two in the De providentia (46, 74).

On the other hand, the elegists occasionally engaged in various types of verbal repetition between the pentameter and the preceding hexameter, or even between the pentameter and the following hexameter;[187] no instances are found in the De providentia.

Homoioteleuton occurs at various points in the pentameter in the De providentia:

carpebas duram, non sine fasce, viam (58)
carpere non cessant ulcera dira pium (78)
dumque pios agimus, vertimur in querulos (20)
confusis quoniam non fuit ordo malis (62)

The "bracketing" effect noted by Siefert,[188] in which a pair of words with similar endings in the second hemistich is encompassed by a second pair of words which are themselves similar in ending, and each word in each pair is in grammatical agreement with the other word in its pair (e.g., exitus est studii parva favilla mei,

Ov., Trist. 5.12.62) is not parallelled exactly in the De providentia, but one verse does approach it:

---

[186]Platnauer, ibid.,14-15: "The extreme scarcity of such lines suggests that they were deliberately avoided." He cites the Ovidian verses semibovemque virum semivirumque bovem (A.A. 2.24), and tempora noctis eunt; excute poste seram (Am. 6.1), among others.

[187]Cf. Platnauer, ibid.,33-35.

[188]Siefert, Meter and Case 37.

et <u>proprios</u> habeant <u>tristia</u> <u>corda</u> <u>modos</u> (6).[189]

Conclusion: The evidence amassed thus far clearly
demonstrates the affinity of the <u>De providentia</u> with the
works of the classical poets of the Golden and Silver
Ages of Latin literature in most metrically significant
respects. If Prosper was the author, Manitius' statement
aptly applies: "Ich kenne wenigstens keinen christlichen
Dichter, dessen Prosodie so rein . . . wäre wie Prosper."[190]
At least, the weight of the metrical evidence seems to
confirm a resemblance between the <u>De providentia</u> and the
<u>De ingratis</u> noted by Moricca: ". . . la lingua e la
tecnica del verso del <u>De providentia</u> concordano con quelle
del <u>Carmen de ingratis</u>."[191] But it is one thing to suggest that Prosper, the author of the <u>De ingratis</u>, could
have composed the <u>De providentia</u>, at least from a metrical
standpoint, and quite another to prove that he did in
fact compose both poems. Therefore the question of authorship remains open; surely the schools of Gaul could have
produced others steeped in the metrical traditions of the
classical poets as Prosper was.

---

[189] For further discussion of rhyming effects in
the elegiac distich, with special reference to the pentameter line, cf. Platnauer, <u>Latin Elegiac</u> Verse 49 (internal rhyme only); Siefert, <u>Meter and Case</u> 21, 37-38 (with
special attention to the second hemistich of the pentameter); and B. O. Foster, "On certain euphonic embellishments in the verse of Propertius," <u>Transactions of the
American Philological</u> Association 40 (1909) 31-62.

[190] Manitius, <u>Geschichte</u> 202.

[191] Moricca, <u>Storia</u> 3.1.41-42.

TEXT AND TRANSLATION

SIGLA

Manuscript

Maz.   Codex Mazarinensis 3896, fol. 162-167^V <u>circa</u> 1535

Editions

Editor	Place	Date
L S. Gryphius	Lyons	1539
B Maurists	Paris	1711
M Migne	Paris	1846

<u>Abbreviations</u> <u>used</u> <u>in</u> <u>Apparatus</u>

<u>in</u> marg.   in margine

<u>om</u>.   omittit, omittunt

CARMEN DE PROVIDENTIA DEI

Maxima pars lapsis abiit iam mensibus anni,
    quo scripta est versu pagina nulla tuo.
quae tam longa tibi peperere silentia causae?
    quisve dolor maestum comprimit ingenium?
quamquam et iam gravibus non absint carmina curis,   5
    et proprios habeant tristia corda modos;
ac si te fracti perstringunt vulnera mundi,
    turbatumque una si rate fert pelagus,
invictum deceat studiis servare vigorem.
    cur mansura pavent, si ruitura cadunt?   10
o felix cui tanta Deo tribuente facultas
    contigit, ut tali tempore liber agat!
quem non concutiat vicina strage ruina,
    intrepidum flammas inter et inter aquas.
nos autem tanta sub tempestate malorum   15
    invalidi passim caedimur et cadimus.
cumque animum patriae subiit fumantis imago,
    et stetit ante oculos quidquid ubique perit,
frangimur, immodicis et fletibus ora rigamus;
    dumque pios agimus, vertimur in querulos.   20
nec parcunt quidam turbatam incessere mentem,
    linguarum et iaculis saucia corda petunt.
'dic,' aiunt, 'causas, qui rerum hominumque labores
    arbitrio credis stare regique Dei,
quo scelere admisso, pariter periere tot urbes?   25
    tot loca, tot populi, quid meruere mali?
si totus Gallos sese effudisset in agros
    oceanus, vastis plus superesset aquis,
quod sane desunt pecudes, quod semina frugum,
    quodque locus non est vitibus aut oleis,   30
quod fundorum aedes vis abstulit ignis et imbris,
    quarum stare aliquas tristius est vacuas.
si toleranda mali labes, heu! caede decenni
    Vandalicis gladiis sternimur et Geticis.
non castella petris, non oppida montibus altis   35
    imposita, aut urbes amnibus aequoreis,
barbarici superare dolos atque arma furoris
    evaluere omnes, ultima pertulimus.
nec querar exstinctam nullo discrimine plebem,
    mors quoque primorum cesset ab invidia,   40
maiores anni ne forte et nequior aetas
    offenso tulerint quae meruere Deo;

5 et iam⌐ etiam <u>uncis</u> <u>includunt</u> B M

ON THE PROVIDENCE OF GOD

With the now declining months the greater part of a
year has passed and during it not a page has been written
in your verse. What has caused you to be silent so long?
What heavy sorrow crushes your talent? But let us not be
without poems even now in our grevous cares; let our sad   5
hearts find their proper expression. Even if the wounds
of a broken world numb you and the troubled sea bears you
on a single bark, still you must keep your strength unim-
paired for your studies.

Why do enduring things tremble with fear if perishable
ones fall? O happy the man who has received such power   10
through God's gift that he can act with free spirit in
such a time! He is not shaken by the ruin around him, but
stands fearless amid the flames and flood.

But we are cut down everywhere under such a storm of
evils and in our weakness we fall. When the image of our   15
smoking fatherland has passed before our mind, and universal destruction stands before our eyes, we are broken and
the tears water our cheeks without restraint. And while
we encourage the faithful, we are confronted by complainers.   20

Some do not hesitate to reproach our troubled spirits
as they attack our wounded hearts with the arrows of their
tongues. "You believe that the works of men and the operations of the universe exist and are governed by the will
of God. Why have so many cities perished together without
being guilty of any crime? Why have so many places, so   25
many peoples deserved such evil?

"If the entire ocean had poured over the fields of
Gaul, more would have survived the vast waters. For the
flocks are gone, the seeds of the fruits are gone, and
there is no place for vines or olive trees; destructive   30
fire and rain have even taken away the buildings on the
farms, while it is still more saddening that some of them
stand empty.

"If we must endure the blows of misfortune, alas! for
ten years we have been cut down by the slaughtering swords
of the Vandals and of the Goths! No forts set on rocks,
no towns on lofty mountains, or cities protected by mighty 35
rivers, not all together have been able to overcome the
wiles of the barbarians and their raging weapons--we have
suffered the ultimate calamity.

"I would not complain that the people were indiscri-
minately destroyed; even the death of leading citizens
would not arouse my wrath. Perhaps men of more ad-   40
vanced years, whose wickedness was greater, have suffered what they deserved from an offended God, but

261

quid pueri insontes, quid commisere puellae,
    nulla quibus dederat crimina vita brevis?
quare templa Dei licuit popularier igni?   45
    cur violata sacri vasa ministerii?
non honor innuptas devotae virginitatis,
    nec texit viduas religionis amor.
ipsi desertis qui vitam ducere in antris
    suerant, laudantes nocte dieque Deum,   50
non aliam subiere necem, quam quisque profanus;
    idem turbo bonos sustulit atque malos.
nulla sacerdotes reverentia nominis almi
    discrevit miseri suppliciis populi;
sic duris caesi flagris, sic igne perusti,   55
    inclusae vinclis sic gemuere manus.
tu quoque pulvereus plaustra inter et arma Getarum
    carpebas duram, non sine fasce, viam,
cum sacer ille senex plebem, usta pulsus ab urbe,
    ceu pastor laceras duceret exsul oves.   60
verum haec belli sileantur turbine gesta,
    confusis quoniam non fuit ordo malis.
forte etenim placidas res mundi, et tempora pacis,
    arbitra dignetur cernere cura Dei.
si cunctos annos veterum recolamus avorum,   65
    et quidquid potuit nostra videre dies,
maximus iniustis locus invenietur in orbe,
    oppressis autem pars prope nulla bonis.
qui fuerit violentus, atrox, versutus, avarus,
    cuius corde fides cesserit, ore pudor,   70
hunc omnes mirantur, amant, reverentur, honorant,
    huic summi fasces, huic tribuuntur opes.
quod si quis iustus castam et sine crimine vitam
    dissimili studio ducere maluerit,
hic inhonorus, inops, odium iuvenumque senumque,   75
    in totis mundi partibus exsul agit.
impius exsultat maturis integer annis,
    carpere non cessant ulcera dira pium.
falsa valent in iudiciis, et vera laborant,
    insontes sequitur poena, salusque reos.   80
ignorata piis illudit adultera sacris,
    blasphemus templi limina tutus adit.
quae si cura Dei celsa spectaret ab arce,
    resque ageret nostras sub dicione sua,
aut non effugerent ultrices crimina poenas,   85
    aut virtus terris sola reperta foret!'

what crime did innocent boys and girls commit, when their
short life span had given them no time or occasion for
sin? Why were the temples of God allowed to be devastated
by fire? Why were the vessels of his holy ministry vio- 45
lated? The honor of their dedicated virginity did not
shield maidens nor did their zeal for religion protect
widows. Even those who were accustomed to spend their
lives in desert caves, praising God by night and day, suf
fered the same death as their worldly fellows. The same 50
tempest destroyed both the good and the wicked. Priests
were not spared the torments of their wretched flocks out
of reverence for the Sacred Name. They too were lashed
with rough scourges, they were burned with fire, and they
groaned with heavily fettered hands. 55

"And you yourself, all covered with dust and carrying your pack, traveled the cruel road amid the wagons
and arms of the Goths, when the aged and holy bishop was
driven from his burning city and led forth his wounded
flock, himself a shepherd in exile. But let us pass 60
over all this in silence in the face of the tempest of
war, since there was no order in such a compounding of
evils.

"Perhaps God in his providential judgment may deign
to decree tranquillity and peace for the world. If we
recall all the years of our ancient forefathers, and all 65
the events we have been able to witness in our own times,
we will find that the unjust have the highest rank on
earth, and that the good have almost nothing, for they
have been overwhelmed. The violent, cruel, crafty and
greedy man, from whose heart faith has departed, and modesty from his countenance--all admire him, all love him, 70
all revere him, all honor him; the highest office is
given to him and riches are bestowed upon him. But if
any just man has chosen with a different kind of zeal to
lead a life pure and without reproach, he is unhonored,
without riches, the scorn of young and old, and spends 75
his life as an exile in all parts of the earth.

"The wicked man enjoys vigorous health, although old
in years, while cruel diseases continually attack the
pious one. Falsehood prevails in judgments and truth is
oppressed; punishment awaits the innocent, and deliverance the guilty. The secret adulteress ridicules sacred 80
things; the blasphemer approaches in safety the thresh-
old of the temple. But if God in his providence observed such happenings from heaven's lofty heights, and
conducted our affairs under his sovereign power, either
crimes would not escape avenging punishments, or virtue 85
alone would have been found on earth."

263

talia cum facilis vulgi spargantur in aures,
  quam multis rudibus lingua maligna nocet!
nec tantus dolor est Scythicis consumier armis,
  quantus ab infidis cordibus ista seri.   90
prome igitur sanctis caelestia tela pharetris,
  et medicis hostem confice vulneribus!
forte aliqui poterunt errorum evadere noctem,
  inque viam, visa luce, referre pedem.
at ne sermo moram patiatur ab impare versu,   95
  heroi numeris porrige pentametrum.
    Ista quidem melius divinis edita libris
cognoscenda forent, ubi legis in aequore aperto
promptum esset ventis dare libera vela secundis.
sed quoniam rudibus metus est intrare profundum,   100
in tenui primum discant procurrere rivo,
qua iacet extremo tellus circumdata ponto,
et qua gens hominum diffusa est corpore mundi.
seu nostros annos, seu tempora prisca revolvas,
esse omnes sensere Deum, nec defuit ulli   105
auctorem natura docens; et si impius error
amisit, multis tribuens quod debuit uni,
innatum est cunctis genitorem agnoscere verum.
hic auctore carens, et tempore, permanet idem
semper, et immensum nec saecula nec loca claudunt.   110
hic nullis mundi causis exstantibus, in se
quidquid vellet habens, cum visum est, omnia solus
condidit ut voluit, formas, numerosque, modosque,
et genera, et vitas statuens et semina rebus.
quidquid inest caelo, quidquid terraeque marique,   115
quidquid quocumque est in corpore, sive animatum,
sive expers animae, calida, humida, frigida, sicca,
uno exstant auctore Deo, qui divite Verbo,
quod Deus est, rerum naturas atque elementa
protulit, et summis opifex intentus et imis.   120
quod vero adversis compugnant condita causis,
atque aliis alia obsistunt, contraria discors
omnia motus alit; dumque illi occurritur illo,
vitalem capiunt cuncta exagitata vigorem;
quae vel pigra situ, vel prono lubrica lapsu,   125
aut cursu instabili, stabili aut torpore perirent.
mollia sic duris, sic raris densa resistunt,
et liquidis solida, et tardis velocia, claro

    95 at⁊ ac L   105-520 exhibet Maz. 110 nec⁊ non B M
121-146 usque ad munere Christi om. Maz.

When such thoughts are poured into the receptive
ears of the crowd, what multitudes of the unlearned are
harmed by an evil tongue! And it is not so great a trial
to be destroyed by Scythian arms, as it is to have these
ideas spread by those who are lacking in faith. Bring   90
forth celestial arrows from their holy quivers, and destroy the enemy with healing wounds! Perhaps some will be
able to escape the darkness of their errors and to return
to the right path once they have seen the light.

But do not let my discussion be delayed by unequal
verse; extend the pentameter to epic meters!   95

What is related in Sacred Scripture would have been
better understood in the open sea of the Law, where it
would be easy to spread free sail under favoring winds.
But because the unlearned are afraid to enter upon the
deep, let them first learn to proceed in a shallow stream,100
where the land lies surrounded by the farthest extremities
of the sea, and the race of men is scattered over the
body of the earth.

Whether you consider our own age, or olden times,
all men have felt that there is a God, and nature did not
fail anyone in teaching them her Author. And if wicked   105
error caused the knowledge of him to be lost, by assigning to many what it owed to one, still it is innate in
all men to acknowledge their true Creator. He, being without author and without time, ever remains the same, and
neither time nor place confines his immensity.   110
There were no other causes of the world's existence, and
he alone, having in himself whatever he desired, created
all things as he willed when it seemed good, and assigned
to them their forms and numbers and measures and kinds,
and their lives and their origins.

Whatever exists in the heavens, or on land or sea,   115
whatever exists in any body, whether it be animate or inanimate, the hot, the moist, the cold, the dry, all exist
with God as their one Author, who by his abundant Word,
which is God, produced the natures of things and the elements, a Creator equally attentive both to the highest
and the lowest.   120

But while created things do battle with opposing
causes and some are in conflict with others, a disharmon-
ious motion sustains all contraries, and while there is
opposition of one to another, all receive their vital
strength through motion. And if they remained sluggishly
in their place, or were slippery in their headlong fall,   125
they would perish either through their unstable course or
through their stationary inactivity. So the soft resist
the hard, and the dense the rarefied; and solid is opposed
to liquid, and swift to slow, and the obscure to the clear,

obscurum obiectum, et dulci contendit amarum.
nec mihi fas dixisse aliquid non rite creatum,   130
aut ullas ausim mundi reprehendere partes,
cum sator ille operum teneat momenta suorum,
et carptim varios in totum temperet usus.
denique quidquid obest, aut causa aut tempore verso,
prodest; et gemino subsistunt cuncta periclo.   135
frigora perpessus, solem cupit; ustus ab aestu,
inter hyperboreas mavult algere pruinas.
iniusto pluviam metuit sub fasce viator,
quam poscit votis sitienti rusticus agro.
caeruleos angues timor isti est visere, at illi   140
intrepida excoctis oneratur mensa chelydris.
quod si forte lupos, lyncasque, ursosque creatos
displicet, ad Scythiae proceres regesque Getarum
respice, queis ostro contempto, et vellere Serum,
eximius decor est tergis horrere ferarum.   145
singula sectari longum est; sed munere Christi
scire datum, quod alit tellus, quod in aequore vivit,
quidquid in arboribus, quidquid variatur in herbis,
in laudem auctoris, certis subsistere causis.
at quae sola nocent, eadem collata mederi.   150
   Est igitur Deus, et bonus est, et quidquid ab illo
effectum est, culpa penitus vacat, atque querela.
omnem autem hanc molem mundi qui condidit, ipse
et regit; utque nihil non ortum sumpsit ab illo,
sic nihil est quod stare queat, factore remoto.   155
nam qui pigra Deo dant otia, credo, verentur
ne curae intentum vigiles durique labores
conficiant, et tanta simul non explicet unus.
o mersi in tenebras, divinique ignis inanes,
et plus corporeis oculis quam mente videntes!   160
qui vestrae aeternum naturae et conditioni
audetis conferre Deum! cui si quid amatis
in laudem pravi adicitis, vestrisque beatum
creditis esse bonis, aut ulla incommoda ferre.
an quia cum magnas urbes populosque tenetis   165
sub vestro imperio, miserum est insomnibus aegram
partiri curis in multa negotia mentem;
cumque graves trepidis incumbant undique causae,

   131 reprendere L 144 et om. B M 154 ortum⁊
horum uncis includunt B M, ad hunc versum in marg.
ponunt Maz. L 156-174 om. Maz.

and bitter is in contention with sweet.

And I have no right to say that something has not been created properly, nor would I presume to find fault 130 with any parts of the world, since the Creator maintains the movements of his works and controls separately their various employments for the good of the whole. Accordingly, whatever is harmful becomes beneficial either by change of time or circumstance, and all things subsist under a double tension. The man who has endured the cold, desires135 the sun; the man who has been scorched by the heat, prefers to be cold amid the northern frosts. The wayfarer beneath his cruel burden fears the rain which the farmer seeks with prayers for his thirsting field. One man is afraid to look upon dark serpents, while the fearless 140 table of another groans under the weight of roasted reptiles. But if we are displeased that wolves and lynxes and bears have been created, look at the chiefs of Scythia and kings of the Goths, who scorn the purple and the Seric fleece, and consider it a special glory to bristle 145 in the skins of wild beasts.

To pursue these matters one by one would be tedious, but by the gift of Christ it has been granted us to know that the produce which the soil nurtures, the creatures that live in the sea, all the different trees and grasses, exist for definite causes and give glory to their Author. Yet those things which by themselves cause harm, when joined together constitute remedies. 150

Therefore God exists, and he is good, and whatever has been made by him is wholly free of fault and of cause for complaint. Moreover, he not only established all this mass of the world, but also governs it, and just as there is nothing that has not received its origin from him, so there is nothing that could remain if the Creator were removed. For those who attribute to God a sluggish ease 155 are afraid, I suppose, that watchful cares and hard exertions may cause him to grow weary in his attentiveness, and that the one could not control and resolve so many difficulties at the same time.

O you that are sunk in darkness and empty of the divine fire, and see with the eyes of the body more than with the soul! You who presume to compare the everlast- 160 ing God to your own nature and condition! Whatever you yourselves love you perversely credit to him, and you believe either that he is wealthy in your kind of goods or else that he suffers discomforts.

When you hold mighty cities and great peoples under165 your dominion, it is difficult to direct your mind to many different tasks, for it is sleepless and stricken with cares. And when fearful men are beset by heavy problems

267

non fert urgentes industria victa labores;
et si animis aegris depulsa est sollicitudo,   170
blanda voluptatem requies creat otia nactis;
de Domino hoc sentire pium est, quem semper eumdem
nil gravat, ex toto nil occupat? effluit aetas
ac venit, et spectant genita et gignentia finem;
ille manet, simul acta tenens et agenda, futuris   175
ulterior, tum praeteritis prior, omnibus unus
praesens, et solus, sine tempore tempora condens.
utque aevi spatia ac numeros praecedit et exit,
sic nullo immensus cohibetur fine locorum.
nilque adeo est magnum, quod non certus modus arcet;   180
et caelum, et terras, et totum denique mundum
limes habet; meta est altis, et meta profundis.
sed nusquam non esse Dei est, qui totus ubique,
et penetrat mundi membra omnia liber et ambit.
haec igitur vis sola potest moderamina rerum   185
dividere, et placidis eadem persistere curis,
quam non effugiant cita, nec remorantia tardent;
quae numquam ignara, numquam longinqua, nec ullis
translata accedens regionibus, absit ab ullis,
nec de noscendis egeat manifesta doceri.   190
haec testis rerum tacita audiat, abdita cernat,
det vitas, adimatque datas, pereuntia salvet,
deiecta attollat, premat ardua, proroget annos
et minuat, mutet corda, et peccata remittat.
        Sed qui virtutem concedunt Omnipotenti,   195
forte voluntatem demant; et magna regentem,
curam hominis renuisse putent, in tempora nati
exigua, et varia sub tempestate relicti.
quo vos sponte iuvat cadere, oblitosque parentis,
in pecudum genus et sortem transire ferarum?   200
incomperta latent naturae exordia nostrae,
aut spem propositam in Christo praesentia turbant?
parcite sublimes aeternae gentis honores
degeneri violare metu, potiusque relictum
immortale decus superato apprendite caelo.   205
nota via est, Christo cunctis reserante magistro,
qui vocat, et secum nos deducturus, et in se.

        190 de noscendis _7 dignoscendis Maz. L
191-211 om. Maz.

on every side, their energy is overwhelmed and they cannot bear the pressing tasks; but if anxiety is cast from
their troubled spirits, the soothing quiet gives them   170
pleasure, once they have obtained a respite. Is it right,
therefore, to think that this is true of the Lord, who is
ever the same, whom nothing burdens, whom nothing wholly
occupies?

Ages come and go, and things begotten and those be-
getting them look toward their end. But he remains, at
once maintaining and controlling what has been done and
what is to be done, ulterior to what is to come as he is 175
prior to what has passed; One present to all, and he alone,
without time, the Creator of time.

And as he precedes and goes beyond the spaces and
numbers of time, so in his immensity he is confined by no
boundaries of place. And nothing that is confined within
an uncertain limit is so mighty. Both sky and lands and 180
indeed the whole world have their boundaries; there is a
limit to the heights and a limit to the depths. But nowhere is there question of God's non-existence; he, being
everywhere in his entirety, both freely penetrates and
encompasses all the parts of the universe.

Therefore only such a power as his can distribute
the government of the world, and this power alone can re- 185
main serene in its concerns. Swiftness does not escape
it and delay does not retard it, never is it without knowledge, never is it distant, and in passing from one region
to another it is not absent from any region; and since it
has full knowledge, it does not need instruction on whatever is to be known. Such a witness of events hears what 190
is silent and perceives what is hidden, grants life and
takes the life that it has given, saves what is perishing,
lifts up what has been cast down, casts down what is elevated, prolongs years and shortens them, changes hearts,
and remits sins.

But those who concede the power to the Omnipotent, 195
perhaps would take from him the will, and imagine that
since he rules the entire universe he had renounced his
providence over man, who is born for a short time and left
to suffer various misfortunes.

Why do you delight to fall by your own choice and,
in forgetfulness of your Father, to pass into the race and
condition of savage brutes? Do the origins of our nature 200
lie hidden and undiscovered, or do present circumstances
disturb the hope set before you in Christ? Refuse to violate the lofty honors of an everlasting race with an ig-
noble fear, but rather surmount the heavens and lay hold
of the immortal glory that awaits you. The way is known, 205
for Christ our Master opens it to all; he summons us, and
he will lead us with himself and to himself.

ac ne vaniloqui spondere incerta putemur,
res monet a primis aperire parentibus ortum
humani generis, causasque evolvere vitae 210
amissae, et rursus, Christo donante, receptae.
dispositis rebus, totum iam conditor orbem
fecerat, et pulchra vernabat origine mundus.
iam sol dimensis in tempora cursibus ibat,
lunaque cum stellis praebebat lumina nocti; 215
iam pecudes tellus, iam pisces pontus alebat,
et liquidum volucres innabant aera pennis.
sed quod divina posset ratione potiri,
nondum erat in terris animal; dedit optimus auctor
hoc homini speciale decus, cumque omnia verbo 220
conderet, hunc manibus, quo plus genitoris haberet,
dignatur formare suis; substantia duplex
iungitur, inque unam coeunt contraria vitam.
namque anima ex nullis, ut cetera, gignitur, expers
interitus, nisi quod Domino cruciabilis uni est, 225
et rea ferre potest poenam, sub nomine mortis;
terrenamque illapsa domum, dat vivere secum
consortem, et pariter divinum haurire vaporem.
nec quia dissimilis rerum natura duarum est,
dispar conditio est; manet exitus unus utrumque, 230
seu potior iuri subdatur posterioris,
seu se maioris virtuti infirmior aequet.
est etenim ambarum vinci, est et vincere posse;
proficere, et minui; regnare, et perdere regnum;
non quia plus cuiquam, minus aut in origine causae 235
nascendi attulerint, aut ulla externa creatos
vis premat, ignarosque agat in discrimina morum;
sed quia liber homo, et sapiens, discernere rectis
prava potest, in se intus habens discrimina rerum,
iusque voluntatis, quo temperat arbitrium mens, 240
si tamen ancipitis caeca inter proelia vitae
non de se tumeat, sed votis tuta modestis,
inde putet totum posse, unde accepit et esse.

237 promat B M

And so that we may not be considered idle prattlers
who promise uncertainties, the importance of this matter
suggests that we recount the origin of the human race from
our first parents, and unfold the reasons for our loss of
everlasting life and for its recovery anew by the gift of 210
Christ.

The Creator had already made the whole universe and
disposed its elements, and the world enjoyed a springtime
in its fair origin. Already the sun was proceeding, its
courses measured out into times, and the moon together
with the stars furnished light to the darkness. Already 215
the land sustained its beasts, and the sea its fishes, and
flying creatures sailed with wings upon the limpid air.

But there was not yet on the earth an animal that
could receive the divine gift of reason. This particular
glory the most excellent Creator gave to man, and although
God established all things by his word, he designed to   220
fashion man with his own hands, that man might have a
greater claim to him as a Father. A two-fold substance
was united, and contraries came together to form a single
life. For the soul is not begotten from anything, as
are all other things, and it is free from destruction,
except that it may suffer torment from the Lord alone,
and, like a criminal, can bear punishment under the title 225
of death. And after it has penetrated into its earthly
home, the Creator allows it to live as a partaker with
himself and to breathe the heavenly air in the same manner. Nor, because the nature of the two elements is
different, is their condition dissimilar; one end awaits
each, whether the strong be subjected to the law of the   230
inferior, or the weaker make itself equal to the strength
of the greater. For it is characteristic of both to be
overcome and to be able to overcome, to advance and to
be diminished, to reign and to lose the sovereignty.

This is not because reasons of birth have been of
greater or lesser help to anyone in his beginnings, or
because any external force exercises its pressure on created men and forces them in their ignorance into different
ways of life, but because man, being free and endowed
with wisdom, can distinguish between right and wrong.
For he possesses deep within himself the ability to dif-
ferentiate among things and the right of choice, by which
the mind regulates its judgment. Yet if amid the dark   240
and uncertain battles of life the mind would not be swol-
len with pride in itself, but would be protected by
moderate aspirations, let it consider that it has all its
power from that Source from whom it has received also its
being.

271

insita sic nobis patriae virtutis imago est,
longo iustitiae quae multum exercita cultu,   245
ceu speculo lumen divinum imitata referret.
cumque bonis positum transisset in artibus aevum,
aeternam victrix arcem mansura teneret.
totaque res effecta Dei, iam nulla subiret
proelia, nec trepide secum decerneret in se,   250
nec vellet quod mox nollet, voluisse, timere,
ignorare, optare, pati iam nescia, nullis
crescere egens cumulis, nullisque obnoxia damnis.
et quo promissis adsit fiducia magnis,
ac spes propositae sit non incerta coronae,   255
munere praesentis vitae documenta futurae
sumit homo, et dandis confidere discit adeptis.
huic caeli volucres, et cuncta animalia terrae
subiecta, et pisces quos nutrit pontus et amnes;
huic solis lunaeque vices, et sidera noctis   260
nosse datum, numerisque dies comprendere et annos,
scire potestates herbarum, et nomina rebus
indere, et ingenium varias augere per artes;
hunc potiorem unum cunctis spirantibus, uni
subiectum servire Deo; nec corporea vi,   265
sed rationis ope, praefortibus imperitare.
        Quod si quis non totus homo haec extendere verbis
me putat, et nondum sese cognovit in istis,
audiat a primis distare parentibus actum
per delicta genus, multa et rubigine morum   270
corrupti exiguum semen superesse vigoris.
utque suae tantum naturae discat honorem,
in summum sancti generis redeat caput, et se
aestimet a manibus Domini afflatuque regente,
qualis Adam, nondum terram damnatus in istam,   275
et liber culpae, paradisi divitis orbem
cultarum locuples virtutum fruge tenebat.
cui cum tanta Deus largitus dona fuisset,
viperei populi princeps invidit, et alta
deiectus regione poli - quia summa tenere   280
non nisi pura potest bonitas - maiora nocendi
concepit verso mutatus corde venena.
qui possessorem tantarum deliciarum

253 que om. Maz.   264 hunc 7 huic Maz.

267-277 om. Maz.

Thus the image of our Father's virtue is implanted
in us, and given much training through a long devotion to
justice, it would have imitated and reflected the divine   245
light as in a mirror. And when a life spent in upright
activities had passed, virtue would remain victorious in
possession of an eternal citadel. And the entire work of
God, once it had been accomplished, would then suffer no
conflicts, nor would it contend fearfully with itself
against itself, nor would it wish what it would soon re-   250
gret having chosen, for then it did not know the meaning
of fear or ignorance or desire or suffering, but lacked
nothing to increase in its growth and was not subject to
any loss.

And so that man might have trust in these great promises, and his hope for the crown set before him might not
be unsure, in the gift of present life he received proofs   255
of future life, and learned to believe in gifts to come
by those that he had already obtained. The birds of the
sky were made subject to him, and all the animals of the
earth, and the fishes that were sustained by the sea and
the rivers. He was allowed to know the alternations of
the sun and of the moon, and the constellations of the
night, and to number the days and the years, to know the   260
virtues of herbs, and to give names to things, and to increase his abilities through various pursuits. For he
alone was more powerful than all living things, but was
bound as a subject to serve God only, and allowed to rule
the very strong, not by bodily force but through the   265
power of reason.

But if anyone is so dull that he thinks that I am
exaggerating these things, and does not yet recognize himself in what I have said, let him listen and learn that
our race has been driven far from its first parents under
the pressure of its sins, and that after much corrosion
in its character only a poor seed of adulterated strength   270
is left. And for him to learn the great honor of his own
nature, let him return to the earliest origins of a holy
people, and consider himself as coming from the hands of
the Lord and from his ruling breath. Such was Adam, not
yet condemned to this earth, and free from sin, when he   275
still possessed the world of a splendid paradise and was
rich in the fruit of the virtues he had cultivated.

And since God had bestowed such gifts upon Adam, the
prince of the serpent throng envied him. For Satan had
been cast down from the lofty realms of heaven, because
only pure goodness can possess its heights, and after his   280
transformation he nursed strong and injurious poisons in
his heart. And because he knew that man, the possessor

273

mandato exclusum quia noverat arbore ab una,
perpulit a vetitis pomum decerpere ramis,   285
queis inerat recti et pravi experientia maior
tunc dicione hominis, quia nondum acceperat hanc vim,
qua posset vitanda suo sine nosse periclo.
his illata dolis, hoc crimine nata subegit
mors hominem, culpa in cunctos manante minores;   290
quae semel antiqua pulsos virtutis ab arce,
non uno tantum transfuso errore parentum
implicuit, sed cum populis nascentibus aucta,
multiplicem lata porrexit strage ruinam.
at quamquam immissa regnaret morte peremptor,   295
nulla tamen placitos Domino non edidit aetas,
cunctaque diversos habuerunt saecula iustos,
quos licet ob meritum vitae bona multa manerent,
in mortem vitiata tamen natura trahebat,
non prius a primi vinclo absolvenda parentis,   300
quam maiestate incolumi generatus in ipsa,
destrueret leti causas et semina Christus,
cuius perpetuam cunctis assistere curam
promptum est exemplis ab origine nosse petitis.
non latet hanc sanctis onerans altaria sacris   305
iustus Abel, qui primitiis ovium grege lectis,
convertit Domini sincera in munera vultum.
nec fallit specie devota religionis
dona Cain reprobanda dicans, cui virus amarum
invidia in fratrem successo felle coquebat.   310
nec revocare ferum Dominus sermone benigno
abstinuit: quantumque nefas strueretur ab ipso
ingessit, formamque dedit qua vincere sese
posset, et insanae regnaret fortior irae.
sed concepta semel facinus crudele peregit   315
impietas, scelere immergens primordia mundi.
at numquid placitum sibi iustum a caede nefanda
non potuit servare Deus? sed finis acerbi
occasum potior vita et tribuenda corona
immodico aeterni superabant pondere honoris.   320
quid, cum viventem de terris transtulit Enoch,
spernebat terrena Deus? namque omnibus illud
proderat exemplum, quo mortis terror abiret,
spemque inconcussam caperet substantia carnis.

295 peremptor proponit Valentin; peremptos Maz. L B M

316 immergens/ immenso Maz. L

of these great delights, had been excluded by command
from one tree, he drove him to pluck a fruit from its forbidden branches, in which there was a greater knowledge   285
of good and evil than was then under man's control. For
man had not yet received the power or ability to know
evils without endangering himself.

Introduced by such deceits, and born of this crime,
death subjugated man, and the fault spread to all his
descendants. And once men were driven from the ancient   290
citadel of virtue, death held them in her grip, not sole-
ly by the transmission of the one sin of their first
parents, but also because she increased with the birth of
multitudes and spread her manifold destruction and
slaughter everywhere.

But although the destroyer now reigned over men with
the introduction of death, no age failed to produce those 295
that were pleasing to the Lord, and all generations had
their various just persons. And although many blessings
awaited them by reason of the merit of their lives, their
tainted nature still brought them to death, for that nature would not be freed from the bonds of our first parent
until Christ, begotten in it without impairment to his   300
majesty, would destroy the causes and the seeds of death.

But through examples derived from man's origins we
can readily understand that God's providence is present
to aid all men, always and everywhere. Just Abel, who
made the altars groan with holy offerings, did not escape
this care, for he chose from his flock the first fruits   305
of the sheep and turned the countenance of the Lord to
his pure gifts. And Cain, who offered gifts that were to
be rejected, did not succeed in his deceit under pious
pretext of religion. Then his animosity was aroused and
out of envy toward his brother he prepared for him a bitter potion. And the Lord attempted to restrain fierce   310
Cain with kindly speech, showed him the magnitude of the
sin that he was contriving, and gave him the precept by
which he could overcome himself and govern his mad wrath
with greater strength. But impiety, once conceived, accomplished the cruel misdeed and immersed in crime the   315
beginnings of the world. Was God unable to preserve from
heinous slaughter a just man who was pleasing to him?
But the crown and better life that were to be granted sur-
passed the calamity of a harsh death in the incomparable
weight of everlasting glory.   320

And when God transported Henoch from the earth alive,
did he show contempt for earthly things? For that was
surely a beneficial precedent for all men so that by it
the dread of death might depart and the substance of flesh

sic alio post multa aevo documenta minores 325
propositae in Christo meruerunt sumere vitae,
cum raptum ignitis per inane iugalibus Helim
scandentem rutilo viderunt aethera curru.
an aberat tum cura Dei, cum effusa per omnes
gens hominum culpas, penitus pietate relicta, 330
dira toris vetitis generaret monstra gigantas?
illa quidem mundi exitium praefata futurum,
tempora larga dedit, queis in meliora reducti
mortales scelerum seriem virtute piarent.
cumque nefas placitum toto persisteret orbe, 335
nec nisi diluvio deleri crimina possent,
sola Noe servata domus, quae libera cladis -
conclusis paribus spirantum de genere omni,
unde forent vacuis reparanda animalia terris -
illaesa, mundo pereunte, superfuit arca; 340
non quia non alios populos Deus edere posset,
sed multis fractus morbis, ut semine ab ipso
idem homo in Christi corpus nascendo veniret,
utque Deo iusto meritorum iudice, partam
nossemus requiem sanctis in clade malorum. 345
nonne etiam in nostram Domini iam tum miserentis
progeniem tendebat amor, cum credulus Abram,
multorum, pariente fide, genitor populorum,
promissum genus innumeris censebat in astris?
aut cum in Pentapolim descenderet igneus imber, 350
nonne prius multo dilata examine venit
iudicis ira Dei, qui promptus parcere, nullas
invenit causas veniae, deque omnibus unum
dissimilem Sodomis incesta in plebe repertum
exemit, parvique dedit dominum oppiduli Loth? 355
cum vero Aegyptum Chananaeaque regna teneret
dira fames, totos septem toleranda per annos,
praestruitur certe patriarchis causa movendis,
et domus externos inter placitura paratur,
quae blande foveat populi incrementa futuri, 360
mystica dum Ioseph prodentem somnia fratres

333 larga⎤ longa Maz.   333 reducti⎤ deducti Maz. L

350 in om. Maz.   350 descenderet⎤ descenderit Maz. L

352 iudicis ira⎤ ira iudicis (additis transpositionis
signis) Maz.

276

embrace steadfast hope.

Later, in another age, their descendants likewise merited to receive many proofs of the life set before   325 them in Christ, when they saw Elias carried by a fiery team through the air and mounting the heavens in a shining chariot.   And was God's providence absent when the race of men indulged in every sort of fault and in utter abandonment of piety begot from forbidden marriages those abom-330 inable monsters, the giants?

Before the impending destruction of the world, God gave ample time for mortal men to return to a better state and to expiate their chain of crimes through the practice of virtue.   And when alluring sin persisted in all the earth, and crimes could be destroyed only by a flood, the   335 household of Noe alone was saved.   For it alone escaped the destruction; while the earth perished, it survived, and the ark was unharmed.   In it pairs of living creatures 340 of every kind were confined and from them animals were to be restored to the empty lands. /Noe's household was saved7 . . . not because God could not create other peoples, but so that man, weakened by many disorders, yet the same from his very seed, might come by birth into the body of Christ. And also, since God is the just judge of merits, we might know that rest had been obtained for the holy in the destruction of the wicked.   345

Even in that early age the Lord took pity, and did his love not extend also to our posterity when believing Abraham, the father of many peoples through fruitful faith, reckoned his promised descendants according to the unnumbered stars?

Or when a rain of fire descended on Pentapolis, did   350 not the anger of God its judge come upon it only after long delay and much consideration?   For he, although prompt to spare, found no reason for forgiveness.   And he took from all of Sodom the only guiltless man found in that incestuous people, and granted that Lot should become master of a small city.   355

Even when dire famine held Egypt and the realms of Chanaan in its grip, and had to be endured through seven whole years, a reason for the migration of the patriarchs was prepared beforehand and a pleasing dwelling was made for them among strangers, to nurture gently the lineage of a future nation.   Meanwhile Joseph's brethren sold him   360 into slavery because he told his mystical dreams, and they then proceeded to deceive their father.   The wantonness of his mistress condemned chaste Joseph to prison, but the king released that prophet and honored him with a place next to his own, once Joseph had explained the

in servum vendunt pretio, falluntque parentem;
dum castum dominae petulantia carcere damnat;
dum rex obscuri narrato aenigmate somni,
exemptum vatem dignatur honore secundo;   365
dumque piis traducta dolis Hebraea iuventus
gaudet adoratum venia cognoscere fratrem.
qui cum multa insons ferret mala, nonne remotum,
resque hominum dedignantem, potuisset inepto
incusare Deum questu, nisi cuncta profundis   370
iudice sub iusto scisset decurrere causis?
quae licet infidas soleant confundere mentes,
non possunt turbare pias, quia tempore in isto
haec posita est virtus, ut libertate potitos,
exiguo in spatio, iusti patiantur iniquos,   375
quos Deus ipse modo dilata sustinet ira.
sic gens cara Deo, et saevo suspecta tyranno,
iniustum imperium regis tolerabat acerbi;
maestarum et matrum fetu potiore necato,
condendas iussos lateres praebebat ad urbes,   380
ut durus labor, et saevae inclementia mortis,
omnes terribilis populi consumeret annos.
sed non ista Deo patribus illata remoto,
ipse docet, curamque sibi probat esse suorum.
nam iubet electum Pharaoni edicere Mosen,   385
ut sinat Aegypto Domini discedere plebem;
ni faciat, multis plectenda superbia plagis,
sentiet excitam quae regni vis habet iram.
ille quidem quoties patitur caelestia tela,
cedit, et obsequium simulat; sed clade remota,   390
duratur parcente Deo, causas pereundi
impius inde trahens, quo posset habere salutem;
donec vi victus laxat fera iura tyrannus,
ditia barbaricis et Moses agmina gazis
promovet, insigni sulco monstrante columna   395
per deserta viam, quae formam in tempus utrumque
temperat, alterna ut tribuat vice commoda castris,
luce tegens et nocte regens, eadem ignis et umbra,
discutiens flammis tenebras, et nube calores.   399
quid loquar et trepidis patribus cum incumberet hostis,
divisum pelagus, solidoque rigore ligatas
instar montis aquas, vacuo cessisse profundo;
quaque gradum illaesae tulerant tot milia plebis,

       377 sic⎤ si B M
       380 condendas⎤ condensas omnes; ⎡condendas⎤ addunt
B M
       403 illaesa B M

meaning of his obscure dream. And the band of Hebrew   365
youth, brought back by a pious trick, fell down before
their brother and were glad to recognize him because of
his forgiveness.

When he, being guiltless, bore many evils, could he
not have made senseless complaints, blaming God for being
distant and for scorning the affairs of men, if he had
not known that all things happen for mysterious reasons   370
under the judgment of a just God? Even if such happenings often puzzle unbelievers, they cannot trouble pious
hearts. And this is the established condition of the
world, that the just should endure the unjust, who have
received full liberty during a short period of time, and
whom God himself permits to live only by deferring his   375
anger.

Thus a people dear to God, but mistrusted by a cruel
tyrant, endured the unjust rule of that harsh king; and
although their male offspring were slain and their mothers
were in sorrow, they continued to provide the prescribed
number of bricks for the building of cities. Hard toil   380
and cruel, merciless death consumed all the years of that
detested race. But God himself showed that he was not
far distant when those wrongs were inflicted on the
fathers, and proved that he exercised his providence over
his own. For he commanded Moses, his chosen one, to
order Pharaoh to allow the people of God to depart from   385
Egypt. If the king should not do so, many blows would
be struck to his pride and he would experience the full
force of the sovereign power whose wrath he had aroused.

As many times as Pharaoh suffered the celestial
weapons, he did indeed yield and pretend compliance. But
once the calamity had passed, he was hardened while God   390
spared him, and he impiously derived the causes of his
own destruction from the very source from which he could
have had deliverance. At last the tyrant was overcome
and forced to relax his cruel laws. Moses led forth his
people in battle array, loaded with foreign treasures,
as a column with a fiery trail showed them the way   395
through the desert. It changed its form according to the
time, to provide the camp with a succession of benefits,
covering it by day and guiding it at night, for it was
both fire and shade, dispelling the darkness with its
flames and the heat with its cloud.

How shall I tell this tale? When the enemy threaten-
ed our anxious fathers, the sea was divided, and the   400
waters, bound firm and solid like a mountain, withdrew
from their deep bed. Where countless thousands of the
chosen people had walked through unharmed, the host of

oppressum Aegypti populum coeuntibus undis?
omnis enim auctori servit natura potenti,   405
quaeque ad opem cedunt, eadem famulantur ad iram.
sed mihi nec vacuum cunctas percurrere formas
virtutum, et gestis oris non aequa facultas.
nam quis tantarum evolvat miracula rerum,
mannae imbrem, et cunctos in caeli pane sapores,   410
siccae rupis aquam, et dulcorem fontis amari,
aut inter deserta actos denos quater annos,
nec membris nocuisse aevo, nec vestibus usu?
    Legis in exemplum iuvat ire, et quaerere ab ipsis
qui curam Domini removent, an tempore ab illo   415
coeperit humanas in vitae foedera mentes
informare Deus; nec per tot saecula mundi
permotus vitiis, tunc ius perscripserit aequum.
ite ipsi in vestrae penetralia mentis, et intus
incisos apices ac scripta volumina cordis   420
inspicite, et genitam vobiscum agnoscite legem.
nam quis erit, modo non pecus agri aut belua ponti,
qui vitiis adeo stolide oblectetur apertis,
ut quod agit, velit ipse pati? mendacia fallax,
furta rapax, furiosum atrox, homicida cruentum   425
damnat, et in moechum gladios destringit adulter.
unus enim Pater est cunctorum, et semine recti
nemo caret, similisque omnes produxit origo.
unde etenim, nondum descripta lege, fuerunt
qui placidum sanctis agerent in moribus aevum,   430
nec summi Patris ignari, nec iuris egeni.
ergo omnes una in vita cum lege creati
venimus, et fibris gerimus, quae condita libris.
nec nova cura fuit nostri, cum tradita Mosi
littera praesenti damnaret crimina poena;   435
sed superadiecta est generi custodia sancto,
qua memor in patriae fidei perstaret honore,
et promissorum Domini succederet heres;
cum tamen et quoscumque eadem sub sacra liceret
ire, nec externos arcerent limina templi;   440
cumque Dei monitu canerent ventura prophetae,
saepe etiam ad varias gentes sint multa locuti.
sic regina Austri cupidis, Salomonis ab ore,
auribus eloquium Domini venerata trahebat.

    418 prescripserit Maz.   426 distringit omnes
    437 prestaret Maz.

Egypt was overwhelmed by the coming together of the
waters. For all nature serves its mighty Author and   405
whatever proves to be a benefit can also execute God's
anger.

But I have not the time to recount all the examples
of God's miracles and the power of my voice is not equal
to his deeds. For who could describe such great wonders
as the rain of Manna, and all the savors in the bread of
heaven, the water of the dry rock, and the sweetness of   410
the bitter fountain, or how the people suffered no harm
to their limbs from age, nor to their clothing from use,
although they were led through the desert forty years?

It is useful to go on to the giving of the Law, and
to ask those who reject the providence of the Lord whether God began only then to fashion human hearts to the   415
laws of life. Although he was aroused by crimes through
so many ages of the earth, did he write out his just law
only then?

Go search the depths of your hearts, look upon the
letters inscribed within and the volumes written there,   420
and know that the law was begotten with you. For who is
there that takes such a stupid delight in notorious vices
that he would himself choose to suffer his own misdeeds?
Not even a beast of the field, or a monster of the sea!
But the deceitful man condemns falsehoods; the rapacious
man, thefts; the violent man condemns the man in a rage;
the homicide condemns the bloodthirsty man; and against   425
the adulterer the adulterer draws his sword.

For there is one Father of all, and no one lacks the
seed of virtue, since all men are produced from a similar
origin. For this very reason, even when the law was not
yet written down, there were persons who followed a peace-
ful and holy way of life, and they were not ignorant of   430
God the Father or destitute of law. Thus we have all
been created in one life together with the law, and in
our hearts we carry what is preserved in books.

And God's providence over us was not new, when the
tablets that were given to Moses condemned offenses to
prompt punishment. Instead, he gave a further protection 435
to his holy people so that by it they would remember to
stand firm in their honorable legacy, the faith of their
fathers, and would take their place as heirs to the
promises of God.

Still any person could lawfully come under the same
holy rites, for the doors of the temple were not closed
to strangers. And since the prophets foretold future   440
events at God's command, they often spoke many things
that applied also to various peoples. Thus the Queen of
the South honored the word of the Lord, and received it

sic Ninive monitis Ionae sub tempore cladis   445
credidit, et tribus in luctu ieiuna diebus,
promeruit morum excidio consistere regno.
verum ne longo sermone moremur in istis,
quae sparsim varieque suis sunt edita saeclis,
neve quod in parte est, in toto quis neget esse,   450
dum solidam Domini divisa negotia curam
velant, et nulla accipitur quae rara videtur.
dicite quem populum, qua mundi in parte remotum,
quosve homines, cuius generis, vel conditionis,
neglexit salvare Deus. vir, femina, servus,   455
liber, Iudaeus, Graecus, Scytha, barbarus, omnes
in Christo sumus unum; non persona potentis,
nec domini, regisve prior; distantia nulla
luminis unius, speculi nisi discrepet usus.   459
namque velut speculum mens est, quae quo mage tersa est
expoliente fide, radiisque intenta supernis,
hoc mage confessi resplendet imagine Christi,
qui cum Patre Deo semper Deus, inque paterna
maiestate manens, miscetur conditioni
humanae; et Verbum caro fit, rerumque creator   465
nascitur, atque annis succedit conditor aevi.
hoc etenim lex, hoc veneranda volumina vatum,
hoc patriarcharum spes non incerta tenebat:
ultima cum mundi finem prope curreret aetas,
venturum ad terrena Deum, qui morte perempta   470
solveret inferni leges, longamque ruinam
humani generis meliore attolleret ortu.
    Sed tu qui geminam naturam hominisque Deique
convenisse vides angusti in tramitis ora,
firma tene cautus vestigia, ne trepidantem   475
alterutram in partem, propellat devius error:
si cernens operum miracula divinorum,
suspicias sine carne Deum; cumve omnia nostri
corporis agnoscas, hominem sine Numine credas.
nulla etenim soli vita est mihi, morsque subactum   480
detinet; et non est quo victus vincere possim,
si non vera Dei virtus mihi consociata est,
aut me non vera Salvator carne recepit,
cuius maiestas stabilis non hoc violatur,
quo redimor; neque se minor est, dum mutor in illo;   485

    478 suscipias Maz. L   485 illo_7 illum proponit
                                   Valentin

with eager ears from the lips of Solomon. And thus
Nineve believed the warnings of Jona during the time of
its calamity, and by fasting for three days in mourning   445
apparel, it merited to continue in its rule through the
overthrow of its evil ways.

But let us not delay with long discussion on such
happenings, which have occurred on various occasions
throughout the ages of history. And let no one say that
what is in the part is not in the whole; for the separate   450
actions of God conceal the entirety of his providence
and man receives no example of it that appears isolated.

Tell what people in any distant region of the earth,
what men, of any race or condition, God has failed to
save. Man, woman, slave, freeman, Jew, Greek, Scythian,   455
barbarian, we are all one in Christ. A wealthy master or
a powerful king enjoys no superiority of place, and there
is no difference in the one Light, unless there is a difference in the mirror that reflects it. For the soul is
like a mirror, and the more it has been rubbed and polish- 460
ed by faith, and been directed toward celestial rays, the
more brightly it shines in the sure image of Christ.

He, with God the Father, is ever God, and while remaining in the majesty of his Father he participates in
our human condition; the Word is made flesh, and the   465
Creator of the world is born, and the author of time submits to the passage of the years. For the law and the
venerable writings of the prophets and the sure hope of
the patriarchs all held that when the last age of the
world had almost run its limit, God would come to earth
to cancel the laws of hell by destroying death, and to   470
raise the human race from its long collapse through a
new birth.

But you see that the two natures, the human and the
divine, have converged at the entrance of a narrow path.
Therefore keep a firm and careful step, so that you do
not wander from the roadway and tumble in fearful uncertainty to one side or the other. Perceiving his won-   475
derful miracles, you may look at the divinity without
the humanity; or recognizing in him all our bodily elements, you may believe in the humanity without the divinity.

Alone, I surely have no life, and death holds me under its dominion. There is no means by which I can   480
overcome, once I have been overcome, unless the true
power of God is joined to me and the Savior receives me
with a true human flesh. For his enduring majesty is not
violated in the manner of my redemption; and he is not

sed mortale meum subit, ut quia morte teneri
vita nequit, pereat mihi mors, et non ego iam in me
vivam, sed Christus, qui se mihi miscuit in se.
victus enim terrenus Adam, transfudit in omnes
mortem homines, quoniam cuncti nascuntur ab illo,   490
et transgressoris decurrit causa parentis.
sed novus e caelis per sacrae Virginis alvum
natus homo est, aliudque bonus mortalibus in se
fecit principium, carnemque refusus in omnem,
et vita functos, naturam participando,   495
edidit, et vivos, vitam mutando, creavit.
utque illos veterum complexa est gratia solos
qui Christum videre fide, sic tempore nostro
non renovat quemquam Christus, nisi corde receptus.
en, homo, quanta tibi est gratis collata potestas!   500
filius esse Dei, si vis, potes; omnipotens te
Spiritus umbratum Verbi virtute creavit.
nec te corporeo patrum de semine natum
iam reputes; pereant captiva exordia carnis.
nil veteris coniunge novo, non hic tibi mundus,   505
non haec vita data est, nulla hic tua, nec tuus ipse es.
emptus enim es, pretiumque tui resolvere fas est,
quo potes, ut solvens sis ditior, et tibi crescant
quae dederis, cedatque tibi pars ipse Redemptor.
nec te difficilis nunc observantia legis   510
sub durum iubet ire iugum; mens libera sanctum
obsequium ratione ferat, quam Spiritus almus
in tabulis cordis describat sanguine Christi.
qui nobis quidquid sermonibus insinuavit,
condidit exemplo, factis praecepta coaequans.   515
rex ille, et rerum dominus; sed pauperis egit
in specie, nec veste nitens, nec honore superbus.
infirmis fortis, rex servis, dives egenis;
iustitia iniustis cedit, sapientia brutis.
sacrilegis manibus percussus, non parat ictum   520
reddere; nulla refert avidae convicia linguae.
damnatur iudex, Verbum tacet, inspuitur lux,
ipse ministerium sibi poenae est; felque et acetum
dulcius ille favis haurit; sanctus maledictum
fit crucis, et moritur Christus, vivente Barabba.   525
impia gens tantum ausa nefas, sentisne furorem

508 quo7 qua uncis includunt B M, ad hunc versum
in marg. ponunt Maz. L   520 desinit Maz.
524-525 sanctus maledictum / fit, crucis et moritur
ligno, vivente Barabba proponit Valentin

less than himself, while I am changed in him. But he   485
submits to my mortality in order that death may perish
for me, because life cannot be possessed by death. And
not I will live now in me, but Christ, who has united himself to me in himself.

For the earthly Adam was overcome, and transmitted
death to all men, since all are descended from him and   490
the sin of our first parent passes down to all. But a
new man was born from heaven through the womb of a holy
Virgin, and being sinless, he made a new beginning for
mortal men in himself. United with all flesh, he both
brought the dead to birth by sharing their nature and   495
created the living by changing life. And as grace extended only to those of the fathers who saw Christ by faith,
so in our time Christ renews no one unless he has first
been received in the heart.

Man, see how great is the power granted to you gra-
tuitously! You are able, if you wish, to be a son of   500
God; the omnipotent Spirit has created you overshadowed
by the power of the Word. And do not suppose now that
you have been born of the corporeal seed of the fathers;
let the captive beginnings of our flesh be destroyed.
Join nothing of the old to the new; this world has not
been given to you, this life has not been given to you,   505
nothing here is yours, and you yourself are not your own.
For you have been bought, and you ought to pay the price
of yourself, insofar as you can, that paying it you may
be richer and that what you have given may increase for
you, and the Redeemer himself may be your portion.

And you are not commanded now to submit to the harsh
yoke of a law which is difficult to keep. But let the   510
free soul offer its holy obedience in accordance with the
rule that the Holy Spirit writes on the tablets of the
heart with the blood of Christ; for whatever Christ commend-
ed to us in words, he established by example, matching his
precepts to his deeds. He was a king, and the master of   515
the world, but he lived in the manner of a poor man, with
neither proud honors nor shining garments. He was strong
to the weak, to servants a king, rich to the poor; Justice
submitted to unjust men, and Wisdom to stupid ones.

When struck by sacrilegious hands, he made no effort
to return the blow; he did not answer abuse from an eager   520
tongue. The Judge was condemned, the Word was silent, the
Light was spat upon, he was himself the agency of his own
punishment. He drank gall and vinegar that was sweeter
than honey; the holy Christ became the curse of the Cross, 525
and died, while Barabbas lived.

Unholy race that dared so great a sin, did you

iam mundo damnante tuum? sol fugit ab orbe,
et medio nox facta die est; concussaque tellus
intremuit, mortemque Deo subeunte, sepulcris
excita sanctorum sumpserunt corpora vitam.   530
velum etiam templi discissum est, ne quid opertum
in sacris adytis iam plebs indigna teneret,
sanctaque pontifices fugerent offensa cruentos.
te vero exstinctae calcantem spicula mortis,
et de carne novum referentem carne tropaeum,   535
tertia discipulis, Iesu, dedit attonitis lux.
nec dubiis Dominum licuit cognoscere signis,
cum documenta fides caperet, visuque manuque
rimans clavorum vestigia, vulnus et hastae;
cumque quater denis firmans promissa diebus,   540
conspicuus multis, saepe et tractabilis esset.
hactenus in nostris te, Iesu, novimus; exhinc
in tua nostra abeunt, nec iam diversa, sed unum
sunt duo, dum vita in vita est, in lumine lumen,
augmento, non fine hominis; quo glorificato,   545
sic homo, sic Deus es, ut non sis alter et alter.
nosque ad te ire iubes sursum, tecumque potiri
luce tua, si calle tamen curramus eodem,
edocti non posse capi nisi de cruce caelum.

      Iamne Dei compertus amor, diffusaque in omnes   550
cura patet? notum et cunctis astare salutem?
et tamen, heu! rursus querulis, homo, garrula verbis
bella moves, iaculisque tuis tua viscera figis.
'cur non sum bonus?' hoc non vis. 'cur sum malus?'
      hoc vis.   554
'cur volo quae mala sunt, et cur quae sunt bona nolo?'
liber es; sed cum recta queas discernere pravis,
deteriora legis, placitisque improvidus haeres.
'erro,' ais, 'et vellem non posse errare.' duobus
subiacet haec votis sententia: nam penitus te,
aut esse exanimum cupis, aut rationis egenum.   560
error enim est eius qui cessit limite recti,
quique potest ad inter, Christo ducente, reverti.
at quem nulla viae suscepit linea, nusquam
declinat; nullumque timent non stantia casum.
numquid cura Deo de bobus? numquid ad ullas   565

533 cruenti _proponit_ Valentin

556 liber es⫽ libere L

perceive your madness when the earth condemned it? The
sun fled from its orbit, and darkness was made in midday;
the earth shook and quaked, and when God submitted to
death the bodies of the saints were called from their
tombs and came to life. The curtain of the temple was   530
torn asunder also, to prevent an unworthy people from
keeping anything hidden in their holy sanctuary any longer, and to allow the violated sanctuaries to escape the
contact of their priests, who were guilty of blood.

But in destroying and treading under foot the stings
of death, you won a new victory by the flesh over the
flesh, and on the third day, O Jesus, you appeared to   535
your astonished disciples. And it was possible to recognize the Lord by sure signs, for faith received its proofs
by examining with both eye and hand the prints of the
nails and the wound of the lance. Confirming his promises,
during forty days he was visible to many and could often 540
be touched.

Thus far, O Jesus, we have known you as one of us.
Henceforth, what is ours becomes yours; and the two are
no longer diverse, but the two are one, while life is in
life, and light in light, through the increase and not
through the end of the human nature. And in its glorifi-
cation you are both man and God, in such a way that you   545
are not one or the other /but both/. And you command us
to go upward to you and possess your light with you, provided that we, taught that Heaven cannot be taken except
through the Cross, hasten by that same path.

Is not God's love known by now, and his all-embrac-
ing providence manifest? And is it not known that salva- 550
tion is at hand for all men?

Alas! Still you stir up strife with your long and
loud complaints, and pierce your hearts with your own
weapons. "Why am I not good?" This you do not will. "Why
am I evil?" This you will. "Why do I will the things
that are evil, and why do I not will those that are good?" 555
You are free, but although you can distinguish the right
from the wrong, you choose the worse, and cling to your
desires without thought of the future.

"I sin," you say, " and I would wish not to be able
to sin." This thought derives from one of two desires,
for you wish either to be utterly lifeless or to be completely devoid of reason. For man goes astray only when   560
he has departed from the path of justice and can return
to the right road with Christ as his guide. But the man
who has recieved no map of the road never turns aside,
and things that do not stand have no fear of a fall.

Does God exercise his providence for cattle? Is   565

fit verbum Domini volucres? num lege tenentur
monstra maris? quae cum faciunt iussa Omnipotentis,
ignorant sese facere, affectumque volendi
sumunt, et quod agunt aliis, sibi cedere credunt.
sic etiam quae non spirant sunt semper in illo   570
in quo sunt formata modo; non plana tumescunt
collibus, aut celsi sternuntur in aequora montes;
non veniunt Alpes in pontum, aut pontus in agros;
saxa iacent, amnes decurrunt, stantque paludes.
et tamen his nihil est mercedis, quae sine sensu   575
dispositos in se praebent viventibus usus.
quod si horum praestare tibi natura videtur,
iam bove mutari velles, vel rupe, vel amne.
'deterior nollem fieri, potior voluissem.'
numquid qui Domino placuerunt moribus almis,   580
displicuere sibi? numquid non semine ab uno
venimus, aut alia est hominum natura bonorum?
non aliter dives quam pauper nascitur, unum est
principium servis et regibus; optimus ille
non plus accepit quam pessimus; aequa creantis   585
mensura est, uno qui lumine luminat omnes.
sed mundum ingressi variis rerum speciebus
suscipimur, mentemque adeunt quaecumque videntùr,
iudicio censenda hominis; stant undique formae
innumerae, possuntque omnes spectando probari.   590
quaedam etiam patulas intrant stipata per aures,
errores veterum studiorum, et vana parentum
dogmata, cum quodam fuco ostentantia veri.
haec modulata sono veniunt, haec levia tactu,
haec blandis late funduntur odoribus, illa   595
conciliant varias in mille saporibus escas.
magno ergo haec homini sunt discernenda periclo,
ne nimium trepidus nullum procedat in aequor,
neu vagus effusis sine lege feratur habenis.
est etenim sanctus rerum usus, quem cohibentes   600
intra modum numeri, et momentum ponderis aequi,
pro cunctis soli Domino reddemus honorem.
omnia quae fecit bona valde, ut non vitiorum
incentiva, sed ut superas caperemus in illis,
hic decertato virtutis agone, coronas.   605
an tibi caelestes illi, quos protulit orbis
fertque, viri non haec eadem tolerasse videntur

the word of the Lord intended for any birds? Are the monsters of the sea bound by the law? When they do the commands of the Omnipotent, they do not know that they are doing them, but desire them by instinct, and what they do for others they imagine they are doing only for their own benefit. So also inanimate objects exist always in the manner in which they have been fashioned; plains do not   570 swell up to hills, nor do towering mountains spread out into level surfaces. The Alps do not come into the sea, or the sea into the fields;stones lie flat, streams flow down, and marshes are stagnant.

And yet these creatures receive no reward at all; in themselves they provide well-ordered benefits to living men, without possessing understanding. But if you think   575 that their nature is superior to yours, you would wish by now to be changed into an ox or a rock or a stream.

"I would not wish to become worse, I would wish to become better." Have men who pleased the Lord by their holy way of life caused displeasure to themselves? Have   580 we not come from one seed, or are good men different by nature? The rich man is not born differently than the poor man; servants and kings alike have one origin. The best man has not received more than the worst; the Creator, who illumines all men with one light, bestows on each an equal measure.   585

But having entered the world, we meet with things of varying appearance, and whatever is seen enters the mind, to be weighed by man's judgment. Innumerable objects stand on every side, and they all can be examined by looking at them. Certain thoughts enter also through the open 590 ears in a dense throng, and these display with some pretense of truth both the errors derived from ancient studies and the false teachings of our ancestors. Some things are melodious in sound, some are smooth to the touch, some are widely diffused by their enticing fragrances, others produce foods in a thousand different tastes. Man   595 must distinguish among all these at great peril, for if he is too fearful, he may not venture on the sea at all, or if he casts aside all restraint, he may wander about aimlessly without any law.

For there is a holy use of things, and if we keep our use of them within the bounds of moderation and ob-   600 serve a true balance, then we shall return honor to God alone for everything. All things which he made are exceedingly good, so that we would receive in them not incentives to vice, but the crowns that are above, after we had fought well the contest here below.   605

Or do you imagine that the saints whom the world produced and still produces have not endured these same

quae patimur, motus animi, affectusque rebelles,
et circumiectis vitia oppugnantia castris?
sed gladio verbi, fideique umbone potenti,   610
vincebant arcus tenebrarum et spicula mortis.
cumque opus hoc mundi magnum pulchrumque viderent,
non mare, non caelum,non ignem, aut sidera caeli,
quae numero subiecta sibi visuque tenebant,
suspexere deos, unum, ratione magistra,   615
auctorem et Dominum rerum, non facta, colentes.
at tu nobilius qui factum te voluisses,
numquid in angelico satus ordine non querereris?
nam cum ille excelso deiectus Lucifer axe
conciderit, rueritque illo pars tertia pulso   620
astrorum, quaero in quanam tunc parte fuisses?
clara Dei semper bonitatis imago maneres,
an castra invidiae sequereris et agmina noctis?
        Sed quo te praeceps rapit orbita? vis bonus esse
absque labore tuo? credis hoc cedere posse,   625
si tibi mutentur natalia sidera, quorum
te pravum decursus agit? quid vana vetusti
perfugia erroris Chaldaeis quaeris in astris?
quamvis sollicitis adeas caelestia curis,
et penitus causas rerum scruteris apertas,   630
non renuis mage nosse Deum, quam cuique elemento
naturam dederit, qua pontum lege moveri
iusserit, aut teneris quam vim conseverit auris,
sidereosque ignes in quae momenta crearit.
qui cum sincerus sit fons aequique bonique,   635
immitem iussis legem praescripsit iniquis,
si prius ipse hominum mores constrinxerat astris.
namque adversa sibi sunt haec, nimiumque repugnant,
exigere insontes actus, delictaque poenis
afficere, et cunctos eadem ad promissa vocare;   640
contra autem natis violentum affigere sidus,
quod nec velle homini cedat, nec posse, sed omnes
desuper ignaros et virtus ducat, et error.
ergo aut aethereis nullum est ius ignibus in nos,
aut si quid nostri retinent, amittere possunt.   645
cum mihi progenito ad vitam mandata salutis
et cordi insinuet bonus auctor et auribus, ac me
currentem mercede vocet, terrore morantem.

        630 opertas <u>posse defendi dicit Valentin</u>
633 consueverit <u>M</u>

evils which we suffer, the disturbances of soul, and the
rebellious passions, and the attacks of the vices encamp-
ed around us? But with the sword of the word and the
powerful shield of faith they overcame the bows of dark-   610
ness and the arrows of death.

And when they saw the world, this great and beautiful work, they did not honor as gods the sea, nor the
sky, nor fire, or even the stars of the sky which they
considered subordinate to themselves, for they could see
and count them. With reason as their teacher they worshipped the one Author and Lord of the universe and not
his works.   615

But you would have wished to be made of nobler
stuff. Would you not complain had you been begotten in
the angelic order? For when Lucifer was cast down from
lofty heaven and fell to earth and a third part of the
stars fell with him in his banishment, I ask on which side620
you would have been then? Would you remain always the
bright image of God's goodness, or would you serve in the
camp of hatred and the cohorts of darkness?

But where does your headlong course carry you?
Do you wish to be good without your own effort? Do you
suppose that this could happen if your birth stars were   625
changed when their declination makes you wicked? Why do
you seek a useless refuge for your old crimes in the astrology of the Chaldaeans?

Although you approach celestial phenomena with
anxious concern, and examine the manifest causes of the
universe with the greatest thoroughness, you admit that   630
God has the greater knowledge of the nature which he has
given to each element, and of the law by which he has commanded the sea to move, and of the force that he has sown
in the gentle breezes, and of the causes for which he has
created the fiery stars.

Now although he is the pure fountain of justice
and of equity, he prescribed a cruel and unjust system of 635
law, if he first bound the conduct of men to the stars.
For it is inconsistent and completely contradictory to de-
mand that man's actions be guiltless, to punish his of-
fences, to summon all to the same promises, and on the   640
other hand to fasten on men at birth a strong and impetuous
star, which allows to man neither will nor power, but which
looks down upon and guides all men in their ignorance,
being itself both virtue and sin.

Therefore either the stars of heaven have no right
over us, or, if they do retain anything of ours, they can
lose it. For when I have been brought forth into life,   645
the good Author of life introduces into my heart and my
ears the commandments of salvation, and encourages me with

'solum,' inquit, 'venerare Deum, solique memento
servire, externas et despice religiones.   650
hoc operis sectare boni, hoc fuge cautus iniqui.
vita beata isto paritur, mors editur illo.
coram adsunt aqua servatrix, populator et ignis;
ad quod vis extende manum, patet aequa facultas.'
quod legis monitus, et vatum scripta piorum,   655
et Deus ipse suo nequidquam promeret ore,
arbitrium nostrum si vis externa teneret.
verum si quid obest virtuti, animosque retardat,
non superi pariunt ignes, nec ab aethere manat,
sed nostris oritur de cordibus; ipsaque bellum   660
libertas movet, et quatimur civilibus armis,
otia cum mollis complexa ignava voluptas
difficili negat ire via, bravioque potitos
ardua quaeque piget pro spe tentare latenti.
cumque haec intus agi prospexit callidus hostis,   665
de studiis vestris vires capit, utque parentis
avertat veri cultum, persuadet ab astris
fata seri, frustraque homines contendere divis.
hinc vario vitae dominos mercantur honore.
error abi, procul error abi! satis agnita prisci   670
sunt commenta doli, monitos quibus Omnipotens nos
elaqueat, cultusque docet vitare profanos.
scimus enim quanta steterit mercede quibusdam
sidus adoratum Rempham, venerataque caeli
militia, et cultus Soli Lunaeque dicatus.   675
nec latet haec verbis hominis subsistere iussa
ad vocem servisse mora, noctisque repulsae
temporibus crevisse diem, cum lux famulata
nesciret nisi quem faceret victoria finem.
novimus et caelo praescriptas conditiones   680
arbitrio quondam sancti mansisse prophetae,
cum positum ad tempus clausos, sitientibus agris,
non licuit rorare polos; ipsumque, vocata
partibus e superis in sancta altaria flamma,
quem dederat sacris ignem immisisse profanis.   685
cuius vis etiam Christi delapsa fuisset
discipulis, poenam hospitii exactura negati,
ni patiens Dominus venia praeverteret iram.
nullum ergo in nos est permissum ius elementis,

663 potiri proponit Valentin

689 est permissum _7 permissum est L

a reward when I hasten, but spurs me with fear when I delay.

"Worship God alone," he says, " and remember to
serve him only and scorn strange religions. Strive after   650
the good work but warily shun the evil. A blessed life is
begotten through the good, but death is produced through
the evil. Saving water and destroying fire are before you;
stretch out your hand to the one you wish--you may choose
either equally." But the commandments of the law, and the
writings of the holy prophets,and God himself,speaking   655
from his very lips, would all express this thought without any purpose if an external force restrained our will.

But in fact, if anything harms virtue and hinders
souls, the stars above do not produce it nor does it issue
from the heavens, but it arises out of our own hearts.
Our freedom itself is the cause of a war, and we are sha-   660
ken by internal strife, when soft pleasure combines with
a slothful ease and refuses to follow the difficult path,
and those who possess the prize become weary of attempting
each height for the sake of its hidden hope. And when the
crafty enemy has perceived this inner conflict, he acquires665
power over you through your own desires. To divert you
from the worship of the true Father, he persuades you that
your fates are arranged by the stars and that it is useless for men to contend with these gods. So with various
honors they seek to buy these lords of life.

Error, depart! Error, depart from us completely!
The snares of your old deceit are known well enough; the   670
Omnipotent has warned us about them and extricates us from
them while he teaches us to shun wicked cults.

For we know that the adoration of the star Rempha,
the veneration of the host of heaven, and the worship
given to the Sun and the Moon cost some men dear. And we   675
are aware that the Sun and Moon were ordered to stand still
by the words of a man, and obeyed his voice by their delay. The day lengthened as the hours of night were held
back, since the light did not cease in the performance of
its service until the victory. We know too that the appointed operations of the sky were once held in abeyance   680
at the will of a holy prophet, when the heavens were closed for a set time and could not drop their rain on the
thirsting fields. And that same prophet called flames
from the upper regions onto the holy altar, and cast upon
the unholy the fire he had bestowed on the holy sacrifice.
His power would have passed down also to Christ's disci-   685
ples, to inflict punishment on those who denied them
hospitality, unless the Lord in his patience had preferred
forgiveness to anger.

Therefore the elements have been granted no power

293

in quae ius hominis; nec possunt condere legem,   690
quae legem accipiunt. solus Deus omnipotens Rex,
omnia qui nostrae dispensat tempora vitae,
nec servire astris vult quos super astra locavit.
nam quoscumque sacro renovavit Spiritus amne,
in Christo genitos, mortali ex stirpe recisos,   695
iam sedes caelestis habet, nec terrea nectit
progenies templum in Domini corpusque redactos.
quod si quis cursu astrorum effectuque notato
contendit naturam hominis vitamque videri,
quaero quid hac trepidis mortalibus afferat arte.   700
'hic,' inquit, 'felix, miser hic erit, hunc rapiet mors
impubem, hic senio transcendet Nestoris annos.'
falsum hoc, aut verum est? si stant praedicta canentis,
nec misero superest spes, nec formido beato.
et quae sideribus danda est reverentia fixis,   705
si quae ferre queunt, nequeunt decreta movere?
dent sese scelerum potius torrentibus omnes:
fallant, diripiant, iugulent, fas omne nefasque
confundant, persistet enim nihilominus astrum,
cuius ab effectu firmato cardine rerum,   710
ut mala non poterunt sancta probitate repelli,
sic bona non fugient perversos debita mores.
at si praedictae sortis mutabilis ordo est,
et declinari possunt ventura, soluta est
omnis ab ancipiti casu vis pendula fati.   715
scrutatis igitur stellarum motibus, hoc est
artis opus, totam subvertere religionem,
dum nullum curare Deum mortalia suadet;
aut dum posse docet votis elementa moveri,
innumeram miseris plebem insinuare deorum.   720
       Sed quia detectis laqueis iam fraudis opertae,
quo captos vanis studiis deduceret error
compertum, superest nunc respondere querelis
quae mundi rebus divinam absistere curam
obiciunt, dum saepe bonos labor anxius urget,   725
et tranquilla fluit cunctorum vita malorum.
dic age, qui nullis Domini moderantis habenis
humanas res ire putas, quid ab ordine cessat
naturae? quae bella movent elementa? quid usquam

    726 cunctorum⟋ laborum L

294

over us, but man has been granted power over them; and
they who receive the law, cannot make the law. God alone   690
is the omnipotent King who controls all the circumstances
of our life, and he does not will that those whom he has
placed above the stars be subject to the stars. For whatever men the Spirit has renewed in the holy torrent, have
been begotten in Christ and cut off from their mortal origin. Now they live in a heavenly dwelling, and they are   695
not bound by their earthly descent, for they have been
brought into the temple and the body of the Lord.

But if anyone asserts that the nature and life of
man is determined by observing the course and operation of
the stars, I ask him what good he does for anxious mortals 700
through this art. "This man will be happy," he says, "and
this one wretched; death will carry off one in his youth,
while another will surpass Nestor in his long span of
years." Is this false, or is it true? If the predictions
of the seer stand, no hope remains for the unfortunate man,
no fear for the fortunate one.

And what reverence should be paid to the fixed   705
stars, if they cannot alter the decrees which they can
propose? Let all men give themselves over to torrents of
crime instead. Let them deceive, let them rob, let them
kill, let them perform every right and wrong action without distinction, for their star will nonetheless remain the
same. And once the course of events has been fixed by its 710
operation, just as it will not be possible to avert evils
through goodness and holiness, so men of wicked character
will not lose their predestined blessings. But if the
above order of destiny is subject to change, and future
events can be avoided, then the entire power of fate,
which depends upon uncertain chance, is broken. And so   715
it is the whole purpose of that art, after examining the
movements of the stars, either to destroy all religion by
urging that no God exercises providence over human affairs,
or else to fasten an innumerable host of gods on wretched
men by teaching that the elements can be moved by prayers. 720

But we have already exposed these snares of hidden
treachery and have ascertained where the pursuit of error
led men who were deceived by false learning. Now we must
answer the complaint that divine providence is absent from
the affairs of the world, while the good are often beset
by hardships and anxieties, and the lives of all the   725
wicked flow serene.

You suppose that human affairs do not proceed under
any restraints imposed by a governing Lord. Then tell me,
what is amiss in the order of nature? What conflicts do
the elements initiate? What exists anywhere that is parted

dissidet a prisco divisum foedere rerum?   730
sic interiecta solis revocatur in ortum
nocte dies, idem est lunae astrorumque recursus,
et relegunt notas subeuntia tempora metas;
non aliter venti spirant, ita nubibus imber;
laeta negant, servantque genus trudentia flores   735
semina quaeque suum; nec abest ab origine rerum
ordo manens, iisdem subsistunt omnia causis.
quae nisi perpetui solers prudentia Regis
astrueret, molemque omnem spirando foveret,
conciderent subita in nihilum redigenda ruina.   740
et cum haec pervigili cura Omnipotentis agantur,
quae certum ad finem devexo limite vergunt,
quis neget in nostram gentem specialius aequum
partiri sua iura Deum? cui perpetis aevi
spem tribuit, propriae largitus imaginis instar.   745
at qui nec poenam iniustis, nec praemia sanctis
restitui ad praesens quereris, vellesne per omnes
ultricem culpas descendere iudicis iram?
et quo magnanimi clemens patientia Regis
distaret saeva immitis feritate tyranni?   750
aut quae pars hominum peccati nescia mundum
possessura foret? vel sanctae quis locus esset
virtuti in terris? cui si praesentia dona
affluerent, caelo potius sublata maneret.
sic mundi meta abruptis properata fuisset   755
temporibus, neque in subolem generanda veniret
posteritas, pariter cum iustos atque nocentes
aut promissus honos aut poena auferret ab orbe.
nunc vero et generis nostri profunda propago
tenditur, ac duplici succedit origine pubes,   760
nata patrum membris, et Christi fonte renata;
et pia dum populis Domini patientia parcit,
in lucem multos de taetra nocte reversos,
ac posita claros peccati labe videmus.
ille per innumeros vultus, et mille per aras,   765
barbatos levesque deos, iuvenesque senesque,
ut quondam fecere, colens, iam errore parentum
abiecto, solum Unigenam submissus adorat.
hic sophicas artes Graecorum et vana secutus

751 aut7 an B M

from the primeval law of the universe or at variance with
it? Thus day follows day after the interposition of   730
night; the recurrence of the moon and of the stars is unvarying, and the advancing seasons retrace their familiar
course. The winds do not blow differently, and the clouds
bring their rain in the same manner. Flowers withhold
their joyous seeds and preserve them, so that each bur-
geons into its own kind, order abides from the very begin- 735
ning of the universe, and all things subsist for the same
reasons. But unless the everlasting King sustained them
in his wise judgment, and nurtured the entire mass by
breathing on it, the whole world would collapse and swiftly be reduced to nothing.   740

    And since all these things come to pass under the
ceaseless providence of the Omnipotent and tend by a steep
path toward a definite end, who would deny that God shares
his rights with us out of a special benevolence for the
human race? For he has granted us the hope of everlasting
life, having imparted to us his own image and likeness.   745

    But you complain that in the present life punish-
ment is not imposed on sinners, nor rewards given to the
holy. Would you then wish that the avenging wrath of our
Judge extend to every fault? And how would the merciful
forbearance of the magnanimous King be different from the
cruel ferocity of the savage tyrant? What portion of   750
mankind would be free of sin and so have been left to possess the world? And what opportunity would there be on
earth for the practice of holy virtue? For if virtue received its rewards at once, the virtuous man would have
been raised up to heaven and would be dwelling there.
Thus the end of the world would have been hastened, the
passage of time been interrupted, and succeeding genera-   755
tions would not continue to beget descendants, since the
good and wicked alike would be taken from the earth, either
to their promised glory or punishment.

    But now the innumerable offspring of our race ex-
tend from generation to generation, and a new people of
two-fold origin follows after them, a people born from the 760
bodies of their parents and reborn from the fountain of
Christ. And while the Lord in his holy forbearance spares
the nations, we perceive the radiant glory of those many
men who have returned from foul darkness to the light and
have rid themselves of the stain of sin.

    One man, who worshipped under countless aspects and
on a thousand altars gods both bearded and beardless, as   765
men once did, now has cast aside the error of his ancestors
and humbly adores the Only-begotten alone. Another, who
followed the sophistic arts of the Greeks and their false

297

dogmata, iam Christo sapere et brutescere mundo   770
gaudet, apostolico doctus caelestia ludo.
quam multos procul a portu rationis in altum
dedecorum turbo abstulerat, quos aequore toto
iactatos, nimiumque vagis erroribus actos,
nunc reduces iuvat excipere, amplexuque paterno   775
confotos, nusquam statione abscedere vitae!
quos si multa inter morum delicta priorum
plectisset propere rigor implacabilis irae,
intercepta forent melioris tempora vitae,
nec standi vires licuisset sumere lapsis.   780
'mortem,' inquit Dominus, 'peccantis nolo, nec ullum
de pereunte lucrum est; redeat magis, inque relictum
mutatus referatur iter, vitaque fruatur.'
et quia virtutum similes vult esse suarum   784
quos genuit, 'vindictam,' inquit, 'mihi cedite; reddam
iudicio quae digna meo; detur locus irae.'
sic dum multorum differtur poena malorum,
nonnulli plerumque probos revocantur in actus,
ac fit quisque sibi iudex ultorque severus,
quod fuerat prius interimens, aliusque resurgens.   790
at qui persistunt errori incumbere longo,
quamvis in multis vitiis impune senescant,
in saevum finem venient; ibi non erit ulla
spes veniae, minimo ad poenam quadrante vocando.
nos etenim quoties causa quacumque movemur,   795
vindictam celerem cupimus, quia rara facultas
non patitur laesis tempus transire nocendi.
at vero aeternum nil effugit, omniaque adsunt
salva Deo; nihil est illi tardumve citumve;
nec dilata umquam, nec festinata putemus   800
quae veniunt, nostris mutantur tempora rebus.
nam quod ubique agitur, quod gestum est, quodque
     gerendum est,
ante oculos Domini puncto subsistit in uno,
una dies cui semper adest cras atque here nostrum.
     Sed quamquam examen Deus omnia servet in illud,805
quo quae nunc occulta latent reserata patebunt,
multa tamen mundum per saecula cuncta regentis
iustitiae documenta dedit, dum maxima bellis
regna quatit, dum saepe urbes, populosque potentes

    778 plexisset B̲ M̲

doctrines, now rejoices to be wise before Christ and
foolish before the world, for he has been instructed in   770
heavenly things in the school of the Apostles.

A whirlwind of vices carried so many persons far
away from the harbor of reason out into the deep! They
were tossed about over all the sea and driven beyond endurance by inconstant errors, but now we rejoice to re
ceive them upon their return, and rejoice too that they
are comforted in the embrace of their heavenly Father and   775
remain in the safe port of true life. But if the stern
and implacable wrath of God had swiftly punished them while
they lived among their many former offenses, the period of
their better life would have been taken from them and,
once they had fallen, they could not have received the
strength to stand.   780

"I desire not the death of the sinner," says the
Lord, "nor is there any gain from one who perishes. Instead let him come back, be converted, return to the path
that he abandoned, and enjoy true life." And because God
wishes those whom he has begotten to practice virtues
similar to his own, he says, "Leave vengeance to me; I will785
repay the deeds that deserve my judgment; let place be
given to my wrath."

Thus while the punishment of many evildoers is being postponed, it frequently happens that some of them return to a virtuous way of life, and each of these becomes
his own judge and stern avenger, destroying his old self,
and rising again a different man. But those who persist-   790
ently indulge in long-continued error, although they grow
old in their many vices without suffering any punishment,
will come at last to a horrible end. Then there will be
no hope of pardon, but retribution will be exacted for the
last penny.

For we mortals desire quick vengeance whenever we
are provoked for any reason; the victims cannot neglect   795
their chance to do harm, so rare is their opportunity.
But nothing ever escapes the Eternal One, and all things
are present before God in their entirety. To him nothing
is slow or swift; and let us not suppose that the course
of events has ever been delayed or hastened--it is only   800
in our world that times change. For whatever happens anywhere, or has happened, or will happen, exists before the
eyes of God in a single moment, and to him our tomorrow
and our yesterday is always present as a single day.

But although God reserves all things for the final
judgment, when the secrets that are now hidden will be   805
plainly revealed, he has still given many proofs of the
justice that controls the world through all ages. He af-
flicts the strongest kingdoms with wars, and frequently

exhaurit morbis, cremat ignibus, obruit undis;   810
dumque inopes ditat, deiectos elevat, auctos
imminuit, solvit vinctos, subigitque superbos.
nec vero hoc nisi cum magna ratione putandum est
accidere, ut quoties iram experiuntur iniqui,
supplicia insontes videantur obire nocentum.   815
multa quidem semper mundo communia in isto
indignos dignosque manent: sol omnibus idem est,
idem imber, pariter subeuntur frigora et aestus.
utque indiscreta est cunctis aqua, lumen, et aura,
sic iniustorum iustos mala ferre necesse est,   820
ut dum multa malis insontes compatiuntur,
sint quorum merito populis parcatur iniquis,
et qui conversos virtutis imagine ducant.
sed cum perdendis indemutabilis instat
finis, non eadem incumbit sententia sanctis.   825
sunt quos diluvium mundi non obruat, et quos
arsuris liceat Sodomis evadere; norat
angelus Aegypti vastator limina signo
scripta crucis, sacro removens a sanguine plagam;
nec rutilo mulier decepta est vellere, cuius   830
sola domus tanta pereunte superfuit urbe;
fit mare per tumidum sanctis via, fitque per·amnem;
et per inane piis gradus est: cibus alite serva
suggeritur, perditque avidus sua fercula messor.
utque Dei servis nihil obsit, vertitur ordo   835
naturae: vinctos labentia vincula solvunt;
carcer sponte patet, sera non tenet obice valvas;
deficit humor aquas, ignes calor, ira leones.
non autem dubium est in magnae turbine cladis
involvi teneros annos, et more parentum,   840
criminis expertes, aliena occumbere culpa.
nam cum homines pontus tegeret, deleta per orbem
multa puellarum et puerorum milia notum est.
nec tamen iniuste terris exempta videtur
progenies auctura malos, cui multus in ipso   845
exitio est collatus honos, quod crimine patrum
occidit ante sua caderet quam noxia culpa.
quod si et iustum aliquem complexa est poena malorum,

    840 more_7 in ore L

destroys powerful cities and peoples through diseases,
consumes them by fires, and overwhelms them by floods.   810
He enriches the poor, raises up the fallen, brings down
the mighty, frees captives, and subjugates the proud.

But whenever sinners suffer his wrath, the innocent seem to suffer the same torments as the guilty,and   815
we must suppose that this happens for a weighty reason.
For there are many experiences in this world which await
the worthy and the unworthy alike; the sun is the same for
all, the rain is the same, and both endure cold and heat
in the same measure. And as all men without distinction
receive water, light, and air, so the just must necessarily bear the punishments of the unjust. Thus, while the   820
innocent undergo many sufferings together with sinners,
there may be some men for whose sake God will spare throngs
of evil-doers, and the former will guide the unjust by
their virtuous example once the latter have been converted.

But when the damned approach their immutable end,
the holy do not fall under the same sentence. Some per-   825
sons were not overwhelmed in the universal flood, and some
were allowed to escape the impending destruction of Sodom
by fire. The angel that devastated Egypt recognized those
lintels marked with the sign of affliction, and spared the
holy people from the plague. And the harlot was not deceived when she trusted in her scarlet cord, for her house-830
hold were the sole survivors of the ruin of a great city.

A path was made for the holy people through the
swelling sea, and a path was made also through the torrent.
Pious men could even step through the air, and food was
supplied through a winged servant while a hungry reaper
was deprived of his own lunch. And so that no harm would
come to the servants of God, the natural order was transformed. Chains fell off and released their captives, the 835
prison stood open of its own accord, for bar and bolt did
not secure the doors. Water had no moisture, fire had
no heat, and lions no wrath.

Moreover, it is certain that young children were
enveloped in the mighty tempest of destruction; although
free of crime themselves, they fell through the sins of
others and died like their parents. For we know that many840
thousands of boys and girls were destroyed throughout the
earth when the sea covered mankind. And yet it does not
appear unjust that a generation which would increase the
number of evildoers was removed from the world. They
received a great reward in their very destruction, because845
they perished through their fathers' crimes before they
could fall fatally through their own guilt.

And even if the punishment of evildoers includes

ne dubites placuisse Deo; nec enim mala mors est
ulla bonis, quibus e vario longoque labore   850
quilibet in requiem patet exitus; aspera vitam
dat via, nec campo capitur, sed fine corona.
verum nos blandis capti, offensique severis,
nec bona iudicio spectamus, nec mala vero,
dum non nostrarum curanda negotia rerum   855
suscipimus, propriisque iuvant aliena relictis.
nec quemquam vitiis miserum, aut virtute beatum
censentes, frustra externis culpamque decusque
iungimus, et caelo ascripti terrena fovemus.
felices dici mos est, quos blanda potestas   860
in summos apices tumidorum evexit honorum,
quos magni quaestus ditarunt, et quibus amplos
congessit reditus totum res fusa per orbem.
laudantur vestes pretiosae, et pulchra supellex,
magnae aedes, famuli innumeri, vigilesque clientes,   865
et quidquid non est nostrum, quodque ut dare quivit
una dies, sic una potest auferre; nec illud
quod speciale bonum est hominis, nullamque timet vim,
amplexi, miseros quibus haec perdentia desunt,
et per mille modos pereuntia, credimus - ac si   870
iustitiam durus labor urgeat, et dolor aegri
corporis, et mortes natorum, et turpis egestas.
non quantas pariat constans tolerantia palmas,
nec quo pugna brevis sit processura videmus,
sed calicem crucis ac vitae libare verentes,   875
vipereum obducto potamus melle venenum.
dulcia sunt etenim gustu, specieque decora,
quae morbos mortemque animae generantque foventque,
canceris et ritu languentia viscera carpunt.
cumque Deus medicam caelo demittere curam   880
dignatur, penitusque putres abscindere fibras,
incusamus opem teneri, et tabescere morbo
malumus, antidoti quam vim tolerare severi.
non igitur mala sunt quae nos mala ducimus, et cum
ulceribus diris non parcit dextra medentis,   885
amplectenda salus, non exacuenda querela est.
iam quos peccantes Deus arguit, hos etiam nunc
diligit, et patrio vult emendare flagello.
meque istis potius societ, quam congreget illis

850 quibus e vario⎤ quibus vario B M

an occasional just man also, do not hesitate to be pleasing to God, for no death is evil to good men. After a long and varied life of toil, it does not matter to them what kind of end leads to their eternal rest. The rough road gives life, and the crown is not taken in the field, but is the prize at the end.   850

But since we are seduced by allurements and repelled by austerities, our view of good or evil is not based on correct judgment. We do not attempt to attend to our own condition as we should but neglect our true interests and find delight in the affairs of others. And we do not consider anyone unfortunate because of his vices or fortunate from his virtue, for we erroneously associate both fault and virtue with externals. We are citizens of heaven, but we love the things of the earth.   855

Usually we say that men are happy when the inducements of power have led them up to the dizzy heights of proud honor, when they have been enriched by huge profits and have accumulated magnificent returns on properties scattered throughout all the world. We admire their costly clothing and fine furnishings, their great houses, countless servants, and watchful clients, and whatever does not belong to us. But just as all this could be given in a single day, so in a single day it could all be taken away. We have not loved the good which is proper to man, and which fears no violence. Therefore we suppose that men are unhappy when they are without these goods that destroy and are themselves destroyed in a thousand ways--as if hard work and the pain of bodily illness and the death of children and abject poverty were an argument against justice.   860   865   870

We do not consider the great rewards that firm endurance brings, or the goal that we will reach through this brief combat, but since we are afraid to taste of the cup of the cross and of everlasting life, we see the honey on the rim and drink the serpent's poison. For these enticements that beget and nurture disease and death for the soul, and devour our feeble organs like a cancer, are indeed sweet in taste and handsome in appearance. And when God is pleased to send down from heaven his healing remedy and to uproot the deeply festering sores, we find fault with his help because we are weak, and prefer to waste away from disease rather than to endure the force of a strong antidote. But those things which we consider evils are not really evils, and when the hand of the physician does not spare our terrible wounds we should set our minds on our health and not intensify our complaining.   875   880   885

303

quos iam submoto permisit verbere, cursu   890
ire voluntatis, propriaque libidine ferri.
hi sunt vero illi, quos inter crimina tutos,
et scelerum dites fructu, impunita senectus
extremas turpis vitae produxit in oras.
hi iustum iniustis odiis pressere; per istos   895
bella excita piis, et flagra medentia tardis.
        Namque eadem cunctos exercent tela fideles
sub duplici causa, dum quo torquentur iniqui,
hoc sancti crescunt; et quod poenam attulit illis
pro culpa, hoc istis dat pro virtute coronam.   900
denique si quidquid mundanis rebus acerbum
accidit excutias, totum iam sponte videbis
anticipasse Dei famulos. gemit ille talentis
argenti atque auri amissis, hunc rapta supellex,
perque nurus Geticas divisa monilia torquent.   905
hunc pecus abductum, domus ustae, potaque vina
afficiunt, tristes nati, obscenique ministri.
sed sapiens Christi servus nil perdidit horum
quae sprevit, caeloque prius translata locavit;
ac si quid mundi sub tempestate laborum   910
incidit, intrepide subiit, manifestus honoris
promissi, et cupidus victo certamine solvi.
at tu, qui squalidos agros desertaque defles
atria, et exustae proscenia diruta villae,
nonne magis propriis posses lacrimas dare damnis,   915
si potius vastata tui penetralia cordis
inspiceres, multaque obtectum sorde decorem,
grassantesque hostes captivae mentis in arce?
quae nisi per cunctas patuisset dedita portas,
inque suam cladem facibus fomenta dedisset,   920
haec etiam quae facta manu speciosa fuerunt,
devoti meritum populi testata manerent.
sed cum deformi iaceant prostrata ruina,
obiciunt nobis casus nostrosque suosque.
hos igitur cineres templorum, haec busta potentum,   925
quae congesta iacent, populati cordis in aula

        894 extremas proponit Valentin; extremae Maz. L B M
921 haec/ hoc B M

Moreover, even now God loves the very sinners whom he rebukes, for he desires to chastise them with a paternal scourge. And may he join me to their company, rather than unite me with those from whom he has already removed his rod, for he has permitted the latter to proceed in the course they have chosen and to be led by their own 890 passions. They are the ones who remain safe amid their offenses, and rich in the fruit of their sins, and in old age they come unpunished to the final extremity of their shameful lives. It is they who have oppressed the just man with heinous injustices; it is through their doing that wars have been stirred up against the devout and 895 healing scourges have fallen upon the slothful.

Truly, the same weapons harass all the faithful for two different reasons, while the unjust are tormented and the just increase in holiness through the same means. What has brought punishment on the former for their sin offers a crown to the latter for their virtue. 900

Therefore if you examine any misfortunes whatever that occur in human affairs, you will readily perceive that the servants of God have already anticipated all of them. One man grieves at the loss of his gold and silver talents, another is tormented by the seizure of his possessions and the distribution of his jewels among Gothic 905 brides. Another is troubled by the stealing of his flock, the burning of his houses, and the drinking of his wines, the misery of his children and the squalor of his servants. But the wise servant of Christ has lost none of these things, for in rejecting them he has already transferred his true riches to heaven. And if any earthly misfortune falls upon him, and he meets with a multitude of sufferings, he 910 faces it with courage, being sure of the glory that has been promised him, and eager with victory won to depart.

But you mourn over your neglected fields and deserted halls, and the destruction of your terraces and the burning of your villa. Could you not shed more tears for your true losses, if you looked instead into the deso-915 late depths of your own heart and saw how its beauty has been concealed by many stains of sin, and how the enemy goes about in your captive mind as in a captive citadel? For if the mind had not been left exposed by the surrender of all its defenses, and had not supplied the torches with the tinder for its own destruction, these splendid 920 possessions which were made by the hand of man would have remained to bear witness to the merit of a devout people. But since they lie on the ground in ugly ruin, they reproach us with our downfall as well as their own.

And so, amid the devastation in the depths of our hearts, let us weep for these ruins of sanctuaries, these tombs of the powerful, which all lie heaped together. 925

305

plangamus captiva manus, nos splendida quondam
vasa Dei, nos almae arae et sacraria Christi,
in quibus argentum eloquii, virtutis et aurum,
et sceptrum captum est crucis, et diadema decoris.   930
nec rabidis iustam moveamus questibus iram,
iudicium culpando Dei, quod mentis et oris
officium multa transcendit maius abysso.
quamvis exiguo hoc fugientis tempore vitae
iniusti tumeant, et tuta pace suorum   935
laetentur scelerum; nonque illos vinea fallat,
non ager; et noceant illaesi, et crimine crescant;
nos, quibus in Christo sunt omnia, non capiant res
occiduae, quas nec nobiscum inveximus orti,
nec discessuri mundo exportabimus isto.   940
sed si quis superest animi vigor, excutiamus
peccati servile iugum, ruptisque catenis,
in libertatem et patriae redeamus honorem.
impia non oberunt cum saevo pacta tyranno,
captiva conscripta manu; resolubile Christo est   945
hoc foedus, quod iure potest subvertere iusto,
aversos revocans et suscipiens conversos,
sanguine quos proprio quaesivit prodigus emptor;
si tamen assertoris opem festina voluntas
praeveniat, fletu Dominum motura fideli.   950
nam ut nemo invitus, somnove quietus in alto,
fit salvus, nec vi petitur qui sponte recessit,
sic pulsata patent redeuntibus atria vitae,
et recipit caeli servatos curia cives.
cuius spem veniae firmato corde foventes,   955
implorate Deum, pugnasque relinquite, fratres,
verborum, et lites de pravis sensibus ortas.
nec quia procidimus fusi certamine primo,
stare, et conflictum vereamur inire secundum.
cuncta licet variis terroribus impleat hostis,   960
et vigili clausas obsidat milite portas,
cum victo tamen est bellum, si carne vetusta
exuti, in Christi renovemur corpus, et omnem
vincendi nobis vim de victore petamus.
qui dum nostra suis sociat, iunxit sua nostris,   965
ut non humanis fidens homo, totus in illum
se referat, sine quo non stant qui stare videntur,
et per quem sparsi coeunt, stratique resurgunt.
        Haec sat erit parvo rudibus scripsisse libello,

For we are a captive band, we who were once the shining
vessels of God, and the holy altars and sanctuaries of
Christ, we who possessed the silver of eloquence and the
gold of virtue and the scepter of the cross and the dia- 930
dem of beauty. And let us not arouse the just wrath of
God with frenzied complaints, or by finding fault with
his judgment, which surpasses our powers of thought and
expression, since it is greater than the mighty deep.

Sinners swell up with pride during this short and
fleeting life, and they delight in their offenses in safety and tranquillity. Their vineyards and their fields do 935
not fail them; they inflict injury while escaping harm
themselves, and they prosper through their crimes. But
let us, who have all things in Christ, not be enslaved by
perishable things, for we neither brought them in with
us when we were born, nor shall we carry them out when we
leave this world. And if we have any strength of spirit 940
left, let us shake off the servile yoke of sin, and, when
we have broken our fetters, return to the honorable liberty
of our fatherland. We will not be prevented by unholy
covenants with the fierce tyrant, even though written in
our captive hand, for Christ can dissolve this bond and 945
he has every right to cancel it, while himself calling
back those who have turned away and receiving those who
have turned toward him.

A prodigal purchaser, Christ bought them with his
own blood and, provided only that the swift will anticipates the aid of its deliverer, it will move the Lord by
its sincere tears of repentance. For as no man is saved 950
against his will, or when he rests in a deep sleep, and
the man who has gone astray of his own volition is not
sought out by force, even so the halls of everlasting life
are open to those who return to them and knock, and the
heavenly court receives as citizens those who have been
saved.

While you cherish with strengthened heart the hope
of that forgiveness, call upon God, my brothers, and give 955
up your battles over mere words and the contentions that
have arisen over wrong interpretations. And let us not be
afraid, because we have fallen down in defeat in the first
contest, to stand firm and enter into a second struggle.
Even though the enemy fills all things with manifold ter-
rors, and his watchful army besieges the gates that are 960
closed against it, still our war is with one who has been
conquered. But we must put off the old flesh, be renewed
into the body of Christ, and seek for ourselves all power
to conquer from Christ the Conqueror.

For while he unites what is ours with what is his,
he joins what is his with what is ours, that man may not 965

307

qui cum sincerum vivo de fonte liquorem   970
gustarint, ipsi profundent flumina ab alvo
cordis, et irriguas praebebunt fratribus urnas.

trust in the things of men, but may return entirely to him. And without him those who seem to stand do not stand, while through him the scattered are united and the fallen rise again.

It is enought to have written these thoughts for beginners in a short book. And when they have tasted the pure stream from the living fountain, they will them-   970 selves pour forth rivers from the depths of their hearts, and will offer brimming vessels of water to their brothers.

1-22. **maxima pars lapsis**, etc.: Cf. Boeth.,Cons. 1
carm. 1.1-22 esp. 1-4:
> carmina qui quondam studio florente peregi,
> flebilis, heu, maestos cogar inire modos,
> ecce mihi lacerae distant scribenda camenae
> et veris elegi fletibus ora rigant.

1. **maxima pars**: Cf. Ov., Met. 1.311; Pont. 1.2.83:
"maxima pars"; Verg., Aen. 7.686; Georg. 2.40; Ov.,Met.
2.672; 6.380; Ars 3.229: "pars maxima"; Verg.,Aen. 2.6:
"pars magna."

lapsis . . . mensibus anni: Cf. Verg., Georg. 1.64:
"tot iam labentibus annis"; Ov., Fast. 3.100; Prud.,
Peri. 11.195: "mensibus annus."

5. **carmina curis**: Cf. Verg.,Ecl. 3.61: "carmina
curae."

11. **cui tanta Deo tribuente facultas**: Cf. Verg.,
Aen. 9.97: "cui tanta Deo permissa potestas."

12. **tali tempore**: Cf. Lucr. 1.93: "in tali tempore."

13-14. **quem non concutiat**, etc.: The Maurist editors and Migne print an interrogation mark at the conclusion of v. 14, but it seems that vv. 13-14 are joined
more closely to vv. 11-12. The Lyons edition supports
the punctuation with a period.

13. **concutiat**: concutere ■ "disturb, alarm" is
mostly Silver and Late, except for the perf. part.,
which appears in this sense in the classical poets.
Cf. TLL 4.120. 16-42 and Young, Studies 64.

17. **animum patriae subiit fumantis imago**: Cf. Verg.,
Aen. 2.560: "subiit cari genitoris imago"; 9.294:
"animum patriae strinxit pietatis imago"; 10.824: "mentem
patriae subiit pietatis imago."

18. **et stetit ante oculos**: Cf. Ov., Am. 1.5.17:
"ut stetit ante oculos"; 3.5.10; Her. 15.162; Paul.
Nol., Carm. 6.114: "constitit ante oculos." Cf. also
C. Weyman, Beiträge 147 and n. 1.

19. **immodicis et fletibus**: Cf. Stat., Silv. 5.1.247-
248: "quid nunc immodicos, iuvenum lectissime, fletus/
corde foves longamque vetas exire dolorem?"

immodicis: immodicus = "unrestrained" appears in
Tir. and Nigid., is used by the classical poets, and taken
over from them by Liv. and Sen. Cf. TLL 7.1.485. 41-43.

fletibus ora rigamus: Cf. Verg., Aen. 6.699: "largo
fletu simul ora rigabat"; 9.251: "vultum lacrimis atque
ora rigabat"; Ov., Met. 11.419; "fletibus ora rigavit";
Pont. 2.11.9: "ora rigabas"; Prud., Peri. 11.194: "fletibus ora rigant."

20. pios: pii, subst. pl. = "the faithful, dutiful
men," is Christian. Cf., e.g., Ambr., Isaac 4.37: "animae
piorum." Cf. Blaise, s.v., and Young, Studies 47.

22. saucia corda petunt: Cf. Prud., Psych. 322:
"saucia . . . capiebat corda."

23. rerum hominumque labores: Cf. Verg., Aen. 2.284:
"hominumque urbisque labores."

30. oleis: The mention of olive trees may suggest
Provence as the place of composition of the De prov.
Cf. Intro., p. 21.

33. mali labes: Cf. Verg., Aen. 2.97: "mali labes."

caede decenni: i.e. 406-415 A.D. Cf. Intro., p. 19.

34. Geticis: The identification of the Getae with the
Goths occurs in the Historia Augusta and appears again in
Isidore of Seville. Cf. Valentin, Saint Prosper 784 n. 5.

35-36. oppida montibus altis / imposita: Cf. Verg.,
Aen. 6.774: "imponent montibus arces."

35. montibus altis: This verse tag is very freq.,
often preceded by a prep. Cf., e.g., Lucr. 4.1020;
5.313, 492, 663; 6.735; Verg., Aen. 3.675; 7.563; 10.707;
12.523; Georg. 4.112; Ecl. 7.66; Ov., Met. 1.133.

36. urbes amnibus aequoreis: The cities may have
been Toulouse and Bordeaux, the river the Garonne. Cf.
Intro., pp. 18, n. 2; 19, n.6.

39. nullo discrimine: This phrase is very freq. in
verse. Cf. Lucr. 5.1314; Verg., Aen. 1.574; 10.108;
12.498, 770; Prud., Ham. 72, 99. Cf. also Ov., Trist.

5.10.29; Prud., Symm. 2.826; "discrimine nullo"; Ov., Met. 1.291: "nullum discrimen."

43. quid pueri insontes, quid commisere puellae: Cf. Verg., Aen. 1.231-232: "quid meus Aeneas in te committere tantum / quid Troes potuere?"

45. templa: templum - "Christian church" appears only from the 4th cent. on. Cf. Blaise and Souter, s.v., and C. Mohrmann, "Le latin langue de la chrétienté occidentale," Etudes 1.62.

46. ministerii: ministerium - "ministry, office in the Church," is freq. in Christian authors. Cf. TLL 8.1006.82-1007.4. For ministerium in Roman law, cf. Berger, Encyclopedic Dictionary 583.

48. religionis amor: Cf. Prud., Peri. 11.192; Symm. 2.591: "religionis amor."

53. nominis almi: For nomen - "name of Christ" cf. Acts 4.12: "nec enim aliud nomen est sub caelo datum hominibus." Cf. also Blaise, s.v. and esp. C. Mohrmann, "A propos de deux mots controversés de la latinité chrétienne: tropaeum-nomen," VC 8 (1954) 167-173.

55. flagris: flagrum appears in Plaut., and thereafter rarely throughout the Latin of all periods; it is lacking in Cic., Verg., Hor., Ov., Tac. Cf. TLL 6.1. 848.47-48, and n. on 896, flagra, below.

57. inter et arma: Cf. Verg., Aen. 9.557: "inter et arma."

58. carpebas duram iniusto sub fasce viam: Cf. Verg., Georg. 3.347: "iniusto sub fasce viam cum carpit."

59. senex: For senex - "bishop" cf. Aug., Epist. 128; 129; Prosp., De ingrat. 187. On the identity of the bishop cf. Intro., pp. 19-20.

64. veterum recolamus avorum: Cf. Verg., Aen. 7.177: "veterum effigies ex ordine avorum"; Prud., Symm. 1.39: "veterum procul absit avorum."

69. violentus, atrox, versutus, avarus: Cf. Prud., Peri. 5.467: "violentus, audax, barbarus"; 10.33: "immitis, atrox, asper, implacabilis."

73. sine crimine vitam: Cf. Verg., Aen. 4.550:

"sine crimine vitam"; Ov., Nux 1: "sine crimine vitae";
Prud., Symm. 1.95: "crimine vitam."

75-76. hic inhonorus, inops, etc.: Cf. Ambr., Off.
1.12.40: "iustos inopes degere, inhonoros, sine liberis";
Prosp., In psalm. 144.14: "iusti inhonori ac pauperes
spernuntur a potentibus mundi."

75. iuvenumque senumque: Cf. Verg., Aen. 9.309;
Ov., Met. 7.612: "iuvenumque senumque"; 8.526:
"iuvenesque senesque"; 12.464; 15.210: "inter iuvenemque
senemque."

78. ulcera dira: Cf. Prud., Ham. 928: "post ulcera
dira."

79. falsa . . . vera: Cf. n. on 703, below.

83. celsa spectaret ab arce: Cf. Verg., Aen. 1.56:
"celsa sedet Aeolus arce"; Prud., Ham. 494: "celsa
stans eminus arce."

85. ultrices . . . poenas: ultrices poenae is
cited for Ambr. in Georges, under ultrix. Cf. n. on
748, below.

86. reperta foret: For foret - esset in pluperf. pass.
cf. L.-Hof. 609-610; K.-Steg. 2.1.167. For further instances cf. De prov. 779 (forent), and Neue-Wagener,
Formenlehre 3.153-155.

87-88. talia cum facilis vulgi spargantur in aures:
Cf. Verg., Aen. 2.98-99: "hinc spargere voces / in
vulgum ambiguas"; 2.119: "vulgi quae vox ut venit ad
aures"; Prud., Peri. 1.78: "per aures posterorum spar-
gerent"; Prosp., De ingrat. 33-34: "talia cum demens
late diffunderet error, / commentisque rudes traheret
letalibus aures."

88. rudibus: For rudis subst. - "ignorant, inex-
perienced" cf. Tert.,Scorp. 1: "multos simplices ac
rudes"; Aug., Catech. 8.12: "rudibus indoctisque."
Christian authors frequently use rudis - "candidate for
baptism"; cf. the title of Aug.'s work, De catechizandis
rudibus, and J. P. Christopher, S. Aurelii Augustini
Liber De Catechizandis Rudibus (CUA Patristic Studies 8;
Washington,1926) passim.

91. prome . . . tela pharetris: Cf. Verg., Aen.
5.501: "depromunt tela pharetris"; App. Verg., Ciris

160: "depromens tela pharetra"; Ov., Met. 1.468:
"prompsit duo tela pharetra"; 5.620; Pont. 3.8.19:
"tela pharetra."

93-94. forte aliqui poterunt, etc.: For similar
joining of the concepts "light" and "darkness" cf. Prosp.,
De ingrat. 681-682: "qui vero tenebris exempti in lumine
vivunt / gaudent." For analysis of the biblical use of
the figures of the way and of Christ the light, cf. Intro.,
pp. 33-34.

95-96. at ne sermo moram, etc.: Explicit avowal by
a poet of the metrical difficulties under which he labors
has precedent in classical poetry, although the difficulty
encountered is ordinarily that of fitting a specific word
into verse. Cf. Siefert, Meter and Case 9, n.5, and
Platnauer, Latin Elegiac Verse 103. To the examples cited
add Rut. Nam. 1.419 f.

98. cognoscenda forent: For forent - essent with fut.
pass. part. cf. L.-Hof. 556-557; K.-Steg. 2.1.168. Cf.
also De prov. 339, forent . . . reparanda.

in aequore aperto: Cf. Verg., Aen. 12.333: "aequore
aperto"; Ov., Met. 4.527; 11.555; "in apertum . . .
aequor."

99. ventis dare libera vela secundis: Cf. Verg.,
Aen. 3.683: "ventis intendere vela secundis"; 7.23:
"ventis implevit vela secundis"; Ov., Her. 16.163
/17.163/: "vela quidem Creten ventis dedit ille secundis."

100. rudibus: Cf. n. on 88, above.

102. tellus circumdata ponto: Cf. Ov., Met. 2.272:
"tellus . . . circumdata ponto."

106. error: error = "paganism, heresy" appears in
Christian authors from Itala and Tert. on. Cf., e.g.,
Tert., Apol. 46.18: "philosophus et Christianus, amicus
et inimicus erroris"; Min. Fel. 3.1; Hier., Epist. 28.5;
Aug., Civ. 6.1; Nat. bon. 42.1-3; Prosp., De ingrat.
praef. xxi. Cf. TLL 5.2.818.18-47.

108. genitorem: genitor appears from Enn. and Acc.
on, primarily in poetry or in prose passages of an elevated tenor. Cf. TLL 6.2.1816.51-59. genitor = "the
Creator," as here, is Christian. Cf., e.g., Iuvenc.,
praef. 4: "genitor rerum." Christian authors also use

genitor = "God the Father" (as opposed to the Son).
Cf., e.g., Iuvenc. 1.320: "genitor dominusque salutis"
(i.e., Father and Son); 1.390; 2.507. On the two latter
usages cf. also TLL 6.2.1819.46-78.

113-129. condidit ut voluit, etc.: For treatment
of similarities between this passage and Ov., Met. 1.7-9,
15-20, cf. Intro.,p. 71.

113-114. condidit ut voluit, etc.: Cf. Prosp.,
Epigr. 91.9-10: /Deum/ fingentem rebus formas, loca,
tempora, motus, / mensuris, numeris, ponderibusque suis."

113. condidit: condere - creare is freq. among
Christian authors. Cf. Aug., Fid. et symb. 4.5: "idem
est condere quod creare . . . cum sine ambiguitate loqui
volumus, non dicimus creare sed condere"; TLL 4.154.30-
55. This usage appears also at De prov. 121, 153, 177,
221. For creare used to denote the creative action of
God, cf. TLL 4.1161.21-74.

numerosque modosque: Cf. Verg., Aen. 11.328:
"numerumque modumque."

114. semina rebus: Cf. Lucr. 1.59: "semina rerum."

114. quidquid inest caelo, quidquid terraeque marique: Cf. Lucr. 4.43: "terrai maris et caeli generisque
animantum"; 6.678: "omnia cum caelo terraque marique";
Ov., Fast. 1.117: "quidquid ubique vides, caelum, mare,
nubila, terras"; Iuvenc. 1.486: "donec caeli terraeque
marisque interitus veniat." The combination heaven-
earth-sea is freq. in Scripture. Cf. Ex. 20.11; Tob.
8.7; Ps.68 (69).35; 134 (135).6; 145 (146).6; Agg. 2.6;
Acts 4.24; Apoc. 5.13; 14.7.

115. terraeque marique: Cf. Lucr. 3.837; 5.219; 6.678:
"terraque marique"; Verg., Aen. 1.598: "terraeque marisque'; 10.162: "terraque marique"; Ov., Met. 2.96:
"terraeque marisque"; Prud., Symm. 2.579: "terraque
marique."

118. Verbo: For Verbum = "the Divine Logos, the
Son of God," cf., e.g., Vulg., John 1.1: "in principio
erat Verbum"; 14: "et Verbum caro factum est." Verbum
in this sense is later than Sermo, which appears in
Itala, Tert., Cypr. Cf. Souter, s.v. sermo, Cf. also
Br. A. Anthony Moon, F.S.C., The De Natura Boni 179:
"In fid. et symb. 3, 3-4, PL 40, 183-184, Augustine

explains why God the Son is called the Word. Verbum, he says, is not used with reference to Christ in the sense of our spoken words, which endure only as long as they sound. The Word remains immutable, for of Him as of Wisdom it is written: In se ipsa manens innovat omnia (Sap. 7.27). The word of the Father is so-called because the Father becomes known through him. When we speak the truth, our mind (animus) becomes known to the listener, and the word-symbols bring out that which has been hidden in our heart to the knowledge of another. Likewise, God the Father, though hidden (secretissimus), becomes known to worthy souls through that Wisdom which He has begotten, and which is then fittingly called His Word. . . . Cf. also conf. 11, 6-9. PL 32, 812-814; epist. 102, 11. PL 33, 374."

119. elementa: elementa pl. - "the (constitutive) elements of the world" is cited for Ov., Plin. Mai., Tac., and is freq. in Christian authors. Cf. TLL 5.2.346.13-63 and, for a survey of the uses of elementum at all periods, H. Diels, Elementum (diss., Leipzig, 1899).

120. protulit: proferre = "bear, produce" is Silver and Late. The use of proferre with reference to the creative activity of God is Christian. Cf. Min. Fel. 32.2: "hostias . . . in usum mei protulit." Cf. Benoist and Blaise, s.v. For proferre = "bear, produce," with reference to the creative power of the earth, cf. n. on 606, below.

121-150. quod vero adversis, etc.: Prosp. applies a similar contrast to the characters of men, who are all fashioned by the same creator while in temperament they may be opposite to each other. Cf. De ingrat. 721-743.

123-124. contraria discors / omnia motus alit: Cf. Verg., Aen. 6.724-726:
    . . . caelum ac terram corpusque liquentis
  lucentemque globum, lunam Titaniaque astra
  spiritus intus alit . . .
127-129. mollia sic duris, etc.: Cf. Prud., Ham. 325-326: "quid durum, quid molle foret, quid lene, quid horrens, / quid calidum gelidumve."

130-131: nec mihi fas dixisse aliquid, etc.: Cf.

Prosp., De ingrat. 740-741: "nec tamen haec inter tam
compugnantia quisquam / arguit auctorem . . ."

130. dixisse: the use of the perf. inf. instead of
the pres. inf. originated after verbs of prohibition and
wish, and was greatly expanded by the elegiac poets for
metrical reasons. Cf. Platnauer, Latin Elegiac Verse
109-112 and K.-Steg. 2.1.133-134. Cf. also De prov. 849,
placuisse.

132. sator: For sator = "creator" cf., e.g., Paul.
Nol., Carm. 10.50; 29.19. Cf. Blaise, s.v. At De ingrat.
891 rerumque sator refers to Christ; at De ingrat. 915
mortis sator denotes Satan.

137. inter hyperboreas . . . pruinas: Cf. Val. Fl.
8.211: "hyperboreas . . . pruinas."

138. iniusto pluviam metuit sub fasce viator: Cf.
Verg., Georg. 3.347: "iniusto sub fasce viam cum carpit,"
Prud., Apoth. 720: "sub fasce minister."

140. caeruleos angues: Cf. Verg., Georg. 4.482:
"caeruleosque angues."

isti: The use of iste - ille = hic - ille is treated
in TLL 7.1.346.4-16. It is almost entirely Silver and
Late, appearing from Val. Max. on.

142. lyncasque: For the acc. pl. termination of
lynx in -as cf. Hor., Carm. 2.13.40; 4.6.34; Ov., Met.
15.413. Cf. also K.-Steg. 1.372.

143. Scythiae: Cf. Courcelle, Histoire littéraire
75 n.4: "Le nom de Scythe est appliqué, au sens péjoratif,
par Oros. /5th cent./, Hist. 7.37.9 p. 539. 14 au Goth
Radagaise--et déjà auparavant aux Wisigoths, par Synesius."

Getarum: Cf. n. on 34, above.

144. queis: This alternative form of quibus occurs
freq. in the poets, but seldom in prose of the classical
period. Cf. K.-Steg. 1.613, and, for an extensive list
of occurrences, Neue-Wagener, Formenlehre 2.469.

Serum: The first allusions to the Seres (Chinese)
who are identified as producers of silk, occur in the
poets of the Augustan Age. Cf., e.g., Verg., Georg.
2.131: "velleraque ut foliis depectant tenuia Seres";
Hor., Carm. 1.12.56; 3.29.27; 4.15.23; Ov., Am. 1.14.6.

The number of references increases in the Silver Age, but by the 5th cent. Seres apparently referred to any distant people. This latter sense appears as early as Lucan 10.292 (the Ethiopians). Cf. Herrmann, "Seres," in RE 2.2.2.1678-1683.

145. decor: decor appears in Laev. and Cic., but is mostly Poetic. Cf. TLL 5.1.206.23-25 and n. on 917, below.

tergis horrere ferarum: Cf. Verg., Aen. 7.20; Ov., Met. 14.66; Prud., Symm. 1.128: "terga ferarum."

147. scire datum: For pass. forms of dare with inf. = licet, fieri potest, cf. K.-Steg. 2.1.675; TLL 6.1. 1689.48-81. Cf. esp. Sen., Epist. 124.20: "quibus datum est scire."

148. quidquid variatur in herbis: Cf. App. Verg., Moretum 106: "tot variatur ab herbis."

149. subsistere: subsistere = "be, exist" is Late. Cf. Blaise and Souter, s.v., and Young, Studies 69. Cf. also De prov. 737, 803. Authors of the Silver Age use subsistere = "persist, endure, remain in the same state"; cf. Benoist and Forcellini, s.v.

156. dant: For dare = "ascribe, attribute" cf. TLL 5.1.1682.7-76; for attribution esp. to gods and heroes, TLL 5.1.1682.56-65.

159. o mersi in tenebras: For the figurative depiction of man as sunk in darkness, cf. Job 37.19: "nos quippe involvimur tenebris"; 1 Tim. 6.9: "desideria . . . quae mergunt homines in interitum et perditionem."

160. corporeis oculis: For other instances of bodily and spiritual illumination cast in figurative terms, cf. Matt. 6.22-23; Luke 11.33-36. For the contrast between "the eyes of the body" and "the eyes of the soul" cf. Ambr., Hex. 1.7.26: "/terra/ visibilis corporeis oculis non poterat"; Paul. Nol., Carm. 31.207: "corporeis oculis divina teguntur"; Rufin. (ob. 470), Adamant. 2.11: "corporei oculi."

166-167. insomnibus aegram / partiri curis, etc.: Cf. Verg., Aen. 1.208: "curisque ingentibus aeger"; 12.487: "diversaeque vocant animum in contraria curae."

174. <u>genita</u> et <u>gignentia</u>: Cf. Verg., <u>Aen</u>. 9.642:
"genite et geniture."

182. <u>meta</u> <u>est</u>: Cf. Ov., <u>Met</u>. 10.597: "meta est."

183-194: <u>sed</u> <u>nusquam</u> <u>non</u> <u>esse</u> <u>Dei</u> <u>est</u>, etc.: Cf.
the description of the works and attributes of Yahweh at
<u>Sir</u>. 42.15-25.

183. <u>esse</u> <u>Dei</u> est, <u>qui</u> <u>totus</u> <u>ubique</u>: Cf. Prud.,
<u>Apoth</u>. 638: "Deus est, qui totus ubique est."

185. <u>moderamina</u> <u>rerum</u>: Cf. Ov., <u>Met</u>. 6.677: "rerumque capit moderamen."

<u>moderamina</u>: The pl. appears from Ov. on, and is
mostly Poetic. Ov. seems to have formed the word as a
metrical equivalent of <u>moderatio</u>. <u>moderamen</u>, sg., appears in prose from Apul. on. Cf. <u>TLL</u> 8.1203.36-39. For
the use of the word in relation to the divine government
of the universe cf., e.g., Apul., <u>Mund</u>. 30: "uno moderamine
contenta omnia"; Paul. Nol., <u>Carm</u>. 8.5: "aeterno . . .
moderamine." Cf. further <u>TLL</u> 8.1204.9-18.

190. <u>de</u> <u>noscendis</u>: Usage of the gerundive of <u>noscere</u>
as a subst. appears to be unexampled, but the same is
true of the alternative reading, <u>dignoscendis</u>, which,
furthermore, does not yield a satisfactory sense.

<u>egeat</u> . . . <u>doceri</u>: Forms of <u>egere</u> with complementary
inf. pass. appear once in Mela, and also at Prosp.,<u>De</u>
<u>ingrat</u>. 885; Resp. ad Gall. 1.8; Resp. ad Gen. 1-3;
C. coll. 15.1, and occasionally in other Christian authors.
Cf. K.-Steg. 2.1.675; <u>TLL</u> 5.2.238.14-29.

<u>manifesta</u>: manifestus - certus is rare, being cited
at <u>TLL</u> 8.310.68-70 only for <u>De</u> <u>prov</u>. 911 and Ennod.,
<u>Epist</u>. 2.19.2.

191. <u>abdita</u>: Cf. Cypr., <u>Laps</u>. 27: "Deus perspicit
abdita et secreta et occulta considerat."

192. <u>det</u> <u>vitas</u> <u>adimatque</u>: Cf. Verg., <u>Aen</u>. 4.244:
"dat somnos adimitque"; Ov., <u>Met</u>. 8.615: "si dant
adimuntque figuras."

<u>salvet</u>: Apart from its use in the medical writer
Garg. Mart., salvare is confined to Christian authors.
Cf. Blaise and Souter, <u>s</u>.<u>v</u>., and Young, <u>Studies</u> 27.

194. <u>peccata</u> <u>remittat</u>: In the O.T. the power to

remit sin is ascribed to Yahweh. Cf. Ps. 31 (32).5:
". . . et tu remisisti impietatem peccati mei"; Ps.
84(85).3: "remisisti iniquitatem plebis tuae, operuisti
omnia peccata eorum"; Sir. 2.13: "et remittet /Deus/
in die tribulationis peccata." For Christ's power to forgive sins, cf. 1 John 1.9; 2.12; for his exercise of the
power, cf. Matt. 9.2; Luke 5.20; 7.47.

195. Omnipotenti: For omnipotens, subst. - "the
Christian God," cf. e.g., Ex. 15.3: "Omnipotens nomen
eius"; Job 34.12: "nec Omnipotens subvertet iudicium";
Prud., Ham. 307; Psych. 815; Prosp., De ingrat. 755;
Epigr. 24.1; Vocat. gent. 1.1. Cf. Blaise, s.v., and
Young, Studies 47.

197-198. hominis . . . in tempora nati / exigui:
Cf. Solomon's portrayal of himself at Wisd. 9.5: "homo
infirmus, et exigui temporis."

200. in pecudum genus et sortem transire ferarum:
Cf. Varro, Rust. 2.1.5: "genera pecudum ferarum."

204. degeneri . . . metu: Cf. Lucan 3.149:
"degenerisque metus."

204-205. potiusque relictum, etc.: Cf. 1 Tim. 6.12:
"apprehende vitam aeternam"; 19: "ut apprehendant veram
vitam."

205. immortale decus: Cf. Prud., Symm. 2.757:
"decus immortale."

208. vaniloqui: Cf. Tit. 1.10: "sunt enim multi
etiam inoboedientes, vaniloqui et seductores."

209-223. res monet a primis, etc.: Cf. Gen. 1.1-27;
2.7-16.

211. Christo donante: Cf. Paul. Nol., Carm. 12.35:
"Christo donante."

212-223. dispositis rebus, etc.: For analysis of
the relationship between this passage and Ov., Met. 1.69-
86, cf. Intro., pp. 69-70.

213. pulchra vernabat origine mundus: Cf. Verg.,
Aen. 1.286: "pulchra Troianus origine Caesar"; 2.336:
"origine mundi"; Lucr. 5.548; Ov., Met. 1.3; Trist.
2.559: "ab origine mundi."

215. praebebat lumina: Cf. Ov., Met. 1.10:
"praebebat lumina."

216. iam pecudes tellus, iam pisces pontus alebat:
Cf. Ov., Trist. 5.2.25: "silva feras quot alit, quot
piscibus unda natatur."

217. liquidum volucres innabant aera pennis: Cf.
/Tib./ Paneg. Messall. 4.1.209: "per liquidum volucris
vehar aera pennis"; Ov., Met. 11.194: "liquidumque per
aera vectus"; 732; Prud., Ham. 816; Psych. 305: "aera
pennis." For citations from Verg., cf. Intro., pp. 53-54.

219-228. nondum erat in terris, etc.: Cf. Drac.,
Laud. Dei /post De prov./ 1.329-332:
   omnibus his genitis, animal rationis amicum
   formatur virtute Dei, limatur in artus,
   ut dominanter eat moderatior omnibus unus,
   naturae iussu quae protulit omnia princeps.

221. plus genitoris haberet: Cf. Prosp., De ingrat.
970: "minimumque operis mortalis habere."

genitoris: Cf. n. on 108, above.

222. substantia duplex: substantia - "substance,
nature," in reference to the union of soul and body in
man, appears to be Late. Cf., e.g., Tert., Paen. 3:
"ex hac duplicis substantiae congregatione confectus homo";
Aug., Nupt. et conc. 2.9.21: "substantia animi et corporis"; Prud., Psych. 909: "duplex substantia." For a
thorough discussion of the various senses of substantia
cf. Blaise, s.v. Contrast the use of substantia at n. on
324, below.

224-230. namque anima ex nullis, etc.: There is
evidence in this passage of vagueness of doctrine on the
individual soul. mortis (226) is to be taken as "spiritual death," as is clear from expers interitus (225-226),
and also from cruciabilis (226), which suggests the idea
of torment. The common departure of soul and body (manet
exitus unus utrumque, 230) is therefore physical death,
and does not imply annihilation of the soul. The phrases
terrenamque illapsa domum, 227, and divinum haurire vaporem,
228, may be derived from Priscillianism, which had itself
borrowed from Plotinus the teaching that the soul enjoyed
a preexistence before its earthly life. Cf. Valentin,
Saint Prosper 779, and, for Priscillianism, Tixeront,
History of Dogmas 2.229-241, and n. on 624-720, below.

The lack of precision in thought is accompanied by a lack of precision in syntax, viz., the anacolouthon at v. 227.

225. cruciabilis: The use of adjs. terminating in -bilis is very much in the Vergilian manner. Cf., e.g., Aen. 2.234; 8.334, ineluctabile; 12.858, immedicabile; 6.27, inextricabilis; 5.591 (nom.), 6.425 (gen.), irremeabilis; 10.467, irreparabile, all cited by A. Cordier, Etudes sur le vocabulaire épique dans l'"Eneide" de Virgile (Paris,1939) 186.

227. terrenamque illapsa domum: illabi with the acc. obj. is mostly Late, being cited at TLL 7.1.334. 24-25 /through the cross references given there/ for Sil., Avien., Paul. Nol., Claud.

dat vivere secum: dare = "allow, permit" with acc. and inf. appears in Verg. and poets of the Silver Age, and in Christian Latin from Itala on. Cf., e.g., Verg., Aen. 3.77: "/tellurem/ immotamque coli dedit et contemnere ventos"; Itala, Isa. 43.28: "dedi perire Iacob." Cf. TLL 6.1.1689.82-1690.32.

229-234. nec quia dissimilis, etc.: The warfare in man between the flesh and the spirit is a Pauline theme. Cf. Rom. 7.13-23; Gal. 5.16-17; 2 Tim. 4.7 The theme appears again at De prov. 660-661; 918-920; 958-964.

230. manet exitus unus utrumque: Cf. Verg., Aen. 10.630: "nunc manet insontem gravis exitus"; Ov., Met. 8.60; 9.726; Prud., Ditt. 159: "manet exitus."

237. premat: promat is metrically impossible here. The poet is generally careful about vowel quantity, and scans forms of promere correctly in the two instances in De prov. where the quantity of the -o is determinable, viz., at vv. 91, 656. Cf. Intro., p 184 n. 11 and Valentin, Saint Prosper 845.

238-240. sed quia liber homo, etc.: Cf. Prosp., De ingrat. 977: "libertate agimus, sed libertate redempta," and Huegelmeyer, Carmen de Ingratis, ad loc. (p. 208): "The actual cooperation of the two /grace and free will/ is a mystery, but it is clear that grace does not destroy free will, nor is free will the same under the influence of grace, as the will of Adam before the Fall. . . . Cf. De prov. 238-240. The liber homo in this passage is 'redeemed man,' whose mens retains ius voluntatis. Cf. C. coll. 8.3."

Antelmy, De veris operibus 406, suspects vv. 238-246 as being unorthodox in doctrine. Valentin, op. cit., 888, upholds vv. 238-240 as an affirmation of human liberty and freedom of conscience against Teuffel, who had challenged them as suspect of semipelagianism. The orthodoxy of the doctrine enunciated in the passage is not challenged by the Maurists.

238-239. discernere rectis / prava: For the contrast between "right" and "wrong" expressed by the substs. rectum and pravum cf. Ter., Phorm. 771: "eis nunc praemiumst, qui recta prava faciunt"; Cic., Ac. 2.11.33: "interesse oportet, ut inter rectum et pravum sic inter verum et falsum"; De orat. 3.50.195: "quae sint in artibus recta ac prava diiudicare." The same contrast occurs at De prov. 286, 556.

239. discrimina rerum: Cf. Verg., Aen. 1.204: "discrimina rerum."

240. voluntatis: Cf. Aug.'s definition of voluntas, De duab. anim. 10.14: "animi motus, cogente nullo ad aliquid vel non admittendum, vel adipiscendum." Cf. also Retract. 1.15.2.

arbitrium: arbitrium is rare among the classical poets, except Hor. and Ov. Cf. TLL 2.1.410.1-3. Forms of the word appear 28 times in the De ingrat., however. For arbitrium as the power of choosing right or wrong cf. TLL 2.1.412.67-413.31.

242-243. non de se tumeat, etc.: Cf. Prosp., De ingrat. 907-909:
non ita pro summis oblectent ultima lapsos,
ut de supplicio tumeant atque ordine verso,
quo sunt effecti miseri, sint inde superbi.

243. inde: inde - a quo is used with reference to persons by Plaut., Ter., Lucr., and appears often in Late Latin. Cf. TLL 7.1.1119.9-46, and esp. Tert., Apol. 30.3: "inde est imperator unde et homo . . . inde potestas illi unde et spiritus." The same construction appears at De prov. 392, q. v. Cf. also n. on 339, unde, below.

244. insita sic nobis patriae virtutis imago est: Cf. Verg., Aen. 9.294: "animum patriae strinxit pietatis

imago"; 10.824: "mentem patriae subiit pietatis imago"; Ov., Pont. 2.8.31: "virtutis imagine natum"; Prud., Psych. 2: "patria virtute."

246. lumen divinum: Cf. n. on 544, below.

249. totaque res effecta Dei: Cf. Prud., Cath. 11. 23-24: "virtute verbi effecta sunt / haec cuncta"; Verg., Aen. 11.14: "maxima res effecta viri."

252. nescia: nescius with the complementary inf. is freq. among the poets. Cf., e.g., Verg., Georg. 2.467: "nescia fallere vita"; Hor., Carm. 1.6.6: "cedere nescii"; Iuv. 11.100: "Graias mirari nescius artes."

253. nullisque obnoxia damnis: Cf. Ov., Met. 15.853: "nullisque obnoxia iussis."

254. quo promissis adsit fiducia magnis: Cf. Verg., Aen. 10.152: "humanis quae sit fiducia rebus"; Ov., Met. 7.309: "quo sit fiducia maior."

255. propositae coronae: Cf. n. on 604-605, ut superas caperemus, below.

258-259. huic caeli volucres, etc.: Cf. n. on 264-266, hunc potiorem unum, below.

260-263. huic solis lunaeque vices, et sidera noctis, etc.: Cf. Verg., Georg. 2.477-478: "caelique vias et sidera monstrent / defectus solis varios lunaeque labores"; Lucr. 5.751: "solis item quoque defectus lunaeque"; 1.1065; Ov., Am. 1.6.44: "sidera noctis"; Prosp., De ingrat. 871-874:

iam cum exercetur /sapientia7 numeris ad sidera caeli
per cursus noscenda suos et scire videtur
defectus solis varios lunaeque labores . . .

261. nosse datum: Cf. n. on 147, above.

"numerisque . . . comprendere" Cf. Verg., Georg. 2.104; Ov., Ars 2.447; 3.151: "numero comprendere"; Trist. 5.11.19: "numerum comprendere."

262. scire potestates herbarum: Cf. Verg., Aen. 12.396: "scire potestates herbarum."

262-263. nomina rebus / indere: For man's prerogative of assigning names to the lower creatures, cf. Gen. 2.19-20.

263. ingenium varias augere per artes: Cf. Verg.,

NOTES

Georg. 1.133: "ut varias usus meditando extunderet
artes"; Prud., Symm. 2.390: "varias agitetur ad artes."

264-266. hunc potiorem unum, etc.: Man's dominion
over the lower animals is mentioned at Gen. 1.26-28;
9.2-3; Ps. 8.6-9; Sir. 17.3-4. Cf. De prov. 258-259.

264-265. uni / subiectum servire Deo: Cf. Prud.,
Peri. 5.172: "ooliquе subiectum Deo."

265. corporea vi: Cf. Paul. Nol., Epist. 16.2:
"mundum istum corporeum vi incorporea gubernari."

266. praefortibus: praefortis is Late, being cited
first in the lexica for Tert. Cf., e.g., Tert., Carm.
Chr. 5; Prosp., De ingrat. 352. Cf. Geroges, Benoist,
and Blaise s.v.

271. corrupti exiguum semen superesse vigoris: Contrast Prosp.'s description of the effects on the integrity
of man's nature if man had not suffered the consequences
of original sin, at De ingrat. 880-888.

273-277. in summum sancti generis, etc.: The special
creation of man, and Adam's condition in paradise, are
described at Gen. 2.7-16.

277. cultarum locuples virtutum fruge: Cf. Prosp.,
De ingrat. 958: "infecundi virtutum et fruge carentes."
Cf. also De prov. 893.

278-288. cui cum tanta Deus, etc.: For the biblical
account of the temptation and fall, cf. Gen. 2.17; 3.1-13.
--A passage of somewhat similar tenor occurs at Prosp.,
De ingrat. 915-919:
    hoc patribus primis mortis sator insinuatus
    consilio est, hoc arte omnes prostravit in uno,
    dum suadet multo praestantius esse quod ipsis,
    non tribuente licet Domino, sponderet habendum
    prudens libertas vetitoque instructa cupido . . .

278. largitus fuisset: The so-called "double" pluperf. of pass. verbs, composed of perf. pass. part. and
pluperf. of sum, appears in the subj. from Cic., and with
increasing frequency in Silver and Late Latin. Cf. L.-Hof.
562; K.-Steg. 2.1.164-165. For further instances with
the subj., cf. Neue-Wagener, Formenlehre 3.139, 145.
Cf. also De prov. 686, delapsa fuisset, and 755, properata
fuisset. For instances with the indic. among the elegiac
poets cf. Platnauer, Latin Elegiac Verse 114-115.

325

279. **viperei populi princeps**: The reference to the viper is scriptural. Cf. Matt. 3.7: "progenies viperarum" (Pharisees and Sadducees); Luke 3.7: "genimina viperarum" (the same); Matt. 23.33: "serpentes genimina viperarum" (Scribes and Pharisees). Cf. also Prosp., De ingrat. 71: "agmen vipereum"; 598: "vipereo . . . susurro"; 804: "viperei . . . sensus"; 934: "viperei calicis." Cf. n. on 876, below.

279-280. **alta / deiectus regione poli**: Cf. n. on 619-621, below.

280. **summa**: **summum**, subst. neut. sg., = "height," is found from Plaut. on; cf. Benoist, s.v. The same usage appears in scripture; cf., e.g., Jer. 51.31: "a summo usque ad summum." The pl. in this sense is rare, appearing in Bell. Afr., Curt., Sen., Mart., Priap.; cf. Benoist and Georges, s.v., and also Vulg., Matt. 24.31: "a summis caelorum usque ad terminos eorum."

285. **perpulit a vetitis pomum decerpere ramis**: Cf. Ov., Met. 5.536: "decerpserat arbore pomum"; Prud.,Cath. 3.109: "stipite carpere poma veto"; Paul. Nol., Carm. 15.291: "decerpere ramo"; Prosp., De ingrat. 919: "vetitoque instructa cupido."

286. **queis**: Cf. n. on 144, **queis**, above.

recti et **pravi**: Cf. n. on 238-239, **discernere recta**, above.

experientia: **experientia** appears from Varro and Cic. but is more freq. among later authors. Cf. TLL 5.2.1651. 69-71.

287. **acceperat hanc vim**: Cf. Verg., Aen. 3.242-243: "neque vim plumis ullam . . . / accipiunt."

289-290. **his illata dolis**, etc.: For the transmission of Adam's sin to his descendants, cf. Rom. 5.12. Cf. also Prosp., De ingrat. 550-552:
. . . uno omnes homines cecidisse ruente,
in quo tota simul series prostrata nepotum
deperiit . . .

hoc crimine nata subegit / mors hominem, etc.: Cf. Rom. 5.2: "per unum hominem peccatum in hunc mundum intravit, et per peccatum mors, et ita in omnes homines mors pertransiit"; Prosp., De ingrat. 155-156: "inciderit mortem peccando, suamque / progeniem culpa et leto devinxerit omnem."

291. antiqua . . . virtutis ab arce: Cf. Verg., Aen. 3.342: "in antiquam virtutem"; Ov., Met. 11.343: "virtutem antiquam."

292. non uno tantum . . . errore parentum: Cf. App. Verg., Ciris 240: "uno . . . errore parentum."

294. multiplicem lata porrexit strage ruina: Cf. Prosp., De ingrat. 889-890: "sed prostrata semel, quanto natura profundo / immersa et quantae sit mole oppressa ruinae."

295-302. at quamquam immissa, etc.: Antelmy, De veris operibus 406, questions the orthodoxy of this passage. Valentin, Saint Prosper 888, defends the passage as meaning that the just persons of the O.T. could receive their reward only after the Incarnation, a perfectly orthodox belief.

295. peremptor: This reading, suggested by Valentin, Saint Prosper 845, has been adopted to avoid the inconcinnity involved in taking as the subject of the subordinate clause the same word, Dominus, which appears as indirect object of the principal clause. peremptor is Silver and Late. For peremptor = "Satan" cf. Prosp., De ingrat. 898: "cuius /Christi/ perimatur morte peremptor"; C. coll. 9.3: "inimicus peremptor." Contrast emptor = "redeemer" at De prov. 948.

302. destrueret leti causas, etc.: Cf. Aug., Pecc. Mer. 1.11.13: "gratia Salvatoris destruit regnum mortis."

305. onerans altaria sacris: Cf. Verg., Aen. 5.101: "onerant aras"; 11.50: "cumulatque altaria donis"; Lucr. 4.1237: "adolentque altaria donis."

305-316. non latet hanc, etc.: The story of Cain and Abel is recounted at Gen. 4.1-8; cf. esp. 4.4: "Abel quoque obtulit de primogenitis gregis sui et de adipibus eorum et respexit Dominus ad Abel et ad munera eius." Cf. also Prud., Peri. 10.828-830:
    ut primitivum crederes fetum geri
    Deo offerendum sancti Abelis ferculo
    lectum ex ovili, puriorem ceteris.

306. **primitiis**: **primitiae** - "first fruits" in freq. in poetry. Cf.,e.g., Ov., Met. 8.274; Fast. 2.520. For the same usage in scripture, cf., e.g., Ex. 22.29: "primitias tuas non tardabis reddere"; 23.19: "primitias frugum terrae tuae deferes in domum Domini Dei tui." For primitiae in a figurative sense, cf., e.g., 1 Cor. 15.20: "primitiae dormientium" (of Christ); Prosp., De ingrat. 282: "crescunt primitiae" (the early Church).

ovium grege: Cf. Paul. Nol., Carm. 14.131: "ovium grege."

lectis: **legere** - "choose (from among several)" is classical, but eligere is preferred. Cf. Benoist and Georges at lego and eligo.

307. **convertit Domini . . . vultum**: Cf. Num. 6.26: "convertat Dominus vultum ad te et det tibi pacem."

309. **reprobanda**: **reprobare** - "condemn" is Late. Cf., e.g., Ps. 32 (33).10: "Dominus . . . reprobat autem cogitationes populorum, et reprobat consilia principum"; 117 (118).22: "lapidem quem reprobaverunt aedificantes, hic factus est in caput anguli"; Tert.,Marc. 4.15; Hier., Epist. 119.11; Prosp., In psalm. 106.40; De ingrat. 791, 792 (in a paraphrase of Ps. 117/118/ .22); Vocat. gent. 1.10. Cf. also Benoist and Blaise, s.v., and Young, Studies 28.

313. **formamque**: **forma** - "rule, precept" occurs as early as Cic. and Varro, but is mostly Late. Cf. TLL 6.1.1085.82-1086.55, and n. on 407, formas, below.

316. **impietas**: The personification of impietas is rare, appearing in Sen., Hil., Aug., Drac. (5th cent.). Cf. TLL 7.1.614.14-19, and add Prosp., De ingrat. 692: "insana impietas." impietas in Christian authors often - "lack of belief in the true God." Cf. TLL 7.1.613. 25-70.

primordia mundi: Cf. Ov., Met. 15.67: "primordia mundi."

319. **tribuenda corona**: Cf. n. on 604-605, ut superas, below.

320. **aeterni . . . honoris**: Cf. App. Verg., Ciris 100: "aeterno . . . honore."

321. **transtulit Enoch**: Henoch's miraculous removal

from the earth is narrated at Gen. 5.24: "ambulavitque
/Henoch/ cum Deo, et non apparuit: quia tulit eum Deus."

324. substantia carnis: substantia = "substance,
matter" is Silver and Late. Cf. Quint., Inst. 7.2.5:
"substantia hominis" (the body). Cf. Benoist and Blaise,
s.v. Contrast substantia at n. on 222, above.

327-328. cum raptum ignitis, etc.: The story of
Elias' removal from earth is narrated at 4 Kgs. 2.11:
"ecce currus igneus et equi ignei diviserunt utrumque et
ascendit Helias per turbinem in caelum." Cf. Prud., Cath.
7.31-32: "sed mox in auras igneis iugalibus / curruque
raptus evolavit praepete"; Verg., Aen. 5.819: "caeruleo
per summa levis volat aequora curru"; App. Verg., Culex
212: "rapior per inania."

ignitis: ignitus is Late, appearing from Gell. and
Apul. on. Cf. TLL 7.1.286.65-69. For ignitus - "fiery,
hot" cf., e.g., Apul., Mund. 1: "aether vocatur non . . .
quod ignitus sit et incensus";Prosp., In psalm. 148.7-8:
"quidquid . . . in coruscationibus apparet ignitum." Cf.
TLL 7.1.286.81-287.44.

329-331. an aberat tum cura Dei, etc.: For the race
of giants, i.e., great sinners, begotten by Adam's descendants, cf. Gen. 6.4; Wisd. 14.6; Bar. 3.26-28.

331. dira toris vetitis, etc.: The text restores the
interrogation mark found at the conclusion of the verse
in the Maurist edition, as against Migne, who omits any
mark of punctuation. Verse 332 is joined closely with
tempora larga in 333, as a general reference to all that
precedes. Granted the giants by their appearance on
earth foreshadowed the destruction that would be effected
by the flood, they were merely the last in a series of
indications of approaching calamity, which began with
Adam's sin.

monstra gigantas: Cf. Ov., Fast. 5.35-36: "terra
feros partus, immania monstra Gigantes / edidit."--For
the acc. pl. termination of gigas in -as cf. Neue-Wagener,
Formenlehre 1.448, citing Ov., Met. 1.152; 5.319; 10.150;
Sen., Oed. 91; Prud., Ham. 499. Cf. also K.-Steg. 1.372.

On the giants cf. E. F. Sutcliffe, S.J., in CCHS at
Gen. 6.4: ."The Nephilim are mentioned Num. 13:34

(MT 33) as a Canaanite race of giants in Moses' time
. . . They are referred to in Wis. 14:6, Ecclus.16:8,
Bar.3:26-8, etc. The term 'giants'does not imply more
than unusually tall stature, and its import is relative
to the average height of the race using it. The Hebrews
were not a tall nation."

333. reducti: The early reading deducti is rejected
by later editors, and is impossible metrically. The poet
employs forms of deducere with the e of the first syllable scanned correctly as long at De prov. 207, 722.

334. scelerum seriem: Cf. Ov., Met. 4.564: "serieque
malorum"; Pont. 1.4.19: "series immensa malorum."

335-340. cumque nefas placitum, etc.: The story of
Noe and the flood is told at Gen. 6.9-8.19; cf. also
De prov. 826, 842-843.

336. diluvio: Cf. n. on 826, diluvium, below.

338. spirantum: The gen. ending of spirans in -um
occurs also at Sil. 10.554; Stat., Theb. 4.559; Auson.,
Mos. 96.   Cf. K. Georges, Lexikon der lateinischen
Wortformen (Leipzig,1890) s.v., and Neue-Wagener, Formenlehre 2.144. Cf. also K.-Steg. 1.353; L.-Hof. 278-279.

339. unde: Employment of the rel. adv. as rel. pro.
is freq. in pre-classical Latin, e.g., Cato, Agr. 5.3:
"duas aut tres familias habeat, unde utenda roget." The
idiom was retained in popular speech, and is freq. in
Late Latin. Cf. L.-Hof. 2.491-492; cf. also, e.g.,
Prosp., De ingrat. praef. xvii-xviii: "nec caput attriti
virosum palpitet anguis, / unde igitur commenta mali
sopita resurgant"; 909: "quo sunt effecti miseri, sint
inde superbi." Cf. n. on 243, inde, above.

forent . . . reparanda: Cf. n. on 98, cognoscenda
forent, above.

340: illaesa: illaesus appears from Tib. and Ov. on.
Cf., eg., Tib. 3.9.18: "illaesus abibit . . . aper";
Ov., Her. 15.168: "illaeso corpore pressit aquas
/Deucalion/"; Aug., Pat. 8.8: "illaeso et intacto"; Prosp.,
In psalm. 141.5; De ingrat. 161, 496, 542, 976; Vocat.
gent. 2.13. Cf. TLL 7.1.336.21-337.34.

343. in Christi corpus: The doctrine of the mystical
body of Christ is a favorite theme in the Pauline epistles,
receiving extensive development at 1 Cor. 12.12-27.

Cf. also Rom. 12.5; 1 Cor. 6.15, 10.17; Eph. 4.1-16, 5.29-30; Col. 1.18,24.

nascendo: The abl. of the gerund is used increasingly in Late Latin to replace the pres. part. (cf. L.-Hof. 599-600; K.-Steg. 2.1.752-753); however, the construction has precedent as early as Plaut. For other instances in De prov. cf. participando, 495; mutando, 496; spirando, 739; culpando, 932.

346-349. nonne etiam in nostram, etc.: For the covenant between God and Abraham, cf. Gen. 15.5-6; 22.15-18.

347. amor: For the use of amor to denote God's love for man cf. Aug., Civ. 14.7: "amorem et dilectionem indifferenter et in bono et in malo apud sacras scripturas inveniri." Cf. the similar use at Prosp., De ingrat. 394: "amor quem conserit ipse /Deus/ est." Cf. also De prov. 550.

348. genitor: Cf. n. on 108, above.

350-355. in Pentapolim descenderet igneus imber, etc.: The account of the destruction of Sodom and Gomorrha and the deliverance of Lot occurs at Gen. 18.16-19.29; Wisd. 10.6-7. Cf. Wisd. 10.7: "descendente igne in Pentapolim"; Paul. Nol., Carm. 28.92: "igneus imber."

350. Pentapolim: The acc. ending of Pentapolis in -im occurs at Vulg., Wisd. 10.7; Amm. 22.16.1 (a city in Cyrenaica); Iord., Rom. /A.D. 551/ 229; Hist. Apoll. /6th cent./ 51. Cf. Neue-Wagener, Formenlehre 4.262.

352. qui promptus parcere: For the principle that God's justice is always mitigated by his mercy, cf., e.g., Prosp., Vocat. gent. 2.22: "ut generali necessitate variata, causas sibi Dominus indulgentiae correptionisque servaret, essetque in uno omnium debito quod et misericors remitteret, et iustus exigeret"; Aug., In psalm. 32.1. 10-12. For the coupling of the divine titles "Justice" and "Mercy" cf. Prosp., De ingrat. 895: "iustitia iniustos tolerat, clementia saevos."

354. Sodomis: In Vulg., the nom. and acc. forms are sg., being Sodoma and Sodomam, respectively. The dat.-abl. form is pl., Sodomis, while the gen. may be either sg. or pl. in form, Sodomae or Sodomorum. Cf. Dutripon, Bibliorum Sacrorum Concordantiae, s.v.

Among later authors there are great divergences in the forms. Cf. Forcellini, s.v. (onom.2); Benoist and Souter, s.v.

355. dedit dominum oppiduli Loth: dare - "make, constitute," with double acc., appears from Cic. and Liv. on, mostly with reference to the selection of public officials. For the construction in Christian Latin, cf., e.g., Itala, 2 Para. 25.16: "consiliarium regis dedi te"; Vulg., Ezech. 3.17: "dabo pueros principes eorum"; Eph. 4.11: "dedit quosdam apostolos"; Paul. Nol., Carm. app. 1.104: "patriae civem me dedit alterius." Cf. TLL 5.1. 1694.21-37.

oppiduli: oppidulum is rare. Cf. Hor., Sat. 1.5. 87: "mansuri oppidulo, quod versu dicere non est"; Cic.,Att. 10.7.1; Quint. frat. 2.12.1; Hier., Epist. 112.21.

356-357. cum vero Aegyptum, etc.: For the account of the seven years of famine, cf. Gen. 41.47-57; for the famine as extending with special severity to Egypt and Chanaan, Gen. 47.13.

357. dira fames: Cf. Verg., Aen. 3.256; Ov., Met. 8.845: "dira fames"; 11.371: "diramque famem."

358-369. praestruitur certe, etc.: On the migration of the Hebrews into Egypt cf. Gen. 46.1-47.12.

360. incrementa: incrementum = "offspring" is rare, being cited at TLL 7.1.1044.60-69 only for Verg., Ecl. 4.49: "cara deum suboles, magnum Iovis incrementum"; Ciris 398: "cara Iovis suboles, magnum Iovis incrementum"; Itala, Gen. 43.8; Ps.-Ambr., Ennod.(ob.521), Inscr. Cf. also Ov., Met. 3.103: "populi incrementa futuri."

361-367. mystica dum Ioseph, etc.: The story of Joseph is recounted at Gen. 37.5-36 (Joseph's dreams; Joseph sold into Egypt;the deception practiced on his father Jacob); 39.1-20 (Joseph's virtue in temptation, and his imprisonment); 41.14-46 (his interpretation of Pharaoh's dreams); 44.1-45.8 (the cup in Benjamin's sack; Joseph's revelation of his identity to his brothers).

364. aenigmate somni: Cf. Cic., De div. 2.64.132: "aenigmata somniorum."

365. vatem: For va̲tes ▪ "prophet (of the Old or New Law)," cf. Blaise, s.v. On the use of vates for propheta by the Christian poets cf. Mohrmann, "La langue et le style" 285. Cf. n. on 441, below.

dignatur honore: Cf. Ov., Met. 1.194: "dignamur honore"; 13.949: "dignantur honore"; Pont. 2.9.23: "dignemur honore"; 4.12.3: "dignarer honore"; Met. 3.521; 8.569: "dignatus honore."

dignatur: The construction with acc. and abl. appears from Verg. and Ov. on. Cf., e.g., Verg., Aen. 1.335: "hand equidem tali me dignor honore." Cf. TLL 5.1.1141. 45-65.

367. venia cognoscere fratrem: Cf. Prud., Ditt. 28: "agnoscunt fratrem veniaque pudescunt"; Lucr. 2.349; Verg., Ecl. 4.60: "cognoscere matrem."

369. dedignantem: dedignari appears from Verg. on. Cf. TLL 5.1.262.6. Use of the pres. part. with the acc. obj. is cited first for the 3rd cent. epitomist Iust., and for Prud. Cf. TLL 5.1.262.7-47.

371. decurrere: decurrere - "happen, take place" appears in Sen. and Quint., but otherwise is Late. Cf. TLL 5.1.231.49-75.

372-373. mentes / non possunt turbare pias: Cf. Verg., Aen. 12.246: "turbavit mentes"; 160: "turbatam vulnere mentis"; Prud., Symm. 2.102-103: "vimque fatigatae mentis . . . / turbari."

377-382. sic gens cara Deo, etc.: The account of the oppression of the Hebrews in Egypt and Pharaoh's command to the Hebrew midwives occurs at Ex. 1.8-22.

377. sic: The reading si would result in a conditional phrase in which the principal member would be omitted. Cf. Valentin, Saint Prosper 830 n.2, 845. The restoration of sic, found in the pre-Maurist editions, gives an acceptable sense.

380. condendas . . . ad urbes: For condere joined with urbs, cf., e.g., the title of Livy's work, Ab urbe condita. The alternative reading, condensas, found in the pre-Maurist editors, is rejected here because the ensuing construction of praebere with ad and the acc. to express indirect object is poor grammatically, and because condendas corresponds to the biblical account, which lays

stress on the construction of cities and reports nothing as to their population. Cf. Ex. 1.11-14.

381. durus labor et saevae inclementia mortis: Cf. Verg., Georg. 3.68: "et labor et durae rapit inclementia mortis"; 2.412: "durus uterque labor"; Lucr. 3.999; 5.1272, 1359: "durum sufferre laborem."

inclementia: inclementia appears from Verg. and Tac. on. Cf., e.g., Verg., Georg. 3.68, cited immediately above, and Stat., Silv. 1.4.50: "gravis inclementia fati." Cf. TLL 7.1.938.1-35.

385-388. nam iubet electum: The narrative of the Lord's command to Moses and the threat of stern judgment, i.e., the ten plagues, is found at Ex. 6.10-13, 28-30; 7.1-7.

387-388. faciat . . . sentiet: For the fut. indic. in the apodosis of the fut. less vivid condition cf. , e.g., Cic., Inv. 2.44: "si diligenter attendamus, intellegemus." Cf. K.-Steg. 2.2.395.

388. sentiet excitam, etc.: Valentin, Saint Prosper 830 n. 2, 845, terms this verse obscure or incomprehensible, and suggests that it ought to be altered. But the verse appears to give an acceptable, if difficult, sense as it stands.

389-392. ille quidem quoties, etc.: Instances of pretended compliance with Yahweh's command to release the Hebrews occur at Ex. 8.4 (second plague), at 24 (fourth plague), 9.27-29 (seventh plague), 10.8-11, 16-20 (eighth plague), 24-25 (ninth plague).

390. obsequium simulat: Cf. Tac., Ann. 12.47: "simulare obsequium"; Hist. 4.56: "simulatum ipsis obsequium."

392. inde: Cf. n. on 243, inde, above.

393-395. donec vi victus, etc.: The story of the Exodus is recounted at Ex. 12.31-51; the manner of getting the gold and silver vessels is foretold at Ex. 3.21-22; 11.1-3.

393. donec vi victus: Cf. Verg., Aen. 12.254: "donec vi victus."

394. __ditia__ . . . __gazis__: Cf. Prud., __Psych__. praef.
24: "gaza dives."

395-399. __monstrante columna__: For the column which
guided the Hebrews in their wanderings, cf. __Ex__. 13.21-
22, esp. v. 21: "Dominus autem praecedebat eos ad ostenden-
dam viam per diem in columna nubis et per noctem in columna
ignis ut dux ooact itineris utroque tempore"; 40.34-38;
__Num__. 9.15-23.

399. __discutiens flammis__ tenebras: Cf. Verg., __Georg__.
3.357: "sol . . . discutit __umbras__"; Sen., __Thy__. 896-897:
"discutiam tibi / tenebras"; Prud., __Peri__. 13.26: "discutit et tenebras."

400-404. __quid loquar et trepidis__, etc.; The crossing
of the Red Sea and the destruction of the Egyptians are
narrated at __Ex__. 14.10-31; __Wisd__. 19.6-8.

400. __quid loquar__: Cf. Verg., __Ecl__. 6.74; Ov., __Her__.
18.39; __Trist__. 2.399; 3.10.25; 5.10.51; Prud., __Ham__. 230;
__Symm__. 1.271; __Peri__. 1.112: "quid loquar."

402. __instar montis aquas__: Cf. Verg., __Aen__. 1.105:
"praeruptus aquae mons"; 2.15: "instar montis"; Prud.,
__Cath__. 5.93: "instar fellis aqua"; __Psych__. 654: "mons
. . . pendentis aquae."

__vacuo__ cessisse __profundo__: Cf. Prud., __Ham__. 471:
"aequoreum pelago cedente profundum."

403. __illaesae__ . . . __plebis__: __illaesae__, found in the
pre-Maurist editions, gives an acceptable sense and is
preferable on metrical grounds. The phrase illaesae
. . . __plebis__ may derive from __Wisd__. 19.6: "ut pueri tui
custodirentur illaesi," which refers to the exodus. Cf.
n. on 340, above.

405. __omnis enim auctori servit natura potenti__: Cf.
Verg., __Georg__. 1.26-28:

. . . te /Caesarem/ maximus orbis
auctorem frugum tempestatumque potentem
accipiat . . .

407-408. __cunctas percurrere formas / virtutum__: Cf.
Verg., __Aen__. 6.626-627: "omnes scelerum comprendere
formas / omnia poenarum percurrere nomina."

407. __formas__: forma = "example" appears in Cic. but
is mostly Poetic, Silver, and Late. The usage in this

sense may be influenced by the employment of forma =
"formula, prescription, law" among the jurists. Cf. TLL
6.1.1080.61-1081.35, and Berger, Encyclopedic Dictionary
474. The usage in the sense of "example" is known to
Prosp. Cf., e.g., De ingrat. 12: "forma nocui non semine
proli"; Epigr. 69.14: "sit forma et speculum, lux et
imago Dei"; In psalm. 119.1; 143.1. Cf. TLL 6.1.1085.17-
81 and n. on 313, above.

408. virtutum: virtutes pl. = "miracles" is Late,
appearing in Christian authors from Tert. on. Cf., e.g.,
Ter., Pud. 10: "si virtutum documenta vidissent"; Vulg.,
1 Cor. 12.10: "operatio virtutum"; Lact., Inst. 4.15.4,
6; 7.17.2 Cf. Blaise and Souter, s.v.

409. miracula rerum: Cf. Verg., Georg. 4.441: "in
miracula rerum"; Prud., Apoth. 138: "miracula rerum."

410. mannae imbrem: For the rain of manna cf. Ex.
16.4-15; Ps. 77(78).24.

et cunctos in caeli pane sapores: Cf. Wisd. 16.20:
"et paratum panem de caelo praestitisti illis sine labore,
omne delectamentum in se habentem, et omnis saporis
suavitatem." For the bread as a type of the Eucharist,
cf. John 6.22-60.

411. siccae rupis aquam: The miracle of the rock of
Horeb is related at Ex. 17.1-7; Num. 20.2-13. Cf. also
Ps. 77(78).15; Wisd. 11.4, and, for the rock as a type
of Christ, the spiritual rock, 1 Cor. 10.4.--Cf. Verg.,
Aen. 5.180: "siccaque in rupe."

et dulcorem fontis amari: For the changing of bitter
water into fresh at Mara, cf. Ex. 15.22-26.

412-413. aut inter deserta, etc.: Mention of the
immunity from aging and from injury to clothing in the
forty-years' wandering appears at Deut. 8.4, 29.4; 2 Esd.
9.21.

419. penetralia mentis: Cf. Paul. Nol., Carm. 6.237:
"sacrae ad penetralia mentis."

420. scripta volumina cordis: Reference to the
Natural Law written in man's heart derives from Rom.
2.15: "opus legis scriptum in cordibus suis" (i.e., the
Gentiles); cf. Prosp., De ingrat. 506: "/legem/ quam
scripta munibat pagina cordis"; 16: "lexque insita
cordibus intus."

426. destringit: For the confusion of destringere and distringere in MSS., cf. TLL 5.1.768.80-81. This verse is cited with destringit at TLL 5.1.770.25.

427-440. unus enim Pater est, etc.: Antelmy, De veris operibus 406, objects to vv. 427-428 on the grounds of unorthodoxy in doctrine. The phrase semina recti, 427, may contain a reference to the semipelagian "seeds of virtue." Cf., e.g., Prosp., De ingrat. 929 et al.; C. coll. 13.4. The entire passage is noted as suspect in the Maurist edition (and therefore in Migne). Valentin, Saint Prosper 889-890, defends these verses on the grounds that they are a statement of God's providential care for all men, and esp. for his chosen people.

430. sanctis agerent in moribus aevum: Cf. Verg., Georg. 4.154: "magnisque agitant sub legibus aevum /apes/."

434-435. cum tradita Mosi, etc.: The giving of the Ten Commandments on Sinai is related at Ex. 31.18, foretold at Ex. 23.12.--Cf. Prud., Ditt. 38-39: "scripta decem verbis saxorum pagina Moysi / traditur."

435. praesenti . . . poena: The exact reference is obscure, but would perhaps apply to the slaying of 3,000 worshippers of the Golden Calf by the Levites by order of Moses, shortly after the giving of the Commandments. Cf. Ex. 32.18-29.

436-438. sed superadiecta est, etc.: For the covenant between Yahweh and Moses made upon the renewal of the Ten Commandments, cf. Ex. 34.10-28.

436. superadiecta est: superadicere is Late and rare, appearing from the 4th cent. on, and cited by the lexica only for Pall., Apic., Macr., Boeth. Cf. Forcellini, Lewis-Short, and Souter, s.v.

438. promissorum Domini succederet heres: Cf. Gal. 3.29: "secundum promissionem heredes."

441. prophetae: propheta, a Greek loan word, is Late and esp. freq. among Christian authors, appearing from Itala on; it appears also in Apul. and Macr. Cf. Blaise, s.v., and Young, Studies 31. For the distinction between propheta (prophet of the Old or New Law) and vates, cf. Lact., Inst. 7.23.5: "non modo prophetae, sed etiam vates

et poetae et philosophi anastasim mortuorum futuram consentiunt." Cf. n. on 365, vatem, above.

442. ad varias gentes: The O.T. uses gentes = "the Gentiles," i.e., those who did not worship Yahweh, e.g., Ps. 95(96).5: "omnes dii gentium." Cf. Blaise, s.v. Contrast De prov. 377: "gens cara Deo" (i.e., the Hebrews).

443-444. sic regina Austri, etc.: The account of the visit of the Queen of Saba to Jerusalem is found at 3 Kgs. 10.1-10. Cf. Prud., Ditt. 82: "regina Austri."

444. eloquium Domini: This expression is freq. in the O.T. to denote "the word of the Lord." Cf. 2 Kgs. 22.31: "eloquium Domini"; Ps. 11(12).7, 17(18).31: "eloquia Domini"; Ps. 106 (107).11: "eloquia Dei." The only Vulg. N.T. instance is Rom. 3.2: "eloquia Dei" (but cf. Itala, 1 Pet. 4.11).---eloquium = "word" is exclusively a Christian usage, except for Iuv. and Ps.-Cic. Cf., e.g., Prosp., In psalm. 118.82: "ad Dei eloquia." Cf. TLL 5.2.415. 38-48; 416.23-32.

445-447. sic Ninive monitis Ionae, etc.: The conversion of Ninive is related at Jon. 3.1-10.

447. promeruit morum excidio, etc.: Valentin, Saint Prosper 845, questions the meaning of this verse, but it appears to give an acceptable sense as it stands.

promeruit: promerere - "merit (and obtain), earn, win" is mostly Silver and Late. The use with the inf.. appears at Sedul., Carm. 5.318. Cf. Blaise and Benoist, s.v.

448. verum ne longo sermone moremur: Cf. Hor., Epist. 2.1.4: "si longo sermone morer."

452. velant: velare - "conceal, cover up," in a fig. sense, is Silver and Late. Cf. Benoist, Georges, and Blaise, s.v., and Young, Studies 71.

453-459. dicite quem populum, etc.: This passage is marked as suspect of unorthodoxy by the Maurists. Valentin, Saint Prosper 890, while admitting that the doctrinal import of the passage approaches semipelagian teachings, nevertheless sees it as reaffirming the universal salvific will of God, and finds similar statements in authors whose orthodoxy is unchallenged. Cf.

Sister M. Alphonsine Lesousky, O.S.U., The De Dono
Perseverantiae 57-58.

454. cuius generis: Cf. Prud., Symm. 2.823: "cuius
generis."

455. salvare: Cf. n. on 192, above.

455-456. vir, femina, servus, etc.: Cf. Gal. 3.28:
"non est Iudaeus, neque Graecus: non est servus, neque
liber: non est masculus, neque femina. omnes enim vos
unum estis in Christo"; Col. 3.11: "ubi non est gentilis
et Iudaeus, circumcisio et praeputium, barbarus et Scytha,
servus et liber: sed omnia, et in omnibus Christus";
Prud., Cath. 12.202-204: "Iudaea, Roma, et Graecia,/
Aegypta, Thrax, Persa, Scytha, / rex unus omnes possidet."

457-459. non persona potentis, etc.: The theme of
impartiality toward persons is biblical. Cf. Lev. 19.15:
"ne consideres personam pauperis nec honores vultum
potentis"; Deut. 1.17: "nulla erit distantia personarum";
Prov. 24.23; Jas. 2.1-13.

459. luminis unius: Cf. n. on 544, below.

461. radiis . . . supernis: Cf. Leo M., Serm. 74.2:
"radii superni." For supernus - "celestial, divine" cf.,
e.g., Ov., Met. 15.128: "numenque supernum"; Lucan
6.430-431: "supernis / . . . deis"; 9.556-557: "supernas
/ ad leges"; Vulg., Phil. 3.4: "supernae vocationis."

462. confessi . . . Christi: Cf. Matt. 10.32: "omnis
ergo qui confitebitur me coram hominibus, confitebor et
ego eum coram Patre meo, qui in caelis est"; Luke 12.8:
"omnis quicumque confessus fuerit me coram hominibus,
et filius hominis confitebitur illum coram angelis Dei."

confessi: The use of confiteri - "to confess
(Christ)," with the acc. obj., is biblical [cf. the examples cited above] and is noted esp. for Prosp. Cf.,
e.g., In psalm 142.5; 144.10; Vocat. gent. 1.9. Cf. TLL
4.231.3-11. Cf. further C. Mohrmann, "Quelques traits
caractéristiques du latin des chrétiens" 446-448.

464-465. miscetur conditioni / humanae: Cf. Phil.
2.7: "sed semetipsum exinanivit formam servi accipiens,
in similitudinem hominum factus, et habitu inventus ut
homo."

For an explanation of the orthodox doctrine of the hypostatic union, cf. Leo M., Serm. 23.1: "Deus itaque Dei Filius par atque eadem de Patre et cum Patre natura, uni- versitatis Creator et Dominus, totus ubique praesens, et omnia totus excedens, in ordine temporum, quae ipsius dis- positione decurrunt, hunc sibi diem, quo in salutem mundi ex beata Virgine Maria nasceretur, elegit, integro per omnia pudore generantis. . . . Hic enim mirabilis sacrae Virginis partus, vere humanam vereque divinam unam edidit prole personam, quia non ita proprietates suas tenuit utra- que substantia, ut personarum in eis possit esse discretio; nec sic creatura in societatem sui Creatoris est assumpta, ut ille habitator, et illa esset habitaculum; sed ita ut naturae alteri altera misceretur. Et quamvis alia sit quae suscipitur, alia vero quae suscepit, in tantam tamen uni- tatem convenit utriusque diversitas, ut unus idemque sit Filius, qui se, et secundum quod verus est homo, Patre dicit minorem /John 14.28/, et secundum quod verus est Deus, Patri profitetur aequalem /John 10.30/.

465-466. et Verbum caro fit, rerumque creator / nascitur: Cf. John 1.14: "et Verbum caro factum est"; Prosp., De ingrat. 891-892: "Verbum homo fit rerumque sator sub conditione / servilis formae dignatur virgine nasci."

465. rerumque creator: Cf. Prud., Peri. 10.469: "rerum creator."

467. volumina vatum: Cf. Hor., Epist. 2.1.26: "volumina vatum"; Prud., Apoth. 219: "voluminibus vatum."

vatum: Cf. n. on 365, above.

469. ultima cum mundi finem prope curreret aetas: Cf. Verg., Ecl. 4.4: "ultima Cumaei venit iam carminis aetas."--Valentin, Saint Prosper 845, questions the mean- ing of this verse. In view of the fact that currere in Christian authors often refers to the contest of life, it seems better to adopt V.'s second alternative, and trans- late curreret as "had run its limit," rather than "had drawn to its end." Cf. 1 Cor. 9.24; Rom. 9.16; Gal. 2.2; Phil. 2.16.

470-471. morte perempta / solveret inferni leges:

NOTES

Cf. Rom. 7.6: "nunc autem soluti sumus a lege mortis."

471. inferni: infernus, subst. = "the lower region,"
appears from Pacuv. on, mostly in epic or elegiac, but increasingly in prose in the Silver Age. Cf. TLL 7.1.1370.
64-70. Christian authors regularly employ infernus - "hell,"
a usage found in Scripture. Cf., e.g., Luke 16.22: "mortuus
est . . . dives et sepultus est in inferno." But infernus
could also refer to the region beyond the grave, i.e., the
hell into which Christ descended to free the patriarchs and
other persons of the O.T. Cf., e.g., Job 17.16; "in pro-
fundissimum infernum descendent omnia mea." For the confusion between the two usages cf. Aug., Quaest. hept.
1.126: "solet esse magna quaestio, quomodo intellegatur
infernus: utrum illu mali tantum an etiam boni mortui
descendere soleant." Cf. TLL 7.1.1372.32-53.

471-472: longamque ruinam / humani generis meliore
attolleret ortu: Cf. Prud., Symm. 1.559-560: "stipemque
superbam / gentis patriciae venturo attollere saeclo."

473: sed tu qui geminam, etc.: The Lyons ed. has
the gloss "contra Eutychem" at this verse. Hincmar, De
praedestinatione dissertatio posterior /PL 125.445/, cites
vv. 497-501 under the title: "in libro contra Eutychen."
While there is some confusion over the content of Eutyches'
teachings, it would appear that they ended in a denial that
Christ possessed a true human nature after the hypostatic
union. Cf. Tixeront, History of Dogmas 3.76-84.

475-476. firma tene cautus vestigia, etc.: Cf.
Prosp., De ingrat. 992-994:
    praecipites semper calles, et devia motu
    ingressura suo, nisi fessam /voluntatem/, tu bone,
                        et aegram
    suscipias, referas, foveas, tuearis, honestes.

476. error: Cf. n. on 106, above.

477. si cernens, etc.: Valentin, Saint Prosper
830 n.2, terms this verse obscure or incomprehensible,
and suggests that it be altered.

operum miracula divinorum: = mira opera divina. For
miracula rerum - mira res cf. TLL 8.1057.5-30.

479. sine Numine: Cf. Lucr. 2.168; Verg., Aen.
2.777; 6.368; Ov., Met. 11.263: "sine numine."

341

480-481. morsque subactum / detinet: Cf. Prosp.,
De ingrat. 531-532: "morsque subactum / detineat."

483. Salvator: For salvator - "savior (Christ),"
cf., e.g., Luke 2.11; Acts 5.31; 2 Pet. 2.20; Prosp.,
De ingrat. 422. Cf. Blaise, s.v., and Young, Studies 16.
C. Mohrmann, Liturgical Latin (Washington, 1957) 44-45,
comments: "The Latins refused to adopt . . . conservator
because it retained a pagan significance. They preferred
to take refuge in a neologism, salvator, derived from
salvare, equally of Christian coinage." But salvator became the fixed term for "savior" only in the 4th cent.,
among Aug., Ambr., Hier. Cf. Lact., Inst. 4.12.6: "Iesus,
qui latine dicitur salutaris sive salvator"; Aug., Serm.
299.6: "Christus, inquit, Iesus, id est Christus salvator.
hoc est enim latine Iesus. nec quaerant grammatici quam sit
latinum, sed Christiani quam verum. salus enim latinum
nomen est. salvare et salvator non fuerunt haec latina
antequam veniret salvator: quando ad latinos venit et
haec latina fecit." Cf. further C. Mohrmann, "Les éléments
vulgaires du latin des chrétiens," VC 2 (1948) 171; "Les
emprunts grecs dans la latinité chrétienne," VC 4 (1950)
203-205; L.R. Palmer, The Latin Language (London, 1954)
192-193.

485. mutor in illo: Valentin, Saint Prosper 485, suggests that illum must be read here. But for in with the
abl. after mutare cf. Vulg., Dan. 7.28; "et facies mea
mutata est in me."

487-488. et non ego iam in me / vivam, sed Christus:
Cf. Gal. 2.20: "vivo autem iam non ego, vivit vero in
me Christus"; John 17.23.

489-490. transfudit in omnes / mortem homines: Cf.
Rom. 5.12: "in omnes homines mors pertransiit"; Prud.,
Apoth. 911-912: "exim tincta malo peccamine principis
Adae / infecit genus omne hominum, quod pullulat inde."

491. transgressoris: transgressor appears only in
Christian authors from Itala and Tert. on. Cf., e.g., Vulg.,
Isa. 53.12: "et cum sceleratis reputatus est, et ipse
peccata multorum tulit, et pro transgressoribus rogavit";
Tert., Res. 39: "transgressor legis"; Cypr., Bon. pat.
11: "Adam . . . datae legis transgressor." Cf. Blaise
and Souter, s.v., and J. Schrijnen, "Le latin chrétien
devenu langue commune" REL 12 (1934) 103.

492-493. sed novus e caelis, etc.: Cf. Verg., Ecl. 4.7: "iam nova progenies caelo demittitur alto"; Prud., Cath. 3.136-137: "ecce venit nova progenies / aethere proditus alter homo."

caelis: Use of the pl. of caelum instead of the sg. by Christian authors is derived from Hebrew practice; this is the only instance in De prov. Cf. J. Schrijnen and C. Mohrmann, Studien zur Syntax der Briefe des hl. Cyprian 1 (Nijmegen, 1936) 64.

493. natus homo est: Cf. Ov., Met. 1.78: "natus homo est."

495-496. et vita functos, etc.: Compare the different play on the ideas "life" and "death" at Heb. 2.14: ". . . that through death he might destroy him who had the empire of death, that is, the devil; and might deliver them, who throughout their life were kept in servitude by the fear of death."

499. renovat: For renovare used to denote spiritual renewal cf. Hebr. 6.6: "renovari ad paenitentiam." Cf. Blaise, s.v. The term, freq. in Christian authors, occurs at De prov. 694, 963.

501-504. filius esse Dei, etc.: The passage is cited by Antelmy, De veris operibus 406, and by the Maurists, as suspect of unorthodox teaching, but is defended by Valentin, Saint Prosper 890, who sees in it a reaffirmation of the doctrine of original sin, esp. at captiva exordia carnis, 504. As V. observes, the author has already shown original sin and its consequences in the preceding verses. Cf. vv. 480-491, esp, et non est quo vinctus vincere possim, 481; et transgressoris decurrit causa parentis, 491; cf. also vv. 269-271. The Pelagians denied the transmission of Adam's sin to his descendants; the semipelagians admitted original sin and the necessity of Baptism. Cf. Sister M. Alphonsine Lesousky, O.S.U., The De Dono Perseverantiae 22, 23.

506-507. nec tuus ipse es / emptus enim es, pretiumque tui,etc.: Cf. 1 Cor. 6.19-20: "et non estis vestri? empti enim estis pretio magno"; 7.23: "pretio empti estis." For Christ as purchaser (emptor) of man, cf. n. on 948, emptor, below.

507. fas est: Cf. Verg., Aen. 1.77; Ov., Trist.

3.5.27; 4.10.89; Ars 3.151: "fas est"; Verg., Aen. 6.63:
"fas erit"; Prud., Apoth. 18: "fas sit."

509. Redemptor: For redemptor = "Christ, the Redeemer,'
as here, cf., e.g., Cypr., Hab. virg. 2; Epist. 55.22;
Prud., Cath. 10.157; Aug., Serm. 130.2. Christian authors
also use redemptor = "liberator, savior" in speaking of
God. For both meanings cf. Blaise and Benoist, s.v.

511. sub durum iubet ire iugum: Contrast Matt. 11.30:
"iugum enim meum suave est."

513. in tabulis cordis describat: Cf. Prov. 3.3:
"describe in tabulis cordis tui."

516. rerum dominus: Cf. Verg., Aen. 1.282: "rerum
dominos"; Ov., Pont. 2.2.12: "in rerum dominos"; Liv.
9.18.16: "domini rerum"; Prud., Apoth. 227: "rerum
dominum."

516-518. pauperis egit / in specie, etc.: Cf. 2
Cor. 8.9: "propter vos egenus factus est, cum esset dives,
ut illius inopia vos divites essetis."

519-525. iustitia iniustis cedit, etc.: Cf. Prosp.,
De ingrat. 894-898:
        vexatur virtus, sapientia ludificatur,
        iustitia iniustos tolerat, clementia saevos;
        gloria contemptum subit et tormenta potestas,
        inque crucis poenam nulli violabilis usquam
        vita agitur . . .

519. iustitia: Cf. Rom. 5.18: "per unius /Christi7
iustitiam in omnes homines in iustificationem vitae";
Prosp., De ingrat. 850: "Christus enim tua iustitia est."

520-533. sacrilegis manibus percussus, etc.: For
an analysis of various incidents accompanying the passion and death of Christ, with verbal similarities between the De prov. and the Gospel accounts, cf. Intro.,
pp. 30-31.--Cf. Prud., Apoth. 199: "sacrilegisque . . .
manibus."

521. convicia linguae: Cf. Ov., Met. 11.601:
"convicia linguae."

522. inspuitur lux: Cf. Itala, Luke 18.32: "/filius
hominis7 tradetur . . . gentibus et illudetur et inspue-
tur."

523. ministerium: ministerium - "instrument," and
applied to persons, is rare, being cited at TLL 8.1014.
8-11 only for Tac., Hil., and the 4th cent. medical writer
Theod. Prisc.

523-524. felque et acetum / . . . haurit: Cf. Prud.,
Apoth. 99: "fel potat et haurit acetum."

524-525. sanctus maledictum, etc.: Cf. Gal. 3.13:
"Christus nos redemit de maledicto legis, factus pro nobis
maledictum." Valentin, Saint Prosper 845, proposes to
read ". . . sanctus maledictum fit, crucis et moritur ligno,
vivente Barabba." The text is intelligible as it stands;
V.'s reading, however, does receive support from Deut.
21.23: "maledictus a Deo est qui pendet in ligno."

524. maledictum: maledictum subst., used to refer to
a condemned man, is rare. Cf., e.g., Hier., Epist. 21.2.5:
"ut . . . /crucis/ fieret maledictum"; Paul. Nol., Epist.
23.15: "ex damnatione maledictum eramus." Cf. TLL 8.170.
36-41. For maledictum = "one who is accursed" cf., e.g.,
Itala, Isa. 43.28: "dedi . . . Israhel in maledictum."
Cf. TLL 8.169.56-65.

526. impia gens tantum ausa nefas: Cf. Ov., Met.
10.232: "gens impia"; Verg., Aen. 6.624: "ausi omnes
immane nefas."

528-529. concussaque tellus / intremuit: Cf. Ov., Met.
1.283-284: "Ipse /Neptunus/ tridente suo terram percussit
at illa / intremuit."

529-530. sepulchris / excita sanctorum, etc.: Cf.
Verg., Ecl. 8.98: "animas imis excire sepulchris."

533. sanctaque: sanctum, subst. sg. = "temple,
sanctuary," appears in Pers. and is freq. in Vulg. Cf.
Benoist, and Dutripon, Bibliorum Sacrorum Concordantiae,
s.v. The pl. subst. sancta is also freq. in this sense
in the Vulg. Cf., e.g., Ex. 39.1: "ministrabat in sanctis";
Lev. 10.18: "intra sancta"; Ps. 133 (134). 2: "extollite
manus vestras in sancta"; 150.1: "laudate Dominum in sanctis
eius."

cruentos: Valentin, Saint Prosper 845, observes that
the verse is acceptable as it stands, but suggests that
cruenti would give a more natural sense.

534. spicula mortis: Cf. 1 Cor. 15.55: "ubi est

mors stimulus tuus?"; Os. 13.14.

535. referentem carne tropaeum: Cf. Verg., Aen.
10.542: "refert . . . tropaeum"; Prud., Psych. 64:
"referens ex hoste tropaeum." For tropaeum - "spiritual
victory" cf. Blaise, s.v.; for a survey of the uses of
tropaeum among Christian authors cf. C. Mohrmann, "A propos
des deux mots controversés de la latinité chrétienne: tropaeum - nomen," VC 2 (1948) 154-167.

536. tertia discipulis, Iesu, dedit attonitis lux:
Appearances of Christ to his apostles and disciples are
mentioned at Mark 16.12 (two of the disciples), 16.13-14
(the eleven apostles), Luke 24.13-31 (disciples traveling
to Emmaus), 36-37 (the eleven apostles), John 20.19-23
(the apostles).--Cf. Prud., Apoth. 531: "maiestate patris
vivum lux tertia reddit"; Verg., Aen. 3.117; 11.210; Ov.,
Fast. 3.713; 4.377, 629, 679: "tertia lux."

537-539. nec dubiis Dominum licuit cognoscere signis,
etc.: Christ's invitation to the apostles to touch his
wounds as a proof of the Resurrection is recounted at
Luke 24.39-40; his invitation to Thomas, at John 20.24-29.
Cf. Verg., Georg. 1.394: "certis poteris cognoscere
signis"; 4.253: "non dubiis poteris cognoscere signis";
App. Verg., Ciris 243: "ut nullo passim cognoscere signo";
Prosp., De ingrat. 816: "non dubiis promptum est cuivis
cognoscere signis" (i.e., the goal and origin of Pelagian
teachings).

539. vulnus et hastae: The piercing of Christ's body
by the lance is mentioned at John 19.34.

540-541. cumque quater denis, etc.: Events of the
forty days between the Resurrection and Ascension are recounted at John 20.24-21.25; Acts 1.1-8.

540. firmans promissa: Cf. Ov., Met. 10.430:
"promissaque numine firmat."

541. tractabilis esset: Cf. Prud., Symm. 2.588:
"quidquid tractabile moribus esset."

544. vita in vita est, in lumine lumen: For the
figure of Christ as light and life cf. John 1.4: "in
ipso vita erat, et vita erat lux hominum"; 9: "erat lux
vera quae illuminat omnem hominem venientem in hunc mundum."
The figure of light and life is found in the O.T. in reference to Yahweh. Cf. Ps. 35 (36).10: "apud te

est fons vitae, et in lumine tuo videbimus lumen." Cf.
also Prosp., De ingrat. 563-564: "sine lumine lumen /
nemo videt, vitam sine vita inquirere mors est." Cf.
De prov. 246, 459, 586.

545. augmento: augmentum appears occasionally in
Silver Latin, but is mostly Late. Cf. Zeno 1.13.8: "non
in damnum hominis . . . sed in augmentum hominis." Cf.
TLL 2.2.1360.41-44; 1362.11-1363.38.

glorificato: glorificare appears only in Christian
writers from Itala, Tert., Vulg. on. Cf. TLL 6.2.2088.
69-71. For glorificare used to refer to Christ as glori-
fied cf., e.g., Itala, John 7.39: "Iesus necdum fuerat
glorificatus"; Vulg., 2 Thess. 1.10: "cum venerit
/Christus/ glorificari"; Tert., Resurr. 47: "nec Christus
glorificatus est ante passionem"; Aug., Serm. 265.7-8:
"/Iesus/ bis glorificatus, resurgendo et ascendendo." Cf.
TLL 6.2.2089.11-52--glorificare may also be used to refer
to the condition of Christians in the state of glory,
e.g., Prosp., In psalm. 131.17: "sancti . . . non in se,
sed in Domino glorificantur"; or to refer to the action
of giving praise to God, e.g., Prosp., Vocat. gent. 1.8:
"glorificarent Deum." Cf. TLL 6.2. 2088.57-2092.67.

546. sic homo, sic Deus es, ut non sis alter et alter:
The Lyons ed. has the gloss "contra Nestorium" opposite
v. 546. Hincmar, De praedestinatione dissertatio posterior
/PL 125.445/ introduces vv. 550-557 under the title
"contra Nestorium." Nestorius failed to explain satisfactorily the hypostatic union, for he held it to be a union
between two persons rather than between two natures. In
orthodox teaching Christ does indeed possess a human nature, but is not a human person in the strict sense. The
questions raised by Nestorius were under discussion in Gaul
prior to Ephesus (A.D. 431). Cf. Intro., p. 21, n. 15, and
Tixeront, History of Dogmas 3.10-57.

In no way does the author intend to confound the two
natures of Christ after his Resurrection, and thus fall
into the errors of both Nestorius and Eutyches. Cf. vv.
473 ff. and n. on 473, above; also augmento, non fine
hominis, 545. The phrase ut non sis alter et alter must
therefore be taken as ▪ sed ut sis uterque, as a vindica-
tion of the two natures in Christ, in accord with the poet's
specific admonition against the errors involved in the
denial of either nature at vv. 475-479, above.

alter et alter: Cf. Prud., Peri. 8.18: "alter et alter."

548. curramus: currere, employed with reference to the Christian's course of life, is scriptural and freq. in Christian authors. Cf. Phil. 2.16: "quia non in vacuum cucurri"; Gal. 2.2.: "ne forte in vacuum cucurrerem, aut cucurrissem"; 1 Cor. 9.24; Rom. 9.16. Cf. also Prosp., De ingrat. 562: "perque ipsam /gratiam/ nisi curratur, non itur ad ipsam"; 567: "currere currentum si non et velle volentum est." Cf. also De prov. 647-648.

550-559. iamne Dei compertus amor, etc.: The passage is marked as suspect of erroneous doctrine in the Maurist edition. Valentin, Saint Prosper 891, sees in it an affirmation of the universal salvific will of God and a defense of human liberty. Cf. n. on 453-459, above-- essentially the same question is involved in both passages.

550. amor: Cf. n. on 347, above.

551. notum et cunctis astare salutem: God's salvific will is universal. Cf. 1 Tim. 2.4: "/Deus/ qui omnes homines vult salvos fieri, et ad agnitionem veritatis venire." Cf. also n. on 781-783, below.

astare: astare with an incorporeal subject, as here, is rare. Cf., e.g., Enn., Trag. 83 (Cic., Tusc. 1.85; 3.44): "astante ope barbarica." Cf. TLL 2.1.955.78- 956.4.

salutem: For a play on the two senses of salus, cf. Aug., Serm. 16.7: "salutem quaeris? contemne et habebis"; 23.3.

552-553. garrula verbis / bella moves: Cf. Ov., Trist. 3.12.18: "cedunt verbosi garrula bella fori."

553. iaculisque tuis tua viscera figis: Cf. Ov., Met. 10.130-131: "hunc puer imprudens iaculo Cyparissus acuto / fixit."

556. sed cum recta queas discernere prava: Cf. nn. on 238-240, 238-239, above.

558. deteriora legis: Cf. Ov., Met. 7.20-21: "video

meliora proboque, deteriora sequor."

'erro,' ais: Cf. Prud., Ham. 509: "'errat,' ait."

559. subiacet: subiacere = "be subject to" is
Silver and Late, appearing from Quint. on. Cf. Benoist
and Blaise, s.v., and Young, Studies 68.

560. rationis egenum: Cf. Prud., Symm. 1.81:
"rationis egenum"; Cath. 10.82: "rationis egenis"; Lucr.
4.502: Verg., Aen. 8.299: "rationis egentem"; Ov., Met.
15.150: "rationis egentes"; Lucr. 5.1211: "rationis
egestas."

561-564. error enim est eius qui cessit limite recti,
etc.: The concept of the path and man straying from it
is biblical. Cf. 2 Pet. 2.15: "derelinquentes rectam
viam, erraverunt"; Prov. 2.13.--Cf. Prosp., De ingrat.
450-451: "quem non recto via limite ducit, / quanto plus
graditur, tanto longinquius errat."

566. fit verbum Domini: Cf. J. L. McKenzie, The
Two-Edged Sword (Milwaukee, 1956) 29: "'The word of the
Lord' is the consecrated phrase which describes the experience of every man who is called a prophet." Cf.,
e.g., 1 Kgs. 15.10: "factum est autem verbum Domini."

lege tenentur: Cf. Verg., Aen. 12.819: "lege tene-
tur"; Ov., Met. 10.203: "lege tenemur"; Prud., Psych.
343: "lege teneri."

567. faciunt iussa: Cf. Verg., Aen. 1.302; Ov.,
Met. 2.798; Fast. 1.379: "iussa facit"; Met. 3.154:
"iussa . . . faciunt."

568. affectumque volendi: Cf. Prosp., De ingrat.
128: "affectumque volendi." affectus in Christian
authors may = "intention"; cf. TLL 1.2.1192.9-31.

570-574. sic etiam quae non spirant: For the relationship of this passage to Lucr. 3.784-786, cf. Intro.,
p. 49.

572. in aequora: For aequor = "level surface,
plain," cf., e.g., Prosp., De ingrat. 477: "/neque/
praesulcet divina manus, quo temperet aequor"; Epigr.
19.6: "et tamen hi calles /virtutis/ . . . quaedam
magnificis aequora sunt animis." Cf. TLL 1.2.1022.84-
1023.70.

574. amnes decurrunt: Cf. Verg., Aen. 12.524: "amnes et in aequora currunt."

577-579. quod si horum, etc.: Contrast the opposite situation, where a beast might wish to be transformed into a man, at Aug., Serm. 26: "si posset loqui pecus et dicere Deo: 'quare istum hominem et me pecudem fecisti?' nonne iuste succenseres et diceres: 'o pecus, tu quis es qui respondeas Deo?';et tu homo es, sed ad Deum pecus es."

580-586. numquid qui Domino, etc.: The Maurists mark this passage as suspect of unorthodoxy. A major difficulty appears at vv. 585-586, aequa creantis / mensura est, uno qui lumine luminat omnes. If mensura refers to grace, then the passage is erroneous in teaching that grace is offered equally to all. Cf. Sister M. Alphonsine Lesousky, O.S.U., The De Dono Perseverantiae 270, citing A. Tanquerey, Synopsis Theologiae Dogmaticae 3 (21st ed., Rome, 1929): "Since grace is necessary for everyone who is saved, and God wills all men to be saved, grace is given to all. But it is not given equally to all, for grace is gratuitous: God pours out His grace on individuals as He wills and according to the disposition and cooperation of each." Cf. further ibid., 270-271. Valentin, Saint Prosper 892, defends the passage as meaning only that salvation is offered to all, with the "light" being reason, conscience, and Natural Law. But these latter are not ordinarily referred to in terms of measurable factors, and it is difficult to avoid taking mensura - "measure of grace."

585. creantis: creans subst. - "creator" is cited at TLL 4.1161.71-74 only for Aug., Civ. 22.24: "bonum quod a creante tribuitur"; Ennod. (ob. 521); Arator (6th cent.); Coripp. (6th cent.). Cf. also Prosp., De ingrat. 727: "iure creantis," and contrast, e.g., De prov. 485, creator.

586. mensura: mensura appears from Cato, and in poetry from Moret., Priap., Ov. on. Cf., e.g., Iuv. 10.98: "ut rebus laetis par sit mensura malorum"; Vulg., Luke 6.38: "date, et dabitur vobis: mensuram bonam ... dabunt in sinum vestrum"; Cypr., Epist. 78.2: "abundans mensura, quam accipies a Domino in die remunerationis." Cf. TLL 8.758.49-50; 767.29-48, and, for the freq. occurrences of mensura in Vocat. gent., Young, Studies 39.

uno qui lumine luminat omnes: Cf. Prud., Symm. 2.8.31:
"luminat omnes."--Cf. n. on 544, above, for the figure of
Christ as light.

luminat: luminare is Silver and Late. Cf. Apul.,
Met. 9.12: "male luminatus" (one who has a narrow view).
For luminare - "illumine (with grace)," as here, cf.,
e.g., Cypr., Dom. orat. 1: "luce gratiae illuminati."
Cf. Blaise, s.v.

587-588. variis rerum speciebus / suscipimur: Cf.
Verg., Georg. 4.406: "variae eludent species"; Ov.,Rem.
526: "mille mali species"; Prud., Apoth. 733: "exiguas
rerum species."

591. patulas intrant stipata per aures: Cf. Hor.,
Epist. 1.18.70: "patulae . . . aures"; 2.2.105:
"patulas . . . aures"; Prud., Apoth. 399: "stolidas
intrare per aures."

593. dogmata: dogma, a Greek loan word, appears
from Cic. on as a general term for any theological or
philosophical tenet. Christian authors may employ dogma
= "theological opinion"(cf. TLL 5.1.1814.5-62); "teaching, true or false" (1814.63-1816.57); "doctrine, dogma"
(1816.58-1817.5). dogma appears here and at v. 770, the
only other occurrence in De prov., as "false teaching";
it appears at De ingrat. 1, 44, 127, 479, 543, the only
instances in that poem, in the same sense, but with
specific reference to Pelagianism or semi-pelagianism in
each instance.

598. nullum procedat in aequor: Cf. Verg., Aen.
10.451: "medium procedit in aequor."

599. effusis . . . habenis: Cf. Verg., Aen. 5.818;
12.499: "omnes effundit habenas."

602. reddemus honorem: Cf. Ov., Met. 13.272:
"reddat honorem"; Fast. 2.555: "redduntur honores."

603. omnia quae fecit bona valde: Cf. Gen. 1.31:
"viditque Deus cuncta quae fecit et erant valde bona";
1 Tim. 4.4: "omnis creatura Dei bona est."

ut non vitiorum: Cf. Prud., Apoth. 934: "sed non
vitiorum."

604-605. ut superas caperemus, etc.: The image of
the Christian life as a contest with the crown as its

reward is biblical. Cf. 1 Cor. 9.25: "omnis autem qui in agone contendit, ab omnibus se abstinuit, et illi quidem ut corruptibilem coronam accipiant; nos autem incorruptam"; 2 Tim. 4.8; 1 Pet. 5.4; Jas. 1.12; Apoc. 2.10. The figure of the crown is freq. in De prov., occurring also at vv. 255, 319, 852, 900.

604. incentiva: incentivum subst. = "incentive" is Late, appearing from Tert. on. Cf., e.g., Aug., In psalm. 2.42: "universa vitiorum incentiva." Cf. TLL 7.1.872.79-874.4.

605. agone: agon appears from Plin. min. on, and is freq. in Christian authors in the sense of "spiritual combat." Cf., e.g., Itala, 2 Tim. 4.7: "agonem bonum decertavi"; Prosp., Vocat. gent. 2.28: "in praesentis autem agonis incerto." For further explanation of the word as understood by Christian authors cf. Tert., Spect. 29: "aspice impudicitiam deiectam a castitate, perfidiam caesam a fide . . .tales sunt apud nos agones." Cf. TLL 1.2.1411. 35-37; 1411.84-1412.60.

606. protulit: proferre = "bear, produce" appears first in Plin. mai. with reference to the creative power of the earth. Cf. Benoist, s.v.

608. motus animi: Cf. Lucr. 4.1072: "animi traducere motus"; Verg., Georg. 4.86: "motus animorum."

610. gladio verbi, fideique umbone: Cf. Eph. 6.10-17 for the image of the armor of God, based on the image of Christian life as a warfare. For the latter, cf. n. on 229-234, above.

611. spicula mortis: Cf. n. on 534, above.

612-616. cumque opus hoc mundi, etc.: References to worship of heavenly bodies and warnings against the practice are freq. in the O.T. Cf. Deut. 4.19, 17.3; 4 Kgs. 23.5; Job 31.26-28; Jer. 19.3; Am. 5.26 (quoted at Acts 7.43). Cf. also De prov. 674-675.

613. sidera caeli: Cf. Verg., Georg. 2.1: "sidera caeli"; Ov., Met. 7.580: "/ad sidera caeli/."

619-621. nam cum ille excelso deiectus Lucifer, etc.: For the account of Satan's banishment from heaven, cf. Apoc. 12.1-9. Cf. also Prosp., De ingrat. 855: "regione poli disiecta superbia."

620-621. pars tertia . . . / astrorum: Cf. Ov., Met.
5.372: "pars tertia"; Vulg., Apoc. 12.4: "cauda eius
trahebat tertiam partem stellarum caeli."

622. clara Dei . . . bonitatis imago: Cf. Prosp.,
De ingrat. 575: "inviolata Dei . . . sublimis imago."

623. castra invidiae ocquereris: For castra alicuius
sequi = "to do one's military service under someone," cf.
Nep., Cato 1.2: "castra secutus est C. Claudii Neronis."
On the distinction between castra and exercitus, cf.
Greg.-M., Hom. Ezech. 1.8.10 /PL 76.858/: "castra enim
multitudines appellantur exercitus, cum in procinctu
pergunt aut in certo quolibet loco in itinere demorantur."

624-720. sed quo te praeceps, etc.: The Christians
rejected astrology in all its forms as superstition, and
also because of its close association with pagan thought.
There was a further danger, however, in that the practice
of astrology constituted a direct attack on the doctrine
of providence by promoting a deterministic system of the
universe, which in turn led to a denial of the efficacy
of grace and of the freedom of the will. It is not surprising, therefore, that attacks against astrology should
appear frequently in Christian authors.

Tert. approaches the subject, not by denying outright
that the stars have any power, but by stressing the subjection of these heavenly bodies to God. Cf., e.g., Nat.
2.3.1-6.7; esp. 2.5: "credere . . . elementorum potestates
et arbitria esse, quae sunt servitutes et officia." At
another point he suggests that the stars may be unfaith-
ful angels or adulterers. Cf. Idol. 9: "non allego,
quod idola honoret, quorum nomina caelo inscripsit, quibus
omnem Dei potestatem addixit, quod propterea homines non
putant Deum requirendum praesumentes stellarum nos im-
mutabili arbitrio agi: unum propono, angelos esse illos
desertores Dei, amatores feminarum, proditores etiam huius
curiositatis, propterea quoque damnatos a Deo. O divina
sententia usque ad terram pertinax, cui etiam ignorantes
testimonium reddunt!"

Aug. himself levelled attacks against the astrologers.
Cf., e.g., Epist. 246.2: "illud sane quanto citius ac
breviter noveris, omnes leges atque instituta omnia dis-
ciplinae, laudes, vituperationes, exhortationes, terrores,

praemia, supplicia ceteraque omnia, quibus humanum genus administratur et regitur, penitus labefactari atque subverti nihilque in eis omnino iustitiae remanere, nisi voluntas sit causa peccandi"; cf. also Civ. 7.15; In psalm. 61 (where the conversion of an astrologer is related); Doct. Christ. 2.21-23.

Leo M., the pope under whom Prosp. served as papal secretary, delivers a number of attacks against astrology and astrologers. In one of his sermons the pontiff denounces the element of fatalism implicit in the worship of the stars, and concludes with an argument similar in thought to De prov. 705-715. Cf. Serm. 27.3: "commentum impium sua ratione destruitur, quia si praedicta non permanent, non sunt fata metuenda; si permanent, non sunt astra veneranda." The passage immediately after the foregoing, Serm. 27 (26).4, contains a denunciation of sunworship, a theme taken up again at Serm. 84(81).2, where the pope vindicates human liberty against astrological fatalism. Finally, in Epist. 15, Leo cites scripture /Col. 2.8, 18; 2Tim. 4.34/ against the Priscillianists, who were accused of holding that the stars have power over men. Leo is here again concerned with the fatalism to which such a belief would lead.

The Priscillianists, followers of the 4th cent. Spanish layman, later bishop, Priscillian, were condemned at the Councils of Sarogossa (A.D. 380), Bordeaux (385), Toledo (411), and Braga (563). Priscillian himself was executed at Trier in 385 by order of the usurping emperor Maximus, after he had been judged guilty of magic. Whether Priscillian held all the doctrines attributed to him is an open question. It is certain that Priscillian and a group of his followers passed through Aquitaine c. 380 A.D. on their way to Rome to appeal to Pope Damasus against the decisions of Sarogossa, and that Priscillianism was popular in Aquitaine around the beginning of the 5th cent. Cf. Tixeront, History of Dogmas 2.229-241, and Valentin, op. cit., 781.

Before and during this period, astrology was esp. popular in Africa, "la patrie, la terre classique de l'astrologie" (Valentin, Saint Prosper 40), and Aug. himself was misled at first (cf. Conf. 4.3) as a result of his own attachment to Neo-Platonic thought. Plotinus had taught that the stars grant men's prayers, although he denied to them all power over the soul. Cf. Plot., Enn. 3.1.1, 5-6; 4.4.40-42. For a general survey of the subject, with special attention to Gaul, cf. Valentin, op. cit. 39-41. Cf. also M.L.W. Laistner, "The Western Church and Astrology during the Early Middle Ages," Harvard Theological Review 34 (1941) 251-275.

The term for practitioners of astrology was mathematici. Cf. Aug., Divers. quaest. 45.1: "non eos appellarunt mathematicos veteres, qui nunc appellantur, sed illos qui temporum numeros motu caeli ac siderum pervestigarunt; . . . nunc appellantur mathematici volentes actus nostros corporibus caelestibus subdere." Cf. also TLL 8.471.81-472.59. The Lyons ed. of De prov. has the gloss contra mathematicos opposite v. 627, leading the Ballerini (1769) to conclude erroneously that the poem was composed primarily against the astrologers. Cf. Intro., p. 12.

624. quo te praeceps rapit orbita: Cf. Prud., Ham. 1: "quo te praecipitat rabies tua?"

630: apertas: Valentin, Saint Prosper 845, suggests that opertas would be a possible reading here, but apertas gives an acceptable sense.

632-633. qua pontum lege moveri / iusserit: Cf. Verg., Georg. 1.130: "iussit pontumque moveri."

633. conseverit: For conserere in a figurative sense, cf., e.g., Prosp., De ingrat. 394: "amor quem conserit ipse /Deus/ est." Cf. Blaise, s.v.--Valentin, Saint Prosper 845, rejects the reading of Migne, consueverit, as not yielding good sense; it appears to be a misprint in the PL text.

634. sidereosque ignes: Cf. Ov., Met. 15.665: "sidereos . . . ignes."

635. sincerus . . . fons aequique bonique: For the figure of God as a fountain, cf., e.g., Aug., Divers. quaest. 8.44: "a Deo, quem fontem aequitatis atque iustitiae credi necesse est"; Prosp., De ingrat. 85: "aeterni fontis"; 952: "summo verorum a fonte bonorum."

640. ad promissa vocare: Cf. 2. Pet. 1.3-4: "per cognitionem eius, qui vocavit nos propria gloria, et

virtute, per quem maxima, et pretiosa nobis promissa donavit."

644. aetheriis . . . ignibus: Cf. Ov., Fast. 1.473: "aethereos . . . ignes."

647. cordi insinuet bonus auctor et auribus: Cf. Hier., In Is. 5.7: "insinuare auribus."

648. currentem: Cf. n. on 548, above.

649-650. 'solum,' inquit, 'venerare Deum' etc.: Cf. Deut. 6.13: "Dominum Deum tuum timebis et ipse ser-vies," cited at Matt. 4.10, Luke 4.8 in the form: "Dominum Deum tuum adorabis, et illi soli servies"; Prud., Symm. 2.244-245: "'soli mihi construe templum / meque unum venerare Deum'."

649. venerare Deum: Cf. Verg., Georg. 1.338: "venerare deos"; Prud., Apoth. 385: "venerata Deum."

651. 'hoc operis sectare boni, hoc fuge cautus ini-qui': Cf. 1 Tim. 6.4-12 for the command to do good and avoid evil, and esp. v. 11 for verbal similarity: "haec fuge: sectare vero"; cf. also Sir. 17.12.

652. vita beata: Among the pagan philosophers, es-pecially the Stoics, vita beata referred to the state attainable by man through the practice of virtue; the Peripatetics made a distinction between the vita beata and the vita beatissima, which was a combination of the vita beata with health and wordly possessions. In the period of Ambr. and Aug., vita beata is adopted into Christian eschatological terminology in the sense of "eternal life." Cf. P. J. Couvée, Vita beata en vita aeterna (Baarn,1947).

653. coram adsunt: Cf. Verg., Aen. 1.595: "coram, quem quaeritis, adsum."

aqua: For aqua = "baptismal water" cf., e.g., Vulg., Matt. 3.11: "ego quidem baptizo vos in aqua in paeni-tentiam"; Tert., Spect. 4: "aquam ingressi Christianam fidem . . . profitemur"; Paen. 6: "inire aquam"; Bapt.1: "in aqua nascimur nec aliter quam in aqua permanendo salvi sumus"; Aug., Conf. 9.13.35: "aqua salutaris"; Prosp., De ingrat. 464-465: "anne ab aquis divina manus renovare receptos / incipit?" Cf. TLL 2.1.361.22-29.

servatrix: servatrix is cited in the lexica for Ter., Cic., Ov., Stat., Apul., Inscr. Cf. Benoist and Georges, s.v.

654. patet aequa facultas: Cf. Prosp., Epist. ad Aug. /Aug., Epist. 225/ 4: "putant /Massilienses/. . . quantum quisque ad malum tantum habeat facultatis ad bonum; parique momento animum se vel ad vitia vel ad virtutes movere, quem bona appetentem gratia Dei foveat, mala sectantem damnatio iusta suscipiat."

655. vatum scripta piorum: Cf. Verg., Aen. 4.464: "vatum praedicta priorum /piorum/," and Intro., pp. 59-60.

vatum: Cf. n. on 365, vatem, above.

657. arbitrium: Cf. n. on 240, arbitrium, above.

vis externa: Cf. Liv. 5.33.3: "externa vis."

660-661. sed nostris oritur, etc.: Cf. n. on 229-234, above.

660-661. ipsaque bellum / libertas movet: Cf. Verg., Aen. 6.820-821: "natosque pater nova bella moventes / ad poenam pulchra pro libertate vocabit"; Ov., Am. 3.15. 8-9: "gentis . . . / quam sua libertas ad honesta coegerat arma."

661. libertas: For libertas - liberum arbitrium cf. Blaise, s.v. libertas is freq. in this sense in Prosp., De ingrat., e.g., at vv. 11-12: "quia libertate male usi / peccarunt."

663. bravioque potitos: bravium is scriptural in origin, being found at 1 Cor. 9.24; Phil. 3.14 in both Itala and Vulg. Cf. TLL 2.2.2153.21-2154.6. For the shortening of i cf. Prud., Peri. 5.538.--Valentin, Saint Prosper 845, suggests the reading bravioque potiri, where bravium might designate worldly pleasures which the voluptuaries are unwilling to sacrifice, but the verse gives an acceptable sense as it stands.--For the image of Christian life as a contest cf. n. on 604-605, above.

664. ardua quaeque piget pro spe temptare latenti: Cf. Verg., Aen. 11.437: "ut tanta quidquam pro spe temptare recusem."

665. callidus hostis: For use of this term to denote Satan cf.,e.g., Gen. 3.1: "sed et serpens erat callidior cunctis animantibus terrae"; Hier.,Epist. 22.29: "variis callidus hostis pugnat insidiis"; Greg. M., (6th cent.) Past. 3.33.

666. vires capit: Cf. Ov., Met. 7.417: "vires cepisse."

668. frustraque homines contendere divis: Cf. Verg., Ecl. 7.69: "victum frustra contendere Thyrsim"; App. Verg., Ciris 329: "neque est cum dis contendere nostrum."

670-671. satis agnita prisci / sunt commenta doli: Cf. Verg., Ecl. 4.31: "priscae vestigia fraudis"; Prosp., De ingrat. 596-597: "cognoscite tandem / antiqui commenta doli."

671. commenta: For commentum ∗ "lie, deceit" cf., e.g., Aug., Civ. 10.10: "quis non videat haec omnia fallacium daemonum esse commenta?"; Prosp., De ingrat. praef. xviii: "unde igitur commenta mali sopita resurgant."

672. elaqueat: elaqueare is Late, appearing from Amm. and Ambr. on. Cf. TLL 5.2.323.20-29.

674. sidus adoratum Rempham: Cf. Acts 7.43: "et sidus dei vestri Rempham"; Am. 5.26: "sidus dei vestri." Rempha, or the Assyrian deity Kaiwan, may be identified with the planet Saturn. The reference may have been introduced into the text of Am. after the fall of the Northern Kingdom of Israel to the Assyrians (721 B.C.); from Am. it was introduced by Stephen into his discourse before the Sanhedrin in Acts. Cf. M. Leahy in CCHS on Am. 5.26.

sidus adoratum: Cf. Verg., Aen. 2.700: "sanctum sidus adorat."

674-675. venerataque caeli / militia, etc.: Cf. Deut. 17.3: "ut . . . adorent eos, solem et lunam et omnem militiam caeli"; 4 Kgs. 23.5; "et soli et lunae et duodecim signis et omni militiae caeli"; Jer. 19.13: "sacrificaverunt omni militiae caeli"; Acts 7.42: "/Deus/ tradidit eos servire militiae caeli." Cf. also n. on 612-616, above.

676-685. nec latet haec, etc.: The examples from Elias might not seem to be to the point, since the nature and operation of celestial bodies is in dispute, and not other celestial phenomena. However, the author here extends the issue to include all celestial phenomena.

680-683. caelo praescriptas conditiones, etc.: Mention of Elias' closing of the heavens from raining appears at 3 Kgs. 17.1; Sir. 48.1-3; Jas. 5.17-18.

680. novimus et: Cf. Verg., Ecl. 3.8; Prud., Ham. 366: "novimus et"; Ov., Pont. 4.13.12: "novimus atque"; Prud., Apoth. 433: "novit et."

681. prophetae: Cf. n. on 441, above.

683-685. ipsumque, vocata, etc.: The account of Elias' challenge to the false prophets appears at 3 Kgs. 18.1-40; cf. Sir. 48.1-3.

684. altaria flamma: Cf. Verg., Ecl. 8.105: "altaria flammis."

685. ignem inmississe profanis: The reference is to fire brought down by Elias against two companies of troops sent to apprehend him. Cf. 4 Kgs. 1.1-15.

686. delapsa fuisset: Cf. n. on 278, largitus fuisset, above.

688. ni patiens Dominus, etc.: The text restores the period found in the Lyons and Maurist editions, but omitted in Migne.

694. renovavit Spiritus: For the teaching that man's salvation comes through the Holy Spirit, cf. Tit. 3.5: "per lavacrum regenerationis et renovationis Spiritus Sancti."

renovavit: Cf. n. on 499, above.

695. mortali ex stirpe recisos: Cf. Verg., Aen. 12.208: "imo de stirpe recisum"; Stat., Theb. 4.747; Prud., Symm. 1.268: "mortali de stirpe."--For the figurative use of the terminology from grafting, cf. Rom. 11.24; "si tu ex naturali excisus es oleastro et contra naturam insertus es in bonam olivam"; Prosp., De ingrat. 937: "/figmentum . . . quod/ stirpe vestustatis discretum est atque recisum."

696-697. nec terrea nectit / progenies: Cf. Verg., Georg. 2.341: "terrea /ferrea/ progenies," and Intro., pp. 59-60.

697. templum in Domini corpusque: Cf. M. Bevenot, S.J., in CCHS 788: "The conjunction of the ideas of the Body of Christ and of a sacred building goes back, it

seems,to Christ himself . . . St. John gives us both his
words and their significance." Cf. John 2.19: "solvite
templum hoc, et in tribus diebus excitabo illud"; 21:
"ille autem dicebat de templo corporis sui." For the development of the two interrelated ideas "body" and "temple"
cf. Eph. 2.14-21; for the idea of "temple" cf. 1 Pet. 2.5.
Cf. also Intro., p. 41.--For the doctrine of the Mystical
Body, cf. n. on 343, in Christi corpus, above.

702. transcendit Nestoris annos: Cf. Sil. 1.226:
"transcendit florentes viribus annos"; 4.226: "annos
transcendere factis."--References to the long lifespan of
Nestor are freq. among the poets of the Silver Age. Cf.,
e.g., Stat., Silv. 1.3.110: "finem Nestoreae precor
egrediare senectae"; Mart. 11.56.13: "ter vivere Nestoris
annos"; Iuv. 10.246-247: "rex Pylius, magno si quidquam
credis Homero, / exemplum vitae fuit a cornice secundae."
Cf. A. Otto, Die Sprichwörter der Römer (Leipzig,1890) 242
s.v. Nestor.

703. falsum hoc, aut verum est: For the contrast between "true" and "false" cf. Ter., Andr. 922: "nam ego
quae dico vera an falsa audierim, iam sciri potest";
Cic., Ac. 1.15.9: "quid verum, quid falsum, quid rectum
in oratione pravumve"; 2.11.33: "rationem veri et falsi."

707. dent sese scelerum potius torrentibus omnes:
Cf. Quint., Inst. 10.7.23: "se inani verborum torrenti
dare."

708-709. fas omne nefasque / confundant: Cf. Verg.,
Aen. 5.800: "fas omne"; Georg. 1.505: "fas versum atque nefas"; Ov., Ars 1.739: "fas omne nefasque"; Met.
6.585-586: "fasque nefasque / confusura ruit"; 9.551-552:
"nefasque / fasque"; Prud., Cath. 3.134: "fasque nefasque."

710. cardine rerum: Cf. Verg., Aen. 1.672: "cardine
rerum."

712. perversos . . . mores: For perversi mores =
homines perversorum morum cf. Quint., Inst. 2.15.32:
"quae si vera essent, pessimorum hominum foret, haec
tam perniciosa nocentissimis moribus dare instrumenta."
Cf. also Prosp., De ingrat. 501-502: "cum peior mos et
corruptior aetas / terrore instanti et formidine mortis
egeret."

716-720. <u>scrutatis</u> <u>igitur</u> <u>stellarum</u> <u>motibus</u>, etc.:
Prosp., in a description of astronomical and astrological
investigations that are inspired by worldly wisdom, also
observes that the same results are derived from them as
are portrayed here, viz., the denial of the Creator and
the substitution of many forms of religious worship. Cf.
<u>De</u> <u>ingrat</u>. 872-879:
    iam cum exercetur /sapientia/ numeris ad sidera caeli
    per cursus noscenda suos et scire videtur
    defectus solis varios lunaeque labores,
    quam speciosa sibi est, et quam vanescit in ipsis!
    quae licet ex primo naturae habeantur honore,
    non tamen ad veram possunt perducere vitam;
    denique ab his praeceps in multas religiones
    decidit et factis haesit factore relicto.
Cf. also n. on 624-720, above, and esp. the attacks
against astrologers cited there.

717. <u>artis</u>: <u>ars</u> - "the deceit, trickery of Satan"
is freq. in Christian authors. Cf., e.g., Hier., <u>Epist.</u>
21.13: "Satanas cum aliquem sua arte deceperit"; 125.19:
"Christus arte non illuditur." Cf. <u>TLL</u> 2.1.659.38-55.
<u>ars</u> in the sense simply of "deceit, trickery" appears
from Sall. on. Cf. <u>TLL</u> 2.1.658.46ff. Contrast the use
of <u>ars</u> = "human activity" at Aug., <u>Quant. an</u> c. 1075.

718. <u>dum nullum curare Deum mortalia suadet</u>: Cf.
Verg., <u>Ecl</u>. 8.35: "nec curare deum credis mortalia
quemquam."

720. <u>plebem</u> . . . <u>deorum</u>: Cf. Ov., <u>Ibis</u> 81-82:
"plebs superum, Fauni, Satyrique, Laresque, / Fluminaque
et Nymphae, semideumque genus"; <u>Met.</u> 1.595: "nec de
plebe deo." Cf. <u>De prov.</u> 765-768.

721. <u>sed quia detectis</u>, etc.: The gloss "contra
Epicureos" appears opposite this verse in the Lyons
edition.

<u>laqueis</u> . . . <u>fraudis opertae</u>: Cf. 1 Tim. 3.7; 6.9:
"in laqueum diaboli"; 2 Tim. 2.26: "a diaboli laqueis";
Lact., <u>Inst.</u> 4.30.2: "in laqueos et fraudes illius
adversarii nostri"; Prud., <u>Psych</u>. 268: "ad fraudis
opertum."

727-745. dic age, qui nullis Domini moderantis habenis, etc.: Cf., in the O.T. narrative, Yahweh's assertion to Job in considerable detail of his powers over all nature, at Job 38-41. These divine powers are considered to be exercised through the maintenance of the balance of contraries, as well as by direct intervention. Cf. De prov. 121-150.

727. moderantis habenis: Cf. Ov., Met. 6.223: "graves moderantur habenas."

728. quid ab ordine cessit: Cf. Verg., Aen. 3.447: "neque ab ordine cedunt."

730. a prisco divisum foedere rerum: The bond which exists between all created things, and the hierarchy among them, are stressed in the first creation account. Cf. Gen. 1.1-2.3.--Cf. Verg., Georg. 1.60-61: "aeternaque foedera certis / imposuit natura locis."

731. solis . . . in ortum: Cf. Verg., Aen. 6.255: "sub lumina solis et ortus"; Georg. 3.277; Ov., Met. 5.455; Ibis 429: "solis ad ortus"; Met. 6.49; Her. 15.143; Pont. 1.4.29: Trist. 5.8.25: "solis ab ortu"; Prud., Peri. 13.102-103: "in ortum / solis."

revocatur in ortum: Cf. Ov., Her. 20.87: "revocavit ad ortus"; Prud., Cath. 10.10: "revocantur in ortus."

734. nubibus imber: Cf. Verg., Aen. 11.548; Georg. 4.312: "nubibus imber"; Ecl. 6.38; Ov., Met. 11.516: "nubibus imbres"; Paul. Nol., Carm. 18.18: "a nubibus imber."

735-736. laeta negant . . . / semina: Cf. Verg., Georg. 1.1: "laetas segetes"; Ov., Trist. 3.10.73: "poma negat regio."--Valentin, Saint Prosper 830 n. 2, suggests that these verses be altered on grounds of their obscurity. The construction is an involved one at this point, and apparently there is no case of a similar involution in the De prov.; passages of similar structure do appear in Vergil and in the other classical poets, however. The point of the passages, taken in context, seems to be that the flowers--along with the sun, moon,

stars, seasons, winds, and rain--serve as an example of
the manner in which the priscum foedus rerum (730) operates in the practical order. The meaning is thus in accord with that expressed by non aliter . . . ita (734),
i.e., "in the same manner (as always)." The flowers close
the series of examples, and the conclusion of the thought
--nec abest ab origine rerum / ordo manens, (736-737)--
follows immediately. Since the reading of the text as it
stands at this point is uniform in all the editions, and
in view of the fact that V. offers no suggested change
nor evidence to support one, it appears that the text
should remain as it stands.

736. nec abest ab origine rerum: Cf. Verg., Georg.
3.48: "abest ab origine Caesar."

737. subsistunt: Cf. n. on 149, above.

739. astrueret: astruere appears from Caes. on, but
is mostly Silver and Late. Cf. TLL 2.1.978.38-42.
astruere = "build" in a literal sense, as here, is rare.
Cf. TLL 2.1.978.43-48. Contrast, e.g., Prosp., Epist.
ad Ruf. 2: "cum enim primum tantam naturae humanae
vellent /Pelagiani/ astruere sanitatem, ut per solum
liberum arbitrium posset assequi Dei regnum," where
astruere means "show, prove, affirm," its usual sense in
Late Latin. For further instances of astruere in the
latter sense, cf., e.g., Ambr., Epist.5.14: "non astruo,
nec verum arbitror"; Aug., Conf. 4.15.24: "exemplis
corporeis astruebam."

molemque omnem spirando foveret: Cf. Gen. 2.7:
"formavit igitur Dominus Deus hominem de limo terrae
et inspiravit in faciem eius spiraculum vitae, et factus
est homo in animam viventem." In Gen. the passage refers
only to the creation of Adam; in De prov. the thought is
extended to apply to the whole physical universe.

743. specialiter: specialiter is Silver and Late,
appearing from Cels., Col., and Quint. on. Cf. Forcellini
and Blaise, s.v.

744. perpetis: Forms of perpes appear at Plaut.,
Amph. 280, 732; Truc. 878. Cf. Neue-Wagener, Formenlehre
2.169. The word is also cited for Pacuv. by Ernout-
Meillet and Benoist. It apparently disappeared from the
literary language during the classical period, only to
reappear among the archaizers of the second cent. A.D.
Cf. Ernout-Meillet, s.v., and the further instances cited
by Neue-Wagener, op. cit., 2.169-170. For perpes =
perpetuus in Christian authors cf., e.g., Prud., Cath.
1.26: "forma mentis perpetis"; 10.42; 11.111; Peri.
10.477.

745. propriae largitus imaginis instar: References
to man's creation in the image of God abound in Scripture.
Cf., e.g., Gen. 1.26-27; 5.1; 9.6; Wisd. 2.23; Sir. 17.1;
1 Cor. 11.7; Jas. 3.9.

746-747. nec poenam iniustis, nec praemia sanctis /
restitui: Prosp. describes the complaint of the Pelagians
against the orthodox teaching on grace in similar language. Cf. De ingrat. 568: "nec vitiis poenam deberi aut
praemia laudi."

748. ultricem . . . iram: Cf. Cassian, Inst. 8.10:
"ultrices irae." Cf. n. on 85, above.

750. saeva immitis feritate tyranni: Cf. Verg.,
Georg. 4.492-493: "immitis rupta tyranni / foedera";
Ov., Trist. 5.7.46: "saevae plus feritatis"; Prud.,
Symm. 1.46: "feritate tyranni."

751. aut: The reading of the pre-Maurist editors
has been restored here. The poets frequently join aut,
-ve, vel, sive in a series of interrogations. Cf. TLL
2.2.1570.72-1571.20. an - aut in disjunctive questions,
but not otherwise. Cf. L.-Hof. 678.

peccati nescia: Cf. Leo M., Serm. 74.1: "qui
/Christus/ peccati erat nescius."

752. possessura foret: For instances of forms of
forem = essem with the fut. act. part. cf. Neue-Wagener,
Formenlehre 3.174-175.

755-758. sic mundi meta, etc.: For the relationship of this passage to Lucr. 5.1026-1027, cf. Intro., pp. 47-48.

755. properata fuisset: Cf. n. on 278, largitus fuisset, above.

757. nocentes: For nocentes subst. - "unjust persons" cf., e.g., Vulg., Ps. 26 (27).2: "dum appropiant super me nocentes, ut edant carnes meas"; Cypr., Epist. 13.4; 67.9.

758. honos: honos and honor are both in use until the Silver Age, and honos is esp. freq. in Cic. After the Silver Age honos is rarely found in prose, and is obsolete by the time of Quint. (cf. Inst. 1.4.13). The poets, however, continue to employ either form. Cf. Ernout-Meillet, s.v., and TLL 6.3.2916.16-50. Contrast, e.g., De prov. 47, honor, and 846, honos; De ingrat. 16, honos, and 96, honor.

759. generis nostri profunda propago: Cf. Prud., Symm. 2.224: "generisque propagine"; 341-342: "nostrae porrecta propago / stirpis."

761. renata: renasci in Christian authors means "to be reborn in baptism." Cf.,e.g., John 3.3: "nisi quis renatus fuerit denuo"; 1 Pet. 1.23: "renati non ex semine corruptibili, sed incorruptibili per verbum Dei vivi." Cf. Blaise, s.v.

767. errore parentum: Cf. App. Verg., Ciris 240: "errore parentum."

768. Unigenam: For Unigena - Christus cf. Paul. Nol., Carm. 5.47; 27.93. For discussion of the origin and use of the word in the classical poets, cf. in addition to the lexica, A. Cordier, Etudes sur le vocabulaire épique dans "l'Enéide" (Paris,1939) 261.

submissus adorat: Cf. Prud., Apoth. 598: "submissus adoro."

769. sophicas: sophicus is cited only for this place before the 6th cent. Cf. Gaffiot, s.v., and Baxter-Johnson, s.v.

770. dogmata: Cf. n. on 593, above.

iam Christo sapere et brutescere mundo: Cf. 1 Cor.
1.17-31, for the contrast between wisdom and foolishness
as each is interpreted by the world and by the follower
of Christ.

772-776. quam multos procul, etc.: For the relationship of this passage to Aen. 1.23-32; 5.35-41, cf. Intro.,
pp. 52-53. Prosp. uses the figure of the sea and the
harbor in reference to the Pelagians at De ingrat. 522-
525:
    haec si non vestris spirant de cordibus, et vos
    non cum damnatis eadem ratis extulit alto
    mergendos pelago, submittite vela tumoris
    nobiscumque humiles placido consistite portu.

772. procul a portu rationis: For the figure of the
harbor as a place of rest and security, cf. Campbell
Bonner, "Desired Haven," Harvard Theological Review 34
(1941) 49-67.

773-774. quos aequore toto / iactatos: Cf. Verg.,
Aen. 1.29: "iactatos aequore toto"; 5.456; 11.599;
12.501: "aequore toto"; Hor., Carm. 4.4.53-54: "gens
. . . / iactata Tuscis aequoribus"; Stat., Theb. 12.12
"adsiduo iactatis aequore."

774. vagis erroribus actos: Cf. Verg., Aen. 6.532:
"erroribus actus"; 7.199: "sive errore viae seu tempes-
tatibus acti"; Ov., Met. 4.567: "longisque erroribus
actus"; 15.771: "longis erroribus actum"; Her. 2.107;
Trist. 4.10.109: "longis erroribus acto"; Met. 4.502:
"erroresque vagos"; Prosp., De ingrat. 851: "vagus
error."

775-776. nunc reduces iuvat excipere, etc. Cf.
Verg., Aen. 5.40-41: "gratatur reduces et . . . /
excipit"; Ov., Her. 13.115: "quando ego te reducem
cupidis amplexa lacertis"; 17.101: "excipis amplexu."

776. confotos: confovere appears only in Apul.
before Late Latin. Cf., e.g., Hier., Epist. 66.5: "in
his Christum confovet"; In Ier. 15.10: "in sanctis atque
pauperibus confovendis"; Prud., Peri. 11.137-138:
"reverendam / canitiem molli confovet in gremio"; Prosp.,
De ingrat. 479-480: "nonne / perspicuum est quantum
damnatos confoveatis?"

778. plectisset: The form is uncertain, since the
perf. tense of plectere = "punish" is apparently unattest-
ed elsewhere. Forcellini cites this verse with

plectisset; however, Georges cites plexisset. Act.
forms are avoided in Latin of the classical period, but
appear from time to time later. Cf. Ernout-Meillet, s.v.,
and Blaise, s.v.

implacabilis irae: Cf. App. Verg., Culex 238: "implacabilis ira nimis"; Ov., Pont. 3.3.63: "non implacabilis ira."

779. intercepta forent: Cf. n. on 86, above.

781-783. 'mortem,' inquit Dominus, 'peccantis nolo,'
etc.: Cf. Ezech 18.32: "'quia nolo mortem morientis,'
dicit Dominus Deus"; 33.11: "dicit Dominus Deus, 'nolo
mortem impii'"; 2 Pet. 3.9: "Dominus . . . nolens ali-
quos perire"; 1 Tim. 2.4:"/Deus/ qui omnes homines vult
salvos fieri, et ad agnitionem veritatis venire."

781. peccantis: peccans, subst. - "offender" appears
from Sen; for peccans = "sinner, offender against God's
law," cf., e.g., Aug., Nat. bon. 7.8-9: "peccantes igitur
in suppliciis ordinantur." Cf. Blaise and Lewis-Short,
s.v.

784. virtutum similes . . . suarum: Cf. Prosp., De
ingrat. 977-978: "Deus est . . . / . . . virtus"; C.
coll. 13.1: "virtus namque principaliter Deus est";
Vocat. gent. 1.8: "totumque quod virtus est, Deus est."

785-786. 'vindictam,' inquit, 'mihi cedite,' etc.:
Cf. Rom. 12.19: "date locum irae. scriptum est enim,
mihi vindicta"; Heb. 10.30: "mihi vindicta"; Deut.
32.35: "mea est ultio, et ego retribuam in tempore."

790. fuerat: On this apparent use of the pluperf.
for a perf. or imperf., cf. Platnauer, Latin Elegiac
Verse 112: "This, again, is not an exclusively poetical
usage. It seems to have sprung from colloquial idiom,
to have been used freely by the elegists, and so to have
passed into ordinary (later) prose. Any pluperfect might
thus be used, though fueram standing for fui or eram is
probably the commonest." Cf. further K.-Steg. 2.1.140-
141.

794. minimo ad poenam quadrante vocando: Cf. Matt.
5.26: "amen dico tibi, non exies inde, donec reddas
novissimum quadrantem"; Luke 12.59; "dico tibi, non exies
inde, donec etiam novissimum minutum reddas."

802-803. nam quod ubique agitur, etc: Cf. Verg.,
Georg. 4.392-393:"novit namque omnia vates / quae sint,

quae fuerint, quae mox ventura trahantur"; Vulg., Sir.
42.19: "cognovit enim Dominus omnem scientiam, et
inspexit in signum aevi, annuntians quae praeterierunt et
quae superventura sunt, revelans vestigia occultorum";
Prud., Cath. 9.12: "quae sunt, fuerunt, quaeque post
futura sunt."

803. ante oculos: Cf. Lucr. 2.113; 3.185; 4.979:
"ante oculos."

subsistit: Cf. n. on 149, above.

804. una dies: Cf. Paul. Nol., Carm. 14.82:
"una dies."

cras . . . here: For cras subst. - "the future,
tomorrow" cf., e.g., Prosp., Epigr. 76.6: "cur dubium
expectat cras hodierna salus." Cf. TLL 4.1100.72-1101.3.
--here subst. = "the past, yesterday" is cited at TLL
6.3.2658.17 only for this verse and Ps.-Aug., Serm. 123.1.

For the ambiguity in pronunciation which resulted in
the use sometimes of here, and sometimes of heri, cf.
Quint. 1.4.8: "neque e neque i plane auditur." Cf. TLL
6.3.2656.16-64.

805-806. sed quamquam examen Deus, etc.: Cf. Prosp.,
De ingrat. 709-711:
   multa etenim bene tecta latent nescitaque prosunt,
   dum mansueta fides quaedam dilata modeste
   sustinet, et nullo ignorat non edita damno.
Cf. also Vulg., Rom. 2.16; 1 Cor. 4.5.

808-809. maxima bellis / regna quatit: Cf. Verg.,
Aen. 9.608: "quatit oppida bello"; Ov., Her. 8.118:
"et sua regna quatit."

810. obruit undis: Cf. Ov., Pont. 3.6.29: "obruerit
cum tot saevis deus aequoris undis."

811-812. dumque inopes ditat, etc.: For accounts of
various manifestations of God's justice cf. Luke 1.46-55
(the Magnificat); 1 Kgs. 2.1-10; Ps. 74(75).8; 112(113).
6-7; 145(146).7-9. Cf. also Iuvenc. 1.102: "humiles
opibus ditavit egentes."

816-820. multa quidem semper, etc.: The principle
that the just and unjust alike receive the same divine
gifts--and undergo the same trials--is grounded in O.T.
thought. Cf., e.g., Eccles. 9.2-3: "eadem cunctis

eveniunt"; Ezech. 21.3-4: "occidam in te iustum et
impium."

816. in isto: Cf. n. on 895, below.

817. indignos dignosque: Cf. Verg., Aen. 12.811:
"digna indigna"; 9.595; App. Verg., Ciris 247: "digna
atque indigna."

818: frigora et aestus: Cf. Dan. 3.67: "frigus et
aestus"; Lucr. 6.364: "frigus et aestum."

823. et qui conversos, etc.: Cf. Aug., In psalm.
54.3: "utinam . . . qui nosmodo exercent convertantur."

824. perdendis: Except for the perf. part., forms
of perdere in the pass. are chiefly Late. Cf., e.g.,
Vulg., Job 20.7, perdetur; Prov. 2.22, perdentur; Aug.,
Epist. 138.14, perderentur. However, cf. Hor., Sat.
2.6.59, perditur.

indemutabilis: indemutabilis is Late, appearing
from Tert. on. Cf., e.g., Tert., Adv. Hermog. 2: "/Deum/
in partes non devenire, ut indivisibilem et indemutabilem";
Pudic. 12: "novissimi testamenti semper indemutabilis
status est." Cf. TLL 7.1.1136. 20-48.

826-827. et quos / arsuris Sodomis, etc.: Cf. n.
on 350-355, in Pentapolim, above.--Cf. Prud., Ham. 725:
"Sodomis ardentibus."

826. sunt quos diluvium mundi: Cf. n. on 335-340,
above.

diluvium: Verg., Aen. 7.228; 12.205, furnish the
first examples of this word. Cf. A. Cordier, Etudes sur
le vocabulaire épique dans l'"Enéide" (Paris,1939) 144.
Both Christian and non-Christian authors use diluvium to
refer to inundation in general. Cf. TLL 5.1.1191.42-1192.
38. diluvium may also be employed in an extended sense,
e.g., Prosp., In psalm. 103.6: "in diluvio persecutionis."

827-829. norat / angelus Aegypti, etc.: The sparing
of the firstborn of the Hebrews from the tenth plague is
recounted at Ex. 12.1-30.

828. angelus . . . vastator: Cf. Leo M., Serm. 55.5:
". . . limina vastator angelus sanguine agni et signo
crucis praenotata non intrat."

830-831. nec rutilo mulier decepta est, etc.: For the story of Rahab the harlot, cf. Jos. 2.1-24; 6.15-25.

832. fitque per amnem: The account of the Hebrews' passage of the Jordan appears at Jos. 3.7-17.

833-834. et per inane piis, etc. For the story of Habacuc, cf. Dan. 14.33-39.

835. vertitur ordo: Cf. Verg., Aen. 3.376: "is vertitur ordo."

836-837. vinctos labentia vincula solvunt, etc.: For the narrative of the deliverance of Peter from prison by an angel, cf. Acts 12.6-11; for the deliverance of Paul and Silas, Acts 16.16-34, and esp. v. 26: "et universorum vincula soluta sunt."--Cf. Ov., Met. 3.699-700: "lapsasque lacertis / sponte sua fama est nullo solvente catena"; Paul. Nol., Carm. 15.263-264: "Petrus sponte sua vinclis labentibus eque / carcere processit clauso."

838. deficit humor aquas: Cf. Verg., Georg. 1.290: "deficit humor"; Ov., Met. 9.567: "linguam defecerat humor."

deficit . . . ignes calor: The reference is to the three young men, Sidrach, Misach, and Abdenago, in the fiery furnace. Cf. Dan. 3.1-97.

deficit . . . ira leones: The story of Daniel in the lions' den is related at Dan. 6.2-29.--Cf. Verg., Aen. 7.15: "iraeque leonum"; Ov., Trist. 4.6.5: "ira leonum"; Met. 10.551: "leonibus ira"; 15.86: "iracundique leones"; Prud., Cath. 4.861 "leonis ira."

deficit: deficere - "desert, abandon" with reference to animals is cited at TLL 5.1.324.48-49 only for Lucr. 5.887; with reference to objects, at TLL 5.1.324.49-57 from Verg. and Ov. on.

840. more parentum: Cf. Verg., Aen. 6.223; Ov., Met. 15.336: "more parentum"; Vulg., Wisd. 12.24: "infantium insensatorum more viventes"; 2 Mach. 10.6: "more bestiarum"; 11: "leonum autem more."--The meaning is, not that the parents fell through the sins of others, but that the children, who fell because of the sins of others, met death in the same manner as the parents.

NOTES

842-843. nam cum homines, etc.: Cf. n. on 335-340, above.

844. terris exempta: eximere is first used in connection with death by Sen., but the usage is mostly Late. Cf. e.g., Prosp., De ingrat. 438: "exempti mundo." Cf. TLL 5.3.1499.34-50.

845. progenies auctura malos: Cf. Verg., Aen. 5.565: "progenies auctura Italos."

846. honos: Cf. n. on 758, above.

847. noxia culpa: Cf. Ov., Ars 1.395: "/noxia culpa/."

849-850. nec enim mala mors est, etc.: Cf. Aug., Civ. 1.8: "quid autem interest, quo mortis genere vita ista finiatur, quando ille cui finiatur, iterum mori non cogitur? mala mors putanda non est, quam bona vita praecesserit; neque enim facit malam mortem, nisi quod sequitur mortem."

849. placuisse: Cf. n. on 130, dixisse, above.

850. quibus e vario: e, omitted by the Maurists, is here restored to the text. Without e the verse would be metrically impossible.

851. asper: For asper in a figurative sense, cf., e.g., Cic., Sest. 100: "viam . . . aut asperam atque arduam aut plenam . . . periculorum"; Sen., Dial. 4.13.1: 4.13.1: "nec . . . arduum in virtutes et asperum iter est: plano adeuntur." Cf. TLL 2.1.808.71-79.

852. nec campo capitur, etc.: Cf. n. on 604-605, ut superas, above.

858. culpamque decusque: Cf. Verg., Aen. 2.89: "nomenque decusque." decus = "virtue" appears in Cic. and Sall., but is mostly Silver and Late. Cf. Aug., Civ. 2.26 (decus opposed to dedecus); cf. TLL 5.1.236.66-237.26.

859. caelo ascripti terrena fovemus: Cf. Phil. 3.19-20: "et gloria in confusione eorum, qui terrena sapiunt. nostra autem conversatio in caelis est"; Heb. 12.22-26.

863. totum res fusa per orbem: Cf. Verg., Aen. 1.457: "totum vulgata per orbem"; Ov., Pont. 2.5.17:

"totum, mihi crede, per orbem"; Met. 5.481: "latum
vulgata per orbem"; 1.727; Am. 1.325: "per totum . . .
orbem"; Prud., Symm. 2.915: "totumque per orbem."

864. vestes pretiosae et pulchra suppellex: Cf. Liv.
21.15.2: "multam pretiosam supellectilem vestemque
missam Carthaginem."

867. una dies . . . potest auferre: Cf. Verg., Aen.
10.508: "haec te prima dies bello dedit, haec eadem
aufert"; Ov., Pont. 1.2.4: "non omnis Fabias abstulit
una dies"; Ibis 132: "/auferet illa dies/"; Paul. Nol.,
Carm. 14.82: "una dies."

868-869. quod speciale bonum est, etc.: Cf. Aug.,
Conf. 1.5.5: "ut unum bonum meum amplectar te."

871-872. durus labor urgeat et dolor aegri / corporis . . . et turpis egestas: Cf. Lucr. 3.999; 5.1272,
1359: "durum suffere laborem"; 4.1079-1080: "dolorem /
corporis"; 3.65: "turpis . . . contemptus et acris
egestas"; Verg., Georg. 1.145-146: "labor omnia vicit /
improbus et duris urgens in rebus egestas"; Aen. 6.276:
"turpis egestas"; Ov., Trist. 4.10.115: "durisque
laboribus"; Vulg., 2 Mach. 6.30: "duras corporis sustineo
dolores."

873. tolerantia: tolerantia appears in Cic., but
otherwise is Silver and Late, and rare in all periods.
Cf. Blaise and Georges, s.v., and Young, Studies 40.

palmas: palma = "eternal reward" is freq. in Christian authors. Cf., e.g., Aug., Nat. et or. 2.10.14:
"perduci ad palmam"; Prosp., De ingrat. 514: "propositam
citius ferret mens libera palmam"; 839: "/ut/ quaesitas
referant palmas." palma is often used in the same general
sense, but with special reference to the martyr's crown.
Cf. Blaise, s.v.

875. calicem crucis ac vitae: For the figure of
Christ's cup of suffering cf. Matt. 20.20-23; Mark 10.35-
40.

876. vipereum obducto potamus melle venenum: Cf.
Lucan 9.635: "vipereumque fluit depexo crine venenum";
Val. Fl. 1.63: "mella veneno"; Prud., Peri. 13.57:
"vipereis . . . venenis." The image of the cup of poison,
disguised in such a way that it appears attractive to the
drinker, is a commonplace in literature. Cf., e.g., Homer,

Odyssey 10.315, an incident retold at Ov., Met. 14.264.
The same image appears a number of times in Prosp. Cf.
De ingrat. 806: "nullo praelevit letalia pocula melle";
934: "viperei calicis gustum procul excutiamus"; C. coll.
7.1: "utque hoc compositionis suae poculum securis audi-
toribus propinaret, exemplis voluit colorare quod miscuit;"
9.3.

877-884. dulcia sunt etenim, etc.: Cf. the passage
of similar tenor at Prosp., De ingrat. 675-677:
. . . tantum nocet error
ut iuvet errare; et veteris contagia morbi
tam blande obrepunt, ut quo languetur ametur.
For sin as bringing about the death of the soul, cf. Jas.
1.15: "peccatum vero cum consummatum fuerit, generat
mortem."

879. canceris: The gen. sg. of cancer appears in
this form at Lucr. 5.617; Arnob., Nat. 1.50. Cf. Neue-
Wagener, Formenlehre 1.261 and Forcellini, s.v.

880-886. cumque Deus medicam caelo demittere curam,
etc.: Cf. Verg., Georg. 3.455-456: "dum medicas ad-
hibere manus ad vulnera pastor / abnegat"; Ov., Met. 1.261:
"medicorum cura"; Verg., Georg. 1.23: "caelo demittitis
imbrem"; Ov., Pont. 1.6.35: "demittere caelo:; Liv. 5.54.
7: "ancilia caelo demissa." The related figure of the
man who rejects medical assistance out of love for his
illness occurs at Prosp., De ingrat. 595-596: "quid
mirum rabido si corde freneticus aeger / morbum amat et
pellit medicum?"; Resp. ad Gall. 6: "amat ergo languores
suos, et pro sanitate habet quod aegrotare se nescit";
Epigr. 42.9-10: "inque putres fibras descendat cura
medentis / ut blandum morbum pellat amica salus."

885. dextra: On the distinction between dexter and
sinister cf. Aug., Locut. Hept. 90: "dextra nominatur
in omnibus bonis; sinistra in malis"; Prosp., In psalm.
136.5: "dextera nostra est vita aeterna . . . quidquid
fit propter vitam aeternam, dextra operatur."

887-888. iam quos peccantes, etc.: The teaching that
God's punishment of sinners is a sign of his love for them
is scriptural. Cf. Prov. 3.12: "quem enim diligit Dominus
corripit, et quasi pater in filio complacet sibi"; Heb.
12.6: "quem enim diligit Dominus, castigat: flagellat
autem omnem filium, quem recipit"; Apoc. 3.19: "ego quos
amo, arguo, et castigo".

888. emendare: emendare = "chastise, punish" is Silver and Late, appearing from Tac. on. Cf., e.g., Itala, Ps. 140(141).5: "emendabit me iustus in misericordia et arguet me"; Prov. 13.24 (Cypr., Testim. 3.105): "ne destiteris parvulum emendare"; Cypr., Hab. virg. 1.17: "si . . . Deus quem diligit corripit et corripit ut emendet." Cf. TLL 5.2.465.51-466.20, and, for emendare in this sense with the instrumental ablative, ibid. 466. 7-16.

flagello: flagellum = "punishment" in a figurative sense, as here, is Late and mostly Christian. Cf., e.g., Aug., Epist. 43.21: "flagellis temporalibus emendari"; Civ. 1.8: "flagellum Dei ad paenitentiam erudit bonos"; Prosp., Sent. 275 (274): "flagellis piae castigationis"; In psalm. 118.43: "sub persecutionis flagello." Cf. TLL 6.1.836.67-837.10.

892-894. hi sunt vero illi, etc.: Cf. Eccles. 7.15: "impius multo vivit tempore in malitia sua."

893. scelerum dites fructu: Cf. n. on 277, above.

894. extremas . . . produxit in oras: Cf. Enn., Ann. 114 (Warmington 121): "tu produxisti nos intra luminis oras." Reference to the luminis orae is freq. in Lucr.; cf. 1.22, 170, 179; 2.577, 617; 5.224, 781, 1455. Valentin, Saint Prosper 845, suggested that extremas be substituted for extremae, which appears in all editions. In support of V.'s reading, here received into the text, may be cited Lucr. 1.969-970: "ad oras / . . . extremas"; 980-981: "oras ubicumque locaris extremas."

895. per istos: The use of iste - hic is treated in L.-Hof. 476-477. For a concise treatment of iste = hic, ille, is, cf. Blaise, s.v.

896. bella excita: Cf. Verg., Aen. 1.541: "bella cient."

flagra: flagrum in a figurative sense is rare. Cf., e.g., Prosp., Epigr. 46.7: "erranti ne parcant flagra timendum est." Cf. TLL 6.1.849.7-10 (cited only for Cypr., Aug., Prosp.), and n. on 55, above.

897. namque eadem cunctos exercent tela fideles: Cf. Verg., Georg. 4.453: "non te nullius exercent

numinis irae."

900. coronam: Cf. n. on 604-605, ut superas, above.

901-902. quidquid mundanis rebus acerbum / accidit:
Cf. Verg., Aen. 12.678: "quidquid acerbi est"; Prud.,
Epil. 33: "quidquid illud accidit"; Lucr. 3.53: "in
rebus acerbis."

903-904. talentis / argenti atque auri amissis: Cf.
Verg., Aen. 10.531: "argenti atque auri . . . talenta";
5.112: "argenti aurique talentum"; Prud., Peri. 14.102:
"argenti et auri."

906. domus ustae: At this point the verse is metrically deficient since the nom. pl. of domus must show the
-u as a long vowel. Cf. TLL 5.1.1951.52-55.

potaque: Both potus and potatus are very freq. as
perf. pass. part. of potare. Cf. Georges,s.v., and the
many occurrences of potus cited in Neue-Wagener, Formenlehre 3.534.

909. caeloque prius translata locavit: Cf. Verg.,
Aen. 12.145: "caelique libens in parte locarim"; Prud.,
Symm. 1.271: "caelesti in sede locatum"; 2.868: "caeli
super astra locare."

911. manifestus honoris promissi: manifestus =
certus is late and rare, being cited at TLL 8.310.68-70
only for this verse and Ennod. (ob. 521), Epist. 2.19.2;
add De prov. 190.

912. cupidus victo certamine solvi: Cf. Phil. 1.23:
"desiderium habens dissolvi, et esse cum Christo."

cupidus: cupidus with the inf. is mostly Poetic, and
infreq. in all periods. Cf., e.g., Prosp., De ingrat.
144-145: "amicis / mentibus et tecum cupidis componere
foedus." Cf. TLL 4.1426.72-1427.2. For both the use of
cupidus and the similarity of thought, cf. Tert., Uxor.
1.5: "cupidi et ipsi . . . saeculo eximi et recipi ad
dominum."

victo certamine: For the use of the verb with a
subst. which expresses an attribute of the subst. concept
already contained in the verb, cf., e.g., Verg., Aen.
10.370: "devictaque bella"; Ov., Her. 15.76: "causam
vincere"; and esp. Vulg., Wisd. 10.12: "et certamen forte
dedit illi ut vinceret." Cf. K.-Steg. 1.277.

914. proscenia: proscenium, a Greek loan word, appears in Plaut., Verg., Liv., and in authors of the Silver and Late periods with the meanings "scene, proscenium, theatre." But proscenium = "terrace," as here, is cited in Benoist and in Blaise only for this verse; Georges cites also for CIL 6.406; 13.3450. Forcellini, Lewis-Short, and Souter do not cite the word in this sense.

916. penetralia cordis: Cf. Prud., Ham. 542: "cordis penetralia."

917. decorem: The poets generally use decor in the oblique cases in the terminal position in the hexameter line. Cf. TLL 5.1.206.23-25, and De prov. 930, decoris.

918-920. grassantesque hostes, etc.: Cf. n. on 229-234., above.

918. captivae mentis: Cf. Ov., Am. 1.2.30: "captiva vincula mente."

921. haec: haec seems more natural than hoc, the reading of the Maurists. If hoc were retained, the phrase quae facta manu speciosa fuerunt would have to be taken as substantival, and hoc would suffer a considerable separation from meritum with no apparent reason and contrary to the usual practice of the author of De prov. Valentin, Saint Prosper 845, agrees with the pre-Maurist editors in supporting haec.

926. congesta iacent: Cf. Prud., Symm. 2.718: "congesta iacent."

cordis in aula: Christian authors freq. use aula in one or another transferred sense, a practice rare in classical Latin. For aula = "depth," as here, cf., e.g., Prosp., De ingrat. 375: "cordis in aula." Cf. TLL 2.2. 1459.11-27. The words aula and cor are closely joined at Ambr., In psalm. 118.21.10: "qui habet in aula sua, corde videlicet suo." For aula - "church, heavenly kingdom," cf., e.g., Prosp., Epigr. 95.14: "regnum peccati respuat aula Dei." Cf. TLL 2.2.1458. 71-1459.8.

928. vasa Dei: The figure of man as a vessel is scriptural. Cf., e.g., Acts 9.15: "vas electionis" (Paul); Rom. 9.22-23: "vasa irae . . . vasa misericordiae;" 2 Tim. 2.21: "vas in honorem sanctificatum." The figure recurs in Christian authors, and is freq. in Aug., e.g.,

Nat. et grat. 5. Cf. also Prosp., De ingrat. 69: "vasa
irae" (Pelagians); 338: "vasque novum ex fracto fingens"
(activity of grace).

arae: For ara = "Christian altar" cf., e.g., Tert.,
Orat. 19; Iuvenc. 1.10. ara = "Christian altar" is rare
in the first centuries of Christianity, more freq. thereafter. In Cypr., ara always = "pagan altar" /cf. Souter,
s.v./. Cf. aras = "pagan altars" at De prov. 765. For
the figurative use of ara, as here, cf., e.g., Aug., Civ.
10.3: "sacrificemus hostiam humilitatis et laudis in
ara cordis." Cf. TLL 2.1.388.11-22.

et sacraria Christi: Cf. Verg., Aen. 12.199: "et
duri sacraria Ditis"; Prud., Symm. 1.379: "sacraria
Ditis."

930. diadema decoris: Cf. Wisd. 5.16: "ideo acci-
pient regnum decoris, et diadema speciei de manu Domini";
Isa. 62.3: "et eris . . . diadema regni in manu Dei tui"
(Jerusalem, the Lord's Bride).

decoris: Cf. n. on 917, decorem, above.

931. questibus: K.-Steg. 1.398-399 gives questibus
as the only form. Neue-Wagener, Formenlehre 1.557 reports questibus for Verg., Georg. 4.515; Sen., Thy. 179;
Herc. O. 1974; Val. Fl. 6.726; 7.195, but reports no instances of questubus. Therefore it would appear that
questibus is to be read here, and also at De ingrat. 148,
where Migne's reading questubus should be corrected.

932-933. iudicium culpando Dei, quod, etc.: Cf. Ps.
35(36).7: "iudicia tua abyssus multa"; Sir. 24.27: "a
mari enim abundavit cogitatio eius, et consilium illius
ab abysso magna."

933. abysso: abyssus, a Greek loan word, is derived
from biblical Latin. For abyssus = "depth, profundity of
thought" cf., e.g., Ps. 35(36).7, cited at 932-933, above;
Aug., Conf. 7.6.10: "ex abysso iusti iudicii tui." Cf.
TLL 1.1.244.52-72, and Mohrmann, "Les emprunts grecs dans
la latinité chrétienne," VC 4 (1950) 210.

934-940. quamvis exiguo hoc fugientis, etc.: The
theme of the prosperity of the wicked is freq. in Christian authors. Cf., e.g., Min. Fel. 37.7: "Deum
nescientes divitiis affluerent"; Lact., Inst. 5.21.8:
"carere iustos vident et affluere iniustos." Cf. also

De prov. 65-82, 853-870. The source is biblical; cf., e.g., Ps. 72(73).1-12.

937. illaesi: Cf. n. on 340, above.

938. nos, quibus in Christo sunt omnia: Cf. Col. 3.11: "sed omnia et in omnibus Christus."

939. occiduae: occiduus - "perishable" is Late. Cf. e.g., Prosp., De ingrat. 405-406: "vanamque decoris / occidui speciem"; Paul. Nol., Carm. 32.304. Cf. Georges, s.v.

inveximus orbi: For the dat. of limit of motion, a characteristic poetic construction in all periods, cf. K.-Steg. 2.1.320; L.-Hof. 419.

940. isto: Cf. n. on 895, above.

941. sed si quis superest animi vigor: Cf. Verg., Aen. 5.363: "nunc si cui virtus animusque in pectore praesens"; Ov., Trist. 1.6.31: "si quid et in nobis vivi fuit ante vigoris"; Her. 16.51: "vigorque animi"; Sil. 15.355: "animorumque vigoribus"; Prosp., De ingrat. 584: "animi vigor."

941-942. excutiamus / peccati servile iugum: Cf. Cic., Phil. 1.2.6: "iugum servile deiecerant."

942. ruptisque catenis: Cf. Verg., Aen. 8.225: "ruptisque immane catenis."

943. in libertatem et patriae redeamus honorem: Cf. Rom. 8.21: "in libertatem gloriae filiorum Dei"; 15.7: "Christus suscepit vos in honorem Dei."

944-946. cum saevo pacta tyranno / . . . foedus: Cf. Verg., Georg. 4.492-493: "immitis rupta tyranni / foedera"; Ov., Met. 6.581: "saevi . . . tyranni"; Prud., Symm. 2.876: "saevo vivens captiva tyranno."

944. tyranno: tyrannus = "Satan" is freq. in Christian authors. Cf., e.g., Prosp., De ingrat. 860: "spoliante tyranno"; Epigr. 65.7: "iura tyranni."

945. resolubile: resolubilis is Late, appearing from Ambr. on. Cf., e.g., Ambr., Serm. 13.20; Prud., Apoth. 515: "resolubile caementum"; Cath. 10.149: "resolubile corpus." Cf. Benoist and Blaise, s.v.

947-954. aversos revocans, etc.: Antelmy, De veris

operibus 406, objects to vv. 949-950, si . . . praeveniat,
on the grounds of unorthodoxy in doctrine. The passage as
a whole, and esp. vv. 949-950; 953, seems to place within the power of the unaided human will the initium fidei,
or first movement of the soul toward God. Valentin, Saint
Prosper 771, defends the orthodoxy of the author by maintaining that since this passage is hyperbolical in tenor
and exhortatory in content precision in dogma is not to
be expected, and further by citing vv. 960-968 as a cor-
rective supplied by the author himself.

For a succinct statement of the views of the Pelagians
and the semipelagians on grace, and the differences between them, cf. Sister M. Alphonsine Lesousky, O.S.U.,
The De Dono Perseverantiae 33-34: "Pelagius denied both
the necessity and the gratuity of grace. St. Augustine
defended both. The Semipelagians admitted the necessity
of grace for some works, but not for the initium fidei
nor for final perseverance, and they denied its absolute
gratuity . . . for they maintained that the beginning of
salvation--and this erroneous doctrine of initium fidei
was the pivot of Semipelagianism--depends on man himself;
man can by his own natural powers make a positive mediate
preparation for grace, petitioning for it, without grace,
by desiring through a pious disposition to believe, by
knocking, by asking. The consent, too, to this initial
grace is entirely man's."

The Augustinian principle is that God anticipates
man's actions with his grace. Cf., e.g., Aug., Nat. et
grat. 38: "misericordia eius praevenit nos." Cf. also
Prosp.'s description of the Pelagians at De ingrat. 799-
800: "praeveniunt cessantis opem, nec ad omne gerendum /
eius egent, sine quo sibi plurima posse videntur." For a
statement of the orthodox doctrine that Christ's grace is
the beginning of all virtue, cf. De ingrat. 979-981;
Vocat. gent. 1.23.

sic pulsata patent: De Labriolle-Bardy, Histoire
2.651, compares the argument of the semipelagian Vincent
of Lerins, Commonitorium /A.D. 426/ 26.8, that non-
Pelagian (orthodox) believers fail to "knock" at the door
/"nec pulsent"/ with this verse. Contrast Aug., Persev.
23.64 /cited by de Labriolle/: "attentant ergo quomodo
falluntur, qui putant esse a nobis, non dari nobis, ut
petamus, quaeramus, pulsemus."

947. aversos revocans et suscipiens conversos: Cf.
Paul. Nol., Epist. 32.23: "ut conversos ad se reficit
lumine, ita aversos afficit caecitate."

aversos: For aversus subst. = "a sinner, one who has
deserted the faith," cf., e.g., the citation immediately
above and Prosp., De ingrat. 32: "quae sint aversis
indebita, debita rectis." Cf. TLL 2.2.1324. 73-79.

conversos: convertere in Christian language means
"to return to penance and embrace the faith." For con-
versus subst. = "one who has returned to the faith" cf.,
e.g., the reference to Paul. Nol. above, and Aug., Nat.
bon. 9.2: "/poena/ cum conversis remittitur." Cf. TLL
4.868.62-869.19.

948. sanguine quos proprio quaesivit, etc.: For
Christ as purchaser of his people, cf. Acts 20.28:
"ecclesiam Dei, quam acquisivit sanguine suo," and n. on
506-507, nec tuus, above.

emptor: emptor, applied to Christ, is rare, appearing also in Aug. and Rufin. (ob. 470). Cf. TLL 5.2.537.27-
32. Contrast peremptor = "Satan" at De prov. 295, where
the reading is doubtful, and De ingrat. 898.

949. assertoris: assertor = "defender, champion"
appears in Quint., but is mostly Late. Cf., e.g., Cypr.,
Epist. 44.3: "se assertorem evangelii et Christi confiteri;" Aug., C. Cresc. 1.5.7: "assertores Christianae
pacis." Cf. TLL 2.1.871.16-84 and Blaise, s.v.

voluntas: Cf. n. on 240, voluntatis, above.

950. praeveniat: praevenire - "anticipate" appears
from Liv. on. Cf. Benoist and Blaise, s.v., and Young,
Studies 67.

fletu Dominum motura fideli: Cf. Verg., Aen. 4.438-
439: "sed nullis ille movetur / fletibus."

951. somnove quietus in alto: Cf. Hor., Sat. 2.1.8:
"somno quibus est opus alto."

952. fit salvus: salvum facere is the idiom used to
express the act of salvation. Cf. Acts 16.30: "ut
salvus fiam"; 1 Cor. 7.16: "salvum facies . . . salvam
facies"; 9.22: "ut omnes facerem salvos"; 1 Tim. 1.15:
"Christus venit . . . peccatores salvos facere." Cf.

Blaise, s.v.

953. pulsata patent redeuntibus atria vitae: Cf.
Matt. 7.7-8: Luke 11.9-10: "pulsate, et aperietur
vobis . . . et pulsanti aperietur."

atria vitae: atria in a figurative sense, as here,
is Late, but characteristic of Prosp. Cf. De ingrat. 687:
"atria vitae"; 813: "atria mortis"; Epigr. 19.1: "ad
atria vitae." Cf. TLL 2.2.1104.52-62.

954. caeli . . . cives: Cf. Paul. Nol.,Carm. app.
1.103-104: "spes igitur mea sola Deus, quem credere
vita est, / qui patriae civem me dedit alterius."

curia: curia - "assembly of the gods" appears in
Sen.; as "court of heaven" it is freq. in Christian authors. Cf. TLL 4.1487.37-65, and Weyman, Beiträge 250.

956-957. implorate Deum, pugnasque relinquite, etc.:
The exact reference is not clear. Valentin, Saint
Prosper 781, pointing out that Pelagians, Priscillianists,
and Arians had tried to base their teachings on Scripture,
sees in this passage a condemnation of the subtle interpretations current among the aforementioned groups.

958-964. nec quia procidimus, etc.: Cf. n. on 229-
234, above.

960-968. cuncta licet variis, terroribus, etc.:
This passage is cited by Valentin, Saint Prosper 771, as
one of several which serve to cast doubt on the alleged
semipelagian influence in De prov. The same passage is
cited by de Plinval, Pélage 241, as one which faithfully
preserves the ideas of Pelagius.

960-964. cuncta licet variis terroribus, etc.: Cf.
Prosp.,Epigr. 66. 17-20:
qui /Christus/ nostri generis carnem cum morte
                receptans,
nostra hosti, ut nobis vinceret, opposuit,
et carne exuta, dominantem perculit hostem:
ut caperet palmam praeda vetusta novam."

960. terroribus impleat hostis: Cf. Verg., Aen.
11.448: "magnisque urbem terroribus implet."

961. et vigili clausas obsidat milite portas: Cf.
Verg., Aen. 3.400: "obsedit milite campos"; 9.159:

"vigilum excubiis obsidere portas"; Ov., Am. 1.6.29-30:
"urbibus obsessis clausae munimina portae / prosunt";
Met. 3.449; Trist. 5.10.21: "clausis . . . portis";
3.14.42; Pont. 1.8.62: "clausaque porta"; Met. 3.560:
"claudere portas."

962-963. carne vetusta / exuti, etc.: The figure of
the "old man," who is to be put aside, is biblical. Cf.
Eph. 4.22: "deponere vos . . . veterem hominem"; Col. 3.9:
"expoliantes vos veterem hominem cum actibus suis, et
induentes novum eum."--Cf. Prosp., Epigr. 69.15-16: "in
Christo factus novus, et iam carne vetusta / exutus."

963. renovemur: Cf. n. on 499, above.

965. qui dum nostra suis sociat, iunxit sua nostris:
Cf. Prosp., De ingrat. 944: "ut nos insereret summis,
se miscuit imis."

966. non humanis fidens homo: Cf. Verg., Aen. 10.152:
"humanis quae sit fiducia rebus."

967. stant . . . stare: stare is regularly employed
by Christian authors from Cypr. on to mean "stand firm
(in the faith)," as opposed to ruere, cadere = "fall
away." Cf. Blaise and Souter, s.v.

968. sparsi: Cf. Matt. 12.30: "qui non congreget
mecum, spargit"; Luke 11.23: "qui non colligit mecum,
dispergit."

969. haec sat erit: Cf. Verg., Aen. 3.602: "hoc
sat erit"; Ov., Am. 3.2.84: "hic satis est"; Met. 11.211:
"haec satis est"; Trist. 3.3.77: "hoc satis in titulo
est"; 4.10.91: "hoc satis est"; Prud., Peri. 12.65: "sat
est"; Apoth. 893: "sat sit."

rudibus: Cf. n. on 88, rudibus, above.

970-972. qui cum sincerum, etc.: A similar figure
of the stream or torrent occurs at Prosp., De ingrat.
110-113 in reference to the books written by Aug. against
the Pelagians and semipelagians:
> istius ore viri fecit Deus, istius ore
> flumina librorum mundum effluxere per omnem,
> quae mites humilesque bibunt, campisque animorum
> certant vitalis doctrinae immittere rivos.

970. vivo de fonte: For analysis of the concept of
the living fountain, cf. Intro., pp. 45-46.

971-972. ab alvo / cordis: For alvus = "depth"
(perhaps by confusion with alveus?) cf., e.g., Prosp.,
De ingrat. 58?: "cordis in alvo"; contrast, e.g., Paul.
Nol., Epist. 21.2: "in alveum cordis." Cf. TLL 1.2.1804.
16-19 and Ernout-Meillet, under alveus and alvus.

INDICES

A. INDEX LOCORUM SACRAE SCRIPTURAE

Gen. 1.1-27: 25; 1.26-28: 25; 1.26-27: 42; 1.31: 38;
2.7-16: 25; 2.7: 42; 2.17: 25; 2.19-20: 25; 3.1-13:
25; 3.1: 40; 4.1-8: 25; 5.1: 42; 5.24: 26; 6.4: 26;
6.9-8.19: 26; 9.2-3: 25; 9.6: 42; 15.5-6: 26; 18.16-
19.29: 26; 22.15-18: 26; 37.5-36: 27; 37.28: 27; 39.
1.20: 27; 41.14-46: 27; 41.43: 27; 41.47-57: 26;
44.1-45.8: 27; 46.1-47.12: 27; 47.13: 332.

Exod. 1.8-22: 27; 1.11-14: 334; 3.21-22: 334; 6.10-13:
27; 6.28-30: 27; 7.1-7: 27; 8.4: 27; 8.24: 27; 9.27-
29: 27; 10.8-11: 27; 10.16-27: 27; 10.24-25: 27;
11.1-3: 334; 12.1-30: 32; 12.31-51: 28; 13.21-22:
28; 13.21: 28; 14.10-31: 28; 15.3: 320; 15.22-26:
29; 16.4-15: 28; 17.1-7: 29; 20.11: 315; 22.29: 328;
23.12: 29; 23.19: 328; 31.18: 29; 32.18-29: 29; 34.
10-28: 29; 39.1: 345; 40.34-38: 335.

Lev. 10.18: 345; 19.15: 36.

Num. 6.26: 46; 9.15-23: 335; 13.34: 329; 20.2-13: 29.

Deut. 1.17: 36; 4.19: 39; 6.13-14: 39; 8.4: 29; 17.3:
39,40; 21.23: 37; 29.4: 29; 32.35: 42.

Ios. 2.1-24: 32; 3.7-17: 32; 6.15-25: 32.

1 Reg. 2.1-10: 43; 15.10: 47.

2 Reg. 22.31: 338.

3 Reg. 10.1-10: 29; 17.1: 32; 18.1-40: 32.

4 Reg. 1.1-15: 32; 2.11: 26; 23.5: 39,40.

2 Par. 25.16 (Itala): 332.

2 Esdr. 9.21: 29.

Tob. 8.7: 315.

Iudith 8.27: 43.

Iob. 17.16: 341; 20.7: 369; 31.26-28: 39,40; 34.12: 320;
37.19: 34.

Psalm. 8.6-9: 25; 11(12).7: 338; 17(18).31: 338; 26(27).1:
34; 26(27).2: 365; 31(32).5: 34; 32(33).10: 328;
35(36).7: 44; 35(36).9-10: 45; 35(36).10: 37; 68(69).
35: 315; 72(73).1-12: 44; 74(75).8: 43; 77(78).15:
29; 77(78).24: 28; 84(85).3: 34; 95(96).11: 142 n.80;
106(107).11: 338; 112(113).6-7: 43; 117(118).22:
328; 133(134).2: 345; 134(135).6: 315; 145(146).6:
315; 145(146).7-9: 43.

Prov. 2.13: 38; 2.22: 369; 3.3: 46; 3.12: 43; 24.23: 36.

Eccles. 7.16: 44; 9.2-3: 43.

Sap. 2.23: 42; 5.16: 44; 9.5: 34; 10.6-7: 26; 10.12: 47;
11.4: 29; 12.24: 370; 14.6: 26; 15.7: 44; 16.20: 28;
19.6-8: 28.

B. INDEX LOCORUM CETERORUM AUCTORUM ANTIQUORUM

INDEX LOCORUM CETERORUM AUCTORUM ANTIQUORUM

Prosper, Carm. de ingrat. praef. xvii-xviii: 330; praef.
xviii: 358; praef. xxi: 314; 12: 336; 32:
380; 41: 125 n.40; 69: 377; 85: 355; 110-113:
382; 144-145: 375; 148: 377; 155-156: 327;
187: 20 n.9, 312; 276: 124 n.38; 282: 328;
352: 325; 394: 331,355; 405-406: 378; 422:
342; 438: 371; 450-451: 349; 464-465: 356;
477: 349, 479-400: 366; 501-502: 360; 514:
372; 522-525: 366; 539: 125 n.40; 550-552:
326; 562: 348; 567: 348; 568: 364; 582: 383;
675-677: 373; 681-682: 314; 709-711: 368;
721-743: 316; 727: 350; 740-741: 317; 755:
320; 791: 328; 792: 328; 799-800: 379; 839:
372; 850: 344; 855: 352; 860: 378; 872-875:
361; 880-888: 325; 885: 319; 889-890: 327; 891-
892: 340; 891: 144 n.83; 894-898: 344; 895:
331; 898: 327,380; 907-909: 323; 915-919: 325;
915: 144 n.83; 929 et al: 337; 944: 382; 952:
355; 979-981: 379; 992-994: 341.
C. coll. 9.3: 327; 13.4: 337; 15.1: 319.
Epigr. 19.6: 349; 24.1: 320; 46.7: 374; 65.7:
378; 66.17-20: 381; 69.14: 336; 76.6: 368; 91.
9-10: 315; 95.14: 376
Epist. ad Aug. 4: 357.
Epist. ad Ruf. 2: 363.
In psalm. 103.6: 369; 106.40: 328; 118.43: 374;
118.82: 338; 119.1: 336; 131.17: 347; 136.5:
373; 142.5: 339; 144.10: 339; 148.7-8: 329.
Resp. ad Gall. 1.8: 319.
Resp. ad Gen. 1-3: 319.
Sent. 275(274): 374.
Vocat. gent. 1.1: 320; 1.8: 347; 1.9: 339; 1.23:
379; 2.22: 331; 2.28: 352.
Prudentius, Apoth. 18: 96; 99: 96; 138: 96; 199: 94;
219: 98; 227: 95; 385: 92; 399: 97; 433:
94; 515: 378; 531: 91; 598: 97; 638: 94;
720: 95; 733: 98; 893: 99; 911-912: 90;
934: 97; 964: 96.
Cath. 1.26: 364; 3.109: 89; 3.134: 99;
3.136-137: 91; 4.86: 97; 5.93: 94; 7.31-32:
89; 9.12: 94; 10.10: 99; 10.42: 364; 10-82:
96; 10.149: 378; 10.157: 344; 11.23-24: 98;
11.111: 364; 12.202-204: 93.

12.678: 66; 12.770: 61; 12.811: 60; 12.819:
64.

Ecl. 3.8: 60; 3.61: 62; 4.4: 57; 4.7: 58; 4.31:
59; 4.49: 67; 4.60: 62; 6.38: 65; 6.74: 60;
7.66: 63; 7.69: 62; 8.35: 55; 8.98: 56;
8.105: 65.

Georg. 1.1: 68; 1.23: 62; 1.26-28: 58; 1.60-61:
56; 1.64: 62; 1.113: 56; 1.130: 65; 1.145-
146: 55; 1.290: 68; 1.338: 62; 1.394: 55;
1.404: 53; 1.406: 53; 1.505: 68; 2.1: 65;
2.40: 66; 2.104: 66; 2.121: 64; 2.341: 60;
2.336: 61; 2.412: 55; 2.467: 324; 2.477-478:
61; 3.48: 62; 3.68:55; 3.277: 65; 3.347: 54;
3.357: 59; 3.455-456: 59; 3.470: 53; 4.86:
67; 4.112: 63; 4.154: 57; 4.253: 55; 4.312:
65; 4.392-393: 57; 4.393: 90 n.18; 4.406: 67;
4.441: 64; 4.453: 57; 4.482: 66; 4.492-493:
65.

Appendix Vergiliana, Ciris, 100: 67; 160: 63; 240:
64,65; 243: 55; 247: 60;
329: 62; 398: 67; 480: 53;
541: 54.

Culex, 212: 58; 238: 68.

Moretum, 106: 64.

Claudius Marius Victor, Aleth. prec. 3: 104; prec. 9-11:
103; prec. 16: 104; prec. 76:
105; prec. 77: 105; prec. 80:
105; prec. 88: 104; prec. 107:
104; prec. 124: 104; 1.5-6:
104; 1.21: 105; 1.85: 104;
1.335: 104; 1.264: 105;
1.419: 105; 1.428: 104; 1.473:
103; 2.1: 104; 2.43: 105;
2.54: 104; 2.63: 103; 2.368-
369: 103; 2.463: 105; 2.524:
104; 3.402: 104; 3.497: 104,
105; 3.539: 104.

Vincentius Lirinensis, Commonit. 26.8: 379.
Zeno Veronensis: 1.13.8: 347.

C. INDEX NOMINUM RERUM ET LOCUTIONUM

Abel: 327, 329.   Adam: 326, 363
Abraham: 331.   Aeneas Silvius Piccolomini
abyssus: 377.   (Pius II): 3.

D. INDEX VERBORUM

Abbreviations

abl.	ablative	loc.	locative
acc.	accusative	m.	masculine
adj.	adjective	n.	neuter
adv.	adverb	nom.	nominative
conj.	conjunction	perf.	perfect
dat.	dative	pl.	plural
enclit.	enclitic	pres.	present
f.	feminine	pron.	pronoun
gen.	genitive	rel.	relative
grd.	gerund	sg.	singular
impv.	imperative	subjunct.	subjunctive
indef.	indefinite	subst.	substantive
inf.	infinitive	v.	verb
interrog.	interrogative	voc.	vocative

Substantival usages of adjectives and participles are regularly listed after the adjectival and participial usages, respectively.

The cases of all substantives, adjectives and participles are noted, except where they are evident from the inflectional terminations. Whenever cases are noted, gender is also noted even if evident, except for nouns. The present and perfect indicatives active of verbs are differentiated whenever the forms coincide.

All variant readings are listed and enclosed in round brackets.

A: 209, 269, 274, 285, 300, 317, 730, 772, 829.

ab: 40, 59, 83, 90, 95, 136, 151, 154, 189, 284, 291, 304, 312, 342, 414, 415, 443, 490, 527, 581, 659, 667, 710, 715, 728, 736, 758, 971.

abdo: abdita subst. n. acc. 191.

abduco: abductum n. nom. 906.

Abel: nom. 306.

abeo: abeunt 543; abiit 1; abiret 323; abi impv. 670, 670.

abicio: abiecto m. abl. 768.

Abram: nom. 347.

abrumpo: abruptis n. abl. 755.

abscedo: abscedere 776.

406

abscindo: abscindere 881.

absisto: absistere 724.

absolvo: absolvenda f.
nom. 300.

absque: 625.

abstineo: abstinuit 312.

absum: abest 736; aberat
329; absit 189; absint 5.

abyssus: abysso abl. 933.

ac: cf. atque

accedo: accedens f. nom.
189.

accido: accidit pres. 902;
accidere 814.

accipio: accipiunt 691;
accepit 243, 585;
acceperat 287; acci-
pitur 452.

acerbus: acerbum n. nom.
901; acerbi m. gen. 318,
378.

acetum: acc. 523.

actus: acc. 639, 788.

ad: 143, 380, 406, 406, 442,
470, 547, 562, 565, 640,
646, 654, 677, 682, 742,
747, 794.

Adam: nom. 275, 489.

adeo v.: adeunt 588, adeas
629. adv. 180, 423.

adicio: adicitis 163.

adimo: adimat 192.

adipiscor: adeptis subst.
n. abl. 257.

admitto: admisso n. abl.
25.

adoro: adoret 768; adora-
tum m. acc. 367; n. nom.
674.

adsum: adest 804, adsunt
653, 798; adsit 254.

adulter: nom. 426.

adultera: nom. 81.

adversus: adversa n. nom.
638; adversis f. dat.
121.

adytum: adytis abl. 532.

aedes: nom. 865; acc. 31.

aeger: aegri n. gen. 871;
aegram 166; aegris m.
dat. 170.

Aegyptus: Aegypti gen.
404, 828; Aegyptum acc.
356; Aegypto abl. 386.

aenigma: aenigmate 364.

aequo: aequet 232.

aequor: acc. 598; aequore
abl. 98, 147, 773; ae-
quora acc. 572.

aequoreus: aequoreis m.
abl. 36.

aequus: aequa f. nom. 408,
585, 654; aequi n. gen.
601; aequum m. acc.
743; aequum n. acc. 418,
aequi subst. n. gen.
635.

aer: aera 217.

aestimo: aestimet 274.

aestus: aestu 136; aestus
nom. pl. 818.

aetas: nom. 41, 173, 296,
469.

aeternus: aeterni m. gen.
320; aeternae f. gen.
203; aeternum m. acc.
161; aeternam 248; ae-
ternum subst. m. acc.
798.

aether: aethera 328; ae-
there 659.

aethereus: aethereis m.
dat. 644.

aevum: aevi gen. 178, 466,
744; aevum acc. 247, 430;
aevo abl. 325, 413.

affectus: affectum 568;
affectus acc. 608.

affero: attulit 899;
afferat 700; attulerint
236.

afficio: afficiunt 907;
afficere 640.

affigo: affigere 641.

afflatus: afflatu 274.

affluo: affluerent 754.

ager: nom. 937; agri gen.
422; agro dat. 139;
agros 27, 573, 913; agris
abl. 682.

agmen: agmina acc. 394,
623.

agnosco: agnoscas 479; agnoscite 421; agnoscere
108; agnita n. nom.

ago: agit 76, 424, 627;
agimus 20; agunt 569;
egit 516; agat 12, 237;
ageret 84; agerent 430;
age 727; agitur 802;
agantur 741; agi 665;
actum n. acc. 269; actos

412, 774; acta subst. n.
acc. 175; agenda subst.
n. acc. 175.

agon: agone 605.

aio: ais 558; aiunt 23.

ales: alite 833.

algeo: algere 137.

alienus: aliena f. abl.
841; aliena subst. n.
nom. 856.

aliquis: aliquem 848; aliquid n. acc. 130; aliqui
m. nom. 93; aliquas 32.

aliter: 583, 734.

alius: 790; alia f. nom.
582; aliam 51; aliud n.
acc. 493; alio n. abl.
325; alios 341; alia
subst. n. nom. 122;
aliis subst. n. dat. 122,
569.

almus: m. nom. 512; almi
n. gen. 53; almae f. nom.
928; almis n. abl. 580.

alo: alit 123, 147; alebat
216.

Alpes: nom. 573.

altaria: acc. 305, 684.

alter: m. nom. 546, 546.

alternus: alterna n. acc.
397.

alteruter: alterutram 476.

altus: alto m. abl. 951;
alta f. abl. 279; altis
m. dat. 35; altis subst.

408

arbitrium: acc. 240, 657;
arbitrio abl. 24, 681.

arbor: arbore 284; arbor-
ibus abl. 148.

arca: nom. 340.

arceo: arcet 180; arcerent
440.

arcus: acc. 611.

ardeo: arsuris n. abl. 827.

arduus: ardua subst. n.
acc. 193, 664.

argentum: nom. 929; ar-
genti 904.

arguo: arguit pres. 887.

arma: acc. 37, 57; armis
abl. 89, 661.

ars: artis 717; arte 700;
artes acc. 263, 769;
artibus abl. 247.

arx: arcem 248; arce 83,
291, 918.

ascribo: ascripti m. nom.
859.

asper: aspera f. nom. 851.

assertor: assertoris 949.

assisto: assistere 303.

asto: astare 551.

astrum: nom. 709; astrorum
621, 698, 732; astris
dat. 693; astra acc.
693; astris abl. 349,
628, 637, 667.

astruo: astrueret 739.

at: 95, 140, 150, 295, 317,
563, 617, 713, 746, 791,
798, 913.

atque: 37, 52, 119, 122,
152, 466, 757, 804, 904;
ac: 7, (95), 174, 178,
208, 255, 420, 647, 760,
764, 789, 870, 875, 910.

atrium: atria nom. 953,
acc. 914.

atrox: m. nom. 69, subst.
m. nom. 425.

attollo: attollat 193;
attolleret 472.

attono: attonitis m. dat.
536.

auctor: 219, 647; auctoris
149; auctori 405; aucto-
rem 106, 616; auctore
109, 118.

audeo: audetis 162; ausim
131; ausa f. voc. 526.

audio: audiat 191, 269.

aufero: abstulit 31; abs-
tulerat 773; auferret
758; auferre 867.

augeo: augere 263; aucta
f. nom. 293; auctos
subst. m. acc. 811:
auctura f. nom. 845.

augmentum: augmento abl.
545.

aula: abl. 926.

aura: nom. 819; auris dat.
633.

auris: aurem 929; auribus
dat. 647; aures acc. 87,
591; auribus abl. 444.

aurum: auri 904.

auster: austri gen. 443.

aut: 30, 36, 85, 86, 126,
126, 131, 134, 134, 164,
202, 235, 236, 350, 412,
422, 483, 560, 560, 572,
573, 582, 613, 633, 644,
645, 719, 751, 758, 758,
857.

autem: 15, 68, 153, 641,
839.

avarus: m. nom. 69.

averto: avertat 667; aversos subst. m. acc. 947.

avidus: m. nom. 834; avidae
f. gen. 521.

avus: avorum 65.

axis: axe 619.

B

Barabbas: Barabba abl. 525.

barbaricus: barbarici m.
gen. 37; barbaricis f.
abl. 394.

barbarus: nom. 456.

barbatus: barbatos 766.

beatus: beata f. nom. 652;
beatum m. acc. 163, 857;
beato subst. m. dat.
704.

bellum: nom. 962; belli
gen. 61; bellum acc. 660;
bella nom. 896; acc. 553,
729; bellis abl. 808.

belua: nom. 422.

bene: adv. melius 97.

benignus: benigno m. abl.
311.

blande: adv. 360.

blandus: blanda f. nom.
171, 860; blandis m.
abl. 595; subst. n. abl.
853.

blasphemus: subst. m. nom.
82.

bonitas: nom. 281; bonitatis 622.

bonus: adj. m. nom. 151,
493, 554, 624, 647; boni
n. gen. 651; bona n. nom.
555, 603; bonorum m. gen.
582; bonis f. abl. 247;
melioris f. gen. 779;
meliore m. abl. 472;
optimus 219, 584.

bonus: subst. bonum n. nom.
868; boni n. gen. 635;
bona n. nom. 298, 712;
bonis m. dat. 68, 850;
bonos m. acc. 52, 725;
bona n. acc. 854; bonis
n. abl. 164; meliora n.
acc. 333.

bos: bove 578; bobus abl.
565.

bravium: bravio abl. 663.

brevis: f. nom. 44, 874.

brutesco: brutescere 770.

brutus: brutis subst. m.
dat. 519.

bustum: busta acc. 925.

C

Cado: cadimus 16; cadunt
10; caderet 847; cadere
199.

caecus: caeca n. acc. 241.

caedes: caede 33, 317.

caedo: caedimur 16; caesi m. nom. 55.

caelestis: f. nom. 696; caelestes m. nom. 606; caelestia n. acc. 91, 389; subst. n. acc. 629, 771.

caelum: caeli 258, 410, 613, 674, 954; caelo dat. 680, 754, 909; caelum acc. 181, 549, 613; caelo abl. 115, 205, 859, 880; caelis abl. 492.

caeruleus: caeruleos 140.

Cain: nom. 309.

calco: calcantem m. acc. 534.

calidus: calida n. nom. 117.

calix: calicem 875.

callidus: m. nom. 665.

callis: calle 548.

calor: nom. 838; calores acc. 399.

campus: campo abl. 852.

cancer: canceris 879.

cano: canerent 441; canentis subst. m. gen. 703.

capio: capit 666; capiunt 124; capiant 938; caperet 324, 538; caperemus 604; capitur 852; capi 549; captum n. nom. 930; capti m. nom. 853; captos 722.

captivus: captiva f. nom. 927; captivae f. gen. 918; captiva f. abl.

945; n. nom. 504.

caput: acc. 273.

carcer: 837; carcere 363.

cardo: cardine 710.

careo: caret 428; carens m. nom. 109.

carmen: carmina nom. 5.

caro: nom. 465; carnis 324, 504; carnem 494; carne 478, 483, 535, 535, 962.

carpo: carpunt 879; carpebas 58; carpere 78.

carptim: 133.

carus: cara f. nom. 377.

castellum: castella nom. 35.

castra: castris dat. 397; castra acc. 623; castris abl. 609.

castus: castam 73; castum subst. m. acc. 363.

casus: casum 564; casu 715; casus acc. 924.

catena: catenis abl. 942.

causa: nom. 358, 491; abl. 134, 795, 898; causae nom. 3, 168, 235; causis dat. 121; causas 23, 210, 302, 353, 391, 630; causis abl. 111, 149, 371, 737.

caveo: cautus 475, 651.

cedo: cedit 390, 519; cedunt 406; cessit 561; cedat 509, 642; cedite 785; cedere 569, 625; cessisse 402.

celer: celerem f. acc. 796.

celsus: celsa f. abl. 83; celsi m. nom. 572.

censeo: censebat 349; censentes m. nom. 858; censenda n. nom. 589.

cerno: cernat 191; cernere 64; cernens m. nom. 477.

certamen: certamine 912, 958.

certe: 358.

certus: m. nom. 180; certum n. acc. 742; certis f. abl. 149.

cesso: cessat 728; cessant 78; cesserit 70; cesset 40.

ceterus: cetera n. nom. 224.

ceu: 60, 246.

Chaldaeus: Chaldaeis n. abl. 628.

Chananaeus: Chananaea n. acc. 356.

chelydrus: chelydris abl. 141.

Christus: nom. 302, 488, 499, 525; Christi 146, 343, 462, 513, 686, 761, 908, 928, 963; Christo dat. 770, 945; Christum 498; Christo abl. 202, 206, 211, 326, 457, 562, 695, 938.

cibus: nom. 833.

cinis: cineres acc. 925.

circumdo: circumdata f. nom. 102.

circumicio: circumiectis n. abl. 609.

citus: citum n. nom. 799; cita subst. n. nom. 187.

civilis: civilibus n. abl. 661.

civis: cives acc. 954.

clades: cladis 337, 445, 839; cladem 920; clade 345, 390.

clarus: clara f. nom. 622; claros 764; claro subst. n. dat. 128.

claudo: claudunt 110; clausos 682; clausas 961.

clavus: clavorum 539.

clemens: f. nom. 749.

cliens: clientes nom. 865.

coaequo: coaequans m. nom. 515.

coeo: coeunt 223, 968; coeuntibus f. abl. 404.

coepi: coeperit 416.

cognosco: cognovit 268; cognoscere 367, 537; cognoscenda n. nom. 98.

cohibeo: cohibetur 179; cohibentes m. nom. 600.

collis: collibus dat. 572.

colo: colens m. nom. 767; colentes m. nom. 616; cultarum f. gen. 277.

columna: abl. 395.

commentum: commenta nom. 671.

committo: commisere 43.

commodus: commoda subst. n. acc. 397.

communis: communia n. nom. 816.

compatior: compatiuntur 821.

comperio: compertus m. nom. 550; compertum n. nom. 723.

complector: complexa f. nom. 497, 662, 848.

comprehendo: comprendere 261.

comprimo: comprimit 4.

compugno: compugnant 121.

concedo: concedunt 195.

concido: conciderant 740; conciderit 620.

concilio: conciliant 596.

concipio: concepit 282; concepta f. nom. 315.

concludo: conclusis n. abl. 338.

concutio: concutiat 13; concussa f. nom. 528.

condensus: (condensas 380).

conditio: nom. 230; conditionis 454; conditioni 161, 464; conditiones acc. 680.

conditor: nom. 212, 466.

condo: condidit 113, 153, 515; conderet 221; condere 690; condens m. nom. 177; condita f. nom. 433; subst. n. nom. 121; condendas 380.

confero: conferre 162; collatus m. nom. 846; collata f. nom. 500; n. acc. 150.

conficio: conficiant 158; confice 92.

confido: confidere 257.

confiteor: confessi m. gen. 462.

conflictus: conflictum 959.

confoveo: confotos 776.

confundo: confundant 709; confundere 372; confusis n.abl. 62.

congero: congessit 863; congesta n. nom. 926.

congrego: congreget 889.

coniungo: coniunge 505.

conscribo: conscripta n. nom. 945.

consero: conseverit 633.

consisto: consistere 447.

consocio: consociata f. nom. 482.

consors: consortem f. acc. 228.

conspicuus: m. nom. 541.

consto: constans f. nom. 873.

constringo: constrinxerat 637.

consuesco: (consueverit 633).

consumo: consumeret 382; consumier 89.

contemno: contempto n.
abl. 144.

contendo: contendit pres.
129, 699; contendere
668.

contingo: contigit 12.

contra: 641.

contrarius: contraria
subst. n. nom. 223;
subst. n. acc. 122.

convenio: convenisse 474.

converto: convertit pres.
307; conversos 823;
subst. m. acc. 947.

convicium: convicia acc.
521.

coquo: coquebat 310.

cor: cordis 420, 513, 916,
926, 972; cordi 647;
corde 70, 282, 499, 955;
corda nom. 6; acc. 22,
194; cordibus abl. 90,
660.

coram: 653.

corona: nom. 319, 852;
coronae gen. 255; coro-
nam 900; coronas 605.

corporeus: corporea f. abl.
265; corporeo n. abl. 503;
corporeis m. abl. 160.

corpus: corporis 479, 872;
corpus acc. 343, 697,
963; corpore 103, 116;
corpora nom. 530.

corrumpo: corrupti m. gen.
271.

cras: 804.

creator: nom. 465.

credo: 156; credis 24,
625; credimus 870; cre-
ditis 164; credunt 569;
credidit 446; credas
479.

credulus: m. nom. 347.

cremo: cremat 810.

creo: creat 171; creavit
496, 502; crearit 634;
creantis subst. m. gen.
585; creatum n. acc.
130; creati m. nom.
432; creatos 142, 236.

cresco: crescunt 899;
crescant 508, 937;
crescere 253; crevisse
678.

crimen: criminis 841;
crimine 73, 289, 846,
937; crimina nom. 85,
336; acc. 44, 435, 892.

cruciabilis: f. nom. 225.

crudelis: crudele n. acc.
315.

cruentus: (cruenti m. nom.
533); cruentos 533;
cruentum subst. m. acc.
425.

crux: crucis 525, 829,
875, 930; cruce 549.

culpa: culpae gen. 276;
culpam 858; culpa abl.
152, 290, 841, 847,
900; culpas 330, 748.

culpo: culpando abl. grd.
932.

cultus: nom. 675; cultum
667; cultu 245; cultus
acc. 672.

cum prep.: 207, 215, 227, 250, 293, 421, 432, 463, 547, 593, 813, 939, 944, 962.

cum conj.: 17, 59, 87, 112, 132, 165, 168, 220, 247, 278, 321, 327, 329, 335, 347, 350, 356, 368, 400, 434, 439, 441, 469, 478, 538, 540, 556, 567, 612, 619, 635, 646, 662, 665, 678, 682, 741, 757, 824, 842, 880, 884, 923, 970.

cumulus: cumulis abl. 253.

cunctus adj.: cuncti m. nom. 490; cuncta n. nom. 258, 297; cunctorum m. gen. 726; cunctos 65, 290, 410, 897; cunctas 407, 919; cuncta n. acc. 807; cunctis n. abl. 264.

cunctus pron.: cuncta n. nom. 124, 135; cunctorum m. gen. 427; cunctis m. dat. 108, 206, 303, 551, 819; cunctos 640; cuncta n. acc. 370, 960; cunctis n. abl. 602.

cupidus: m. nom. 912; cupidis f. abl. 443.

cupio: cupis 560; cupit 136; cupimus 796.

cur: 10, 46, 554, 554, 555, 555.

cura: nom. 64, 83, 329, 434, 551, 565; curam 197, 303, 384, 415, 451, 724, 880; cura abl. 741; curae nom. 157; curis abl. 5, 167, 186, 629.

curia: nom. 954.

curo: curare 718; curanda n. acc. 855.

curro: curramus 548; curreret 469; currentem m. acc. 648.

currus: curru 328.

cursus: cursu 126, 698, 890; cursibus abl. 214.

custodia: nom. 436.

D

Damno: damnat 363, 426; damnaret 435; damnatur 522; damnatus m. nom. 275; damnante m. abl. 527.

damnum: damnis dat. 253, 915.

de: 172, 190, 242, 321, 338, 353, 503, 535, 549, 565, 660, 666, 763, 782, 957, 964, 970.

debeo: debuit 107; debita n. nom. 712.

decennis: decenni f. abl. 33.

decerno: decerneret 250.

decerpo: decerpere 285.

decerto: decertato m. abl. 605.

decet: deceat 9.

decipio: decepta f. nom. 830.

declino: declinat 564; declinare 714.

decor: nom. 145; decoris 930; decorem 917.

decorus: decora n. nom.
877.

decretum: subst.: decreta
acc. 706.

decurro: decurrit pres.
491; decurrunt 574;
decurrere 371.

decursus: nom. 627.

decus: acc. 205, 220, 858.

dedecus: dedecorum 773.

dedignor: dedignantem m.
acc. 369.

dedo: dedita f. nom. 919.

deduco: deduceret 722;
(deducti m. nom. 333);
deducturus 207.

deficio: deficit 838.

defleo: defles 913.

deformis: deformi f. abl.
923.

degener: degeneri m. abl.
204.

deicio: deiectus 280, 619;
deiectos 811; deiecta
subst. n. acc. 193.

delabor: delapsa f. nom.
686.

deleo: deleri 336; deleta
n. acc. 842.

deliciae: deliciarum 283.

delictum: delicta acc. 270,
639, 777.

demitto: demittere 880.

demo: demant 196.

deni: denos 412; denis abl.
540.

denique: 134, 181, 901.

densus: densa subst. n.
nom. 127.

depello: depulsa f. nom.
170.

descendo: descenderet 350;
(descenderit 350);
descendere 748.

describo: describat 513;
descripta f. abl. 429.

desero: deserta n. acc.
913; desertis n. abl.
49; deserta subst. n.
acc. 396, 412.

despicio: despice 650.

destringo: destringit 426.

destruo: destrueret 302.

desum: desunt 29, 869;
defuit 105.

desuper: 643.

detego: detectis m. abl.
721.

deterior: m. nom. 579;
deteriora subst. n. acc.
557.

detineo: detinet 481.

Deus: nom. 119, 151, 278,
318, 322, 341, 376, 417,
455, 463, 546, 656, 691,
805, 880, 887; Dei 24,
45, 64, 83, 183, 249, 329,
352, 441, 473, 482, 501,
550, 622, 835, 903, 928,
932; Deo dat. 156, 265,
377, 565, 799, 849; Deum
50, 105, 162, 370, 470,
478, 631, 649, 718, 744,
956; Deo abl. 11, 42, 118,
344, 383, 391, 463, 529.

deus: deorum 720; deos 615,
766.

devexus: devexo m. abl.
742.

devius: m. nom. 476.

devotus: devoti m. gen.
922; devotae f. gen. 47;
devota f. abl. 308.

dextra: f. nom. 885.

diadema: nom. 930.

dicio: dicione 84, 287.

dico: dicans m. nom. 309;
dicatus 675.

dico: dic 23, 727; dicite
453; dixisse 130; dici
860.

dies: nom. 66, 732, 804,
867; diem 678; die 50,
528; dies acc. 261;
diebus abl. 446, 540.

differo: differtur 787;
dilata f. abl. 351, 376;
n. acc. 800.

difficilis: f. nom. 510;
difficili f. abl. 663.

diffundo: diffusa f. nom.
103, 550.

dignor: dignatur 222, 365,
881; dignetur 64.

dignosco: (dignoscendis
subst. n. abl. 190).

dignus: digna n. nom. 786;
dignos subst. m. acc.
817.

diligo: diligit 888.

diluvium: nom. 826; dilu-
vio abl. 336.

dimetior: dimensis m. abl.
214.

diripio: diripiant 708.

diruo: diruta n. acc. 914.

dirus: dira f. nom. 78,
357; diris n. dat. 885;
dira n. acc. 331.

dis, ditis: Cf. dives.

discedo: discedere 386;
discessuri m. nom. 940.

discerno: discrevit 54;
discernere 238, 556;
discernenda n. nom. 597.

discindo: discissum n.
nom. 531.

discipulus: discipulis
dat. 536, 687.

disco: discit 257; discat
272; discant 101.

discors: m. nom. 122.

discrepo: discrepet 459.

discrimen: discrimine 39;
discrimina acc. 237,
239.

discutio: discutiens f.
nom. 399.

dispar: f. nom. 230.

dispenso: dispensat 692.

displiceo: displicet 143;
displicuere 581.

dispono: dispositos 576;
dispositis f. abl. 212.

dissimilis: f. nom. 229;
dissimilem m. acc. 354;
dissimili n. abl. 74.

distantia: nom. 458.

disto: distaret 750; dis-
tare 269.

distringo: (distringit 426).

dito: ditat 811; ditarunt
862.

diversus: diversa n. nom.
543; diversos 297.

dives: m. nom. 518; divitis
m. gen. 276; divite
m. abl. 118; dites: m.
acc. 893; ditia n. acc.
394; ditior m. nom. 508;
dives subst. m. nom. 583.

divido: dividere 186; di-
visum n. nom. 730; n.
acc. 401; divisa n. nom.
451, 905.

divinus: divini m. gen.
159; divinum m. acc. 228;
divinam 724; divinum n.
acc. 246; divina f. abl.
218; divinorum n. gen.
477; divinis m. abl. 97.

divus: divis subst. m.
dat. 668.

do: dat 227, 852, 900;
dant 156; dedit 219, 313,
333, 355, 536, 808; de-
derat 44, 685; det 192;
dent 707; dederis 509;
dederit 632; dedisset
920; detur 786; dare 99,
866, 915; data f. nom.
506; datum n. nom. 147,
261; datas 192; danda
f. nom. 705; dandis
subst. n. abl. 257.

doceo: docet 384, 672, 719;
doceri 190; docens f.
nom. 106; doctus 771.

documentum: documenta acc.
256, 325, 538, 808.

dogma: dogmata acc. 593,
770.

dolor: nom. 4, 89, 871.

dolus: doli gen. 671;
dolos 37; dolis abl.
289, 366.

domina: dominae gen. 363.

Dominus: nom. 311, 688,
781; Domini 274, 307,
346, 386, 415, 438, 444,
451, 566, 697, 727, 762,
803; Domino dat. 225,
296, 580, 602; Dominum
537, 616, 950; Domino
abl. 172.

dominus: nom. 516; domini
gen. 458; dominum 355;
dominos 669.

domus: nom. sg. 337, 359,
831; domum 227; domus
nom. pl. 906.

donec: 393.

dono: donante m. abl. 211.

donum: dona nom. 753; acc.
278, 309.

dubito: dubites 849.

dubius: dubium n. nom.
839; dubiis n. abl.
537.

duco: ducimus 884; ducat
643; ducant 823; duceret
60; ducere 49, 74; du-
cente m. abl. 562.

dulcis: dulcia n. nom.
877; dulcius n. acc.
524; dulci subst. n.
abl. 562.

ire 414, 440, 511, 547, 663, 728, 891.

ergo: 432, 597, 644, 689.

erro: 558; errare 558.

error: nom. 106, 476, 561, 643, 670, 670, 722; erroris 628; errori 791; errore 292, 767; errorum 93; errores acc. 592; erroribus abl. 774.

esca: escas 596.

et: 5, 6, 14, 16, 18, 19, 22, 31, 34, 41, 57, 63, 66, 73, 79, 92, 103, 106, 109, 110, 114, 114, 114, 120, 120, 128, 128, 129, 133, 135, 144, 151, 151, 154, 158, 160, 161, 170, 174, 174, 175, 177, 178, 181, 181, 181, 182, 184, 184, 186, 194, 194, 196, 198, 200, 207, 207, 211, 213, 217, 226, 228, 233, 234, 234, 238, 243, 254, 257, 258, 259, 259, 260, 261, 262, 263, 268, 270, 273, 276, 279, 286, 302, 314, 319, 359, 377, 379, 381, 390, 394, 398, 398, 399, 400, 408, 410, 411, 414, 419, 421, 426, 427, 433, 438, 439, 446, 452, 465, 481, 487, 491, 495, 496, 508, 516, 523, 525, 528, 535, 539, 541, 546, 551, 552, 555, 558, 569, 575, 584, 592, 601, 609, 611, 616, 623, 630, 640, 643, 647, 647, 650, 653, 655, 656, 661, 675, 680, 705, 714, 726, 733, 741, 749, 759, 761, 762, 765, 769, 770, 784, 818, 819,

823, 826, 833, 840, 843, 848, 859, 862, 864, 866, 870, 871, 872, 872, 879, 882, 884, 888, 893, 896, 899, 912, 914, 928, 929, 930, 930, 932, 935, 937, 937, 943, 949, 954, 957, 959, 961, 963, 968, 972.

etenim: 63, 233, 429, 467, 480, 600, 795, 877.

etiam: (5), 346, 442, 531, 570, 591, 686, 887, 921.

evado: evadere 93, 827.

evalesco: evaluere 38.

eveho: evexit 861.

evolvo: evolvat 409; evolvere 210.

ex: prep. cf. e.

exacuo: exacuenda f. nom. 886.

exagito: exagitata n. nom. 124.

examen: acc. 805; examine 351.

exanimus: exanimum m. acc. 560.

excelsus: excelso m. abl. 619.

excidium: excidio abl. 447.

excio: excitam 388; excita n. nom. 530, 896.

excipio: excipere 775.

excludo: exclusum m. acc. 284.

excoquo: excoctis m. abl. 141.

excutio: excutias 902; excutiamus 941.

exemplum: nom. 323; acc. 414; exemplo abl. 515; exemplis abl. 304.

exeo: exit 178.

exerceo: exercent 897; exercita f. nom. 245.

exhaurio: exhaurit 810.

exhinc: 542.

exigo: exigere 639; exactura f. nom. 687.

exiguus: exiguum n. acc. 271; exiguo n. abl. 375, 934; exigua n. acc. 198.

eximius: m. nom. 145.

eximo: exemit 355; exempta f. nom. 844; exemptum m. acc. 365.

exitium: acc. 332; exitio abl. 846.

exitus: nom. sg. 230, 851.

exordium: exordia nom. 201, 504.

experientia: nom. 286.

experior: experiuntur 814.

expers: f. nom. 224; n. nom. 117; expertes m. acc. 841.

explico: explicet 158.

expolio: expoliente f. abl. 461.

exporto: exportabimus 940.

exstinguo: exstinctae f. gen. 534; exstinctam 39.

exsto: exstant 118; exstantibus f. abl. 111.

exsul: nom. 60, 76.

exsulto: exsultat 77.

extendo: extende 654; extendere 267.

externus: externa f. nom. 236, 657; externas 650; externis subst. n. dat. 858; externos subst. m. acc. 359, 440.

extremus: (extremae f. gen. 894); extremo m. abl. 102; extremas 894.

exuo: exuti m. nom. 963.

exuro: exustae f. gen. 914.

F

Facilis: n. gen. 87.

facinus: acc. 315.

facio: faciunt 567; fecit 494, 603; fecere 767; fecerat 213; faciat 387; faceret 679; facere 568; facta f. nom. 528; factum m. acc. 617; facta n. nom. 921.

factor: factore 155.

factum: subst. facta acc. 616; factis abl. 515.

facultas: nom. 11, 408, 654, 796.

fallax: subst. m. nom. 424.

fallo: fallit 308; fallunt 362; fallat 936; fallant 708.

falsus: falsum n. nom. 703;

falsa subst. n. nom. 79.

fames: nom. 357.

famulor: famulantur 406; famulata f. nom. 678.

famulus: famuli nom. 865; famulos 903.

fas: nom. 130, 507; acc. 708.

fascis: fasce 58, 138; fasces nom. 72.

fatum: fati 715; fata acc. 668.

favus: favis abl. 524.

fax: facibus dat. 920.

fel: acc. 523; felle 310.

felix: m. nom. 11, 701; felices m. nom. 860.

femina: nom. 455.

ferculum: fercula acc. 834.

feritas: feritate 750.

fero: fert 8, 169, 607; tulerant 403; ferat 512; ferret 368; tulerint 42; feratur 599; ferre 164, 226, 706, 820; ferri 891.

ferus: fera n. acc. 393; ferum subst. m. acc. 311; ferarum subst. f. gen. 145, 200.

festino: festinata n. acc. 800.

festinus: festina f. nom. 949.

fetus: fetu 379.

fibra: fibras 881; fibris abl. 433.

fidelis: fideli m. abl. 950; fideles subst. m. acc. 897.

fides: nom. 70, 538; fidei gen. 437, 610; fide 348, 461, 498.

fido: fidens m. nom. 966.

fiducia: nom. 254.

figo: figis 553; fixis n. dat. 705.

filius: nom. 501.

finis: nom. 825; gen. 318; finem 174, 469, 679, 742, 793; fine 179, 545, 852.

firmo: firmans m. nom. 540; firmato m. abl. 710; n. abl. 955.

firmus: firma n. acc. 475.

fio: fit 465, 525, 566, 789, 832, 832, 952; fieri 579.

flagellum: flagello abl. 888.

flagrum: flagra nom. 896; flagris abl. 55.

flamma: abl. 684; flammas 14; flammis abl. 399.

fletus: fletu 950; fletibus abl. 19.

flos: flores nom. 735.

flumen: flumina acc. 971.

fluo: fluit 726.

foedus: nom. 946; foedere 730; foedera acc. 416.

fomentum: fomenta acc. 920.

fons: nom. 635; fontis 411; fonte 761, 970.

forma: formam 313, 396;
formae nom. 589; formas
113, 407.

formido: nom. 704.

formo: formare 222; formata
f. nom. 571.

forte: adv. 41, 63, 93, 142,
196.

fortis: m. nom. 518; for-
tior m. nom. 314.

foveo: fovemus 859; fovent
878; foveat 360; foveret
739; foventes m. nom.
955.

frango: frangimur 19; fractus 342; fracti m. gen.
7.

frater: fratrem 310, 367;
fratres voc. 956; nom.
361; fratribus dat. 972.

fraus: fraudis 721.

frigidus: frigida subst.
n. nom. 117.

frigus: frigora nom 818;
acc. 136.

fructus: fructu 893.

fruor: fruatur 783.

frustra: 668, 858.

frux: fruge 277; frugum
29.

fucus: fuco abl. 593.

fugio: fugient 712; fugit
perf. 527; fugerent 533;
fuge 651; fugientis f.
gen. 934.

fumo: fumantis f. gen. 17.

fundo: funduntur 595; fusa
f. nom. 863; fusi m.
nom. 958.

fundus: fundorum 31.

fungor: functos subst. m.
acc. 495.

furiosus: furiosum subst.
m. acc. 425.

furor: furoris 37; furo-
rem 526.

furtum: furta acc. 425.

G

Gallus: Gallos 27.

garrulus: garrula n. acc.
552.

gaudeo: gaudet 367, 771.

gaza: gazis dat. 394.

geminus: geminam 473;
gemino n. abl. 135.

gemo: gemit 903; gemuere
56.

genero: generant 878;
generaret 331; generatus
301; generanda f. nom.
756.

genitor: nom. 348; geni-
toris 221; genitorem
108.

gens: nom. 103, 330, 377,
526; gentis 203; gentem
743; gentes acc. 442.

genus: generis 210, 273,
454, 472, 759; generi
436; genus acc. 200,
270, 349, 735; genere
338; genera acc. 114.

gero: gerimus 433; gestum
n. nom. 802; gesta subst.
n. nom. 61; gestis subst.
n. dat. 408; gerendum n.
nom. 802.

Getae: Getarum 57, 143.

Geticus: Geticas 905;
Geticis n. abl. 34.

gigas: gigantas acc. 331.

gigno: genuit 785; gignitur
224; gignentia subst. n.
nom. 174; genitam 421;
genitos 695; genita
subst. n. nom. 174.

gladius: gladio abl. 610;
gladios 426; gladiis
abl. 34.

glorifico: glorificato m.
abl. 545.

gradus: nom. sg. 833;
gradum 403.

Graecus: subst. m. nom.
456; Graecorum subst.
m. gen. 769.

grassor: grassantes m.
acc. 918.

gratia: nom. 497.

gratis: adv. 500.

gravis: graves f. nom. 168;
gravibus f. abl. 5.

gravo: gravat 173.

grex: grege 306.

gusto: gustarint 971.

gustus: gustu 877.

H

Habena: habenis abl. 599,
727.

habeo: habet 182, 388, 696;
habuerunt 297; habeant
6; haberet 221; habere
392; habens m. nom. 112,
239.

hactenus: 542.

haereo: haeres 557.

hasta: hastae gen. 539.

haurio: haurit 524; hau-
rire 228.

Hebraeus: Hebraea f. nom.
366.

Helias: Helim acc. /= Eliam/
327.

herba: herbarum 262; her-
bis abl. 148.

here: 804.

heres: nom. 438.

herous: heroi subst. m.
gen. 96.

heu: 33, 552.

hic adj.: m. nom. 505;
haec f. nom 185, 191,
374, 506, 559; hoc n.
nom. 946; hanc f. acc.
153, 287; hoc n. acc.
220, 612, (921); hoc
m. abl. 289; hac f. abl.
700; hoc n. abl. 289,
934; haec n. nom. 61;
hos m. acc. 925; haec
n. acc. 607, 925; his
m. abl. 289.

hic pron: m. nom. 75, 109,
111, 701, 701, 702, 769;
hoc n. nom. 703, 716,
813; huic m. dat. 72, 72,
258, 260, (264); hunc m.
acc. 71, 221, 264, 701,
904, 906; hanc f. acc.

305; hoc n. acc. 172;
467, 467, 468, 554, 554,
625, 651, 651, 900; hoc.
n. abl. 462, 484, 899;
hi m. nom. 892, 895; haec
n. nom. 594, 594, 595,
597, 638, 741, 869, 921;
horum n. gen. (154), 577,
908; his n. dat. 575; hos
m. acc. 887; haec n. acc.
267, 665, 676; 969.

hic adv: 506, 605.

hinc: 669.

homicida: nom. 425.

homo: nom. 238, 257, 267,
343, 493, 500, 546, 552,
966; hominis: 197, 287,
473, 545, 589, 676, 690,
699, 868; homini 220,
597, 642; hominem 290,
479; hominum 23, 103,
330, 369, 582, 637, 751;
homines acc. 454, 490,
668, 842.

honor: nom. 47; honos nom.
758, 846; honoris 320,
911; honorem 272, 602,
943; honore 365, 437,
517, 669; honorum 861;
honores acc. 203.

honoro: honorant 71.

horreo: horrere 145.

hospitium: hospitii 687.

hostis: nom. 400, 665, 960;
hostem 92; hostes acc.
918.

humanus: humani n. gen. 210,
472; humanae f. dat. 465;
humanas 416, 728; huma-
nis subst. n. dat. 966.

humidus: humida subst. n.
nom. 117.

humor: nom. 838.

hyperboreus: hyperboreas
137.

I

Iaceo: iacet 102; iacent
574, 926; iaceant 923.

iacto: iactatos 774.

iaculum: iaculis abl. 22,
553.

iam: 1, 5, 212, 214, 216,
216, 249, 252, 346, 487,
504, 527, 532, 543, 550,
578, 696, 721, 767, 770,
887, 890, 902.

ibi: 793.

ictus: ictum 520.

idem adj: m. nom. 52, 109,
343, 732, 817, 818;
eadem f. nom. 186, 825;
eumdem m. acc. 172;
eodem m. abl. 548; ea-
dem n. nom. 897; eadem
n. acc. 439, 640; iisdem
f. abl. 737.

idem pro: eadem f. nom.
398; eadem n. nom. 406;
eadem n. acc. 150, 607.

ieiunus: ieiuna f. nom.
446.

Iesus: Iesu voc. 536, 542.

igitur: 91, 151, 185, 716,
884, 925.

ignarus: ignara f. nom.
188; ignari m. nom. 431;
ignaros 237, 643.

impono: imposita n̲. no̲m̲. 36.

improvidus: m̲. no̲m̲. 557.

impubes: impubem m̲. ac̲c̲. 702.

impune ad̲v̲: 792.

impunitus: impunita f̲. no̲m̲. 893.

imus: imis su̲b̲s̲t̲. n̲. dat. 120.

in ac̲c̲.: 20, 27, 87, 94, 133, 149, 159, 163, 167, 197, 200, 207, 214, 223, 237, 273, 275, 290, 299, 307, 310, 333, 343, 346, 350, 362, 396, 414, 416, 419, 426, 474, 476, 494, 543, 550, 572, 573, 573, 598, 634, 644, 684, 689, 690, 697, 731, 740, 743, 756, 763, 772, 782, 788, 793, 805, 851, 861, 894, 920, 943, 963, 966.

ab̲l̲.: 49, 67, 76, 79, 98, 101, 111, 116, 147, 148, 148, 202, 219, 235, 239, 247, 250, 268, 301, 326, 345, 349, 354, 373, 375, 410, 430, 432, 437, 446, 448, 450, 453, 457, 463, 485, 487, 488, 493, 517, 532, 542, 544, 544, 570, 571, 576, 596, 604, 618, 621, 628, 695, 753, 792, 803, 816, 839, (840), 845, 918, 926, 929, 938, 951.

inanis: inanes m̲. vo̲c̲. 159; inane su̲b̲s̲t̲. n̲. ac̲c̲. 327, 833.

incentivus: incentiva su̲b̲s̲t̲. n̲. ac̲c̲. 604.

incertus: incerta f̲. no̲m̲. 255, 468; subst. n̲. ac̲c̲. 208.

incesso: incessere 21.

incestus: incesta f̲. ab̲l̲. 354.

incido: incidit pr̲e̲s̲. 911.

incido: incisos 420.

inclementia: no̲m̲. 381.

includo: inclusae f̲. no̲m̲. 56.

incolumis: incolumi f̲. ab̲l̲. 301.

incommodus: incommoda su̲b̲s̲t̲. n̲. ac̲c̲. 164.

incompertus: incomperta n̲. no̲m̲. 201.

inconcussus: inconcussam 324.

incrementum: incrementa ac̲c̲. 360.

incumbo: incumbit 825; incumbant 168; incumberet 400; incumbere 791.

incuso: incusamus 882; incusare 370.

inde: 243, 392.

indemutabilis: f̲. no̲m̲. 824.

indignus: indigna f̲. no̲m̲. 532; indignos su̲b̲s̲t̲. m̲. ac̲c̲. 817.

indiscretus: indiscreta f̲. no̲m̲. 819.

indo: indere 263.

industria: no̲m̲. 169.

ineo: inire 959.

ineptus: inepto m̲. ab̲l̲. 369.

infernus: subst.: inferni gen. 471.

infero: illata f. nom. 289; n. acc. 383.

infidus: infidas 372; infidis m. abl. 90.

infirmus: infirmior f. nom. 232; infirmis subst. m. dat. 518.

informo: informare 417.

ingenium: acc. 4, 263.

ingero: ingessit 313.

ingredior: ingressi m. nom. 587.

inhonorus: m. nom. 75.

iniquus: iniqui n. gen. 651; iniquis m. dat. 822; n. abl. 636; iniqui subst. m. nom. 814, 898; iniquos subst m. acc. 375.

iniuste adv.: 844.

iniustus: iniustum n. acc. 378; iniusto m. abl. 138; iniustis n. abl. 895; iniusti subst. m. nom. 935; iniustorum subst. m. gen. 820; iniustis subst. m. dat. 67, 519, 746.

innascor: innatum n. nom. 108.

inno: innabant 217.

innumerus: innumeram 720; innumeri m. nom. 865; innumerae f. nom. 590; innumeros 765; innumeris n. abl. 349.

innupta: subst.: innuptas acc. 47.

inops: m. nom. 75; inopes subst. m. acc. 811.

inquam: inquit 649, 701, 781, 785.

insanus: insanae f. gen. 314.

insero: insita f. nom. 244.

insignis: insigni m. abl. 395.

insinuo: insinuavit 514; insinuet 647; insinuare 720.

insomnis: insomnibus f. abl. 166.

insons: m. nom. 368; insontes m. nom. 43; m. acc. 639; subst. m. nom. 815, 821; subst. m. acc. 80.

inspicio: inspiceres 917; inspicite 421.

inspuo: inspuitur 522.

instabilis: instabili m. abl. 126.

instar: acc. 402, 745.

insto: instat 824.

insum: inest 115; inerat 286.

integer: m. nom. 77.

intentus: m. nom. 120; intenta f. nom. 461; intentum m. acc. 157.

inter: 14, 14, 57, 137, 241, 359, 412, 777, 892.

nom. 337, 511; n. acc.
99; liber subst. m. nom.
456.

liber n.: libris abl. 97,
433.

libere: adv. (556).

libertas: nom. 661; libertatem 943; libertate 374.

libido: libidine 891.

libo: libare 875.

licet: 298, 372, 960;
licuit 45, 537, 683; li-
ceret 439, 827; licuisset
780.

lignum: (ligno abl. 525).

ligo: ligatas 401.

limen: limina nom. 440;
acc. 828.

limes: nom. 182; limite
561, 742.

linea: nom. 563.

lingua: nom. 88; linguae
gen. 521; linguarum 22.

liquidus: liquidum n. acc.
217; liquidis subst. n.
dat. 128.

liquor: liquorem 970.

lis: lites acc. 957.

littera: nom. 435.

loco: locavit 693; 909.

locuples: m. nom. 277.

locus: nom. 30, 67, 752,
786; loca nom. 26, 110;
locorum 179.

longinquus: longinqua f.
nom. 188.

longus: longum n. nom.
146; longo m. dat. 791;
longam 471; longo m. abl.
245, 448, 850; longa n.
acc. 3, (333).

loquor: loquar 400; locuti
m. nom. 442.

Loth: acc. 355.

lubricus: lubrica n. nom.
125.

Lucifer: nom. 619.

lucrum: nom. 782.

luctus: luctu 446.

ludus: ludo abl. 771.

lumen: nom. 544, 819; luminis 459; lumen acc.
246; lumine 544, 586;
lumina acc. 215.

lumino: luminat 586.

luna: nom. 215; lunae gen.
260, 732; dat. 675.

lupus: lupos 142.

lux: nom. 522, 536, 678;
lucem 763; luce 94, 398,
548.

lynx: lyncas acc. 142.

M

Maestus: maestum n. acc.
4; maestarum 379.

magis: 782, 915; mage 460,
462, 631.

magister: magistro abl.
206.

magistra: abl. 615.

magnanimus: magnanimi m.
gen. 749.

mensis: mensibus abl. 1.

mensura: nom. 586.

merces: mercedis 575; mercede 648, 673.

mercor: mercantur 669.

mereo: meruerunt 326; meruere 26, 42.

mergo: mersi m. voc. 159.

meritum: acc. 298, 922; merito abl. 822; meritorum 344.

messor: nom. 834.

meta: nom. 182, 182, 755; metas 733.

metuo: metuit pres. 138.

metus: nom. sg. 100; metu 204.

meus: meum n. acc. 486; meo n. abl. 786.

miles: milite 961.

militia: nom. 675.

mille: acc. 765, 870; abl. 596; milia acc. 403, 843.

minister: ministri m. nom. 907.

ministerium: nom. 523; ministerii gen. 46.

minuo: minuat 194; minui inf. 234.

minus: cf. parum.

miraculum: miracula acc. 409, 477.

miror: mirantur 71.

misceo: miscuit 488; miscetur 464.

miser: m. nom. 701; miserum n. nom. 166; miseri m. gen. 54; miserum m. acc. 857; miseros 869; misero subst. m. dat. 704; miseris subst. m. dat. 720.

misereor: miserentis m. gen. 346.

moderamen: moderamina acc. 185.

moderor: moderantis m. gen. 727.

modestus: modestis n. abl. 242.

modo adv.: 376, 422.

modulor: modulata n. nom. 594.

modus: nom. 180; modum 601; modo abl. 571; modos 6, 113, 870.

moechus: moechum 426.

moles: molem 153, 739.

mollis: f. nom. 662; mollia subst. n. nom. 127.

momentum: acc. 601; momenta acc. 132, 634.

moneo: monet 209; monitos 671.

monile: monilia nom. 905.

monitum: monitis dat. 445.

monitus: nom. 655; monitu 441.

mons: montis 402; montes nom. 572; montibus dat. 35.

monstro: monstrante f. abl. 395.

monstrum: monstra nom. 567; acc. 331.

mora: moram 95; mora abl. 677.

morbus: morbo abl. 882; morbos 878; morbis abl. 342, 810.

morior: moritur 525.

moror: moremur 448; morantem m. acc. 648.

mors: nom. 40, 290, 480, 487, 652, 701, 849; mortis 226, 323, 381, 534, 611; mortem 299, 490, 529, 781, 878; morte 295, 470, 486; mortes nom. 872.

mortalis: mortali f. abl. 695; mortale subst. n. acc. 486; mortales subst. m. nom. 334; mortalibus subst. m. dat. 493, 700; mortalia subst. n. acc. 718.

mos: nom. 860; more 840; morum 237, 270, 447, 777; mores acc. 637, 712; moribus abl. 430, 580.

Moses: nom. 394; Mosi dat. 434; Mosen acc. 385.

motus: nom. sg. 123; acc. 608; motibus abl. 716.

moveo: moves 553; movet 661; movent 729; moveamus 931; movemur 795; movere 706; moveri 632; 719; motura f. nom. 950; movendis m. dat. 358.

mox: 251.

mulier: nom. 830.

multiplex: multiplicem f. acc. 294.

multum adv.: 245; multo 351; plus 160.

multus adj.: m. nom. 845; multa f. abl. 270, 917, 933; multa n. nom. 298; multorum m. gen. 348, 787; multis m. dat. 88; multa n. acc. 167, 325, 368, 777, 807, 843; multis m. abl. 342; f. abl. 387; n. abl. 792.

multus subst.: multa n. nom. 816; multis m. dat. 107, 541; multos m. acc. 763; 772; multa n. acc. 442, 821; plus nom. 28; acc. 221, 235, 585.

mundanus: mundanis f. abl. 901.

mundus: nom. 213, 505; mundi gen. 7, 63, 76, 103, 111, 131, 153, 184, 316, 332, 417, 453, 469, 612, 724, 755, 826, 910; mundo dat. 770; mundum 181, 587, 751, 807; mundo abl. 340, 527, 816, 940.

munus: munere 146, 256; munera acc. 307.

mutabilis: m. nom. 713.

muto: mutet 194; mutor 485; mutantur 801; mutentur 626; mutari 578; mutatus 282, 783; mutando abl. grd. 496.

435

mysticus: mystica n. acc.
361.

N

Nam: 156, 224, 322, 385,
409, 422, 460, 559, 619,
638, 694, 802, 842, 897,
951.

nanciscor: nactis: subst.
m. dat. 171.

narro: narrato n. abl. 364.

nascor: nascitur 466, 583;
nascuntur 490; nascen-
tibus m. abl. 293; natus
m. nom. 493; nata f.
nom. 289; 761; nati m.
gen. 197; natum n. acc.
503; nati subst. m. nom.
907; natorum subst. m.
gen. 872; nascendi grd.
236; nascendo abl. grd.
343.

natalis: natalia n. nom.
626.

natura: nom. 106, 229, 299,
405, 577, 582; naturae
gen. 201, 272, 729, 836;
dat. 161; naturam 473,
495, 631, 632, 699;
naturas 119.

ne conj.: 41, 95, 157, 208,
448, 450, 475, 531, 598,
849.

    enclit.: 526, 550, 578.

nec: cf. neque

necesse: 820.

neco: necato m. abl. 379.

necto: nectit 696.

nefandus: nefanda f. abl.

317.

nefas: nom. 312, 335; acc.
708.

neglego: neglexit 455.

nego: negat 663; negant
735; neget 450, 743;
negati n. gen. 687.

negotium: negotia nom.
451; acc. 167, 855.

nemo: nom. 428, 951.

nequam: nequior f. nom.
41.

neque: 485, 756; nec: 21,
39, 48, 89, 105, 110,
110, 130, 187, 188, 190,
229, 250, 251, 265, 308,
311, 336, 407, 413, 413,
417, 431, 431, 434, 440,
458, 503, 506, 510, 517,
517, 537, 543, 642, 642,
659, 676, 690, 693, 696,
704, 704, 736, 746, 746,
780, 781, 800, 800, 813,
830, 844, 849, 852, 854,
854, 857, 867, 874, 931,
939, 940, 952, 958.

nequeo: nequit 487; ne-
queunt 706.

nequidquam adv.: 656.

nescio: nesciret 679.

nescius: nescia f. nom.
252, 751.

Nestor: Nestoris 702.

neu: 599.

nex: necem 51.

ni: 387, 688.

nihil: nom. 154, 155, 575,
799, 835; nihilum

nullus adj.: nulla f. nom.
2, 53, 68, 296, 458, 480,
563; nullum n. nom. 644,
689; nullam 868; nullum
n. acc. 564, 598, 718;
nullo m. abl. 179; n. abl.
39; nullas 352; nulla n.
acc. 44, 249, 521; nullis
m. abl. 252; f. abl. 111,
727; n. abl. 253.

pron.: nulla f. nom. 452;
n. nom. 506; nullis n.
abl. 224.

num: 566.

numen: numine 479.

numerus: numeri gen. 601;
numero abl. 614; numeris
dat. 96; numeros 113,
178; numeris abl. 261.

numquam: 188, 188.

numquid: 317, 565, 565,
580, 581, 618.

nunc: 510, 723, 759, 775,
806, 887.

nurus: acc. pl. 905.

nusquam: 183, 563, 776.

nutrio: nutrit 259.

O

O: 11, 159.

ob: 298.

obduco: obducto m. abl.
876.

obeo: obire 815.

obex: obice 837.

obicio: obiciunt 725, 924;
obiectum n. nom. 129.

oblecto: oblectetur 423.

obliviscor: oblitos 199.

obnoxius: obnoxia f. nom.
253.

obruo: obruit pres. 810;
obruat 826.

obscenus: obsceni m. nom.
907.

obscurus: obscuri m. gen.
364; obscurum subst. n.
nom. 129.

obsequium: acc. 390, 512.

observantia: nom. 510.

obsido: obsidat 961.

obsisto: obsistunt 122.

obsum: obest 134, 658;
oberunt 944; obsit 835.

obtego: obtectum m. acc.
917.

occasus: occasum 319.

occido: occidit perf. 847.

occiduus: occiduae f. nom.
939.

occultus: occulta n. nom.
806.

occumbo: occumbere 841.

occupo: occupat 173.

occurro: occurritur 123.

Oceanus: nom. 28.

oculus: oculos 18, 803;
oculis abl. 160.

odium: nom. 75; odiis abl.
895.

odor: odoribus abl. 595.

offendo: offenso m. abl.
42; offensi m. nom. 853;
offensa n. nom. 533.

officium: acc. 933.

olea: oleis dat. 30.

omnipotens adj.: m. nom.
501, 691.

Omnipotens subst.: nom.
671; Omnipotentis gen.
567, 741; Omnipotenti
dat. 195.

omnis adj.: f. nom. 405,
715; omnem f. acc. 153,
494, 739, 963; omne n.
acc. 708; omni n. abl.
338; omnes m. acc. 382,
489; f. acc. 329, 747;
692.

pron.: omnes m. nom. 38,
71, 105, 432, 456, 707;
f. nom. 590; omnia n.
nom. 603, 737, 798, 938;
omnibus m. dat. 176, 322,
817; omnes m. acc. 428,
550, 586, 642; omnia n.
acc. 112, 220, 478, 805;
omnibus m. abl. 353.

onero: oneratur 141; onerans m. nom. 305.

operio: opertae f. gen.
721; (opertas 630); oper-
tum subst. n. acc. 531.

opifex: nom. 120.

oppidulum: oppiduli 355.

oppidum: oppida nom. 35.

opprimo: oppressum m. acc.
404; oppressis m. dat.
68.

oppugno: oppugnantia n. acc.
609.

ops: opem 406, 882, 949;
ope 266; opes nom. 72.

opto: optare 252.

opus: nom. 717; operis 651;
opus acc. 612; operum
132, 477.

ora: oras 894.

orbis: nom. 606; orbem 212,
276, 842, 863; orbe 67,
335, 527, 758.

orbita: nom. 624.

ordo: nom. 62, 713, 737,
835; ordine 618, 728.

origo: nom. 428; origine
213, 235, 304, 736, 760.

orior: oritur 660; orti m.
nom. 939; ortas 957.

ortus: ortum 154, 209, 731;
ortu 472.

os: oris 408, 932; ore 70,
443, 656,(840); ora acc.
19, 474.

ostento: ostentantia n.
nom. 593.

ostrum: ostro abl. 144.

otium: otia acc. 156, 171,
662.

ovis: ovium 306; oves acc.
60.

P

Pactum: pacta nom. 944.

pagina: nom. 2.

palma: palmas 873.

peto: petunt 22; petamus 964; petitur 952; petitis n. abl. 304.

petra: petris dat. 35.

petulantia: nom. 363.

Pharao: Pharaoni dat. 385.

pharetra: pharetris abl. 91.

pietas: pietate 330.

piger: pigra n. nom. 125; n. acc. 156.

piget: 664.

pio: piarent 334.

piscis: pisces nom. 259; acc. 216.

pius: pia f. nom. 762; pium n. nom. 172; piorum m. gen. 655; piis n. dat. 81; pias 373; piis m. abl. 366; pium subst. m. acc. 78; piis subst. m. dat. 833, 896; pios subst. m. acc. 20.

placeo: placuerunt 580; placuisse 849; placitum n. nom. 335; m. acc. 317; placitis subst. n. dat. 557; placitos subst. m. acc. 296; placitura f. nom. 359.

placidus: placidum n. acc. 430; placidas 63; placidis f. abl. 186.

plaga: plagam 829; plagis abl. 387.

plango: plangamus 927.

planus: plana subst. n. nom. 571.

plaustrum: plaustra acc. 57.

plebs: nom. 532; plebis 403; plebem 39, 59, 386, 720; plebe 354.

plecto: plectisset 778; (plexisset 778); plectenda f. nom. 387.

plerumque adv.: 788.

plus: cf. multum adv.; multus subst.

pluvia: pluviam 138.

poena: nom. 80, 758, 787, 848; poenae gen. 523; poenam 226, 687, 746, 794, 899; poena abl. 435; poenas 85; poenis abl. 639.

polus: poli gen. 280; polos 683.

pomum: acc. 285.

pondus: ponderis 601; pondere 320.

pono: posita f. nom. 374; positum n. acc. 247, 682; posita f. abl. 764.

pontifex: pontifices acc. 533.

pontus: nom. 216, 259, 573, 842; ponti gen. 422; pontum 573, 632; ponto abl. 102.

populator: nom. 653.

populor: popularier 45; populati n. gen. 926.

populus: populi gen. 54, 279, 360, 382, 922; populum 404, 453; populi nom. 26; populorum

348; populis dat. 762,
822; populos 165, 341,
809; populis abl. 293.

porrigo: porrexit 294;
porrige 96.

porta: portas 919, 961.

portus: portu 772.

posco: poscit 139.

possessor: possessorem
283.

possideo: possessura f.
nom. 752.

possum: potes 501, 508; potest 185, 226, 239, 281,
562; possunt 373, 590,
645, 690, 714; poterunt
93, 711; potuit 66, 318;
possim 481; posses 915;
posset 218, 288, 314,
341, 392; possent 336;
potuisset 369; posse 233,
243, 549, 558, 625, 642,
719; cf. potens.

post adv.: 325.

posterior: posterioris
subst. f. gen. 231.

posteritas: nom. 757.

potens: potenti m. dat.
405; m. abl. 610; po-
tentes m. acc. 809;
potentis subst. m. gen.
457; potentum subst. m.
gen. 925; cf. possum.

potestas: nom. 500, 860;
potestates acc. 262.

potior: potiri 218, 547,
(663); potitos 374;
subst. m. acc. 663.

potis adj.: potior m. nom.
579; f. nom. 231, 319;
potiorem m. acc. 264;
potiore m. abl. 379.

potius adv.: 204, 707, 754,
889, 916.

poto: potamus 876; pota n.
nom. 906.

praebeo: praebent 576;
praebebat 215, 380;
praebebunt 972.

praecedo: praecedit 178.

praeceps: f. nom. 624.

praeceptum: praecepta acc.
515.

praedico: praedictae f. gen.
713; praedicta subst. n.
nom. 703.

praefor: praefata n. acc.
332.

praefortis: praefortibus
subst. m. dat. 266.

praemium: praemia acc. 746.

praescribo: praescripsit
636; (prescripserit 418);
praescriptas 680.

praesens: m. nom. 177; praesentis f. gen. 256; prae-
senti f. abl. 435; prae-
sens subst. n. acc. 747;
praesentia subst. n. nom.
202, 753.

praesto: (prestaret 437),
praestare, 577.

praestruo: praestruitur
358.

praeterita subst.: prae-
teritis dat. 176.

praevenio: praeveniat 950.

praeverto: praeverteret 688.

pravus: pravum m. acc. 627; pravi m. nom. 163; pravis m. abl. 957; pravi subst. n. gen. 286; prava subst. n. acc. 239; pravis subst. n. abl. 556.

premo: premat 193, 237; pressere 895.

pretiosus: pretiosae f. nom. 864.

pretium: acc. 507; pretio abl. 362.

primitiae: primitiis abl. 306.

primordia: acc. 316.

primores subst.: primorum gen. 40.

primum adv. 101.

primus adj.: primi m. gen. 300; primo n. abl. 958; primis m. abl. 209, 269.

princeps: nom. 279.

principium: nom. 584; acc. 494.

prior adj.: m. nom. 176; f. nom. 458; priorum m. gen. 777.

priscus: prisci m. gen. 670; prisco n. abl. 730; prisca n. acc. 104.

prius adv.: 351, 637, 790, 909.

priusquam: 300-301 /in tmesi/

pro: 602, 664, 900, 900.

probitas: probitate 711.

probo: probat 384; probare 590.

probus: probos 788.

procedo: procedat 598; processura f. nom. 874.

proceres: acc. 143.

procido: procidimus perf. 958.

procul: 670, 772.

procurro: procurrere 101.

prodigus: m. nom. 948.

prodo: prodentem m. acc. 361.

produco: produxit 428, 894.

proelium: proelia acc. 241, 250.

profanus: profanos m. acc. 672; profanus subst. m. nom. 51; profanis subst. m. dat. 685.

profero: protulit 120, 606.

proficio: proficere 234.

profundo: profundent 971.

profundus: profunda f. nom. 759; profundis f. abl. 370; profundum subst. n. acc. 100; profundo subst. n. abl. 402; profundis subst. n. dat. 182.

progenies: nom. 697, 845; progeniem 347.

progigno: progenito m. dat.
646.

promerco: promeruit 447.

promitto: promissus 758;
promissi m. gen. 912;
promissum n. acc. 349;
promissorum subst. n.
gen. 438; promissis
subst. n. dat. 254; pro-
missa subst. n. acc. 540,
640.

promo: (promat 237); pro-
meret 656; prome 91;
promptus 352; promptum
n. nom. 99, 304.

promoveo: promovet 395.

pronus: prono m. abl. 125.

propago: nom. 759.

prope: 68, 469.

propello: propellat 476.

propere adv.: 778.

propero: properata f. nom.
755.

propheta: prophetae gen.
441; nom. 681.

propono: propositae f. gen.
255, 326; propositam
202.

proprius: propriae f. gen.
745; proprio m. abl. 948;
propria f. abl. 891;
propriis n. dat. 915;
proprios 6; propriis
subst. n. abl. 856.

prorogo: proroget 193.

proscenium: proscenia acc.
914.

prospicio: prospexit 665.

prosterno: prostrata n.
nom. 923.

prosum: prodest 135; pro-
derat 323.

prudentia: nom. 738.

pruina: pruinas 137.

pubes: nom. 760.

pudor: nom. 70.

puella: puellae nom. 43;
puellarum 843.

puer: pueri nom. 43;
puerorum 843.

pugna: nom. 874; pugnas
956.

pulcher: pulchra f. nom.
864; pulchrum n. acc.
612; pulchra f. abl. 213.

pulso: pulsata n. nom. 953.

pulvereus: m. nom. 57.

punctum: puncto abl. 803.

purus: pura f. nom. 281.

puter: putres f. acc. 881.

puto: putas 728; putat 268;
putet 243; putemus 800;
putent 197; putemur 208;
putandum n. nom. 813.

Q

Qua adv.: 102, 103, 403, 508.

quadrans: quadrante 794.

quaero: 621, 700; quae-
sivit 948; quaerere 414.

quaestus: nom. pl. 862.

quondam: 681, 767, 927.

quoniam: 62, 100, 490.

quoque adv.: 40, 57.

quoties: 389, 795, 814.

R

Rabidus: rabidis m. abl. 931.

radius: radiis abl. 461.

ramus: ramis abl. 285.

rapax: subst. m. nom. 425.

rapio: rapit 624; rapiet 701; rapta f. nom. 904; raptum m. acc. 327.

rarus: rara f. nom. 452, 796; raris subst. n. dat. 127.

ratio: rationis 266, 560, 772; ratione 218, 512, 615, 813.

ratis: rate 8.

rea: nom. 226; cf. reus.

rebellis: rebelles m. acc. 608.

recedo: recessit 952.

recido: recisos 695.

recipio: recipit 954; recepit 483; receptus 499; receptae f. gen. 211.

recolo: recolamus 65.

rectus: recti subst. n. gen. 286, 427, 561; recta subst. n. acc. 556; rectis subst. n. abl. 238.

recursus: nom. sg. 732.

reddo: reddam 785; reddemus 602; reddere 522.

Redemptor: nom. 509.

redeo: redeat 273, 782; redeamus 943; redeuntibus subst. m. dat. 953.

redigo: redactos 697; redigenda n. nom. 740.

redimo: redimor 485.

reditus: acc. 863.

reduco: reducti m. nom. 333.

redux: reduces m. acc. 775.

refero: refert 521; referat 967; referret 246; referatur 783; referre 94; referentum m. acc. 535.

refundo: refusus 494.

regina: nom. 443.

regio: regione 280; regionibus dat. 189.

regno: regnaret 295, 314; regnare 234.

regnum: regni gen. 388; regnum acc. 234; regno abl. 447; regna acc. 356, 809.

rego: regit 154; regi 24; regens f. nom. 398; regentis f. gen. 807; regentem m. acc. 196; regente m. abl. 274; cf. rectus.

relego: relegunt 733.

religio: religionis 48, 308; religionem 717; religiones acc. 650.

relinquo: relinquite 956;

448

relicti m. gen. 198; re-
lictum n. acc. 204, 782;
relicta f. abl. 330;
relictis n. abl. 856.

remitto: remittat 194.

remoror: remorantia subst.
n. nom. 187.

removeo: removent 415; removens m. nom. 829; re-
motum m. acc. 368, 453;
remoto m. abl. 155, 383;
remota f. abl. 390.

Rempham: nom. 674.

renascor: renata f. nom.
761.

renovo: renovat 499; renovavit 694; renovemur 963.

renuo: renuis 631; renuisse
197.

reparo: reparanda n. nom.
339.

repello: repelli 711; repulsae f. gen. 677.

reperio: reperta f. nom.
86; repertum m. acc.
354.

reprehendo: reprehendere
131; (reprendere 131).

reprobo: reprobanda n.
acc. 309.

repugno: repugnant 638.

reputo: reputes 504.

requies: nom. 171; requiem
345, 851.

res: nom. sg. 209, 249,
863; nom. pl. 938; rerum
23, 119, 185, 191, 229,

239, 409, 465, 516, 587,
600, 616, 630, 710, 730,
736, 855; rebus dat.
114, 262; res acc. 63,
84, 369, 728; rebus abl.
212, 724, 801, 901.

resero: reserante m. abl.
206; reserata n. nom.
806.

resisto: resistunt 127.

resolubilis: resolubile
n. nom. 945.

resolvo: resolvere 507.

respicio: respice 144.

resplendeo: resplendet
462.

respondeo: respondere 723.

restituo: restitui inf.
747.

resurgo: resurgunt 968;
resurgens m. nom. 790.

retardo: retardat 658.

retineo: retinent 645.

reus: reos 80; cf. rea.

reverentia: nom. 53, 705.

revereor: reverentur 71.

revertor: reverti 562;
reversos 763.

revoco: revocatur 731;
revocantur 788; re-
vocare 311; revocans
m. nom. 947.

revolvo: revolvas 104.

Rex: nom. 691; Regis 738,
749.

rex: nom. 364, 516, 518;
regis 378, 458; reges

acc. 143; regibus dat. 584.

rigo: rigamus 19.

rigor: nom. 778; rigore 401.

rimor: rimans f. nom. 539.

rite: 130.

ritus: ritu 879.

rivus: rivo abl. 101.

roro: rorare 683.

rubigo: rubigine 270.

rudis: rudibus subst. m. dat. 88, 100, 969.

ruina: nom. 13; ruinam 294; 471; ruina abl. 740, 923.

rumpo: ruptis f. abl. 942.

ruo: ruerit 620; ruitura subst. n. nom. 10.

rupes: rupis 411; rupe 578.

rursus: 211, 552.

rusticus: subst. m. nom. 139.

rutilus: rutilo m. abl. 328; n. abl. 830.

S

Sacer: m. nom. 59; sacri m. gen. 46; sacrae f. gen. 492; sacro m. abl. 694, 829; sacris n. abl. 532; sacris subst. m. dat. 685; subst. n. dat. 81; sacra subst. n. acc. 439; sacris subst. n. abl. 305.

sacerdos: sacerdotes acc. 53.

sacrarium: sacraria nom. 928.

sacrilegus: sacrilegis f. abl. 520.

saeculum: saecula nom. 110, 297; acc. 417, 807; saeclis abl. 449.

saepe: 442, 541, 725, 809.

saevus: saevae f. gen. 381; saevo m. dat. 377; saevum m. acc. 793; saevo m. abl. 944; saeva f. abl. 750.

Salomon: Salomonis gen. 443.

salus: nom. 80, 886; salutis 646; salutem 392, 551.

Salvator: nom. 483.

salvo: salvet 192; salvare 455.

salvus: m. nom. 952; salva n. nom. 799.

sanctus adj.: m. nom. 524, 600; sancti m. gen. 681; n. gen. 273; sanctae f. dat. 752; sancto n. dat. 436; sanctum n. acc. 511; sancta f. abl. 711; sancta n. acc. 684; sanctis m. abl. 430; f. abl. 91; n. abl. 305.

subst.: sancti m. nom. 899; sancta n. nom. 533; sanctorum m. gen. 530; sanctis m. dat. 345, 746, 825, 832.

sane: 29.

sanguis: sanguine 513, 829, 948.

sapiens: m. nom. 238, 908.

sapientia: nom. 519.

sapio: sapere 770; cf. sapiens.

sapor: sapores acc. 410; saporibus abl. 596.

satis: 670; sat 969.

sator: nom. 132.

saucius: saucia n. acc. 22.

saxum: saxa nom. 574.

scando: scandentem m. acc. 328.

scelus: scelere 25, 316; scelerum 334, 707, 893, 936.

sceptrum: nom. 930.

scio: scimus 673; scisset 371; scire 147, 262.

scribo: scripsisse 969; scripta f. nom. 2; n. acc. 420, 829; subst. n. nom. 655.

scrutor: scruteris 630; scrutatis m. abl. 716.

Scytha: m. nom. 456.

Scythia: Scythiae gen. 143.

Scythicus: Scythicis n. abl. 89.

sector: sectare impv. 651; sectari 146.

secundus: secundum m. acc.

959; secundo m. abl. 365; secundis n. dat. 99.

sed: 100, 146, 183, 195, 218, 238, 242, 266, 293, 315, 318, 343, 383, 390, 407, 436, 473, 486, 488, 492, 516, 543, 556, 587, 604, 610, 624, 642, 660, 721, 805, 824, 852, 875, 908, 923, 941.

sedes: nom. sg. 696.

semel: 291, 315.

semen: acc. 271; semine 342, 427, 503, 581; semina nom. 29; acc. 114, 302, 736.

semper: 110, 172, 463, 570, 622, 804, 816.

senectus: nom. 893.

senesco: senescant 792.

senex adj.: senes m. acc. 766.

subst.: senex m. nom. 59; senum m. gen. 75.

senium: senio abl. 702.

sensus: sensu 575; sensibus abl. 957.

sententia: nom. 559, 825.

sentio: sentis 526; sentiet 388; sensere 105; sentire 172.

septem: 357.

sepulcrum: sepulcris abl. 529.

sequor: sequitur 80; sequereris 623; secutus 769.

sera: nom. 837.

series: seriem 334.

sermo: nom. 95; sermone 311, 448; sermonibus abl. 514.

sero: seri 90, 668; satus 618.

Seres: Serum 144.

serva: abl. 833.

servatrix: nom. 653.

servilis: servile n. acc. 942.

servio: servit 405; servire 265, 650, 693; servisse 677.

servo: servant 735; servet 805; servare 9, 318; servata f. nom. 337; servatos 954.

servus: nom. 455, 908; servum 362.

seu: 104, 104, 231, 232.

severus: m. nom. 789; severi: n. gen. 883; severis subst. n. abl. 853.

si: 7, 8, 10, 27, 33, 65, 83, 106, 142, 162, 170, 241, 267, (377), 477, 482, 501, 548, 577, 626, 637, 645, 657, 658, 698, 703, 706, 713, 753, 777, 848, 870, 901, 916, 941, 949, 962.

sic: 55, 55, 56, 127, 127, 155, 179, 325, 377, 443, 445, 498, 546, 570, 712, 731, 755, 787, 820, 867, 953.

siccus: siccae f. gen. 411; sicca subst. n. nom. 117.

sidereus: sidereos 634.

sidus: nom. 674; acc. 641; sidera nom. 626; sideribus dat. 705; sidera acc. 260, 613.

signum: signo abl. 828; signis abl. 537.

silentium: silentia acc. 3.

sileo: sileantur 61.

similis: f. nom. 428; similes m. acc. 784.

simul: 158, 175.

simulo: simulat 390.

sincerus: m. nom. 635; sincerum m. acc. 970; sincera n. acc. 307.

sine: 58, 73, 116, 117, 177, 288, 478, 479, 575, 599, 967.

singuli: singula subst. n. acc. 146.

sino: sinat 386.

sitiens: sitienti m. dat. 139; sitientibus m. abl. 682.

situs: situ 125.

socio: sociat 965; societ 889.

Sodoma: Sodomis abl. 827; loc. 354.

sol: nom. 214, 527, 817; solis 260, 731; soli 675; solem 136.

soleo: soleant 372.

solers: f. nom. 738.

solidus: solidam 451; so-
lido m. abl. 401; solida
subst. n. nom. 128.

sollicitudo: nom. 170.

sollicitus: sollicitis f.
abl. 629.

solus: m. nom. 112, 177,
691; sola f. nom. 86,
185, 337, 831; soli m.
dat. 480; 602, 649;
solum m. acc. 649, 768;
sola n. nom. 150; solos
497.

solvo: solvit pres. 812;
solvunt 836; solveret
471; solvi inf. 912;
solvens m. nom. 508;
soluta f. nom. 714.

somnium: somnia acc. 361.

somnus: somni gen. 364;
somno abl. 951.

sonus: sono abl. 594.

sophicus: sophicas 769.

sordes: sorde 917.

sors: sortis 713.

spargo: spargantur 87;
sparsi subst. m. nom.
968.

sparsim: 449.

spatium: spatio abl. 375;
spatia acc. 178.

specialis: speciale n. nom.
868; n. acc. 220.

specialiter: specialius
743.

species: specie 308, 517,

877; speciebus abl. 587.

speciosus: speciosa n.
nom. 921.

specto: spectamus 854;
spectant 174; spectaret
83; spectando abl. grd.
590.

speculum: nom. 460; spe-
culi gen. 459; speculo
abl. 246.

sperno: spernebat 322;
sprevit 909.

spes: nom. sg. 255, 468,
704, 794; spem 202, 324,
745, 955; spe 664.

spiculum: spicula acc.
534, 611.

Spiritus: nom. 502, 512,
694.

spiro: spirant 570, 734;
spirantum subst. n.
gen. 338; spirantibus
subst. n. abl. 264;
spirando abl. grd. 739.

splendidus: splendida n.
nom. 927.

spondeo: spondere 208.

sponte: 199, 837, 902,
952.

squalidus: squalidos 913.

stabilis: f. nom. 484;
stabili m. abl. 126.

statio: statione 776.

statuo: statuens m. nom.
114.

stella: stellarum 716;
stellis abl. 215.

sterno: sternimur 34;
sternuntur 572; strati
subst. m. nom. 968.

stipo: stipata n. nom. 591.

stirps: stirpe 695.

sto: stant 574, 589, 703,
967; stetit 18; steterit
673; stare 24, 32, 155,
959, 967; stantia subst.
n. nom. 564; standi grd.
780.

stolide: 423.

strages: strage 13, 294.

struo: strueretur 312.

studium: studio abl. 74;
studiorum 592; studiis
abl. 9, 666, 722.

suadeo: suadet 718.

sub acc.: 439, 511.

abl.: 15, 61, 84, 138,
166, 198, 226, 371, 445,
898, 910.

subdo: subdatur 231.

subeo: subit 486; subiit
17, 911; subiere 51;
subiret 249; subeuntur
818; subeunte m. abl.
529; subeuntia n. nom.
733; cf. subitus.

subiaceo: subiacet 559.

subicio: subiectum m. acc.
265; subiecta n. acc.
259, 614.

subigo: subigit 812; sub-
egit 289; subactum m.
acc. 480.

subitus: subita f. abl.
740.

sublimis: sublimes m. acc.
203.

submitto: submissus 768.

submoveo: submoto n. abl.
890.

suboles: subolem 756.

subsisto: subsistit 803;
subsistunt 135, 737;
subsistere 149, 676.

substantia: nom. 222, 324.

subverto: subvertere 717,
946.

succedo: succedit 466, 760;
succederet 438.

succendo: succenso n. abl.
310.

suesco: suerant 50.

suggero: suggeritur 834.

sui: sibi m. dat. sg. 317,
384, 523, 789; se m. acc.
sg. 273, 488, 967; f.
acc. sg. 232; sese m.
acc. sg. 27, 268, 313; se
m. abl. sg. 111, 207, 207,
227, 239, 485, 488, 493;
f. abl. sg. 242, 250, 250;
sibi m. dat. pl. 581, 614;
n. dat. pl. 569, 638;
sese m. acc. pl. 707; n.
acc. pl. 568; se n. abl.
pl. 576.

sulcus: sulco abl. 395.

sum: 554, 554; es 506, 507,
546, 556; est 2, 30, 32,
89, 100, 103, 108, 112,
116, 119, 140, 145, 146,
151, 151, 152, 155, 166,
170, 172, 180, 182, 183,
206, 225, 229, 230, 233,

tergum: tergis abl. 145.

terra: terrae gen. 258;
terram 275; terrae loc.
115; terris dat. 339;
terras 181; terris abl.
86, 219, 321, 753, 844.

terrenus: m. nom. 489;
terrenam 227; terrena
subst. n. acc. 322, 470,
859.

terreus: terrea f. nom.
696.

terribilis: m. gen. 382.

terror: nom. 323; terrore
648; terroribus abl. 960.

tertius: tertia f. nom.
536, 620.

testis: nom. 191.

testor: testata n. nom.
922.

timeo: timet 868; timent
564; timere 251.

timor: nom. 140.

tolerantia: nom. 873.

tolero: tolerabat 378;
tolerare 883; tolerasse
607; toleranda f. nom.
33, 357.

tollo: sustulit 52; sub-
lata n. nom. 754.

torpor: torpore 126.

torqueo: torquent 905;
torquentur 898.

torrens: torrentibus dat.
707.

torus: toris abl. 331.

tot: 25, 26, 26, 403, 417.

totus: m. nom. 27, 183, 267,
966; tota f. nom. 249;
totum m. acc. 181, 212,
863; totam 717; toto m.
abl. 335; n. abl. 773;
totos 357; totis f. abl.
76; totum subst. n. acc.
133, 243, 902; toto subst.
n. abl. 173, 450.

tractabilis: m. nom. 541.

trado: tradita f. nom. 434.

traduco: traducta f. nom.
366.

traho: trahebat 299, 444;
trahens m. nom. 392.

trames: tramitis 474.

tranquillus: tranquilla f.
nom. 726.

transcendo: transcendit
pres. 933; transcendet
702.

transeo: transisset 247;
transire 200, 797.

transfero: transtulit 321;
translata f. nom. 189,
n. acc. 909.

transfundo: transfudit 489;
transfuso m. abl. 292.

transgressor: transgressoris
491.

trepide adv.: 250.

trepido: trepidantem m.
acc. 475.

trepidus: m. nom. 598;
trepidis m. dat. 400;
700; subst. m. dat. 168.

tres: tribus m. abl. 446.

Unigena: Unigenam acc. 768.

unus adj.: m. nom. 230, 427;
una f. nom. 804, 867,
867; unum n. nom. 583;
unius n. gen. 459; uni
m. dat. 225, 264; unum
m. acc. 264, 615; unam
223; uno m. abl. 118,
292, 581; una f. abl. 8,
284, 432; uno n. abl.
586, 803.

pron.: unus m. nom. 158,
176; unum n. nom. 457,
543; uni m. dat. 107;
unum m. acc. 353.

urbs: urbe 59, 831; urbes
nom. 25, 36; acc. 165,165,
380, 809.

urgeo: urget 725; urgeat
871; urgentes m. acc.
169.

urna: urnas 972.

uro: usta f. abl. 59; ustae
f. nom. 906; ustus subst.
m. nom. 136.

ursus: ursos 142.

usquam: 729.

usus: nom. sg. 459; usu
413; usus acc. 133, 576,
600.

ut: 12, 113, 154, 178, 224,
272, 342, 344, 374, 386,
397, 424, 486, 497, 508,
546, 603, 604, 666, 711,
767, 814, 819, 821, 835,
866, 951, 966.

uterque: utrumque n. acc.
230, 396.

Vaco: vacat 152.

vacuus: vacuum n. nom.
407; vacuo n. abl. 402;
vacuis f. dat. 339;
vacuas 32.

vagus: m. nom. 599;
vagis m. abl. 774.

valde: 603.

valeo: valent 79.

valva: valvas 837.

Vandalicus: Vandalicis
n. abl. 34.

vaniloquus: vaniloqui m.
nom. 208.

vanus: vana n. acc. 592,
627, 769; vanis n. abl.
722.

vapor: vaporem 228.

varie adv.: 449.

vario: variatur 148.

varius: vario m. abl. 669,
850; varia f. abl. 198;
varios 133; varias 263,
442, 596; variis m. abl.
960; f. abl. 587.

vas: vasa nom. 46, 928.

vastator: nom. 828.

vasto: vastata n. acc.
916.

vastus: vastis f. dat. 28.

vates: vatem 365; vatum
467, 655.

-ve enclit.: 4, 450,454,
458, 478, 799, 799, 951.

vel: 125, 125, 454, 578, 578, 752.

vellus: vellere 144, 830.

velo: velant 452.

velox: velocia subst. n. nom. 128.

velum: nom. 531; vela acc. 99.

velut: 460.

vendo: vendunt 362.

venenum: acc. 876; venena acc. 282.

veneror: venerare impv. 649; venerata f. nom. 444, 674; veneranda f. nom. 467.

venia: veniae gen. 794, 955; venia abl. 367, 688.

venio: venit pres. 174; veniunt 573, 594, 801; venient 793; venit perf. 351; venimus perf. 433, 582; veniret 343, 756; venturum m. acc. 470; ventura subst. n. nom. 714; subst. n. acc. 441.

ventus: venti nom. 734; ventis dat. 99.

verber: verbere 890.

Verbum: nom. 465, 522; Verbi 502; Verbo abl. 118.

verbum: nom. 566; verbi 610; verbo abl. 220; verborum 957; verbis abl. 267, 552, 676.

vereor: verentur 156;

vereamur 959; verentes m. nom. 875.

vergo: vergunt 742.

verno: vernabat 213.

vero adv.: 121, 356, 534, 759, 798, 813, 892; cf. verum.

versus: versu 2, 95.

versutus: m. nom. 69.

verto: vertimur 20; vertitur 835; verso n. abl. 134, 282.

verum adv.: 61, 448, 658, 853; cf. vero.

verus: vera f. nom. 482; verum n. nom. 703; veri m. gen. 667; verum m. acc. 108; vera f. abl. 483; vero n. abl. 854; veri subst. n. gen. 593; vera subst. n. nom. 79; cf. vero, verum.

vester adj.: vestrae f. gen. 419; f. dat. 161; vestro n. abl. 166; vestris n. abl. 163, 666.

vestigium: vestigia acc. 475, 539.

vestis: veste 517; vestes nom. 864; vestibus abl. 413.

veto: vetitis m. abl. 285, 331.

vetus: veterum m. gen. 65; n. gen. 592; veteris subst. n. gen. 505; veterum subst. m. gen. 497.

vetustus: vetusti m. gen.
627; vetusta f. abl. 962.

via: nom. 206, 832, 852;
viae gen. 563; viam
58, 94, 396; via abl.
663.

viator: nom. 138.

vicinus: vicina f. abl.
13.

vicis: vice 397; vices acc.
260.

victor: victore 964.

victoria: nom. 679.

victrix: nom. 248.

video: vides 474; videmus
764, 874; videbis 902;
viderunt 328; videre
perf. 498; viderent 612;
videtur 452, 577, 844;
videntur 588, 607, 967;
videantur 815; videre
inf. 66; videri 699;
videntes m. voc. 160;
visum n. nom. 112; visa
f. abl. 94.

vidua: viduas 48.

vigil: vigili m. abl. 961;
vigiles m. nom. 865;
f. nom. 157.

vigor: nom. 941; vigoris
271; vigorem 9, 124.

villa: villae f. gen. 914.

vincio: vinctos subst. m.
acc. 812, 836.

vinco: vincebant 611; vincere 233, 313, 481; vin-
ci 233; vincendi grd.
964; victus 393, 481,

489; victa f. nom. 169;
victo n. abl. 912;
subst. m. abl. 962.

vinculum: vinclo abl. 300;
vincula nom. 836; vin-
clis abl. 56.

vindicta: vindictam 785,
796.

vinea: nom. 936.

vinum: vina nom. 906.

violentus: m. nom. 69;
violentum n. acc. 641.

violo: violatur 484; vio-
lare 204; violata n.
nom. 46.

vipereus: viperei m. gen.
279; vipereum n. acc.
876.

vir: nom. 455; viri nom.
607.

virginitas: virginitatis
47.

Virgo: Virginis 492.

virtus: nom. 86, 374, 482,
643; virtutis 244, 291,
605, 823, 929; virtuti
232, 658, 753; virtu-
tem 195; virtute 334,
502, 857, 900; virtutem
277, 408, 784.

virus: acc. 309.

vis: nom. 31, 185, 237,
388, 657, 686, 715; vim
287, 633, 868, 883, 964;
vi 265, 393, 952; vires
acc. 666, 780.

viscus: viscera acc. 553,
879.

viso: visere inf. 140.

visus: visu 538, 614.

vita: nom. 44, 319, 480, 487, 506, 544, 544, 652, 726; vitae gen. 210, 241, 256, 298, 326, 416, 669, 692, 776, 779, 875, 894, 934, 953; vitam 49, 73, 223, 496, 530, 646, 699, 851; vita abl. 432, 495, 544, 783; vitas 114, 192.

vitalis: vitalem m. acc. 124.

vitio: vitiata f. nom. 299.

vitis: vitibus dat. 30.

vitium: vitiorum 603; vitia acc. 609; vitiis abl. 418, 423, 792, 857.

vito: vitare 672; vitanda subst. n. acc. 288.

vivo: vivit 147; vivam pres. subjunct. 488; vivere 227; viventem m. acc. 321; vivente m. abl. 525; viventibus subst. n. dat. 576.

vivus: vivo m. abl. 970; vivos subst. m. acc. 496.

voco: vocat 207; vocet 648; vocare 640; vocata f. abl. 683; vocando m. abl. 794.

volo: 555; vis 501, 554, 554, 624, 654; vult 693; 784, 888; voluit 113; velit 424; vellem 558; velles 578, 747; vellet 112, 251; voluissem 579; voluisses 617; velle 642;

voluisse 251; volendi grd. 568.

volucris: volucres nom. 217, 258; acc. 566.

volumen: volumina nom. 467; acc. 420.

voluntas: nom. 949; voluntatis 240, 891; voluntatem 196.

voluptas: nom. 662; voluptatem 171.

votum: votis dat. 559; abl. 139, 242, 719.

vox: vocem 677.

vulgus: vulgi 87.

vulnus: acc. 539; vulnera nom. 7; vulneribus abl. 92.

vultus: vultum 307; vultus acc. 765.